ANNE JAMISON

Why Fanfiction Is Taking Over the World

An Imprint of BenBella Books,
Dallas, Texas

Smart Pop is an imprint of BenBella Books, Inc.
10300 N. Central Expressway, Suite 530
Dallas, TX 75231
www.benbellabooks.com
www.smartpopbooks.com
Send feedback to feedback@benbellabooks.com

Printed in the United States of America
10 9 8 7 6 5 4 3 2 1

Library of Congress Cataloging-in-Publication Data
Jamison, Anne Elizabeth, 1969–
   Fic : Why Fanfiction Is Taking Over the World / Anne Jamison.
     pages cm
   Includes bibliographical references and index.
   ISBN 978-1-939529-19-0 (trade paper : alk. paper)—ISBN 978-1-939529-20-6 (electronic) 1. Fan fiction—History and criticism. 2. Literature and the Internet. I. Title.
   PN3377.5.F33J36 2013
   809.3—dc23

                                     2013029129

Copyediting by James Fraleigh
Proofreading by Chris Gage and Brittany Dowdle
Text design and composition by John Reinhardt Book Design
Printed by Bang Printing

Distributed by Perseus Distribution
www.perseusdistribution.com

To place orders through Perseus Distribution:
Tel: 800-343-4499
Fax: 800-351-5073
E-mail: orderentry@perseusbooks.com

Significant discounts for bulk sales are available.
Please contact Glenn Yeffeth at glenn@benbellabooks.com or 214-750-3628.

Copyright Acknowledgments

Contents

PART FOUR

Art isn't your pet—it's your kid. It grows up and talks back to you.

—Joss Whedon

Foreword

In 1966, three things happened that changed the way we think about fiction.

First, Jean Rhys published *Wide Sargasso Sea*, her feverish reimagining of the story of Bertha Mason, Mr. Rochester's first wife, from Charlotte Brontë's novel *Jane Eyre*. That same year saw the first performance, at the Edinburgh Fringe Festival, of Tom Stoppard's *Rosencrantz and Guildenstern Are Dead*, which expands and improvises upon the brief lives of two hapless supernumeraries from Shakespeare's *Hamlet*.

The third thing that happened that year was the premiere—on September 8, 1966—of *Star Trek*. It would run for only three seasons, but *Star Trek* was one of the first shows to attract not only an audience but a fan community, a group of people who collectively discussed it and analyzed it and criticized it and obsessed over it. Eventually the *Star Trek* fandom became so intense that the canonical fabric of the show itself was no longer enough for it. The fans needed more than the show's creators could give them.

So they staged a revolution—they seized, as revolutionaries do, the means of production. They began publishing and circulating mimeographed zines about *Star Trek*, with names like *Spockanalia* and *T-Negative* (it's Spock's blood type), containing—along with articles, essays and editorials, and fan art—fanfiction: original, unsanctioned stories about the characters from the show, set in the world of the show.

It's unlikely that Jean Rhys or Tom Stoppard would have been much tempted to contribute to the pages of *Spockanalia*, had they even known it existed, but in a way they and the Spockanalians were engaged in very much the same project: the breaking down of a long-standing state of affairs that made stories and characters the exclusive province of their authors, and that locked readers and viewers into a state of mute passivity. In *Spockanalia* the fans dared to raise their voices and speak back to the TV screen—in the TV screen's language, the language of narrative—just as Rhys spoke back to Brontë and Stoppard spoke back to Shakespeare.

They turned reading and viewing from an act of silent consumption into one of active conversation.

In doing so they changed our whole relationship to story. They were coming at it from opposite directions—Rhys and Stoppard were tunneling through from above, as it were, via high culture, and the *Star Trek* fans were working from below—but the goal was the same. Like *Wide Sargasso Sea* and *Rosencrantz and Guildenstern Are Dead,* fanfiction asserts the rights of storytellers to take possession of characters and settings from other people's narratives and tell their own tales about them—to expand and build upon the original, and, when they deem it necessary, to tweak it and optimize it for their own purposes.

Not that they were the first to do it. They had plenty of forerunners. Fans have been engaging in illicit, unsanctioned interactions with other people's characters and stories since at least the nineteenth century. Jane Austen's niece once wrote her a letter addressed to Georgiana Darcy. In 1893, no less a fan than J. M. Barrie wrote a story starring Sherlock Holmes and Dr. Watson. Holmes was a particular focus for early fanfiction: when an American actor named William Gillette wrote a stage play about Holmes, he contacted Arthur Conan Doyle asking for permission to marry Holmes off. Doyle replied, accommodatingly enough, "You may marry him or murder him or do whatever you like with him."

Not everybody is that enlightened about fanfiction. The mainstream understanding of it, to the extent that there is one, is that it's (a) slavishly adoring of its subject matter and (b) pornographic. We'll get to (b) in a second, but it's even more important to correct the record about (a). It's not about simply churning out more and more iterations of existing characters and worlds, or rather, it's not just about that. It's about doing things with those existing characters and worlds that their creators couldn't or wouldn't do. It's about boldly going where no man or woman has gone before, because oh my God, who would even have thought of that?

There's a famous work of *Star Trek* fanfiction called "Visit to a Weird Planet," by Jean Lorrah and Willard F. Hunt, that sends Kirk, Spock, and Bones back to Earth (via "a multiparallel space-time inversion"), and not just to Earth but to the set of *Star Trek,* where they meet the actors who play them on the show, who are in fact busy filming an episode of *Star Trek.* Misadventures and misunderstandings ensue, in a vein that can only be called Stoppardian, but the point is, fanfiction isn't just an homage to the original—it's subversive and perverse and boundary-breaking, and *it always has been:* "Visit to a Weird Planet" appeared in 1968, in

Spockanalia #3. It's about twisting and tweaking and undermining the source material of the fanfiction, and in the process adding layers and dimensions of meaning to it that the original never had.

Hence also the porn. "A Fragment Out of Time," the founding document in slash fanfiction, appeared in 1974 in a zine called *Grup* (short for "grownup," a reference to a *Star Trek* episode about feral children). As the first depiction of a love scene between Kirk and Spock, it wasn't just hot; it was a way of making visible the hidden thread of attraction that runs through the complex bond between the two characters. It elevated subtext to text. In doing so it gave rise to an entire writhing, sweating universe of romantic and sexual pairings. But slash isn't just about making porn out of things that weren't already porn. It's also about prosecuting fanfiction's larger project of breaking rules and boundaries and taboos of all kinds.

At this late date, fanfiction has become wildly more biodiverse than the canonical works that it springs from. It encompasses male pregnancy, centaurification, body swapping, apocalypses, reincarnation, and every sexual fetish, kink, combination, position, and inversion you can imagine and a lot more that you could but would probably prefer not to. It breaks down walls between genders and genres and races and canons and bodies and species and past and future and conscious and unconscious and fiction and reality. Culturally speaking, this work used to be the job of the avant garde, but in many ways fanfiction has stepped in to take on that role. If the mainstream has been slow to honor it, well, that's usually the fate of aesthetic revolutions. Fanfiction is the madwoman in mainstream culture's attic, but the attic won't contain it forever.

Writing and reading fanfiction isn't just something you do; it's a way of thinking critically about the media you consume, of being aware of all the implicit assumptions that a canonical work carries with it, and of considering the possibility that those assumptions might not be the only way things have to be. It's what David Foster Wallace was getting at in his famous speech, "This is Water": "Learning how to think...means being conscious and aware enough to choose what you pay attention to and to choose how you construct meaning from experience. Because if you cannot exercise this kind of choice in adult life, you will be totally hosed." Fanfiction is about exercising this choice. It helps us not to get hosed.

In doing this, fanfiction is breaking new ground, but it's also trying to retake ground that was lost centuries ago. Before the modern era of copyright and intellectual property, stories were things held in common, to be passed from hand to hand and narrator to narrator. There's a reason Virgil was never sued by the estate of Homer for borrowing Aeneas from the *Iliad* and spinning him off in the *Aeneid*. Fictional characters and worlds were shared resources. For all its radically new implications and subversions, which are masterfully theorized in the pages that follow, fanfiction also represents the swinging back of the pendulum toward that older way of thinking. When *Star Trek* fans published *Spockanalia*, they weren't just discovering a new way to tell stories. They were helping us all to remember a very old one.

LEV GROSSMAN
August 2013

INTRODUCTION

The Theory of Narrative Causality

"Things happen because the plot says they should."

TO BE HONEST, I had to click the link at least five times before it...clicked.

"The Theory of Narrative Causality." The story was recommended all over—but the links kept dumping me in this random fan opinion posting board. Some Sherlock Holmes fan going off about some other Sherlock Holmes fan going off about the Guy Ritchie/Robert Downey Jr. movies. Sherlockian A wasn't a fan of this Johnny-come-lately fandom, and let his opinions be known. Everywhere. Sherlockian B wasn't a fan of these opinions...and on and on.

OK. Fine. Lots of Sherlock Holmes purists disliked Ritchie's entertaining alternate universe steampunk fanfic of a film. I am anything but a purist—I thought it was fun—and fandoms ranting about various reboots or pro-fic (licensed, sanctioned, moneymaking fanfiction, called "pastiche" when published as Sherlock Holmes stories, called "movies" when large entertainment corporations are behind it) is nothing new in *any* fandom. Fan commentary can be insightful, sometimes astonishingly so, but it wasn't surprising that a fan of the Doyle canon and Jeremy Brett's classic Holmes wouldn't like Downey. It wasn't *new information*.

I was looking for the brilliant fan commentary that was also smart, well-written fiction. That's kind of my kink.

"The Theory of Narrative Causality." It kept coming up, site after site, rec after rec. I clicked again, hoping *this* link would be fixed. The title sounded so promising—at least, you know, to a fan of "theory" and "narrative," and, well, David Hume. (OK, fine, to fans of Terry Pratchett, too.)

But no. Same fanboard. Fans making a "meta" post (self-reflexive critical commentary, we'd call it in my business) complaining about the arrogant fan "Consulting Detective" and his arrogant ways. It wasn't completely uninteresting, but there comes a point where you've seen one fan v. fan conflict, you've seen them all.

3

Disappointing, but it happens. Links break. Sites change, fall away, or get repurposed. When amateur writers post their fiction online, free of charge, chapter by chapter, sometimes they finish it, sometimes they don't. Sometimes you go back to a story, and it's gone: a change of heart, worry about work or family ramifications—a host of reasons to stop hosting. The archive failed (Geocities, once the third most browsed site on the web and home of many a fanfic archive, was just taken down one day—October 26, 2009—and most of its content was lost). Someone flounced—left the fandom in a huff, or a panic, or for a paid publication. You just never know.

That's also partly what this book is about: not knowing. In various ways, fanfiction resembles all storytelling, ever. People like to swap stories, period, and the internet is like a big electronic campfire. These continuities with past forms and traditions as well as with contemporary sources can (mis)lead us into believing that fic is a known quantity, familiar ground. It isn't always, despite the fact that by its very nature, fic revisits known material.

That isn't all it does.

Fanfiction also responds to—and even helps bring about—very specific shifts in technology and culture, and it does so more quickly, nimbly, and radically than anyone who benefits from the commercial status quo is ever likely to. Yet commercial culture—with its massive distribution, which helps create the fan communities that become fanfiction communities—is also an integral part of the fanfiction equation.

Example: Sherlock Holmes stories first begin to see mass distribution in *The Strand* in 1891. The mimeograph was invented in 1890. Sherlock Holmes fueled the imaginations of the first fanfic fandom; the mimeograph was to become the engine of fanwriting publication and distribution for decades.

Example: Broadcast television brought science fiction material to vast new audiences, including many more women. The fandom that grew up around the show quickly adapted to use phones, electric typewriters, photocopiers, and soon personal computers and desktop publishing to create networks, lobby the show's creators and producers, and ultimately distribute their fanworks, creating the mechanisms of fanfic culture that lasted until…the internet.

Example: Fan culture was ahead of all commercial enterprises in using the internet as a creative space for the production, distribution, and promotion of writing. The publication of *Fifty Shades of Grey* drew the world's attention to this enormous yet somehow still shadowy online culture, and the world is still trying to figure out what it all means.

Today, right now, the contracts (social and literal, explicit and only implied) between writers, readers, and publishers are changing along paths first established in fanwriting communities. When one of my undergraduate classes recently conducted an experiment in reading self-published "indie" fiction commercially available online, I asked them to imagine systems that would distribute, rate, and edit such fiction, making it easier to connect suitable readers, writers, and stories. The system students came up with resembled not commercial publishing but fanfiction communities: collectives in which readers and writers took on varied and active roles.

The way my students imagined it, these roles and expectations would be spelled out: readers, for example, might collect credits for edits or comments offered to writers; credits would grant them access to new material. In amateur online writing communities, however, these contracts governing expectations are often not explicit, and so...wires cross. Links break, get redirected. So you click on the story everyone's raving about, and it's *not there.* "Yeah, you should've been there," internet fandom shrugs sympathetically in your direction, "back in the day. When things were good. Last year. Last month. Last week."

My frustration and disbelief at not finding fanfiction where the internet said it would be reflects outmoded expectations of physical continuity. For a long time, the physicality of reading a story, putting it down, and coming back to it was predictable. We have a book, we put it on the shelf, and, unless someone steals it, it stays there. We might not remember where we put it, but it doesn't *move.* Such an experience has long seemed basic to us, but like so many of our assumptions about how literature is created, disseminated, and consumed, this expectation is a relatively recent development.

For most of human history, of course, stories were not a matter of reading and writing. Written manuscripts and initially even printed books were not only extremely rare but also useless to most of the population. As print and paper technology evolved and literacy increased, cheaply produced abridged and illustrated versions of existing stories and histories were distributed in chapbooks and other ephemera, publications that did not always make an obvious distinction among genres, or even between fact and fiction.

Imagine that. It wasn't always clear exactly what kind of thing you were reading.

Even as mass print culture began to resemble what we're now used to, and the novel began to assume the commercially dominant role in fiction it occupies today, *owning* these books was not part of most readers' experience. Paper was not cheap and binding was exorbitant, so novels were published by subscription, in costly volumes available from circulating libraries for a fee (see Jane Austen's send-up of novel-reading culture in *Northanger Abbey*), or in serial publication (see Charles Dickens). It was long rare for any but the most affluent readers to have their hands on more than one volume of a novel at a time.

For well over a century, though, we've expected to be able to buy a book, a discrete object of more or less uniform size and shape that would, upon purchase, take up residence on our shelves and *stay put*. We owned that copy—or maybe we borrowed it, but still. It might burn, it might wander, we could certainly lend it, but it didn't simply vanish out of existence.

Not so with the internet, I thought, staring at the Sherlock Holmes fandom discussion with chagrin. The vaunted story, "The Theory of Narrative Causality," was simply not where the internet said it was going to be, forever replaced by a posting on a fandom discussion site that didn't even seem interested in the show (BBC's *Sherlock*) whose fans kept linking me to it.

This kind of commentary is an integral part of the online reading environment fanfiction helped create. In fact, my interest in fanfiction per se started with fan commentators, not their stories. I first discovered fanboards when I was a TA teaching *Buffy the Vampire Slayer* in a course at Princeton (Tamsen Wolff's course on musical theater, inspired by "Once More, with Feeling," the series' musical episode). Fans, it often seemed, were paying more attention and saying smarter things than my Ivy League students (or, for that matter, than their TA). Plus the fans did it for fun. They *enjoyed* attending closely and making arguments based on their observations. For all I knew, some of these fans *were* my students, but how could I get students to do this stuff *as* students?

It was in quite serious pursuit of this teaching question that I initially engaged fan culture. As I moved on to the kind of commentary that could be found in fic—a slow development, because first forays into fanfiction seem invariably to turn up nearly unreadable texts—I began to connect this kind of writing with other research interests. I've been interested in the ways fanfiction blurs a whole range of lines we (mistakenly) believe to be stable: between reading and writing, consuming and creating, genres and genders, authors and critics, derivative and transformative works.

"The Theory of Narrative Causality." In a way, by using that absent fic's title as my own, I'm ficcing it—twisting it, taking it out of context. Perhaps as revenge. It *bothered* me. The history of the Sherlock Holmes fandom *is* interesting (I promise), but I wanted to write about the *fiction,* not fandom dynamics. I do write about fandom dynamics, and I do find them relevant to fanfiction as a writing culture, but there's been a lot of ethnographic study of fandom done already, and I'm your literature professor, dear, not your anthropologist. However, since I planned to be writing about *Sherlock* fic for this book, I thought it wouldn't hurt to brush up on some of the personalities of the greater Holmes-related fandoms.

So. Sherlock Holmes Fandom Dynamics 101. "Theory of Narrative Causality" kept linking to the following conflict: Consulting Detective is clearly one of those "Big Name Fans" (BNFs) common to any fandom— he's an artist, an illustrator. Other fans love his work, but they are sick of his telling everyone what's good, what's bad, what to post, what not to post. Fandoms are full of these self-appointed arbiters of good taste (their own, of course). I couldn't read Consulting Detective's actual opinions on other matters, because a lot of the links on this page were weirdly inactive, although it was a fairly recent post. The discussion did link to some recent Conan Doyle–inspired fanfiction. I love this. I love that people are still writing for Sherlock Holmes. J. M. Barrie wrote Sherlock Holmes fanfiction when he wasn't busy writing *Peter Pan* or collaborating with Arthur Conan Doyle on a failed drama. Rex Stout was in this fandom and wrote genderswap "meta," infamously claiming that "Watson was a woman"; some speculated that Stout's Nero Wolfe was Holmes' son. It's like Conan Doyle wrote the best writing prompts ever.

This discussion page helpfully glossed some of the basics of this fandom history:

> So Sherlock Holmes fandom has been small and refined for the longest time. (Many would have it that it's the First Fandom Ever, and that Holmes/Watson is the first slash ship sailin' the seven seas, back when all fapping [masturbating] material fans had were 'zines and mail chains.) The original stories have been adapted left, right, and center — see Basil Rathbone and Bumblin' Nigel Bruce, or the scrumptious Jeremy Brett and his <u>two</u> <u>Watsons</u>. And then there's been the '09 movie by Guy Ritchie, starring

Robert Downey Junior as a disheveled, scruffy Sherlock Holmes and Jude Law as gambling, gun-savvy John 'REALLY FUCKING HOT' Watson.

Fandom, as a result, <u>exploded</u> <u>in many</u> <u>and various</u> <u>ways</u>. <u>Fanfic</u> <u>was</u> <u>written</u>. <u>Fanart</u> <u>was</u> <u>drawn</u>. <u>Discussions</u> <u>were</u> <u>had</u>. <u>There</u> <u>were</u> <u>challenges</u>. And at least <u>two</u> <u>kink memes</u>.

Online, each of those underlines acts as a link that takes you to a different corner of the Sherlock Holmes fandom. (I can't do that in a book.) It's a snapshot of an internet fandom reinvigorated but also dismayed by a new reworking of its source material.

The rest of the discussion also gets at some of that multifaceted writing culture, how it transpires among and around sites and authors and artists, responding to prompts and challenges (to give a famous example from the *X-Files* fandom: "Exactly five hundred words and an eggbeater"). Sometimes, at some of its best times, fanfiction is a game writers play for the game's own sake. A great game, even.

Sherlock Holmes fans have long played something they call the Great Game, which entails very intently insisting on the "fact" that a real biographer named John Watson chronicled the real adventures of a real detective. In the game, these chronicles are known as "the Sacred Writings," for which Sir Arthur Conan Doyle served as literary agent, and they are discussed exhaustively in these terms. The Great Game is itself a kind of participatory fiction—a roleplaying game (RPG) in which the fans play exaggerated versions of themselves, taking their obsession seriously and ironically at the same time.

This fandom post mentions another kind of game, though, one less tweedy and respectable: the kink meme. This game ushers us into the nitty-gritty of online fic-writing today, a writing underground where stories start and percolate. Sometimes these stories evolve and make it on to less chaotic archives, sometimes not. Sometimes they are finished, sometimes not. It's a very mixed bag. The furthest thing from pure.

A kink meme typically posts a pairing, or grouping—whatever floats the poster's boat—with a "kink." The kink doesn't have to be kinky in the sexual sense, though of course it often is; it could simply be a kink as in twist, or plot element (the eggbeater, for example, in the *X-Files* challenge). Writers then fill the requests. So a kink meme prompt could be Sherlock Holmes and John Watson and a seabird, specifying fluff (that is, sweet, not upsetting, a happy ending), or it could be Sherlock Holmes and John Watson and the implied sexual abuse of a seabird, with the stipulation that Sherlock is asexual.

Although not, to my knowledge, actually written for a kink meme, the latter is a superb short *Sherlock* fic by A. J. Hall titled "Breakfast at 221B." (Summary: "Anyway. Enough of my embarrassing sibling brothel stories. Tell me yours.") The story draws not just on the new BBC production but on deliciously arcane Holmesiana. The cormorant (the variety of seabird in question) has a rich Holmesian history, in the fan-authored pastiche "The Adventure of the Trained Cormorant," originally published in *Black-wood's* in 1953. This story (and the many that have since followed) is a "fill" for one of the cases Watson refers to but does not recount—in "The Adventure of the Veiled Lodger," he threatens those who have attempted to destroy his archive: "The source of these outrages is known, and if they are repeated I have Mr. Holmes's authority for saying that the whole story concerning the politician, the lighthouse, and the trained cormorant will be given to the public." This untold story in turn hearkens back to Doyle's own 1881 (pre–Sherlock Holmes) photographic sketch "After Cormorants with a Camera," which details the author's own adventures photographing seabirds near a lighthouse. You don't need to know the trivia about cormorants—but if you do, you get rewarded. A. J. Hall's title also taps into the original stories' beloved Holmes/Watson breakfast scenes—even casual fans of Doyle's stories will recognize this allusion. The best fic writers are fantastically close readers, and they write layered stories for layered audiences. If not, there's still the brothel story. That's the game.

So, a kink meme is also a game—sometimes, a kink meme is a great game—but the writings it produces aren't sacred, nor are they put up to be. It is really no place for purists. This Consulting Detective fellow would not feel at home in one. Consulting Detective embraces canon, and the much-loved Jeremy Brett, and not much else. He has scathing critique for the Ritchie movie franchise:

> The Ritchie movie is nothing more than American-bait with many explosions and basic appeals at the impressionable human psyche with supernatural stupidities

> How To Butcher A Strong Female Character, or why they turned the most intelligent woman of the entire stories into a trousers-wearing,

fighting-savvy, men-dominated femme fatale with red lipstick and no
brains of her own

I liked those movies, but you could see Consulting Detective's logic. Fandom can be pretty exacting on matters of gender representation.

At this point, the whole discussion devolves into an account of an
enormous wank—not, despite the terminology, a group masturbation
session, but rather a blanket term for a particular kind of fandom drama:
usually, fans in a terrible race to take down other fans. It's a pattern familiar to anyone who's spent any time around a fandom. The site fandom_
wank (from which this post is apparently a page) is explicitly dedicated
to mocking "self-aggrandizing posturing. Fannish absurdities. Circular
ego-stroking." Seeming to take seriously the activity to which you devote
hours of your life can be a kind of fandom high crime. You can see how
this Consulting Detective would be a prime target.

This, too, is familiar territory. The disagreement starts, then the
insults, then a moderator comes in and tries to calm everyone down. In
this case, the moderator is called "let_us_trade"—heh. Lestrade. Police
officer. Keeping the peace. Cute. Someone else steps in to recommend fic
by "jumperfucker," apparently another Big Name Fan, but this one with
a Martin Freeman icon. At least someone here likes the BBC *Sherlock*—
Martin Freeman is a fabulous Watson, seamlessly honors and updates
canon, and does look adorable in his jumpers.

But wait. Now I'm in the middle of his LiveJournal post . . . not on
the same fanboard, but on the same page, that is, the same web page, the
same address, I was on before. It's confusing. It's not the usual way of
things, not protocol. And then . . . I'm in the middle of a private message
exchange between jumperfucker and Consulting Detective, discussing
how they've been paired in something called the Sherlock Holmes Big
Bang, a collaborative fiction and art challenge and exchange and...

The game is afoot. Or rather, as BBC *Sherlock*—whose fandom I am
apparently in after all—puts it, the game is *on*. This *is* the metafiction I've
been looking for.

The Theory of Narrative Causality. It's fiction, it's theory, no, wait—
since when do I think that's an either/or question? I feel like my students
must when in literary theory class I assign them Borges' "Pierre Menard"
and they write saying they read the Don Quixote essay but couldn't find
the story. I let my judgment about what I was reading be swayed by the
context I found it in, and the form that context led me to expect. Of all

people, I should know that like art in the blood, fanfiction is liable to take the strangest forms. But I didn't. Isn't it *glorious*?

As it turns out, there's an explanatory post; I just didn't see it. "The Theory of Narrative Causality" started life on the BBC *Sherlock* kink meme. It is named after a trope—a popular culture and fandom convention— on the website TV Tropes, to which it also links from time to time. In fact, the story uses a range of TV Tropes to define its characters and advance its plot. It even creates a fake entry on the real TV Tropes site for Consulting Detective, an entry that in turn proceeds to confuse the readers of the real site, who did not sign on to become a part of a fanfiction.

"The Theory of Narrative Causality" is what fandom calls "meta." It is fiction as cultural criticism and self-commentary. It not only evokes but eventually performs in the internet formats via which fanfiction—not just its writing, but its community activity—is created and disseminated. It is a fanfiction about fanboys writing fanfiction, and the fanfiction they write closely resembles the fanboy-penned (legal, professional) fanfiction of a television show that "Theory" is fic for. "Theory's" own source—this Sherlock Holmes fanboy–penned show—is famous for expanding what is meant by "canon." What is more, it does so from within the first fandom to use the word "canon" in its current, more restrictive sense of the official, authorized storyline. Referring to the fifty-six stories by Sir Arthur Conan Doyle as "The Sacred Writings," and subsequently "canon," was the Sherlockian Great Game's (and hence modern fandom's) original defining gesture. But *Sherlock* creators Mark Gatiss and Steven Moffat explicitly include all Sherlock Holmes' many film, play, and pastiche iterations: "There's an enormous amount of stuff and everything is canonical, the Billy Wilder film [*The Private Life of Sherlock Holmes*], the Basil Rathbone films—they can all be drawn upon as a *Sherlock* source."[1] One of *Sherlock's* finest episodes is named after the Great Game. Fandom is canon. It's *all fine*.

"The Theory of Narrative Causality" spins an irreverent alternative origin story for the irreverent BBC *Sherlock*—but it doesn't just riff on plot and character. It fics *Sherlock's* method: its relationship to authorship, media, and source material. Where *Sherlock* updates investigative and communicative technologies (John blogs; Sherlock prefers to text) and its mode of storytelling (highly produced effects, John Watson's blog actually being on the internet), "Theory" twists internet fandom technologies into both plot device and narrative medium. It creates and links to the fic and art of its characters; it stages "watchalongs" of prior Sherlock Holmes productions so (fictional) community members can comment on their own predecessors while advancing their own plot. It features BBC *Sherlock*'s characters as fandom personalities playing key internet-appropriate roles: Sherlock's brother, Mycroft, and Scotland Yard's Inspector Lestrade as moderators; supervillain Moriarty and his various sock puppets (aliases) as obsessive internet trolls; Mike Stamford as the man who introduced John to the fandom—all ultimately contributing, according to the logic of the fanfiction, to the creation of their own story.

As in any internet fandom, in "Theory," anonymously authored "wanks" stir up drama about the BNFs. In this fanfiction, the drama arises around fanfiction, specifically "Real Person Fic" (RPF)—fanfiction about real people rather than created characters—written about the BNFs themselves. In "Theory's" fictional fan community, RPF is banned and derided—as it is on many other fanfiction forums in real (virtual, online) life. When the (fictional) "real persons" jumperfucker and Consulting Detective themselves OK RPF and even start writing it themselves, about themselves, the plot, well, thickens. And, in a common enough sequence of events after thickening, the plot disperses, spreads itself around.

The characters in this fictional world have "real" social media accounts—active virtual identities. These accounts have comments, some from fictional characters, some from nonfictional characters (from real people, or at least from real internet personae. Real virtual people, then). But these fictional accounts of fictional characters weren't recruited by the "original" author of the "original" "derivative" "origin story" (that is to say, of the initial fanfiction "The Theory of Narrative Causality"). Readers created them, and started playing along—taking the fiction in different directions than the "original" (first?) author ever intended. It's hard to know which are the fictional and which are the "real" readers, where one author/character/reader stopped and another took over. The visual codings that signal our (virtual) presence in these (virtual) virtual venues are exact enough to fool experts—not just professional observers, like myself, but people who have actually run Sherlock Holmes communities (I asked around). (The (real, nonfictional) author did not do these codings, but rather enlisted a friend.)

As part of its plot and part of its telling, "The Theory of Narrative Causality" gives a snapshot of fandom activity, fiction exchange, and typical fandom relationships. It also transposes the story of its source and inspiration in the terms and dynamics of its own online media. And in rewriting BBC *Sherlock*'s "origin" as taking place among fans, it only tells the truth: *Sherlock*'s creators are gleefully creating fic for fic for fic.

Of course they are. As Jacques Derrida (frequently cast by detractors as a literary supervillain) might say if he stumbled into a *Sherlock* fic, that's what writers *do*.

But "The Theory of Narrative Causality" doesn't stop there; it goes all Roland Barthes, and the readers take over. The story morphs into a multi-player internet RPG. It continues outside itself, as successful stories and characters have always done—but with a difference. However similar to past forms of collective storytelling, this is something new.

This newness has to do with technology, speed, format, and the conventions and forms these changes enable. Fanfiction communities collect people who may be very far apart in physical space and connects them, in "close" proximity in virtual space, through near-simultaneous activities of authoring, editing, responding, and illustrating. Neither the codex nor our contemporary notion of literary authorship could accommodate the models of authorship we see in "The Theory of Narrative Causality." It's the fic that is not one. The author is not dead; the author is *legion*.

I can't help but think of "Theory" in terms of, well, theory—the literary and critical kind. I know that stuff; I teach it. I like it. I'd bet that some of the "Theory" writers and readers and collaborators know it, too, though I'd also bet that many of them don't. All that theory didn't keep this fiction from completely surprising me, again and again—despite the fact that knowing the structure of the show meant I knew what would happen in a fic where "things happen because the plot says they should." *How* the fiction reached these points was an endless surprise.

This element of surprise is what I love about fanfiction generally, which in "Theory" is concentrated and made explicit and maybe too postmodernly clever for a lot of readers. But they don't have to like this one—there's plenty of other fic in the sea. Similar dynamics unfold in more traditional fic, especially when taken as a large body of collected, interactive, related narratives rather than fixed, isolated stories. Most fan readers read around in fandoms; some read around in taste groupings similar to genres (hurt/comfort, slash, gen, fluff, BDSM, PWP, plot-driven, etc.), but they read *around,* often following many unfolding stories simultaneously. These stories are read comparatively; they riff on one another, borrow back and forth. Plot threads cross, become confused, create patterns—if not in the individual stories, then often in the readers' minds. Fic experienced in this way is more like a web (appropriately enough) than like a series.

Plenty of literary theorists would say this is what's always happening in literature. They'd use a word like *intertextuality* (if they were Julia Kristeva) or *palimpsest* (if they were Gérard Genette). Then they'd remember, along with Walter Benjamin, that *text* comes from the Latin word for web and they'd hug themselves and smile. Fanfiction makes all that theory very, very apparent, and makes those theorists appear a bit redundant.

A good deal of the literary theorizing of the past half-century has been devoted to dismantling the ideology of the single, autonomous work of art as a literary standard. But no fic *pretends* to be an autonomous work of art. Fic makes no claims to "stand on its own." It doesn't need anyone to point out its props and sources because it doesn't hide them; it celebrates them. A work of fic *might* stand on its own as a story—it might be intelligible to readers unfamiliar with its source—but that's not its point. Asking whether fic stands on its own is "interrogating the text from the wrong perspective"—to put a famous quote by the well-known fic-opponent Anne Rice to a use she would likely hate. Fic can be uncomfortable for writers who believe they create autonomously in a void. Fic lets its seams show in ways other works that also build from sources and predecessors may be at pains to hide—even, apparently, from their authors (later in the same text, a response to an Amazon review, Rice claims that for her, "novel writing is a virtuoso performance. It is not a collaborative art." Someone should let Bram Stoker and John Polidori know).

I began this book with "The Theory of Narrative Causality" because it condenses the universe of fanfiction: it feeds on its predecessors and its contemporaries, interacts with them, makes them new. It is in a constant state of conversation and exchange. It is often unclear where its boundaries are. It is often unclear who is a writer and who is a reader and what the difference is. It sometimes references actual "real world" events; it sometimes custom-crafts fictional elements masquerading as real. It extracts what usually transpires over many texts and places them in a partly real, partly fictional virtual network. It's also funny and romantic and erotic at times. It showcases complex relationships, which are sometimes fraught and angsty and sometimes very sweet. Like its important predecessor, *Tristram Shandy*, "The Theory of Narrative Causality" is at once entirely typical and not at all typical of its genre.

OK. "The Theory of Narrative Causality" impresses me because—much like fanfiction, but in a very condensed way—it broke my mind a little bit. But I have peculiar tastes in these matters.

The wages of sin, Watson, the wages of sin.

Images from "The Theory of Narrative Causality." This story began life on the BBC Sherlock kink meme. The author falling voices credits user misha0529 for "formatting and coding what was previously a terrible mess of fake hyperlinks and html confusion into actual LJ entries, TV tropes articles, and gmail chat." (LiveJournal has been a popular platform for fic writers and readers since 2000, and continues to be used today.)[A]

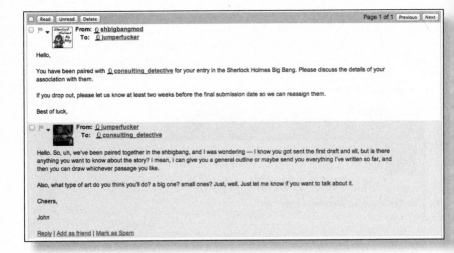

From: Ω shbigbangmod
To: Ω jumperfucker

Hello,

You have been paired with Ω consulting_detective for your entry in the Sherlock Holmes Big Bang. Please discuss the details of your association with them.

If you drop out, please let us know at least two weeks before the final submission date so we can reassign them.

Best of luck,

From: Ω jumperfucker
To: Ω consulting_detective

Hello. So, uh, we've been paired together in the shbigbang, and I was wondering — I know you got sent the first draft and all, but is there anything you want to know about the story? I mean, I can give you a general outline or maybe send you everything I've written so far, and then you can draw whichever passage you like.

Also, what type of art do you think you'll do? a big one? small ones? Just, well. Just let me know if you want to talk about it.

Cheers,

John

Reply | Add as friend | Mark as Spam

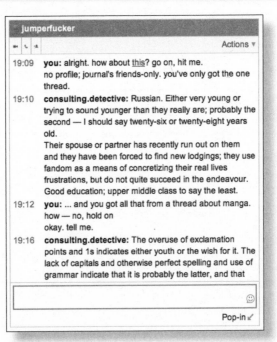

jumperfucker

                                                 Actions ▾

19:09   **you:** alright. how about this? go on, hit me.
        no profile; journal's friends-only. you've only got the one thread.

19:10   **consulting.detective:** Russian. Either very young or trying to sound younger than they really are; probably the second — I should say twenty-six or twenty-eight years old.
        Their spouse or partner has recently run out on them and they have been forced to find new lodgings; they use fandom as a means of concretizing their real lives frustrations, but do not quite succeed in the endeavour. Good education; upper middle class to say the least.

19:12   **you:** ... and you got all that from a thread about manga.
        how — no, hold on
        okay. tell me.

19:16   **consulting.detective:** The overuse of exclamation points and 1s indicates either youth or the wish for it. The lack of capitals and otherwise perfect spelling and use of grammar indicate that it is probably the latter, and that

☺

Pop-in ⟋

Why Fic?

WHY FIC? Why *Fic*?

Fic. Fan writers call it "playing in someone else's sandbox" or "borrowing someone's toys." I call it "writing." Opponents call it "stealing"—and I call that bullshit. Whatever else we call it, though, today we largely understand fanfiction as writing that continues, interrupts, reimagines, or just riffs on stories and characters other people have already written about. Fanfiction means writers getting their feet wet, their hands dirty—and if in their stories other body parts are sometimes getting wet and dirty, too, that doesn't mean those same stories can't be smart. If we call a piece of writing fanfiction, we usually (though not always) understand that it wasn't published for profit.

I've been studying fanwriting communities for a while now, but I never really was part of one, not from the inside. I wrote a few fics eventually, but they started as thank-you gifts for a community I was looking in on with an academic interest. I've been a fan of Sherlock Holmes since grade school, but I just loved the stories and movies, mostly memorized them, then moved on. I might have read Sherlock zines when I was younger, if I'd known they existed—much later, I listened to and admired fan-produced works for the Grateful Dead—but the way my fannishness worked was more academic: I like Kundera, so I'd best learn Czech. I'd written things that amounted to fanfiction for classes that didn't call it that—narrate *Notes from Underground* from the prostitute's point of view! Write Ten Ways of Looking at Socks!—but like many writers who have done such things alone in the isolation of a notebook, I didn't refer to this kind of writing by any special name. Unlike many who call themselves "aca-fans" (and I don't), I was not a fan first. (Well, there were those years following the Grateful Dead around, but we didn't write Jerry/Bobby slash, an omission that may well evidence the existence of a merciful God.)

Fanfiction is an old story. Literally, of course: fanfiction takes someone else's old story and, arguably, makes it new, or makes it over, or just simply makes more of it, because the fan writer loves the story so much they want it to keep going. But fanfiction is also an old story in that people have been doing this since—to borrow a phrase I absolutely disallow my students—the Dawn of Time. Reworking an existing story, telling tales of heroes already known to be heroic, was *the* model of authorship until very recently. This book is organized to highlight both this kind of continuity with the past, and also what I see fanfiction doing that I believe to be new. Often, what is new in the history of fanfiction—as in the history of writing itself—comes down to writing's relationship to technology and media. New technologies enable new and different kinds of stories to be told—and read—by different kinds of people. Paradoxically, fanfiction, the cultural enterprise apparently dedicated to revisiting familiar ground, ends up leading us to new models of publishing, authorship, genre, gender . . . and to voyeuristic aliens who resemble lava lamps, vampire peaches, sex pollen, and an entire universe based on the structure of a canine penis. None of that is in Homer (lotus flowers just made people drowsy).

Sex pollen aside, part of what is new in fic in recent years simply comes down to scale. Look at some of the 500,000-plus works of Harry Potter fic on FanFiction.Net alone. Remixings, crossovers, astonishing Lego-like recombinations (if you can find a "tab A" on any character, it's been in the "slot B" of some other character in fic), but also serious alternate point-of-view or alternate-ending retellings: what-ifs, could-have-beens, or (more often) should-have-beens, rewritten because the original writer, from the fan's point of view, lost her way, got it wrong, needs correcting. Or suggested a different path she couldn't or wouldn't see or fully explore on her own. Or maybe her characters should end up in space, or in a TARDIS, or just in a coffee shop—alternative worlds imagined and populated with familiar, loved voices.

Who writes this stuff? Kids. Parents. Teachers. Married couples—together. Professional writers moonlighting, free from market forces. Tweens working out sexual and writerly grammar online, simultaneously: fumbling "first time" stories written, fumblingly by and about middle-schoolers writing for the first time. And, lest we forget them, legions of fan writers horrified by all the sex, fearful that with the publication of *Fifty Shades*, sex is all their work will be known for. The world of fanfiction is a very big, very mixed bag.

The majority of this not-for-profit writing is written by women, or if not by women, then by people who are willing to be (mis)taken for women. I've spoken with a number of male fanfiction writers—some at length—and with a number of fanfiction writers who refuse to identify in terms of gender binaries. Gender online is far from transparent in the ways we (mistakenly) sometimes believe offline gender to be. Importantly, fic increasingly offers a space where gender, like sexuality, is not an either/or phenomenon, and gender and sexual dissent, even rebellion, has long been a part of fic's story. A favorite fan writer of mine (wordstrings, interviewed here) has been writing an erotic romance about an asexual character. It's hardly the only one. Just tonight I clicked on a rec and the summary warned me: "This is not an after-school special about trans folk." Male/male erotic romance by straight women for straight women was just the beginning. Fanfiction transforms assumptions mainstream culture routinely makes about gender, sexuality, desire, and to what degree we want them to match up. Sometimes not matching is precisely the point—there are all kinds of possibilities we might like to imagine or look in on, even (especially?) where preference or plumbing would preclude our actual participation.

About those gender binaries that still govern the world most of us live in: it's important that in fanfiction, women are largely running the show. Where else is that true? Today, less than 30 percent of television writers are women;[2] in film, that figure is below 20 percent.[3] Oscar-nominated women directors? Four. In 2012, women comprised roughly 30 percent of the writers reviewed by the combined forces of the *New York Times Book Review,* the *Times Literary Supplement,* the *New Yorker,* the *Atlantic Monthly*, and the *Paris Review*.[4] Women dominate in romance writing (sometimes, even in the romances themselves)—only to have their accomplishments derided or ignored by the broader literary culture whose efforts their profits nonetheless help underwrite. In sum, those numbers mean there's a lot of variously talented women we haven't been hearing from. A great many of these women are writing fic.

Again, it's not *just* women, and I really cannot emphasize this enough: fic provides a venue for all kinds of writers who are shut out from official culture, whether by demographic or skill or taste. It makes sense, however, that those who are less shut out from established systems of economic and cultural credit and prestige turn less often to a cultural form that has been not only unpaid, but actively stigmatized. I know many men who write fic, but I know even more men who write fic-like stories, in fic-like ways. When they do it, though, they sell it, get written up in the *Times*, call it *postmodernism* or *pastiche* or simply *fiction*. My study of fic communities has underscored how gender imbalance in literary and mass cultural production doesn't just affect venue, opportunity, and reception for active writers; it affects people even wanting to try. It affects people even *claiming* to be trying. Fanfiction has given many writers permission and encouragement to do something they'd never imagined they could do—in part because they can do it in private, without seeming to arrogantly lay claim to the culturally valued and vaunted status of "writer." Furthermore, fanfiction communities can provide a supportive network for beginning writers in a way that no commercial enterprise possibly can. Today, hundreds of thousands of new writers—young people, children—are growing up writing not in isolation, but with a ready-made community of readers and commentators who already love the characters and worlds they're writing about. That's very different.

It's also true that the world of fanfiction is not all happy anarchy. Academics can tend to emphasize fanfiction's potential for collaboration, nonhierarchical relations, dissent, and resistance. That's not all she (or he, or zie) wrote. Fic may be known for creating worlds in which anything goes (Men can get pregnant! Why not?), but communities and individuals can police these worlds and their boundaries with tremendous vigilance. More than one writer for this volume pulled an essay to protest the inclusion of another writer or a point of view—in some cases my own—that they felt violated the basic tenets of fandom, or even of common decency. Another writer declined to participate in any way because he felt my standard formula when asking after online personae ("identify as") was offensive—a shame for the volume, as he's one of the best writers I've seen. Wars over character relationships, about what kind of stories should be told about what characters and why, can tear friendships apart. For all that many fan writers can be shy about revealing their fic activities in real life, they can be a very opinionated, outspoken bunch—and they don't speak with one voice.

In considering how to do this book, one thing was clear to me: I did not want fanfiction to be represented by a single voice, least of all mine, when at its very essence, fanfiction challenges that model of authorship. When *Fifty Shades* was getting a lot of press and much of it consulted me, I felt my influence on this topic was a bit disproportionate, and that was a little uncomfortable. Fan studies is a field, not just one professor. Fanfiction is a collective tradition, not just one book from one fandom. Many published writers have come out of fanfiction, not just in the past two years. Many accomplished fanfiction writers have no desire to publish traditionally. I wanted *Fic* to reflect both of these groups, and more;

literary and commercial writers who've had no connection with fanfiction can use some pretty fic-like techniques. I also wanted to examine, from a variety of perspectives, why and when it seems acceptable to appropriate, adapt, or recycle elements of existing works or lives, and why and when such a practice gives rise to scorn, or the threat of legal action. (I also want to do all of that without weighing in on the legal questions myself. Not my area.)

The desire to host this conversation leaves *Fic* somewhere between monograph and edited collection. It might help to think of it as a tour through a curated exhibit that I've arranged and guided and shaped— more, in all honesty, than I originally intended, but editors are part of authorship, too, and mine is excellent and usually right. In the end, while *Fic* doesn't transform authorship to the extent that "The Theory of Narrative Causality" does, I do hope it hosts a conversation in keeping with the spirit of its unwieldy and wide-ranging subject. I have tried, in the process, to tread lightly, to leave voices intact. The "rant" is a fandom genre as much as fic is. I do not want to smooth over its rough edges.

That said, fanfiction is a subject that, like some of its favorite characters, really needed hard limits. A book cannot be coextensive with the entire history of literature and the current expanse of the internet. I limited the topic, as I've suggested, to written fanfiction: its production, its dissemination. *Fic* is not about fanart and it's not about video, although I acknowledge that these forms are increasingly interrelated and integrated with written fanwork. *Fic* is organized around what I see as pivotal moments of change that also illustrate a continuity with their predecessors. I've largely restricted the discussion to literary- and media-based fandoms, thereby excluding a number of vast, productive areas such as anime and manga (which have their own distinctive cultures) and sports. Even within its area of focus, *Fic* could hardly be exhaustive; there are many vast franchises the volume doesn't address as well as a seemingly infinite number of smaller, fascinating fandoms. Inclusion here should not be considered as a verdict on importance, quality, or even my own preference—*Veronica Mars* inspired some of my favorite-ever fics (a dazzling H. P. Lovecraft crossover decisively stole my heart), but it didn't mark a sea change in fic's relationship to technology or to broader cultural norms. I focused on fandoms that did. In an attempt to illustrate how fanfiction operates collectively and interactively with its sources and with other fics, I opted to focus on different aspects of very few fandoms as opposed to trying to represent the dizzying range of sources that attract fic. Lastly, since the material of fanfiction remains unfamiliar to many readers, I emphasized fandoms with enough cultural resonance that the thematic terrain, at least, would be familiar to many, even if the mode of engaging it seemed foreign.

Some limitations I did not need to impose; they were unavoidable. Not every fan writer wants to be in print; some guard their privacy or do not approve of any commercialization of fic. Among fic writers I approached, a disproportionate number of self-identified men and people of color declined to participate for a variety of reasons, including professional concerns or simply time. Time was also a limiting factor in other ways, some of them media-specific. Part four, which offers a snapshot of elements and issues in fanfiction today, was compiled with the knowledge that "today" would be yesterday by the time anyone read it, and a few months is ancient history in internet terms. This discrepancy between time frame in print publishing and internet posting helps illustrate the speed at which fanfiction evolves.

This rapid evolution—or rather, change, to avoid any implication that I'm telling a story of progress rather than flux—is driven by experiments, by which I mean not just the process of creation and its product, but the collective, porous way fanfiction is published and read. Yet fanfiction communities and their writing, however diverse these may be, hardly fit anyone's image of experimental writers or avant-gardes, and with good reason. Literary avant-gardes tend to attract and be discovered by those who already evince a marked distaste for both the literary and commercial entertainment status quo. Fanwriting communities enjoy and consume commercial culture voraciously, celebrate it, even as they challenge and transform its products for their own sometimes radical purposes. Experimental writing in fanfiction is found and enjoyed by people who share at least one popular taste, a taste that *has* been catered to by mass culture. Many of these readers, however, also have tastes mass culture does *not* satisfy, tastes they may first discover by reading fic. Persuaded by the presence of favorite characters, even the least adventurous readers sometimes embrace stories featuring alternative sexualities and genders or enjoy more stylistically and thematically challenging material than they would otherwise have turned to. Yet fanfiction is largely driven by a love of the very elements—narrative and character—that much experimental writing of the past half-century has targeted for disruption and critique.

At the same time, fanfiction has demonstrated that many of the values of the literary and commercial establishment—economy, continuity, pacing, "show, don't tell," clarity of style and of genre (what shelf in the bookstore it will go on)—can be jettisoned or systematically and purposefully violated as long as other tastes and agreements are being met: always warn for triggers, character death, specific kinds of sex; specify endings as happy or not; clearly indicate relationship pairings. And while fanfiction *can* be nearly indistinguishable from commercially published books in content, style, and structure, it usually is not. A fic can represent relationships and characters that would be deemed insufficiently universal or popular to justify a publisher's investment of time and capital— and it can do so in 250 or 250,000 words. Driven by an engagement with commercial culture but free from that culture's market constraints, fanfiction can experiment with the popular—with no need for backers, no need to sell the product before it's been realized, and with the luxury of an audience that is already eager to see its works.

As we've recently seen, some of these experiments in fanwriting have turned out to have enormous commercial value. Taken as a collective, some are changing how we see commercial culture and literature in general— how we see authors, readers, producers, and consumers. Not just economic, but cultural capital—that nebulous nonfinancial wealth of credit, knowledge, and access—is shifting in ways that have been trailblazed by those who didn't have it or, in some cases, by those who had it and shrugged it off for the pleasure and fun of writing fic.

Fanfiction is also transforming how readers find material. Archives increasingly are using a variety of tags or labels that help readers to sort and locate stories. Long before Amazon, fan readers and authors had found new ways of categorizing their fiction, thereby allowing it to occupy more than one "shelf" at a time (by kink, by pairing, by disability, by lack of sexual pairing, by adventure, by particular crossover source). Stories can also be made to order, written as part of games, exchanged as gifts, written to prompts and challenges. New habits of writing and reading have been created that are now shared by communities of fan writers and readers, which, taken as a whole, dwarf the number of readers for all but the most wildly successful commercially published works of fiction. Most individual fanfiction stories are likely not commercially viable for one reason or another—including the preferences of the fan writers themselves—but to measure their influence and importance in commercial terms entirely misses the point.

There's been worry that the commercialization of fan culture will lead to its destruction. Even excluding potential challenges from rightsholders,

introducing the potential for individual profit into what had been a collective enterprise can disrupt the balance. I've devoted an entire section
of the book to these discussions. Most of these questions come up around
what I'm calling here "megafandoms" (those large enough to drive online
readership for a select few fics to millions of hits), or around for-profit
writing sites such as Wattpad or Kindle Worlds, the platform recently
announced by Amazon for the limited licensing of fic. At least for now,
most fanfiction does not work in this way. There's only one *Fifty Shades*,
but even for every more moderate publishing success to come out of
fanfic, there are literally hundreds of thousands of fics that are not on the
market and never have been. For every vast franchise, there are dozens
of niche fandoms—the Michigan *Beauty and the Beast* group that's been
meeting monthly since the late 1980s comes to mind—whose intensity
and commitment is all the higher for their small numbers.

It seems inevitable that fanwriting cultures will change in response to
the broader culture's relationship to them. They will continue to change
in response to whatever publishing or posting media technologies and
arrangements arise; there is no one way of writing or posting fic, and so
far its venues only continue to proliferate. Commercial forces are bound
to have an effect—as they always have. One thing seems clear to me,
however, having now talked to hundreds of fan writers and having edited
perhaps more than my fair share of them as well: they don't seem to be
showing any signs of shutting up soon.

part one

WRITING FROM SOURCES

From Mimesis to the Sherlock Holmes Fandom

A Prehistory of Fanfiction

"It's writing, Jim, but not as we know it, not as we know it, not as we—" LOL my bad. It's totally writing as we know it. We just don't *know* we know it.

—Mashup: "Star Trekking" and my internet persona

1.

Aristotle was a Greek philosopher who theorized that art was primarily an imitation of nature. (He had a lot more to say, and his theories are readily available all over the internet, but that's the soundbite version.) Dionysius of Halicarnassus was a Greek historian and rhetorician who came a few hundred years after Aristotle, and he saw things differently. He held that art—at least the art of writing—was more truly a matter of imitating other good writers who'd gotten it right before you. But that's the way of the world. Writing communities and the way they see their work change. We might say that writing is a community whose only constant is change, but then we'd immediately have to amend our cliché to include the constant wank—a term that's recently evolved to designate irritable and strident discussion—that the constant change causes. (But don't worry. We don't get to that particular sense of *wank* for a couple of millennia.)

Anyway, Dionysius (not the wild, sexy god, but the historian) saw good writing as *imitatio,* and this understanding all but totally replaced the Aristotelian conception, *mimesis*, among Latin writers of the day. In fact, Dionysius' theory held sway for a lot longer than most people today have any idea of. This conflict between imitatio and mimesis plays out with greater or lesser intensity until right this very minute, where on a blog near you an Edward/Bella fic writer is taking down a Rob/Kristen fic writer with something akin to extreme prejudice.

26

It could get down and dirty in the eighteenth century, too—as we see in debates surrounding the work of Charlotte Smith, who appropriated lines of Shakespeare and others into her influential sonnets. Was she engaging in the elegant tradition of imitation? Or was she *plagiarizing*?

Writing. The community whose only constant is the extreme glee with which one writer tells another writer, YOU'RE DOING IT WRONG. It's what Plato told all the poets, after all.

2.

Del CHEVALIER DE LA CHARRETE
Comance Crestiens son livre;
Matiere et san li don et livre
La Contesse, et il s'antremet
De panser, si que rien n'i met
Fors sa painne et s'antancion

Here Chrétien begins his book about the Knight of the Cart. The Countess furnishes him with the source material and overall spin she'd like him to give it, and he undertakes to think how to put it all together. All he's really adding is his own hard work and some ideas about context and narrative.

—Chrétien de Troyes, approx. 1171; writer's note to *Lancelot de la Charette* from the "Arthur material" kink meme, my translation

The well-known medieval romance *The Knight of the Cart* announces itself as a fill for Countess' prompt, apparently a request for Arthur/Lancelot/Guinevere with a cart (the exact wording of the request has been lost). There's some evidence to suggest Chrétien added the whole adultery plot, which has since become canon. There's no evidence, however, to prove Chrétien didn't invent the request to begin with (a request from a countess makes you look pretty important, after all). Chrétien plays down his own role, as is expected of fan writers, and pays plenty of deference to his source and The Powers That Be. But, as sometimes happens, it seems that Chrétien's version was more compelling than its source, if we are to judge by longevity. It's hard to judge on merit, since Chrétien's source has been lost. As we all know in the age of the internet, it happens all the time; texts just explode. Natural causes.

My own translation (transposition?) from the Old French into a contemporary global fanfiction English is incredibly free. Like, *way*. So free, in fact, we might consider it fic for the original—but then, translation is what we call it when very serious people rewrite and generally mess with other people's words *in another language*, which makes it all very respectable. We even talk about the difference between faithful and free translation in a way that maps handily onto discussions about canon (the story as told by the original author) and alternate universe (AU) in fanfiction. My version of Chrétien is most definitely AU, but isn't that true of all contemporary readings of Chrétien? A thousand years is a long time, and none of us has a TARDIS.

3.

Sometime around 1600, give or take, William Shakespeare wrote fic for the Ur-Hamlet. But, again, as sometimes happens, it seems that Shakespeare's version was more compelling than its source—hard to judge, though, since his original has been lost. As we all know, in the age of the internet and apparently in other ages, too, it happens all the time; texts just explode. Natural causes.

We *say* Shakespeare wrote *Hamlet*. When I call that into question just a bit, it's not to suggest that some other guy wrote it, as the conspiracy theorists who are invariably seated by me on planes and at weddings like to argue, but rather that Renaissance dramatic authorship was a more porous and collaborative affair than we imagine. Recent research points to how Shakespeare's plays incorporated the innovations of actors and others involved with his company, the King's Men, as well as multiple sources, including histories, romances, and other plays. No one really minded because you didn't make your money as a playwright by selling copies of your own written intellectual property (if that had been the case, figuring out exactly what makes up the text of any of Shakespeare's plays wouldn't be such a complicated affair). If anyone was making money selling copies of plays, it was the stationer. You made money as a playwright by having your entertaining plays performed—so the more entertaining you could make them, the better. For that reason plays were (and still are) amended after early performances, adjusting for audience reaction.

Shakespeare was and is a brand, then, a name that indicated a certain standard and style of entertainment, but also the guy who did most of the heavy writerly lifting and thus deserves the most credit. It works this way in a lot of industries today—all kinds of labor goes into writing a film script or a television show, but typically only one or maybe two writers get the credit.

4.

In 1614, Alonso Fernández de Avellaneda (a sock for some unknown writer) wrote a sequel to Miguel de Cervantes' *Don Quixote*. This sequel may or may not have helped inspire Cervantes to write his own continuation. In his dedication of that continuation (whatever its inspiration), the real Cervantes claims that the real Quixote is "'with his spurs, and on his way'...so as to dispel the loathing and disgust caused by another Don Quixote who, under the name of Second Part, has run masquerading through the whole world."[5] That's pretty much how Anne Rice feels about fanfiction, too.

On the other hand, as the internet commentator "Berk" argues, "I wouldn't call [the 'dodgy' Quixote] fanfic, even jokingly—I think the guy's main idea was to cash in on the popularity of Cervantes's masterpiece, not to pay homage to characters he loved or anything like that; that's the impression I remember getting from the notes to the versions I read at least."[6]

In the late sixteenth century, though, writing based on another writer's work wasn't necessarily *homage;* it was just, as we've seen, standard practice. What sets this "False Quixote" apart is that Avellaneda was publishing his work *as the real sequel*—not as an alternative version, an explicit parody, or homage, as Quixote himself was doing with the romance tradition. Had copyright law existed in those days, Cervantes probably could have sued, but it didn't, so he had no choice but to write his own, better sequel, in which the real (fictional) Quixote discovers and mocks his imposter. From a *literary* perspective, this solution worked out better than a lawsuit anyway.

5.

In 1748, a lady fan calling herself Belfour writes to Samuel Richardson about his novel *Clarissa*, concerned about the fate of his characters— she is worried about spoilers, having "heard that some of [Richardson's] advisers, who delight in horror...insisted upon rapes, ruin, and destruction."[7] She pleads for a better end. As it turns out, this fan's main concern is not with the heroine, but with her potential rapist: "but you must know (though I shall blush again), that if I was to die for it, I cannot help being fond of Lovelace. A sad dog! why would you make him so wicked, and yet so agreeable?"

Another constant: we love bad boys, but also love to imagine that they are actually good on the inside—maybe so we don't have to blush so hard. Belfour rewrites Lovelace accordingly: "He says, sometime or other he designs being a good man...and, in excuse for my liking him, I must say, I have made him so, up to my own heart's wish: a faultless husband I have made him." She takes a characteristic that Richardson teases, and runs with it. As Joss Whedon later advised—perhaps in similar circumstances—if you don't like the way a scene goes, rewrite it yourself.

Like many a fangirl, Belfour would prefer that canon worked out her way, and she has strategies other than pleading: "If you disappoint me...May the hatred of all the young, beautiful, and virtuous for ever be your portion! and may your eyes never behold anything but age and deformity!" Ageist curse notwithstanding, Belfour would also rather not be associated with the wrong demographic: "Perhaps you may think all this proceeds from a giddy girl of sixteen; but know I am past my romantic time in life, though young enough to wish two lovers happy in a married state." Middle-aged fangirls of all eras hate to be mistaken for teenagers—at least, on the basis of their reading and writing.

Thus begins a lengthy correspondence, because Richardson is smart enough to be flattered by such intense engagement with his story. He takes this correspondence with an anonymous female interlocutor who threatens to curse him *extremely seriously*. He expresses regret for the pain he's caused, acknowledges that he feels it himself and that she is not "*particular*" in her desire for "a happy ending, as it is called," but he nonetheless proceeds to explain why he has decided to give his audience not what they want, as Whedon would later put it, but what they *need*. Richardson confesses that it has been a matter of surprise "and indeed of some concern" that a character he set up as so very wicked from the first letter "has met with so much favour from the good and virtuous." This same concern, he says, helped convince him of the "necessity" of the "catastrophe" he in fact wrote.

How, Richardson argues, could he set up a rake like Lovelace to rape and seduce virtuous young women to his heart's content throughout his youth, and then, when he had the luck to meet ~~the Chosen One~~ a paragon of peerless virtue, reward him with her, and reward her, even more unfairly, with him? Indeed, "there cannot be a more pernicious notion, than that which is so commonly received, that a reformed ~~vampire~~ rake makes the best husband. This notion it was my intent to combat and expose."

Still, Richardson the author really doesn't want Belfour to flounce his novel. He is "discouraged and mortified" when she says she won't accept "the volumes when completed, if the catastrophe be not as [she wishes]." He sends the next volume anyway—she reads, she regrets, she berates. The correspondence continues, and takes a heartbreaking turn; when the ruin of Clarissa is accomplished, Belfour announces she's flouncing again, and Richardson writes, essentially, that he can't be expected to put too great a premium on earthly happiness when he himself has lost six sons, a wife, and two daughters. Clarissa is going to Heaven. Isn't that enough?

Point taken.

Richardson also wants to make it clear that he sees himself as an advocate for women, a defender of their worth against those who would dismiss it, and that it really bothers him that he's inadvertently created a bad, bad man who nonetheless attracts them. He probably wasn't the last male writer to be so perplexed.

Ultimately, Belfour—the *Clarissa* fandom identity of one Lady Bradshaigh—settled for the same remedy that so many *Fic* contributors did: she rewrote the damn novel so she liked it better. So, as Elizabeth Judge explains, did Lady Bradshaigh's sister, Lady Echlin, with whom Richardson also corresponded but whose preference for a slightly less tragic ending he likewise resisted, although he "jokingly wrote the latter that Lovelace may as well have been made governor of an American colony."[8] (Which is, for that matter, exactly how he would have ended up, if Richardson had lived a century later and been called "Dickens," whose works were likewise parodied and pastiched.)

Judge, a scholar of intellectual property law who also holds a literature PhD, has written more extensively on these and other instances of eighteenth-century fanfiction, and goes into greater detail on Richardson's and other authors' responses to character "kidnappings." As courteous as he was to "Belfour" and other fan correspondents, Judge explains, Richardson was tremendously displeased with the many bawdy rewritings and continuations of his first novel, *Pamela*. In fact, his distaste at seeing his earlier heroine so ill used led him to kill off his next. It's a lucky thing, then, that he never lived to see the most notorious "fanfic" for *Pamela, or Virtue Rewarded:* the Marquis de Sade's *Justine, or the Misfortunes of Virtue.* In comparison, Richardson might have been happy to settle for any of Belfour's alternate comic happy endings, which Justine decidedly doesn't get. As an erotic fic writer on a roll can tend to do, @TheDivineMarquis let his fic (Justine/Everyone—NC-17, NSFW, warnings for every single thing you can imagine and then some) go on for hundreds of thousands of words.

By that point in history, authorship was growing to resemble something closer to what we understand it to be today. The beginnings of copyright had been in place since 1710's Statute of Anne; literacy had increased exponentially, creating an expanding popular audience; circulating libraries and periodicals had brought down the costs of reading; and intellectual property was something you (or the publisher you sold to) might profit from by circulating copies of your work. Whether Richardson (if he'd lived that long) could have sued the Marquis de Sade for infringement is debatable, but highly unlikely—the emerging standard established by British case law was developing a notion of fair use that argued more on the basis of labor put into a particular book than on the originality of said book. (Plus, not only was Richardson dead, but *Justine* was published in revolutionary France in 1791, at which time England and France had issues to sort out besides international copyright.) A copyright lawsuit would have made little difference to Sade's ultimate fate, in any case. He had already been imprisoned (he wrote *Justine* in the Bastille before the Revolution), released, and would ultimately be rearrested and committed as insane on the order of Napoleon Bonaparte. The Emperor had heard about *Justine.* In fact, he called it "the most abominable book ever engendered by the most depraved imagination" and ordered it destroyed. (Unless I'm confusing that with what some outraged women's advocates said about *Fifty Shades of Grey* before they held their book burning. People can get so *testy* about erotic fic. If Simone de Beauvoir concluded we didn't need to burn Sade, though, I doubt she would have had much time for burning Sade lite.)

6.

In an epigraph to a chapter of *Middlemarch,* her much-adored and near-perfect novel, George Eliot tells a story about two child readers we know to be based on herself. It's a familiar story—at least to many fic writers. These children fall in love with a book, its world, and its author, whose name "rose on their souls and stirred such motions there" and "[made] the little world their childhood knew/Large"—large not just with new, wild landscapes, but with "wonder love belief/Toward Walter Scott."

In other words, long before Mary Ann Evans became George Eliot, one of the most respected, serious literary novelists of all time, she was a historical romance fangirl. But the poor thing had fallen in love with a borrowed book! It was returned before she could finish it! What's a baby novelist to do? Finish it herself, of course, "in lines," she tells us somewhat opaquely, "that thwart like portly spiders ran."

That's right. George Eliot fangirled, and then she wrote fic.

It wasn't all that good, she suggests. We'll never know; those spiders ran clear away from us. George Eliot's early fic is gone. And like Naomi Novik, the author and former historical fiction fanfic writer (for the *Master and Commander* series), I feel that this lost fic is an important part of literary history, and I wish it had been preserved. To avoid this spidery fate for future fanfiction, Novik helped organize the nonprofit Organization for Transformative Works, which not only provides an independent and stable archive (Archive of Our Own), but also informs fan writers about their legal rights regarding their fanworks. Of course, many writers continue to do everything they can to erase their fanfiction origins.

It's OK. We still have fourteen-year-old Jane Austen's pastiche of the sentimental novel and the Brontë children's Duke of Wellington stories to go on with.

Is this, then, the story of fanfiction, its path to legitimacy and respect? The literary apprenticeship of young novelists learning their future craft, cutting their teeth on the worlds of others until they grow up and stand on their own two feet? A number of writers in this volume still see their early fanfiction careers in this way: a phase to be passed through, a childhood playground—or sandbox, as the convention goes (fanfiction authors' notes often explain they are playing "in another writer's sandbox").

It's actually not that simple—not in the nineteenth century, and not today.

A novelist colleague of George Eliot's—one well into adulthood—had similar designs on Sir Walter Scott's characters. Like many, many readers, William Makepeace Thackeray was unsatisfied with the romantic outcome of Scott's beloved novel *Ivanhoe*. Thackeray knew he had company; *everyone* wanted the hero to pick the plucky Jewish heroine, Rebecca, and not the boring blonde. So Thackeray wrote for like-minded fans, and specifically addresses them in an author's note: "Well-beloved novel readers and gentle patronesses of romance, assuredly it has often occurred to every one of you, that the books we delight in have very unsatisfactory conclusions, and end quite prematurely with page 320 of the third volume."[9] Thus Thackeray succumbs—and only partly tongue in cheek—to the siren call for "more" that has motivated so many generations of fan writers. "More," to be sure, but also, "more of what *I* want."

Thackeray had loved Rebecca since childhood—but this continuation was no child's apprenticeship. Like S. E. Hinton today, who has been a respected, published novelist since the age of seventeen but is known to write fanfiction "outtakes" and missing scenes for her favorite TV show, *Supernatural*, Thackeray wrote fic *after* the publication of his best-known work, *Vanity Fair* (whose famous heroine, Becky Sharp, is another Rebecca). Thackeray wrote for a set of reasons familiar to fic writers—a combination of wish fulfilment, criticism, parody, and fun. Like so many fic writers I have read and taught, Thackeray had several serious points to make, among them dissatisfaction with his own genre. He was frustrated with the novel's conventional end at marriage and with the dearth of any heroes and heroines over the age of thirty: "I would ask any of you whether it is fair to suppose that people after the above age have nothing worthy of note in their lives . . . Let us have middle aged novels, then." He goes on to lament that so many of his contemporaries abandon their most interesting and admirable characters when they are still "mere chits," and hopes that those writers still living will agree to give readers more themselves.

But Walter Scott is dead, and Rebecca has always been one of those characters readers want to hear more of. Thackeray also *can't* "believe that such a woman . . . could disappear altogether before such another woman as Rowena, that vapid, flaxen-headed creature, who is, in my humble opinion [IMHO], unworthy of Ivanhoe, and unworthy of her place as heroine." William Makepeace Thackeray was obviously a total shipper. But Thackeray, like his Kirk/Spock, Johnlock, and (in the early years) "Sculder" descendants, must confront the sticky problem of canon: "After all, she married Ivanhoe. What is to be done? There is no help for it. There it is in black and white at the end of the third volume." Are readers really forced to accept that their beloved Ivanhoe could "sit down contented for life by the side of such a frigid piece of propriety as that icy, faultless, prim, niminy-piminy Rowena?"

Not if Thackeray has anything to say about it. Rowena, in his continuation, knows full well that she was outclassed by "the Jewess," and as a wife "she was always flinging Rebecca into Ivanhoe's teeth." The pious Rowena becomes an anti-Semitic shrew, a nag—in fact, a stock character in fanfiction, almost a template for the kind of punishing characterization generations of fan writers have inflicted on the hapless (if often canonically successful) rivals that threaten their One True Pairing. I've read this character—this same character, with minor adaptations—as Angel *or* Buffy, Bella *or* Jacob, and even, in slash fic, Scully—again, and again, and again. Thackeray insists he's writing a "middle aged novel," but here he sounds every bit the teen fangirl. Not—and I really mean this—that there's anything wrong with that.

7.

None of these earlier literary practices are *exactly* the equivalent of what we understand as fanfiction today. The reasons for this difference are, I hope, clear from the examples themselves as I've explained them: our understanding of the key relationships—those that exist variously among writer, written, reader, publisher, object published, and source—changes over time. What doesn't change, or rather, what never disappears, is the writerly habit of writing from sources. Writers have always entered into and intervened in familiar stories and styles and collaborated on authorship through discussion or other forms of influence. Despite this multiplicity of source and process, we have long given (or ceded) credit, ultimately, to a single authorial name—and fanfiction, with all its collaborative glee, continues that tradition. We talk about work by Ivy Blossom or Nautibitz or tby789 or Snowqueens Icedragon, even though these writers were always incorporating suggestions and drawing from a body of other writings—like other writers do. Fic just doesn't hide it.

Today, some of these historically established practices are called "fanfiction," others "adaptation," "sampling," "appropriation," "inspiration," or "homage." Differences in nomenclature have to do with copyright, ownership, authorial attitude, and final product. These names *can* suggest important creative as well as legal differences, and I don't want to ignore these, although I don't find them reliably distinguished by these words. Like many of the contemporary works that could be described by these more neutral, familiar terms, the historical instances I've discussed are *related* to what we understand as fanwriting (and there are many, many other examples; I would go so far as to suggest that there are as many examples as there have been writers in history). What we call fanfiction today is something else, though: it's no longer just writing stories about existing characters and worlds—it's writing those stories for a community of readers who already want to read them, who want to talk about them, and who may be writing them, too.

The Look of Fic: 1800s

A page from the Brontë children's Duke of Wellington "fanfiction," as printed in their household family magazine, a pastiche of the influential *Blackwood's Magazine* [MS Lowell 1 (7). Houghton Library, Harvard University.]

The first fanwriting fandom, and one that's going stronger
today than ever

The Sherlock Holmes Material:
A Study in Fanfic

SHERLOCK HOLMES practically began in mass media—although really, *only* practically. The first, longer Holmes adventures—*A Study in Scarlet* (1887) and *The Sign of the Four* (1890)—were published as books and met only modest success. But beginning in 1891, Sherlock Holmes short stories began appearing in *The Strand* magazine, and the detective immediately began to drive sales. In his 1924 autobiography, Doyle claimed he began writing the shorter forms as a way into *The Strand*—the form thus modified by the opportunities of the market:

> Considering these various journals with their disconnected stories it had struck me that a single character running through a series, if it only engaged the attention of the reader, would bind that reader to that particular magazine...Looking around for my central character, I felt that Sherlock Holmes, who I had already handled in two little books, would easily lend himself to a succession of short stories.[10]

He did. A succession of fifty-six *Strand* stories, often illustrated, followed, and quickly helped build the magazine's circulation to 500,000. Dickens' most popular novels sold that many (and some, more) over the course of his entire lifetime; Doyle was reaching that many readers simultaneously, and repeatedly, over many years.

This material's close relationship to the media, and to the newest and most cutting-edge form of media distribution, has continued. Sherlock Holmes has produced the most spin-offs, pastiches, and adaptations, in the most media, ever. It is the first formal fandom—with rules. With a *constitution*. ("Article III: All persons shall be eligible for membership who pass an examination in the Sacred Writings set by officers of the society.") The Baker Street Irregulars—this very formal, exclusive fan club—is still making news, recently filing suit against Doyle's estate, claiming that Sherlock Holmes is in the public domain and, in effect, belongs to all of us.

Legal wrangling aside (and for the most part, this book holds it at arm's length—I'm a literature professor, not an intellectual property lawyer), Sherlock Holmes helped establish an enormously popular genre: the detective story. He is part of our vernacular, and when I say "our,"

I mean it in a global sense. Early German film adaptations date from the teens; *O Xangô de Baker Street* finds him in Rio. There are Sherlock Holmes radio dramas in Hindi, a Japanese cartoon called *Sherlock Hound.* Soviet television produced a highly regarded Russian adaptation. Today, Sherlock Holmes is familiar worldwide even to many who've never read a word of Doyle's original stories. The sheer number of major adaptations now running—three enormous media franchises (the Guy Ritchie/ Robert Downey Jr./Jude Law movies; the BBC's *Sherlock*; and CBS' genderswapping *Elementary*)—guarantees a certain contemporary currency, but that's just our own historical moment. Sherlock Holmes has generated a vast history of similarly successful adaptations. William Gillette's iconic stage Holmes. John Barrymore. Basil Rathbone and Nigel Bruce. Raymond Massey. John Gielgud on the radio. Leonard Nimoy on the stage. Peter O'Toole in voiceover. Christopher Plummer. Michael Caine. John Cleese. Billy Wilder's *Private Life of Sherlock Holmes,* about Holmes' long-repressed and ambiguous sexuality. *The Seven-Per-Cent Solution* on cocaine addiction and psychoanalysis. The classic Granada Television series starring Jeremy Brett, whose dedication to his role tragically damaged his mental and physical health. *The Return of Sherlock Holmes*, with its female Watson. *Young Sherlock Holmes. The Great Mouse Detective.*

I grew up watching Sherlock Holmes. So did my mother and father. And their parents. My teenage daughter has *Sherlock* earrings. The previous century made adapting, continuing, transposing, and reinterpreting Sherlock Holmes familiar and popular enough to support our own century's current cultural obsession. We are long used to recognizing Sherlock Holmes in multiple versions, by multiple authors. So if thinking about writing and authorship in these terms when we call it "fanfiction" and read it online still seems foreign to some readers, we might remind ourselves that for commercial culture and amateur writers alike, Sherlock Holmes has been "one fixed point in a changing age." From a creative standpoint, how do these impulses to retell him and reframe him differ?

The Early Adventures of the Apocryphal Sherlock Holmes

IN THE WORLDS of literary fanfiction, two names dominate: Jane Austen and Sherlock Holmes.

Already, it looks like a false parallelism. And it is.

Austen fans are "Janeites." They display a reverence around the author herself, "the Divine Jane," whereas Sherlock Holmes fans are "Sherlockians" or (in an earlier, more formal designation) "Holmesians." A tenet of Holmes fandom (an official one, in fact) is to insist on the primacy of the characters, to understand Arthur Conan Doyle as literary agent for the true author, John Watson, who was simply, as the stories claim, recording his adventures with his detective friend. These fans have little if any interest in the "agent's" other, non-Holmesian works of fiction.

Doyle famously saw something of the kind coming, and had no wish to be eclipsed by his creations. He was writing serious historical fiction—*Micah Clarke* (1888), for example, or *The White Company* (1891)—and he didn't intend to spend his career being remembered for his potboilers. If there was ever a writer who knew the deep truth of Joss Whedon's dictum that "art isn't your pet," it's Doyle. Really, what he most wanted out of Sherlock Holmes and John Watson was to make a buck. He had fun with them. I am sure he was fond of them, enjoyed taking them out to play. People came to know him by his "pets" (as we who frequent dog parks know happens) and he feared that soon, they would know him by nothing else: "I saw that I was in danger of being entirely identified with what I regarded as a lower stratum of literary achievement."

So he tried to kill Holmes off. And it didn't work.

Of course, in some ways, it worked too well. News spread fast. The December 1893 publication of "The Final Problem" chronicled Holmes' fall into a ravine at Reichenbach Falls in Switzerland. Newspapers ran obituaries for this fictional character. People marched on the streets wearing black armbands. People also continued to do as they had been doing: buying not nearly as many of Doyle's other works, respected as they were in his day, while bringing Holmes to life in other ways: on the stage and in parodies and pastiches—some fully legal, some merely unchallenged.

In 1893 (before Holmes' death initiated the period fans call The Great Hiatus), *Punch* magazine published eight stories and pastiches under the title "The Adventures of Picklock Holes," including one by a liberal Member of Parliament. Also in 1893, J. M. Barrie of *Peter Pan* fame—who had worked with Doyle on an unsuccessful play—wrote a parody that pleased Doyle so much, he included it in his autobiography. "The Adventure of the Two Collaborators" begins with Holmes and Watson in their rooms at Baker Street, Watson was writing, Holmes "amusing himself with a little revolver practice. It was his custom of summer evening to fire round my head...until he had made a photograph of me on the opposite wall." Watson invariably "springs up to the ceiling" in perpetual amazement, while Holmes spots two "literary characters" and recognizes one as "that big fellow" who has taken credit for most of Holmes' own achievements (Doyle was not a small man). Doyle and Barrie gain entrance and demand that Holmes deduce why the public refuses to attend their failed play, and the detective brilliantly does so: "they prefer to stay away." His author tries to force his creation to attend and, upon his refusal, kills him off. Holmes' last words: "Fool, fool! I have kept you in luxury for years. By my help you have ridden extensively in cabs, where no author was ever seen before. *Henceforth you will ride in buses!*"

Eventually, in response to popular demand (and, perhaps, to riding in buses), Doyle eventually "found" some more of Watson's writings. The detective's first return, *The Hound of the Baskervilles,* appeared serially in *The Strand* in 1901–1902 but was set before Holmes' death—Holmes was back, in other words, but not from the dead. Finally, however, a full decade after attempting to kill him off, Doyle brought Holmes back to life in "The Adventure of the Empty House" (he shows up, Watson faints, but Mrs. Watson has conveniently died, so it's all for the best).

Holmesians have been "finding" new cases ever since, often filling out the various oblique allusions with which Watson peppered his original write-ups—cases politically or socially too sensitive to be related to the public or those for which, like the Giant Rat of Sumatra, "the world was not yet ready." Many of these stories, as was the case with one of the best-known pastiches, Vincent Starrett's 1920 "Adventure of the Unique Hamlet," were printed privately and circulated among friends before later being collected in volumes such as Ellery Queen's 1944 *Misadventures of Sherlock Holmes*. Parodies continued apace: A. A. Milne's first sale was "The Rape of the Sherlock" (the title's a riff on Alexander Pope's satirical poem, not some non-con prompt on a kink meme) and everyone from Mark Twain to O. Henry to Bret Harte to John Lennon seems ultimately to have written one. Very often such "apocryphal" cases were published under more or less thinly veiled name changes (Schlock Holmes, Solar Pons) or were licensed by the Doyle estate; while in other instances, genuine confusion has arisen as to whether a "found" story was actually by Doyle or not. At least once, Doyle himself inadvertently contributed to such a case of mistaken identity.

In his introduction to *The Further Adventures of Sherlock Holmes*, Richard Lancelyn Green recounts the incident of one such story that was "Found!" as William Randolph Hearst's *Cosmopolitan* magazine proclaimed in a 1948 headline. However, as Sherlockians read this supposed story, they were less than impressed with its quality, and soon rumors swirled that it was a forgery, or an imitation by Doyle's (much resented) son, Adrian. As it turns out, it was neither. An architect named Arthur Whitaker had written it in his spare time and sent it to Doyle in 1911, hoping they might collaborate on new Holmes stories. Doyle responded in a letter of March 17, 1911: "Dear Sir, I read your story. It is not bad and I don't see why you should not change the names and try to get it published yourself. Of course you could not use the names of my characters."[11]

Doyle further explained that among his reasons for declining, collaboration with another writer would cause his editors to lower his commanding price by 75 percent. He also, however, offered to buy the idea for the story, something he'd done for other would-be Holmes authors, provided that Whitaker agreed to relinquish all rights and credit and understood Doyle made no commitment to use the idea. Doyle recommended again that Whitaker publish it himself, but instead Whitaker took Doyle up on his offer to purchase the concept. Buoyed by this success, Whitaker went on to write several other stories, one of which he published, using the detective name "Harold Quest." This incident explains the story's confusion of origin, and also illustrates how the question of "filing off the serial numbers"—revising fanworks to publish them as "original" à la *Fifty Shades*—has not always generated the same controversy and upset it often does today. Similarly, August Derleth, founder of the genre fiction publisher Arkham House, began his obviously Holmes-inspired Solar Pons series as "The Adventure of the Circular Room," a full-blown Sherlock Holmes pastiche, in the *Baker Street Journal* in 1946. In 1951 he published it, character names changed, in *The Memoirs of Solar Pons*.[12]

Genderswapping, another common practice in fanfiction that's currently finding commercial success (on CBS' *Elementary*), seems to have begun in the Sherlock Holmes fandom with Rex Stout's (somewhat) tongue-in-cheek address to the Baker Street Irregulars, "Watson Was a Woman." Stout (better known for his massive Montenegrin detective Nero Wolfe) made waves with this close reading, finding abundant evidence in "The Sacred Writings" of Watson's female gender in her nagging Holmes about drugs and smoking and pestering him to talk—and if that weren't enough, "Imagine a man asking another man to play him some of Mendelssohn's *Lieder* on a violin!"

Initially, Stout worries whether the couple lives in sin: "It was unquestionably a woman speaking of a man, yes, but whether a wife of a husband, or a mistress of a lover...I admit I blushed. I blushed for Sherlock Holmes, and I closed the book." He assuages his worry about the morality of Doctor Watson's and Sherlock Holmes' intimacy by deducing that they are married with further observations drawn from the text: Watson's assertion that he is "the most long-suffering of the mortals" and his complaint that he had become "habit" to Holmes—"as an institution I was like the violin, the shag tobacco, the old black pipe, the index books, and others perhaps less excusable."

As to the question "who was this person whose nom de plume was 'Doctor Watson?' Where did she come from?" Stout, in a quite dazzling anagramatic tour de force of cipher-discovering and decoding, teases out the name "Irene Watson." Of course, the one who was always known as "*the* woman," as the Sherlock Holmes short story "A Scandal in Bohemia" asserts, was known as Irene Adler. Adler, Stout asserts, "one who...addles. Befuddles. Confuses." From there, it's effortless for Stout to "deduce" the wedding—Holmes was present at her marriage, after all:

> It is related that he was there as a witness, but that is pure poppycock. Holmes himself says "I was half-dragged up to the altar, and before I knew where I was I found myself mumbling responses..." Those are not the words of an indifferent witness, but of a reluctant, ensnared, bulldozed man—in short, a bridegroom.[13]

Stout concludes by speculating that further research may shed light on the parentage of another literary detective, Lord Peter Wimsey.

Stout is in essence playing classic "Great Game," applying the methods of "the higher criticism" to "the Sacred Writings" with all the seriousness due to the Bible. Lord Peter's author (if not his mother), Dorothy L. Sayers, was also a noted Game player, and famously explained that "it must be played as solemnly as a county cricket match at Lord's." She also wrote extensively about Holmes' "parentege" or influence on her chosen genre, if not her character, but also had the two detectives meet in a radio drama for the BBC. Sherlock Holmes appears in Rex Stout's work, too. Not only do Stout's own genius misogynist detective Nero Wolfe and his Watson-like sidekick and chronicler Archie Goodwin live together, but a picture of Holmes hangs over Archie's desk.

In his final years, Doyle was much more concerned with the lives of fairies than with consulting detectives. He also had a very serious interest in the afterlife. But the ones with the really remarkable afterlife are, of course, his detective and his long-suffering friend.

Unlike most of the material in this volume, the history I've just presented has been minutely studied and written about in popular, professionally published books as well as in the various amateur and professional journals devoted to Sherlockiana. Pastiches in the classic canon style are still being published, but that isn't the focus of most internet Sherlock Holmes–related fanfic today. Rather, that focus is the BBC's *Sherlock*, which attracts an eclectic and very talented group of writers, some of whom have written in other Sherlock Holmes fandoms and thus maintain an explicit connection with previous incarnations—much like the BBC show itself. The rules of the game and the playing field, as we learn from the contemporary Sherlock fandom, have considerably changed. But the game is most definitely on.

The Look of Fic: 1920s

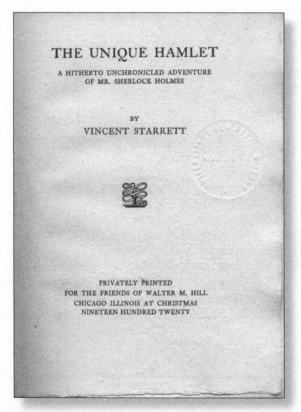

THE UNIQUE HAMLET

A HITHERTO UNCHRONICLED ADVENTURE
OF MR. SHERLOCK HOLMES

BY

VINCENT STARRETT

PRIVATELY PRINTED
FOR THE FRIENDS OF WALTER M. HILL
CHICAGO ILLINOIS AT CHRISTMAS
NINETEEN HUNDRED TWENTY

Privately printed Sherlock Holmes pastiche

Starrett, Vincent. 1920. *The unique Hamlet: a hitherto unchronicled adventure of Mr. Sherlock Holmes.* Chicago, Illinois: Privately printed for the friends of Walter M. Hill. [Title page courtesy of Center for Southwest Research, University Libraries, University of New Mexico.]

With over 400,000 words of fanfiction published in the last two years, Atlin Merrick may be one of the busier fish in the bustling pond of Sherlock fandom. As she apparently attempts to exceed Arthur Conan Doyle's own 600,000-word output about Holmes, she also "splashes around in the Twitter and Tumblr ponds, creating and reblogging things you really ought not to be looking at when you're working."

Here, Atlin Merrick introduces us to the world of contemporary Sherlock fanfiction, highlighting some of its more notable breaks with the sepia-toned tradition of Victorian pastiche. She also argues, however, that contemporary fandom's focus on the close relationship between the BBC's reimagined Sherlock and John builds on a foundation clearly established in Doyle's stories.

Mad as a Box of Frogs

Wendy C. Fries (Atlin Merrick)

Quick, what comes to mind when I say Sherlock Holmes?

Six-foot men pacing crime scenes in five-inch stilettos?

Talking skulls giving sex advice?

Doctors doing detectives in between chases and cases and clues?

What? Oh, I'm sorry. You were thinking gaslight and deerstalkers, horse-drawn carriages and foggy moors, weren't you?

Well pass the lube, Toto, I don't think we're in Kansas anymore.

Birth of a Brilliant Legend

For a man over 125 years old—the first Sherlock story was published in 1887—the world's only consulting detective is looking fantastically fit. That is, if the cut of British actor Benedict Cumberbatch's jib is anything to go by, and judging from his sudden giddy rise to fame it double-damn-well is.

The BBC TV series *Sherlock* brings the detective and his army doctor into London's twenty-first century, trading top hats for texting and cobblestones for black cabs, but the modernization has retained the charms that have helped these characters endure for over a century.

Rebirth of a Brilliant, *Sexy* Legend

Now, given his time and place, it's unlikely Doyle thought of John and Sherlock as more than friends, yet that didn't stop him from writing, across four novels and fifty-six short stories, something very like a love affair.

Because, honestly, only true love could account for a man as irritable as Holmes willingly taming his tongue for a friend, and only a deep and abiding affection could prevent an ex-soldier like Watson from strangling the cranky genius in their bed.

Did I say *their* bed?

Well, that seems to have brought us back to sex, skulls, high heels...and fanfiction.

When Doyle sent Sherlock and his archenemy, Moriarty, to their deaths over Reichenbach Falls over 100 years ago, devotees of the detective resurrected him with their pens long before Doyle did, ten years later. Because it's what humans do: we take beloved myths and keep them going long after the storytellers stop. We tell *stories*.

Peek at a few fiction websites for *Sherlock* and you'll find tales of a mantel-bound skull that talks; an army doctor who's also a werewolf, or vampire, or teacher; a consulting detective with wings, or grease and gears instead of flesh and bone; and again and again you'll find two men who give their hearts—and bodies—to their one and only friend. And, though there's plenty of kid-friendly fic, there's also sex, sex, so *much* sex.

That Doyle never said Watson and Holmes were lovers is forever beside the point. In these, our slightly more tolerant times, those of us who wish it so have written the untold stories, rambunctious tales of romance and rutting, of adventure and love and need.

Then, with the help of fanfiction websites like Archive of Our Own and LiveJournal, *Sherlock* fans have created dozens of tropes, from the expected—an army doctor probably *would* be a BAMF (bad ass motherfucker)—to the possibly unhinged—that same man as a jam-loving, sweater-wearing cat?

As if that weren't enough, some *Sherlock* writers also format their fictions in unusual ways. A 5 + 1 story— "Five Times Sherlock Moaned John's Name and One Time He Sang It," for example—would consist of five vignettes where Sherlock did the first, and end with a single vignette in which he did the second.

The boys of 221B Baker have also inspired an addictive storytelling style called the 221B. These tiny tales are full-fledged stories told in exactly 221 words, with the final word beginning in B.

Adding fuel to the fiction fire, Tumblr—a sort of community blog—has proven fertile ground for fizzing up ideas. A mostly photo- and art-centric website, Tumblr fanworks have repeatedly given rise to silly but beloved fandom tropes—John Watson wears red underpants, Sherlock Holmes loves stilettos, both are fond of dog tags—that then find their way into wee Tumblr fics, which often then give rise to new art and so it goes and goes and…

Whew.

So, what's at the root of this craze of creativity?

Mad as a Box of Frogs, Seriously

There are several reasons why fans of BBC's *Sherlock* are utterly mad, incredibly creative, and horny as hell.

First and foremost, they are hungry.

Devotees of American TV dramas get twenty-two episodes a year. Fans of most British dramas enjoy six, eight, maybe a dozen.

The *Sherlock* fandom gets three. The *Sherlock* fandom gets three television episodes every eighteen to twenty-four months. The *Sherlock* fandom is deeply, abidingly, and very inventively *starving*. With three #@%$& episodes doled out every year and a half it's clear *someone's* got to fill in the gaps.

And fill them we do, with stories of the Baker Street boys in love and in lust. They may be married or dating or dads. Sometimes they're on a case in London, or searching for clues at the Louvre or Hogwarts, or in America. And everywhere you look they're having sex. Sex *everywhere.*

There's not one lonely little kink left unloved in the *Sherlock* fandom. Have a fetish for a slim man in high heels, perhaps wearing a tailored suit and striding around a crime scene? This fandom's got you covered.

Care to see that same alluring creature in thigh-high stockings and indecent knickers? Done.

Maybe you have a thing for height differences, riding crops, army fatigues, dragons? Perhaps you're partial to public sex, slow sex, fast sex, loud sex, silent sex? Do you like dirty talk, golden showers, food porn? There's an app for—uh, there are dozens of fanfictions for that.

And the stories are so often superb. Possibly because, unlike those fine TV shows with the king and the wizard, the forever-shirtless teenage wolves, or the brothers and the angel, this fandom's drawn a huge post-thirty and over-forty following, a surprising number of whom write actual books by day and then unwind by writing *Sherlock* fanfiction by night.

Yet hunger isn't the only thing firing the creative furnace of *Sherlock* fans. The humanity of the characters is also a draw.

Second, Sherlock's a superhero who pays a price.

In *Sherlock* nothing's free. Annoy your nemesis and he straps a bomb to your best friend. Continue to rattle the madman's cage and he'll convince you to jump from a roof to save the lives of those you love. For every case Sherlock closes via his heroic deductions, there are those who insist the genius planted the evidence, cobbled together the clues, that he damn well put the dead body there himself.

Nothing comes without strings for this brilliant idiot with the superhuman ability to deduce so much from so little, but who often has the emotional intelligence of a child. And there's something profoundly empowering about that.

When you write about this modern-day Sherlock, he can metaphorically fly, soaring over everyone as his fast-blink gaze takes in *everything*. But after telling tales of the near-impossible, you have to come down to earth and talk about his heart, how what he does affects people, how it sometimes hurts more than it heals.

It's a brilliant combination, to give free rein to your imagination, to invent poisons and improbabilities and at the same time bring it back to the real world because the creators, the actors, everyone involved with *Sherlock* has done just that—they've rooted the magic in mundane reality, where brothers are disappointed in you, where best friends stalk off in a huff, and where you're on a ledge and weeping because there's so much to say but no time left to say it.

To quote *Sherlock* fandom's most well-known fanfiction writer: "Sherlock just feels...*real.*" Verity Burns knows Sherlock Holmes isn't, but that hasn't stopped her from writing four novel-length mysteries for *Sherlock,* and it hasn't stopped hundreds of others from writing thousands of stories. For so many of us, these fantastical and fragile characters feel complex and believable even as they fly, but especially when they fall.

Another reason I think the *Sherlock* fandom is as fantastically creative as it is:

The actors and writers give us so much to work with.

Have you seen Benedict Cumberbatch?

A rising star who's in every other blockbuster lately—*Star Trek* baddie, war hero in *War Horse,* deep-voiced dragon in *The Hobbit*—Cumberbatch's gifts go far beyond his pretty face.

As Sherlock Holmes, he's taken an unsocial genius and, through sheer acting skill, made the man breakable and bold, annoying and endearing, tender, tough, a bit bad *and* beautiful.

Then there's Martin Freeman as John Watson.

Freeman's gift is a splendid ability to seem real. As good-looking as Cumberbatch but in a more down-to-earth way, you'll forget Freeman's *not* John, and catch yourself railing each time he puts up with Sherlock's jibes, or cheering when he takes out the villain with a single shot.

Then there's the writing. Everything starts with the writing.

Mark Gatiss and Steven Moffat, the cocreators of *Sherlock* and its chief scriptwriters, adore their source material, grew up reading the stories, and as longtime writers for *Doctor Who,* too, they also have a flair for the fantastic.

Their Sherlock doesn't just know London; he's got every road flashing like a neon-bright map in his head. He doesn't just run; he sails over rooftops, long coat flapping like wings. He isn't just blindingly brilliant; he's broken, too, so hobbled by his own genius that, until John Watson comes along, the closest he comes to an endearment is when a cranky colleague calls him a freak.

And then John Watson does, indeed, come along.

In *Sherlock,* John not only calls Sherlock on his antisocial eccentricities, he also praises his gifts. He helps Sherlock with The Work when he can and strives to keep up when he can't. In exchange Sherlock gives an invalided ex-army doctor the excitement of the battlefield, but with far fewer bullets and a lot more blogging.

So complementary is their union that nearly from the moment they meet, just about every other character on the show presumes they're lovers and they *say so.* Is it any wonder so many fanfiction writers delightedly get these two in bed the moment it's fictionally feasible to do so?

Last, it's always about love.

We don't fall in love with explosions or spaceships or mysteries. We fall in love with people. So many fanfiction-writing Sherlockians have fallen in love with the love between these characters, whether they choose to express it with sex and stilettos or mad dashes through London's night-dark streets.

Maybe the *Merlin, Supernatural, Avengers,* and other fandoms offer the same riches, but I'd be surprised. This fandom's hunger, its wide age range, and the gifts and passions of its creators have helped fan creativity absolutely flourish.

I've met more than one *Sherlock* fan writer who's gone on to write and sell original fiction, and I've met gifted artists who make money on their beautiful, *Sherlock*-inspired work. There are many boons to this fandom: the community it creates, the friends made, but its most beautiful has been this fire it's lit in so many of us, this heart-thrumming belief that *we can.*

We can step out of our quiet world and start talking to people who love this thing we do. We can create stunning works of art or edit Hollywood-quality fan videos. And most of all, we can write and write and find an audience who wants, appreciates, absolutely *relishes* what we've made.

Ultimately, like any passion, whether fanfiction or football, wine tasting or marathons, if it brings joy, if it grows you, who cares what anyone else thinks? Joy is joy and if it brings us together it's worthy, whatever form it takes.

In the end, that joy can be an astonishing inspiration. As Atlin Merrick, I've written over 400,000 words of *Sherlock* fanfiction in the last two years, and because of that I have met and made lifelong friends, written original work, and had wonderful doors open for me—the opportunity to write this essay, to write a TV documentary, and to inspire other writers at conventions and meetups are just a few. All because I sat down one night to watch a little TV show called *Sherlock* and thought to myself after, *I wonder . . .*

Excuse me now, there's a crazy fandom out there and I want to get back to it. Memes are being made, stories are being written, dreams are being formed. Some silly, some sexy, but all of them burning with a fine fire.

Come join the madness. (Bring your own frogs.)

"Love Is a Much More Vicious Motivator"

He is the Napoleon of crime, Watson.

—Arthur Conan Doyle's Sherlock Holmes

You are the Edgar Allan Poe of love.

—wordstrings' John Watson

WRITERS HAVE BEEN ADDING a touch of romance to their mystery plots since...Arthur Conan Doyle did it in his second Holmes novel. In the opening scene of *The Sign of the Four*, the characters themselves haggle over the question of mingling genres. As we've seen, the consulting detective in his various incarnations—including this first one—tends to be something of a purist. Unsurprisingly then, Holmes takes issue with generic confusion, faulting Watson's write-up of *A Study in Scarlet:*

> "Detection is, or ought to be, an exact science, and should be treated in the same cold and unemotional manner. You have attempted to tinge it with romanticism, which produces much the same effect as if you worked a love-story or an elopement into the fifth proposition of Euclid."
>
> "But the romance was there," I remonstrated. "I could not tamper with the facts."

This fascinating discussion of genre is interrupted by the arrival of Watson's love interest, Mary Morstan. How meta. In *The Sign of the Four,* of course, the courtship of John Watson is a minor B-plot. No bookseller need doubt whether to shelve Sherlock Holmes stories with the genre he helped establish. Clear generic identity is an important convention of contemporary publishing, the question of "where is it going to go on the shelf" being a constant reality check to writers who envision various kinds of crossover appeal.

Fanfiction doesn't have to draw such clear lines—the use of tags can easily classify a story into many categories at once without insisting on a hierarchy among them. There are excellent *Sherlock* fics that focus on mysteries—Verity Burns' "The Green Mile" is among the best known and most successful case fics, incorporating as it does a compelling plot and extensive deduction scenes while also exploring the platonic but intense relationship between Sherlock and John. Many others follow romance and mystery plots with equal attention; several that I discuss here fall into that category.

My primary goal here, however, is to show how *Sherlock* fics that center on romantic and sexualized relationships also explore innovative narrative, representational, and psychological territory. These fics serve to remind us that romance, largely ignored by major review outlets and derided by literary writers, can be literary in its telling and engage a wide range of topics and motivations, as can works with erotic content. At the level of representation, too, *Sherlock* fandom often favors romance of the nontypical, exploring the possibilities of love as experienced by neurological or physical disability, mental illness, and addiction, as well as through gradations of asexuality, bisexuality, demisexuality, and other forms of queerness. Nor are these forms of difference posed simply as plot or character devices. They are explored, sometimes shockingly, for their romantic, erotic, and stylistic possibilities—with a complexity, pacing, and nuance that would be difficult to place in commercial genre publishing, but would likely, on genre grounds, be excluded from the literary publishing world as well. At its best, the *Sherlock* fandom lives up to the literary promise of online fanfiction—consistently producing experiments in topic and form that a dedicated audience is willing to try and, often enough, embrace for the fresh perspectives and twists on beloved characters and scenes they offer.

Sherlock fanfiction takes its inspiration for much of this from a show "canon" that's making similar moves, if giving somewhat less emphasis to the erotic (though it did reimagine Irene Adler as a dominatrix—in plenty of detail). Sherlock the canon character (much like his pantheon of sources) combines analytic genius and perceptive overload with a sometimes debilitating lack of emotional intelligence; an enthusiasm for experiment and risk with extreme guardedness; a rejection of all things bodily with a constant need for stimulation—all of it filtered through the unprecedented quality of his observation and the precision with which he insists these observations be related. Unlike Doyle's original, however, the BBC series hints at diagnosable thought and affective disorders. In the fanfiction *Sherlock* inspires, the ins and outs of human relationship—of romance, whether sexual in nature or not—are defamiliarized by what amounts to Sherlock's outsider perspective.

This arresting detail, and the unusual filter of the consciousness that must sift through it, are the boons that Sherlock's hyper-intense perception gives writers. Sherlock's close observation defamiliarizes the familiar but doubles as an exercise in character development. He helps fic writers do for character, voice, and even erotica what Viktor Shklovsky wanted of art: "to impart the sensation of things as they are perceived and not as they are known."[14] Sherlock is the *ostranenie* of romance.

Case in point: Ivy Blossom's "The Progress of Sherlock Holmes" begins with Sherlock waking up. Lots of stories begin with the main character waking up—it's a trope, one that's been long decried in professional publishing contexts as stale, clichéd. This isn't:

> Half second of disorientation that dissolves sharply into perfect awareness. Pain radiating from my face. Stabbing ache in ribs like a punch in the gut. Broken rib, probably. More than one? Uncertain. Hurts on inhale, exhale. Morning.

> Strange dream lingers: John with teacups for eyes, disposable razor blades for fingers: disturbing. Odd sensation coiled up in chest, like breath not caught. Distress.

> [. . .]

> Don't want to open my eyes yet; reality is never quite as interesting as the insides of my head. Teacups for eyes? How bizarre. John was naked in that dream. Naked and fourteen-feet tall. Still irrelevant. I was tiny; he could hold me in the palm of his hand, trap me with his disposable razor blade fingers. My subconscious is mad.

> Eyes are gummy, nose feels flattened and sore, mild ache in left mandibular lateral incisor. Probe it with my tongue. Loose, but won't fall out.

This is our restricted view for the entire course of the story: a cracked if sometimes maudlin Sherlock in the style of Beckett's *Watt*, a consummate observer who cannot help but recognize in himself "the signs and symptoms of being desperately, hopelessly in love."

> Imagine an anchorite, hidden away in a cave for decades, living a life of sleep and prayer, not speaking to a soul for years and years, then trying to form words with vocal chords that have been so disused they've forgotten their purpose; the human body needs to be used to fully function. *Like your heart,* says the third man, my knowing subconscious. *Like your heart, Sherlock.* Like an anchorite trying to speak. Metaphor: not really my area.

By her own account, Ivy Blossom's primary interests in writing fiction are voice and character. There's plot, but it's not what my formalist and structuralist forebears would call "foregrounded." Her longer story "The Quiet Man" relates John's attempts and ultimate inability to cope with Sherlock's loss, a loss compounded by John's equally debilitating inability to comprehend his own centrality to Sherlock. In the slow, excruciating space of grief and longing, John incorporates his dead friend's peculiar filter into his own thinking. As he does, the narration shifts between first and second person, the "you" always being the absent friend, the missing person John recreates as a more articulate and romantic figure than he was in life—even as John worries that these psychological compensations are erasing the singular personhood of his beloved. As a writer, Ivy Blossom is interested in experiments in voice *as* plot, and she puts the *long* in *longing*. When the action does come, the consciousness that filters it is thick. Ivy Blossom finds a welcoming audience for these efforts; in fanfiction, the difficult, the long, and the complex often coincide not only with the romantic and the erotic, but with the popular. This audience has, after all, already decided more is better.

thisprettywren experiments differently. Taken, as many in the Sherlock community are, with perceptive differences and differing abilities, thisprettywren created a "disability!verse" (called the SenseVerse) in which the only "freaks" (an insult frequently thrown at Sherlock in the series and its fic) are those with all five senses. In "Quintessential," Sherlock lacks the ability to feel touch, while John, the transcriber, the blogger, has no voice—an avox, historically the target of the greatest derision. In the new era of more politically enlightened thinking (at least officially), such ableist prejudices only reflect badly on those who hold them.

We learn of this world and its rules through a series of mockup memoranda and other bureaucratic detritus—pages from official university

handbooks, for example—that explain in the neutral language of government how the various abilities and their absence are to be discussed and
treated. Mycroft Holmes, MP, Undersecretary of State for Public Health,
distributes a memorandum on "Annual Amendments to the Compre-
hensive Senso-Variant Registry Handbook" that stipulates various test-
ing requirements. University College London handouts on, for example,
"Your Anoptic Peers," list do's (do "report blinking lights on echolo-
cation devices") and don'ts (don't "hesitate to invite anoptic students
to art galleries and other events; there is always a variant-appropriate
interpretation for them to enjoy!"). All this material converges around a
Baskervilles-related plot, conveyed to the story's characters as well as the
readers in large part via blog and text message, since John can't speak.

Following the lead of the technologically updated BBC *Sherlock* itself
(which took its own lead from canon Holmes' interest in the latest methods and technologies), the fic author greywash has also experimented
with new digital forms of storytelling: visual codings of text, blog, Wiki-
pedia entries, Google searches, and other diverse internet formats. greywash's fic "the sensation of falling just as you hit sleep" also chronicles
the familiar territory of Sherlock's post-Reichenbach absence (aka The
Great Hiatus). Sherlock tries to communicate with John without disclos-
ing his survival to his enemies, and tracks these enemies by the same
technology. There's always a pseudonym, and (as is true of all our electronic communications) we can never be sure of the identity behind it. In
this fic, in fact, the identity shifts. We see John receive these communications and doubt their disembodied reality—a play on disembodiment
that is grotesquely but still somehow poignantly reversed when John falls
in love with a photograph of Sherlock's corpse—which turns out to be as
fake as it is naked. With the help of some skilled coding, we see all this
unfold in various electronic formats. There's even a soundtrack. John and
Sherlock are reunited, and as the fic shifts in focus to their newly (hyper-
consciously) sexual relationship, it abandons electronic formatting for
more (much more) personal communications and interior monologues:

> While they kiss, John's hands move a lot. He touches: Sherlock's hair (more
> or less constantly, with one hand or the other), Sherlock's neck (12% of
> the time), Sherlock's shoulders (between 15 and 22% of the time, depend-
> ing on precisely where he draws his lines), Sherlock's chest (between
> 21 and 24% of the time, same reason), Sherlock's back (between 34 and
> 38% of the time, and how Sherlock loathes imprecision), Sherlock's hips

(3% of the time), and what are inarguably Sherlock's buttocks (8% of the time, though a nontrivial amount of the time John's hands spend on his back makes Sherlock feel shivery enough that he feels like that particular dividing line should be moved substantially upwards, anatomical realities be damned).

Detatched precision in describing erotic content isn't exactly *new* information. The Marquis de Sade long ago catalogued a near-exhaustive collection of sexual recombinations with all the passion of an encyclopedia, but Sade is the very antithesis of romance. The larger point here, though, is that greywash used electronic storytelling methods when it made sense for her story, and other methods when it didn't. greywash's style isn't a gimmick, it's integrated into the storyline and characterization.

Updating storytelling to a more twenty-first-century visual and technological context is of a piece not only with *Sherlock*'s update of late Victorian Holmesiana, but also with the BBC series' updated techniques: its visual presence, its stylish editing, its use of texts and blogs. These innovations, in turn, are in keeping with the *series* source. In other words: the inspiration is not just content. By publishing in *The Strand*, Arthur Conan Doyle used mass media to the outer extreme of its capabilities in the 1880s—just as his characters used the latest detection technologies. Throughout his life, Doyle authorized and collaborated on stage and early film adaptations; similarly, *Sherlock* not only represents but also maintains a transmedia presence. The blogs featured in the series—The Blog of John Watson and Sherlock's The Science of Deduction—are online, comment on each other, and even include Doyle's conceit of referencing stories that aren't actually told—by Doyle, that is—but that have been told by others ever since. A series companion volume even records John and Sherlock's interaction via yellow sticky note—it reads like visual fic for its own series.

Like greywash's multimedia storytelling method, the plot of greywash's fic directly responds to the BBC series, but much less in the spirit of *homage* than in the tried and trusted fandom spirit of irritation. Apparently greywash had some problems with *Sherlock*'s season 2 and wondered what "to jettison" so as to be able to embrace the season in fic. And then, a change of heart:

I told myself to stop being a weenie, and then I told myself I had to keep *some* of it, and then I kind of found myself with my head cocked to one side, asking, what if I keep *everything*? What if I take the stuff that bothers me and make it be *central*?[15]

Accordingly, greywash's plot is convoluted: Sherlock overthinks everything and is crippled by an adolescent understanding of love; the characters who love each other most lie most to each other. Taking dissatisfaction for inspiration is a common and very productive strategy in fanfiction, but it is also one of the least understood by outsiders.

Frustration may also, of course, be shared by some of the characters. Sherlock fic often presents its various lovestruck John Watsons with a kind of dangerous gambit: the exciting scrutiny that defamiliarizes the dependable and comfortable and makes it exotic, erotic, and exciting is often the scrutiny of the mad. No one—by which I mean, no one who I know of writing today in any venue, not just in the Sherlock fandom—explores this gambit with more narrative, lexical, and emotional precision than wordstrings.

wordstrings' Paradox Series is stunning, spinning. This Sherlock reminds us of what we use the thick filters of convention to help us forget: that life gives us "shocking amounts of detail to sift through." George Eliot—whom we've already met as a writer of Sir Walter Scott fanfiction—had room for more in her novel *Middlemarch* than an epigraph-length homage to her fangirl childhood. She also wrote, a bit more famously, about what life might be like without those filters of convention:

> If we had a keen vision and feeling of all ordinary human life, it would be like hearing the grass grow and the squirrel's heart beat, and we should die of that roar which lies on the other side of silence.

wordstrings' Sherlock lives in that roar:

> Just for an instant, *let there be nothing,* he thinks.

> And there was nothing.

> For exactly three seconds, there was nothing at all.

> *God had it entirely backwards, didn't he, all the things in the world, all the useless, petty, undusted, uncared-for, forgotten, overlooked things in the world, it's an utter sham isn't it, the way there are so many individual things with*

> *their individual smells and textures, and half of them warped and cracked,*
> *and green and teal being so different and there being a thousand varieties of*
> *blue at the minimum, I ask you do we need it all, and God probably doesn't*
> *exist anyway, but if He did, that would be a joke, wouldn't it, leaving someone*
> *alone here who can see all of it at once and knows that pink tastes different*
> *from vermillion in a certain way,*

Mad Humbert Humbert brings to *Lolita* something of this kind of attention, this kind of discomfort, but John Watson is no fourteen-year-old girl. He's *middle-aged*. So we can feel less creepy about watching a self-diagnosed sociopath's obsession with him unfold. Maybe. John is a willing, desperately eager object of this obsession. His only fear is that the obsession will fade. He gets angry, of course:

> John touches his tongue to his lower lip, still staggeringly furious. It's like
> watching National Geographic, Sherlock thinks, when something very
> small and furry and soft suddenly seems made of teeth.
>
> It's relatively quiet in his head at the moment, but that's temporary. So
> he thinks over what he should bring back to John by way of apology for
> being who he is.

For anyone who has struggled with mental illness, or loved someone who struggled with it, wordstrings' series resonates, as its comments section attested. For those who haven't, it gives a taste. John is not the only object of this Sherlock's scrutiny; the most unrelenting examinations catalogue his own aberrant desires, his feared moral failings, and his terror at his organic inability to distinguish right from wrong. He rigorously transcribes and categorizes his various desires into two lists, which he labels "Fine" and "Not Fine"; one of the central conflicts of the series is that he cannot reliably tell the difference. At one point, after Sherlock has eviscerated all of the Ten Commandments in his journey to become a more high-functioning person, John convinces him to share the full contents of the lists (readers only ever get samples) and then insists on moving several of them around. (Divorce, for example, which Sherlock had categorized as "Fine" because it's normal, in that lots of people do it, John moves emphatically to the "Not Fine" list.) We watch these agonies unfold from the inside, through the distorting lens of Sherlock's mental illness (or neuro-atypicality), and from the outside, from the midst of John's helpless adoration of someone he believes to be "The William Shakespeare of Atrociously Skewed Morals."

In wordstrings' erotic scenes as in many others, Sherlock's observational and deductive skills—in most canonical and official versions, a largely asexual character particular—have been a boon. Even devoted readers of erotica complain that such scenes have a tendency to become stale, rote. This can hold even more true when the scenes repeatedly unfold between (versions of) the same characters. As in fanfiction.

Or, you know, in monogamy.

Fanfiction Sherlock and John's erotic and romantic dealings offer hope that, under the right kind of scrutiny, with the right kind of attention paid, even an average person might continue to be full of surprises.

In this way, "Johnlock" as a romantic pairing often lives up to, albeit in a different configuration, Thackeray's dream of "middle-aged" romance. The BBC Sherlock and John are in their mid- to late thirties, but in the Doyle stories, they age together. They visit each other in retirement. This long partnership—of which readers never tired, even if their author did—presents a relationship that remains (sometimes) exciting and fulfilling into old age, even if it also—as Rex Stout pointed out—sometimes felt like habit. Retirement fic is its own *Sherlock* subgenre. As a whole, Johnlock fic depicts long-term exclusivity in a complex light, and with an attention that much professionally produced culture seems to find impossible or unattractive. Yet all the Johns and Sherlocks continue to find each other fascinating, irritating, and uniquely sustaining—much as the originals seemed to do over their (first) decades of fictional partnership.

The Slasher Who Is Not One
(An Interview with Katie Forsythe
and wordstrings)

TWO OF THE MOST ADMIRED and well-loved writers in the vast, multilayered Sherlock Holmes universe(s) are Katie Forsythe, who has been writing pitch-perfect Victorian-style erotica for many years, and wordstrings, discussed previously. Katie Forsythe's Fanlore entry[16] calls her "probably the most-recced writer of book-canon Holmes/Watson stories." These stories prompted another fan (damned_colonial) to propose the term *Forsythian* as an alternative to the terms *Doylist* (in which continuity breaks in canon are due to author error) or *Watsonian* (in which continuity breaks in canon are due to Watson's mistake or strategy):

> A Forsythian perspective interprets the text from the standpoint of the text *as written by Watson while trying to divert attention from his and Holmes's homosexual relationship.* Any discrepancies, such as jumps in time, gaping plot holes, or bizarre non-sequiturs (as, for instance, Holmes's musings on a rose during The Naval Treaty) are due to this attempt to rewrite history. The more irreconcilable the discrepancy, the hotter the sex being covered up.[17]

The Fanlore entry for wordstrings' Paradox Series is more extensive, incorporating text from several lengthy online reviews and samples from the large quantity of fanart, video, music mixes, and translations the series has inspired—all of which the author welcomes, and about which she declares herself "staggered and flattered."

Despite their vastly divergent styles, settings, and characterizations, Katie Forsythe and wordstrings' distinctive written universes share a driving interest in the intricacies of codependency, mental illness, and addiction. Each also attends with a kind of haunting precision to the particularities of individual desires and the perplexing failings of language to communicate—especially when caught up in these desires—exactly when and what we most need it to.

These shared preoccupations make it less surprising that Katie Forsythe and wordstrings are the same person, a fact that became fully public knowledge only recently, when she announced it on her profile page. After this interview was conducted, wordstrings deleted her LiveJournal account, where all the thousands of comments to her fiction were housed, for the stated reason that the huge personal response to her stories and characters had become too much for her. Her work as wordstrings is at Archive of Our Own; her work as Katie Forsythe is at liquidfic.org.

What first drew you to write about Sherlock Holmes?

I read the stories as a child, like a lot of people did. Even when I was very young, my favorite books all featured what I sort of characterize as "I'd die for you" male friendships—*Lord of the Rings*, Sherlock Holmes, et cetera. Something about the abundance of love in the canon really drew me into the world of Holmes and his doctor friend.

When I was about seventeen or eighteen—seventeen, I think, I'm only in my thirties now—I discovered that classic H/W site However Improbable. And as far as I can recall it, sex hadn't really entered into my slashy little consciousness yet, at least as far as Holmes and Watson were concerned. I'd imagined them in all kinds of dangerous hurt/comfort-creating situations, but I didn't know other people were writing material that directly appealed to me—fic writers like Pandapony and Irene Adler. I took a stab at it myself and the result was "The Sign of Change," the first part of which is still up on However Improbable. Before I quite knew what was happening, there was a hell of a lot of material.

My background was very, very conservative Catholic—I was pent up about all kinds of things sexually, bisexual without really realizing it, genderqueer on a spectrum I've never really scrutinized too closely. Meanwhile, I look like a tiny über-feminine girl (I somewhat resemble that most loathed of characters from *The L Word*, Jenny Schecter), and slash was a way to unload a ton of angst and personal conflict.

Do you write other kinds of work—fiction, poetry, nonfiction—or is your writing mostly focused on fic?

I'm a fic girl.

In canon-verse, your vocabulary—including historically appropriate slang for homosexuality—is very accurate and authentic. What kinds of research do you do, or have you been so immersed in period literature that it comes naturally at this point?

I think the latter. I love period literature, so I don't find myself having to do a great deal of research, although there have certainly been occasions I've used slang dictionaries. And I equally love the history of queer culture, so that isn't too challenging. As for the rest of the historical settings, "The Presbury Letters," for instance, God bless Google.

Why did you choose to write under a new pseudonym?

Oh dear, and not everyone knows I'm Katie Forsythe, though most people do (I wasn't exactly keeping a tight lid on it). Well, for one thing, my canon 'verse stuff is exactly that, canon 'verse, and I was keen to keep it that way. For another, and this is going to sound awful, I was getting a bit frightened at the level of response to my work, and feeling a rather strange responsibility for creating ever more of it, and I wanted a nice quiet little LJ [LiveJournal] where I could post utterly mad BBC *Sherlock* fic and no one would see it. In all seriousness, that was the plan.

I sent messages to about fifteen of my closest fandom acquaintances, telling them I'd be posting under wordstrings and then I crossposted the fic to the BBC *Sherlock* group and to Cox & Co. It worked like a charm until "The Death and Resurrection of the English Language," and then I opened my inbox one day and had something like 300 comments. It was completely unexpected. I literally stepped away from my laptop in shock.

Have you written fic for other versions or offshoots of Arthur Conan Doyle's world? If so, which ones? If not, what in particular about the BBC *Sherlock* inspired you to take on a new style and identity?

No, just canon and BBC. BBC *Sherlock* just captures the intensity of their relationship so well. And it's far more serious in tone than the Warner Bros. version, though I love that, too. I don't know; there's just such a light in their eyes when they're off adventuring together. I was a bit sick of filling in canonical blanks in high Victorian style, and I thought it would be fun times to play over in the BBC yard. All sunshine and daisies and fuzzy jumpers. Then a lot of things happened in my personal life, and the world of the Paradox 'verse took a sharp turn for the dark.

Commentators describe your Sherlock as "neuro-atypical." Do you have a diagnosis you prefer?

Do they really? Well, most of my work relies on the series to inform it, though many, many people have informed me (and I entirely agree with them) that my Sherlock is darker and madder than the one on the show. I admit, when season two came along and Sherlock drugged John and locked him in a lab making demon dog noises, I was like, yep, there you are, my favorite crazed sociopath. To be clear, I don't think the Sherlock of the show is in fact a sociopath, but the Sherlock of the Paradox 'verse posits that he is. He's also simply a genius, and suffers from synesthesia and episodes resembling bipolar disorder, a topic with which I am regrettably familiar. Other things, like the white letters, are completely inspired by the production design.

Your Sherlock is sometimes overwhelmed by particulars and believes himself to be unique—do you agree? Is he "Sherlock-atypical" in the same way he is "John-sexual"—an entirely fictional singularity?

If he were entirely fictional, if he weren't based on real humans, no one would respond to the series the way they have—which is to say, very, very enthusiastically, for which I am eternally grateful for their generosity of spirit. Sherlock's set of issues are unique to him, yes, but I think everyone experiences shades of acting selfishly even though they know better, wishing you could turn your head off, hurting the people you love without wanting to. He's a character who is deeply uncomfortable inside himself, and I relate to that, and it turns out a lot of other people do as well. My Sherlock just takes those feelings and ramps them up to eleven.

Are there negative experiences you've had as a result of this fic (people upset over content, for example when Sherlock is stereotypically "shamming gay," or simply too much internet fame)?

Plenty. I don't blame anyone for it, but my stories tend to bring out a lot of feelings and people tend to want to express them to me directly. For instance, one of the reasons I slowed way down in my canon 'verse is because very kind people were sharing with me all sorts of aspects of their own experiences with mental health problems, addiction, and abuse, and here I was trying to write the crazies out of my head for myself, and the whole process turned into another animal entirely. I've had multiple people inform me that I've stopped them from suicide. Now, that's an enormous honor and an incredibly brave statement and completely unbelievable and something I'll carry with me for the rest of my life. It justifies my existence on the planet in some ways. But the volume was turned up way too high for me, through no direct fault of anyone's.

My Paradox Sherlock has his admirers and his detractors, but I've been very clear since the series took an edgier turn that he isn't a role model. He's just a very screwed-up fellow who can still love and be loved in return. A few people were livid over the gay shamming scene, partly because I didn't warn them in advance, but that's okay and legitimate and we talked it through. My Sherlock is simply demisexual, so he doesn't see himself as being gay. He sees himself as loving John. Which is why later, when he rather adores Irene, I think his statement that he's not exactly gay and might have had sex with a woman if presented with the right one comes to full completion. A few people wanted to see him as a queer advocate, and he's in fact a lunatic. So they were destined for disappointment. They were destined for more disappointment at the climax of "Entirely Covered in Your Invisible Name" when they wanted him to be a nice, harmless sociopath and he isn't. But it's fiction; it's not a guide to life any more than *Lolita* is. Then there was the great BDSM kerfuffle, which squicked some people, but I'm kinky, so . . . it is what it is.

The fandom fame is something I try to downplay as much as possible by talking as little about myself as I can and only posting fic when it exists—I'm no arbiter of taste, and I don't step into arguments or fandom drama very often. I read, I write, I lurk. I admire others from afar. This interview is something of an aberration for me.

Sherlock has difficulty with ethics. John is "good at" right from wrong—but not always where Sherlock is concerned. Do you ever feel similarly torn about the ethics of what you are representing? Or have people challenged you on the ethics of representing an ethically challenged but ethically conscious (even ethically obsessed) relationship?

Yes and no. Yes, people have told me or have mentioned in rec lists that the relationship is borderline abusive and absolutely dysfunctional. I agree with those people. And yes, people have gotten into conversations with me about the ethics of portraying that. But I also get a ton of correspondence from people who like that it's morally complicated, that no one is wholly innocent or wholly unforgiveable, that these are utterly screwy people who still deserve love. All my stories are about love. If the love wasn't there, if it was just Sherlock threatening to kill his partner or John calling himself one of Sherlock's "things" or any of the other completely unhealthy aspects of the stories, I can't imagine anyone would read them. And Sherlock, for all his terrible faults, is well-intentioned, and I think that John can work with that.

Why do you prefer posting online to publishing traditionally?

Because the stories aren't for readers, they're for me and my noisy, noisy head, and then when people happen to read them and enjoy them or even come away feeling a bit better, that's a completely unexpected bonus. Charging money for them would be like having heart surgery and then billing the doctor for the privilege of working on me. Sometimes I need to write these mad tales in order to get rid of all the muck in my chest, and I'd never dream of charging anyone money for the results. That's the reason I allow adaptations of the Paradox 'verse without having to ask my permission as well . . . the same reason you can podfic anything I write as wordstrings or Katie Forsythe, or print it on a T-shirt, or translate it or what you will, and without my knowledge (though I'd love the link, if it comes to that). I already accomplished the therapy by writing the fic, and it was written for selfish reasons. Then I put it online and it belongs to everyone; take it or leave it as you will.

This isn't to say that I don't appreciate my readers, on the contrary. I adore my readers. They bring me great joy. But I, Katherine of various LJ names, didn't expect them. They are a perennial happy surprise.

Are your stories ever influenced by community response? Do you have pre-readers?

No, and no. Because again, they're for me and what I need. I think one of the unintended side effects of that isolation is that it's made me rather fearless regarding both style and substance. I'm not frightened of showing Sherlock and John in a bad light, and I'm not nervous about trying stylistic tricks that might not work. On the other hand, if I did have a beta, my scribblings would certainly be less riddled with typos.

I find your fic incredibly intense. I wonder if writing Sherlock this way brings the mind of the writer uncomfortably close to the madness described. Does that ever happen?

To an enormous extent, these people are loco because I am loco. For instance, I am a very highly functioning addict, and so is the Holmes over in my canon worlds. Now, no, I'm not a sociopath nor a genius nor a synesthete nor a solider with PTSD. But I am a nutcase, and my brain runs on multiple tracks with no off switch. I write to scrape ugly feelings off my chest, and then I put them on the internet and run away. Writing someone who's still madder than I am on the continuum, really madder by far, seems to be good for my mental health. Which is why I write them this way. They are little catharses wrapped in a bow.

Usually your universes are very distinct (the way the men refer to each other as "friends" was one commonality I saw). Do you ever intend for your ACD-verse to bleed into the Sherlock-verse? Do you see these verses as connected?

They don't bleed on purpose. I have three versions of Holmes, essentially (my Watsons tend to vary less). First, the classic prickly gent from the canon stories, the way he's always been slashed— aloof, can't express emotion, loves Watson desperately but works it obliquely, about as good at relationships as a steamed head of cabbage. Next, the Holmes in my *Love* collection, who was conceived as niceboyfriend!Holmes after I'd been writing the prickly gent for too long and thought, What if I'm giving this guy a bad rap? And then Sherlock, who is madder than a bag of ferrets.

But I think at heart, in their heart of hearts, Sherlock and John and Holmes and Watson are friends first. I'm a slasher, so they're also banging, but it's about this massive, uncontainable love they have for each other, so yes...I think they're always friends. That part bleeds over from story to story because that's what draws me to them in the first place. They're the best set of friends I've ever seen.

part two

A SELECTIVE HISTORY
OF MEDIA FANDOM

An Illustrative Narrative of Technology,
Continuity, and Change

Science Fiction, *Star Trek*, and the Birth of Media Fandom

Here we learn what it means to be a fan. Our hero, Jophan, is woken to a new life by his discovery of fanzines. He moves through a symbolic landscape populated by people with symbolic names, in search of "The Enchanted Duplicator," with which he will be able to publish the perfect fanzine and become a True Fan. Eventually our Everyfan survives technical difficulties, his own inexperience, harsh criticism, and over-kind praise, and becomes a True Fan when he knows himself, when he can automatically give back to others what he has received.

—Andy Sawyer, of "The Enchanted Duplicator"

FANFICTION IS FUELED by relationships, and it fuels relationships. It creates them. When fanwriting was predominantly a solitary activity, the primary relationships were between writer and source, and then writer and story. Family magazines similar to those created by the young Brontë children were not uncommon, but they did not circulate widely, as reproduction was a matter of hand copying. As the twentieth century progressed, fans—primarily of Sherlock Holmes or, alternatively, science fiction—found they might join societies, receive and contribute to journals, and, eventually, make their own small publications, or zines. In the case of Sherlock Holmes, some critic-fans published pastiche, as we've seen, but most early fanzine writing was critical and historical in nature. In science fiction fandoms, zines were dominated by commentary—and published writers often took part as well. Many professionals also counted themselves as fans or began as fan writers before going on to publish professionally.

Before the 1960s, fanfiction as a term (or rather "fan fiction," with a space) designated original fiction by amateur writers published in fanzines. It was many years before fanfiction in the sense of stories based on existing worlds and characters began to fill science fiction zines (although there are anecdotal stories of such zines being produced and circulated on a very small scale). Nonetheless, the importance of zine culture to the development of fanfiction as it exists today cannot be overemphasized. Zine publication may not sound as sexy as coming up with the Kirk/Spock erotica that eventually gave birth to, for one thing, the contemporary genre of male birth fic (they didn't mean to), but when you talk to early science fiction fans, even early media fans, what they want to talk about are zines: writing content to ensure they could get their hands on copies. The tactile experience of the hand-made objects. The high prices they were sometimes willing to pay. Making them. Stapling them. The collating parties. The potlucks. I have heard these stories many times over now, both from those who left fandom after the rise of the internet and those who embrace internet culture wholeheartedly. Zines were the first step in creating fan-produced culture; as soon as fans had the means of production, they produced.

At first, fandom culture and its zines—in early days, called amateur magazines—were almost entirely male-dominated. What zines meant, and what fanfiction meant, changed as fandom sources shifted from print (literary) to media-based interests. Fanwriting culture also changed in response to technology, which increasingly allowed fanwriting to reach more readers, just as broadcast television ultimately reached more fans— at least more fans simultaneously—than print could. Some of this culture looks familiar, but some elements would be surprising to many active in fandoms today.

As is especially apparent in today's larger fandoms, there can be a good deal of discontent about BNFs growing too big for their britches. I've seen incredible anger expressed toward fans who fancy themselves "real writers" or "real artists" or otherwise put themselves on a par with the creators of the fandom's source. In 1950s science fiction communities, though, writers often *were* active fans. Ray Bradbury, for example, was a lifelong fanboy; he wrote to artists and authors he admired for autographs throughout his career—long after he became not just a writer but a global public institution in his own right. In her essay here, Jacqueline Lichtenberg details interacting from a young age with the writers she was reading through letters of comment in zines, and later continuing to use those letters columns to receive communication from her own fans. In earlier days, science fiction fandom as a whole could seem less like us (fans) v. them (creators/rightsholders) and more like us (science fiction world) v. them ("mundanes" or nonfans).

So it's here that we start our highly selective history of media fandom and its fanfiction: with a different definition of fanfiction and an earlier set of fans, as well as the *Star Trek* fanfiction fandom, long considered the first modern fic-writing group, that emerged from it.

Andy Sawyer, librarian of the Science Fiction Foundation Collection at the University of Liverpool Library, science fiction scholar, teacher, editor, and fan, relates a forgotten era and entirely different meaning for "fan fiction," one that dates from 1950s Ireland.

Enormous fandom controversies today arise around both Real Person Fic (RPF, or fanfiction based on real people rather than characters) and Big Name Fans (BNFs). Such conflicts are fictionalized in the Sherlock fic "The Theory of Narrative Causality" and they resurface as topics throughout this volume. Yet in a largely forgotten element of fanfiction history, one that introduces the specificity of local fandom culture to an emerging international zine exchange, we see that some of the earliest science fiction fanfiction was essentially RPF of BNFs—and was received unscathed and scandal-free.

The internet has done away with many of the distinctive local cultures that arose around particular fandoms in particular places. This group preserved some of itself for us, in fictionalized form, in science fiction zines that were circulated throughout the UK and America.

Fables of Irish Fandom
Fan Fiction in the 1950s and '60s

Andy Sawyer

For much of the history of science fiction fandom, fan fiction did not represent fiction set in the universe of a fan's favorite book/TV series/film. Rather, it was either fiction written by fans and published in fanzines (as opposed to that by professional writers published in professional magazines) or fiction *about* fans and fandom, written as a joke for the people who were made gentle fun of. One of the greatest exponents of this was John Berry, whose "Fables of Irish Fandom" were published in a number of British and American fanzines between 1954 and 1965, and reprinted in five volumes by British fan Ken Cheslin between 1998 and 1999.[18] Eventually publishing around sixty of these "Fables," Berry described the lives of Northern Ireland's Belfast group, in a kind of soap opera of fannish lives.

Archie Mercer, a British science fiction fan who wrote his own fiction (*Meadows of Fantasy*) in which lightly disguised members of fandom appear, once wrote to Berry, telling him, "When he started to read my Irish Fandom Stories, everything seemed to be perfectly orderly and rational, yet when he'd finished reading the articles, he felt he had been transported into a fantasy world, but he had been unable to finger the transition" ("Down Memory Lain"[19]). Berry, a prolific writer,[20] was a member of the fan group that centered around Walter ("Walt") and Madeline Willis in the 1950s. His accounts started as a joke, one that was sometimes carried too far; Berry also noted that "the lead players became rather irritated by my frequent revelations." They remain an affectionate and amusing picture of a subculture and individuals still revered by certain sections of British fandom. Through Berry's stories, fans in the rest of Britain and America got to know the "Belfast Group." But this knowledge was built upon the way fans know one another, an acquaintance that differed from the usual ways in which people know their friends. Communication here was rarely in person—attendance at science fiction conventions was relatively infrequent for many fans—and usually through the exchange of fanzines. Berry's fables allowed you to feel that you were part of the group.

The context within which Berry was writing is best put by him, in his 1958 story "Star Struck."[21] Here, he talks of "the fundamental facets of a true science fiction fan." He continues: "I had considered myself pretty well indoctrinated in all the basic necessities...nurtured on THE ENCHANTED DUPLICATOR . . . a concentrated course of QUAN-DRY, OOPSLA and SLANT . . . followed by high pressure appreciation of GRUE...reading ASTOUNDING, GALAXY, etc...mad about the pro's...STURGEON, BLISH, BRADBURY, WHITE and SHAW, etc..."[22] When Berry started reading science fiction in the late-1940s "golden age," American magazines were central (it was not until after the war that British magazines such as *New Worlds*, *Nebula*, and *Authentic* offered science fiction to fans in the United Kingdom). *Astounding*, established in 1930 and edited by John W. Campbell, was fundamental. *Galaxy Science Fiction*, founded in 1950 by H. L. Gold, was one of a number of magazines that successfully challenged *Astounding* during the 1950s. The American professional writers Berry name-checks—Theodore Sturgeon, James Blish, Ray Bradbury—were rooted in the magazines, but their novels appeared in book form on both sides of the Atlantic throughout the 1940s and '50s. Two other names in that last list, James White and Bob Shaw, were fellow members of Irish Fandom who had gone on to become professionals in their own right, and whose work was just starting to be published during the early 1950s.

It is significant, however, that Berry begins his list of "fundamental facets of a true science fiction fan" with references to fanzines and fannish activity rather than actual science fiction. *Quandry*, *Oopsla*, *Slant*, and *Grue* were popular fanzines of the time, written by fans and distributed in return for trades of other fanzines, contributions, or letters of comment. In them, science fiction was often discussed but, increasingly, the focus was the activity of fandom itself. The defining document of this activity was *The Enchanted Duplicator*, a mock-epic allegory published by Walter Willis and Bob Shaw in 1954 as a mimeographed booklet.[23]

Here we learn what it means to be a fan. Our hero, Jophan, is woken to a new life by his discovery of fanzines. He moves through a symbolic landscape populated by people with symbolic names, in search of "The Enchanted Duplicator," with which he will be able to publish the perfect fanzine and become a True Fan. Eventually our Everyfan survives technical difficulties, his own inexperience, harsh criticism, and over-kind praise, and becomes a True Fan when he knows himself, when he can automatically give back to others what he has received.

Walter Willis, acknowledged leader of the Belfast Group and the main instigator of *The Enchanted Duplicator*, was, when John Berry got to know him, working for the Northern Ireland Civil Service. He was born in Belfast to a Protestant family who had moved from southern Ireland. Although its most violent times were to come, Northern Ireland was troubled by sectarian division between Protestant and Catholic communities, and Willis, who died in 1999, must have worked through some of the region's most difficult years. He therefore kept his life as a civil servant separate from his life as a fan. Fandom was a hobby, and when it ceased being quite so fulfilling, or the pressures of daily life began to impinge, he scaled down. John Berry's day job was in the police force, so similar pressures may have applied to him. Although he continued to correspond with individual fans, most of his fan activity was over by the mid-sixties. He died in 2011.

The Willises were SF readers—indeed, they told the story of how they met in a shop selling SF magazines[24]—but they were unaware of fandom until Walter discovered a US edition of *Astounding* in a secondhand bookshop, and realized that the British editions he had been reading were in fact heavily abridged. Above all, they lacked what made fandom possible: the letters column, where readers expressed opinions and through which (as postal addresses were usually printed) they could contact each other. By the end of 1948, Willis and White had issued their first fanzine, *Slant*, followed by thirty-six issues of *Hyphen* from 1952 to 1965. Apart from a regular column on fandom in *Nebula* from 1952 to 1959, a coauthored short story, a 1972 reprint of *The Enchanted Duplicator* in *Amazing*, and a book, *The Improbable Irish* (Ace, 1969, under the name Walter Bryan), virtually all of Willis' writing appeared as amateur fanwriting.

Although Willis was certainly not the only fan who emphasized humor and satire and a focus on fan personalities rather than a desire to write or criticize science fiction, he was quickly identified as a master of the quip and the humorous column. His light yet incisively intelligent style made him popular on both sides of the Atlantic. He loved what he read, but did not take it seriously, if by "seriously" one means "solemnly." In fact, because he took what he read very seriously indeed, Willis encouraged mocking the idiosyncrasies of fandom and of science fiction itself.

We first meet the Belfast Group in "Coming Up for the Third Time," first published in Willis' *Hyphen* (1954). Berry, an Englishman who had moved to Northern Ireland in 1949 to be with his fiancée, Diane, had joined the police force and was posted to Belfast. Discovering references to a fan group in the city, Berry wrote to Willis and was invited to meet him. In "Coming Up" he describes his nervousness in meeting WALT WILLIS (his capitals). At first distracted by a prominently displayed picture of Marilyn Monroe (mild salaciousness is a constant presence in his stories), Berry settles into conversation with Willis and is invited back to meet the rest of the group: Bob Shaw, James White, and George Charters, described here as an inveterate punster, but who in later stories is teased (as the oldest member of the group) as being a hard-of-hearing, senile old buffer in a wheelchair.

Berry's stories are usually opportunities to tease his friends rather than specifically plotted fictions: each of them are given specific personae. They are slippery stories because they start with the assumption that their readers are familiar with these personae, and then gently satirize them. They are not a stable source for biography. Charters was older, but not that much older. "Bob Shaw" is surrounded by decrepit machinery and greedily devours Madeline's cakes. James White worked for a clothing store, and is therefore depicted as being sartorially elegant and always ready to sell a friend a suit of clothes. Each writer is both admired for being a "pro" and teased for their prolific output: "If I hurry home now," says James White in "Star Struck," "I'll just have time enough to bash out another chapter for Carnell before Peggy wakes up."[25] Willis is the group's "genius" and natural leader. Berry himself is the "neo," naïvely hero-worshipping his new friends. In "Arrested Development" (*Triode*, 1955; collected in *A Time Regained*), he writes about how Bob Shaw intends to join the police force, and how Walt Willis invents a fiendishly difficult "examination paper" for him. Berry addresses Shaw as "Mr. Shaw" throughout and Willis as "Sir."

A typical story is "Bob and the Typewriter" (*Oopsla*, 1957; collected in *The If Files*[26]), which plays upon the connection between Shaw and machinery. Berry expresses a desire for a typewriter. Willis sets things in motion by remarking, "Here's a client for your typewriter, Bob." We are set up for the joke by Shaw's salesman-like actions as he prepares the innocent for the kill. Berry stresses the difference in status between neophyte and professional author: "What a glorious opportunity, I thought. Me, getting a pro-author's typewriter." Shaw offers Berry an opportunity to test it. An experienced if slow typist ("I can do it blindfolded so there was no need for me to remove the layer of scum off the keys"), Berry tries and fails to type the test word. Shaw covers up his typewriter's failure by technical gobbledygook ("something wrong with the gribble draw-back lever"), and finally offers to sell it "dirt cheap." When Shaw suggests three pounds for an object Berry has already calculated would cost several times that amount to fix, Berry is torn between not wanting to be cheated and their bond as fans. The joke, of course, is that Bob is offering him three pounds to "take the bloody thing away."

More fictionalized are the Goon Defective Agency stories,[27] in which John Berry rewrites himself as "Goon Bleary," a bumbling private eye who investigates cases in which fandom and fanzines appear prominently. Spoofing the hard-boiled detective stories of Raymond Chandler, the stories also owe something to the surreal British radio comedy *The Goon Show*, which aired from 1951 to 1960. "Goon," of course, is also a slang expression for a dim-witted thug, and Goon Bleary solves his cases more by luck than judgment. "This Goon for Hire" (whose title echoes the 1942 film *This Gun for Hire*) recasts Irish Fandom as characters in a noir novel. The Goon is summoned to the Willis residence by a telegram from Walt:

Madeline opened the door.

"What gives, sister?" I growled.

She looked at me. She was pale, apprehensive.

"Upstairs," she breathed.

I pushed past her, then halted. I thought I heard machine-gun fire. I tiptoed to a door on my left...listened. The staccato noise stopped.

"Page ninety-two of my new story just completed," I heard a tired voice gasp.[28]

(The writer churning out fiction at high speed is Bob Shaw.) Goon Bleary enters Willis' study and is offered a new case: someone has stolen Willis' autographed copy of the fanzine *Star Rockets*. The joke here is that *Star Rockets* was, as a note to the story in Ken Cheslin's reprint tells us, a fanzine that was "fabulously awful." The Goon solves his case and claims his reward—although Willis backtracks on his offer of a set of smutty magazines and thrusts upon him a complete set of—*Star Rockets*.

Another story, "The Fan Who Never Was,"[29] mingles the confusion of identity from the 1956 film *The Man Who Never Was*, about the wartime planting of a corpse with forged letters to fool the Germans into thinking the planned Allied invasion of Sicily would take place elsewhere, with a hoax famous among British fandom in the 1950s. Goon Bleary is called in by the security service to investigate a problem at the War Office. Central here is "Sergeant H. P. Sanderson"—who was, as Berry's readers would have immediately grasped, a fan named "Sandy" Sanderson who was a sergeant in the army. There are opportunities for in-jokes when the security agent fails to understand what Bleary means when he quotes fanzine titles and fannish expressions, but eventually Bleary is planted, disguised as a typist in the Women's Royal Army Corps, in Sanderson's office. The opportunity here for salacious sniggering is not lost ("He looked me up and down. 'Come in, my deah,' he said, sort of throbbing like."[30]), but more important is the plotting, which is among Berry's most skilful. Just as an agent is trailing Sanderson, someone is trailing the agent. It turns out to be Bleary's assistant, Art, who is helping a young woman, grievously wronged by Sanderson, to get her revenge.

The woman's name, Joan Carr, is the clue. In 1952, the "real" Sanderson had decided to hoax fandom by inventing a completely fictitious fan. Partly because there were few women in fandom at the time, and partly because it would highlight his ingenuity if he succeeded, he decided to make this fan a woman. So "Joan Carr" was born. "Joan" was, like

Sanderson, a member of the armed forces, serving abroad, so her absence from conventions was not unusual. "She" engaged in correspondence with other fans and eventually became one of the editors of *Femizine*, along with Sanderson's coconspirator, Frances Evans. The hoax was eventually revealed in 1956.

For "The Fan Who Never Was," Berry invents a real Joan Carr who "knew she couldn't go to conventions and write to people and say she was Joan Carr, because they would laugh."[31] Joan goes on to say that "they would laugh at her, revile her, maybe even suggest she was a hoax and was using the name for notoriety." It has certainly been argued that the hoax, while well-intentioned, made it more difficult for women to become involved in fandom for more or less those reasons.

Joan has arranged for Sanderson to be posted to the Pacific, destroying his life in fandom. Goon Bleary solves the case by making the agent an offer he can't refuse (the phone number of a woman who does "artistic poses"), but also saves Joan Carr from being prosecuted by the authorities for illegal entry and forgery by pointing out the logic of the situation. If she were to be caught and prosecuted by the authorities for illegal entry and forgery, it would be possible to provide documentary proof and hundreds of witnesses who would swear she does not exist.[32]

Through their own writing, and Berry's fiction, the core of Irish Fandom—the Willises, Bob and Sadie Shaw, White, George Charters, Berry himself, and a few "honorary members" like the artist Arthur Thomson (Atom)—become personalities. It is a very much a male group. Madeline Willis and Sadie Shaw, and more rarely, Peggy White, occasionally take part in social activities. Madeline supplies tea and cakes for their gatherings in the Willises' home, Oblique House (a reference to the fanzine *Slant*, but also a pun on Charles Dickens' *Bleak House*). But Berry's wife, Diane, is specifically identified as "non-fannish," and none of the women seem very interested in science fiction. It's a world linked through shared rituals—playing ghoodminton (a legendary fannish version of badminton in which we are told that "rules were non-existent"[33]), trading "prozines," writing and publishing—and heavy-handedly affectionate teasing. It's a world fandom today has, rather sadly, lost.

I Am Woman, Read My Fic

IN THE HISTORY OF FANFICTION, *Star Trek* fulfilled its stated mission: to boldly go where no (f)an had gone before. While fanzines focusing on commentary were the norm in science fiction fandom in the 1960s, zines devoted to fanfiction, in the sense of amateur-authored stories set in an already created universe, were not. As Andy Sawyer explained, science fiction fandom had "fan fiction" that treated fans as characters; zines also published original science fiction stories by fans as opposed to commercially published writers. But while individual texts that resembled what we would now call fanfiction had been around for a *long* time, they were not an element of early science fiction zines. With *Star Trek,* they exploded onto the scene.

Star Trek, and even more so its body of fanworks, created science fiction centered on relationships, whether platonic, romantic, or (controversially) sexual. *Star Trek* was not, as we've seen, the first fanfiction fandom, nor the first driven by a close relationship between two men. There was, in fact, significant overlap between these early fic fandoms. Several of the central *Trek* fandom pioneers were also active in Sherlock Holmes circles: Ruth Berman, who founded *T-Negative*, was behind *SH-sf Fanthology* (1967–1973), a zine that collected a variety of writings about Sherlock Holmes and science fiction; the third issue of *Spockanalia* includes speculation by Sherlockian John Boardman on the Holmesian origins of Mr. Spock; and Roberta Rogow (editor of the zine *Grip* as well a filk singer and fandom archivist) has written a number of published Sherlock Holmes pastiches. But *Star Trek was* the first fandom where fanfiction became so central it could sustain multiple fanzines devoted exclusively to fic. With *Star Trek,* fanfiction becomes a true collective...enterprise, the kind of super-social community affair it is today.

Mass-media broadcasts of the source material, increasing access to technologies of reproduction (initially mimeographs, then offset printing, photocopying, and desktop publishing), the sexual revolution, and even Women's Lib all combined to create the conditions for these women fans to take charge. Largely through their efforts, beginning in the late 1960s, fanfiction became a vibrant, active, eclectic, and even driving sector of fan activity. *Star Trek* fanfiction is not the exclusive terrain of women, and never has been, but *Star Trek* was the first sci-fi fandom to engage a really substantial number of them. Women formed a large majority of *Star Trek* fic writers.

As *Star Trek* fic culture evolved, it began the trend of including erotic content in fanfiction (although certainly, bawdy or porny adventures using existing characters and story is nothing new—see "A Prehistory of Fanfiction" and the fates of Samuel Richardson's virtuous heroines). As Jacqueline Lichtenberg explains in her essay "Recollections of a Collating Party," however, this fanfiction trend coincided with and mutually influenced the growing inclusion of sexuality in mainstream science fiction and fantasy literature. Most controversially of all, *Star Trek* also inspired the first slash fandom (slash here and throughout this volume defined as homoerotic romance, usually between characters canonically portrayed as straight), although this element was hardly embraced or even tolerated by the majority of fans.

In the focus of their interest, female *Star Trek* fans surprised the show's creators from the outset. They had thought Captain Kirk would be the big draw and had structured the show accordingly, but Spock got the biggest fan reaction, especially among women. The first zines, *Spockanalia* and *T-Negative* (named after Spock's blood type), reflect this enthusiasm. The show's creators kept up with such zines as a valuable source of insight into fan taste and concerns, and occasionally even contributed in the form of letters from cast members—usually in character.

Like Samuel Richardson before them, *Star Trek*'s creators soon learned the wisdom of engaging seriously with the tastes and interests of the show's assertive, vocal female fans. For example, at the suggestion of Isaac Asimov (a close friend of Roddenberry's), the show sought to help Kirk share in some of the female interest in Spock by making this friendship even more central to the series. This response, in turn, gave "Enterprising Women" (to borrow the title from Camille Bacon-Smith's groundbreaking work) even more material to work with.

Focusing on this central relationship dramatically influenced the dynamic of the show and the fanfiction it inspired. Kirk's relationship to women followed the model of the "lone womanizer," always available to a new romantic interest—and to the fantasies of the female viewer: an established and long-standing formula for male leads in television. With Spock, however, Kirk sustained a complex, long-term commitment of affection and mutual respect. Spock, the withholding, logical one (always a turn-on, apparently), maintained and valued such a relationship with Kirk—but not with a woman (though Nurse Chapel certainly tried). Their relationship *fascinated* viewers—and more than forty years later, continues to do so.

While *Star Trek* fanfiction explores many relationships, Kirk–Spock (and later, Kirk/Spock) had the greatest impact and proved the greatest draw. A common account of the evolution of slash explains that women fans wanted to explore the possibilities of a romantic or sexual pairing in the context of a long-term, complex relationship between equals: a structure mainstream culture was nowhere offering, and certainly not on *Star Trek*. The show allowed for the possibility of such a relationship, but its model of sustained intimacy, trust, and love was between men. When heterosexual liaisons intervened (or, some might argue, interfered) in the Kirk-Spock friendship, as in the pon farr Vulcan mating ritual (e.g., "Amok Time": Spock is overpowered by the need to mate and believes he has killed Kirk) or on the sex pollen planet (e.g., "This Side of Paradise": Spock falls in love as a result of spores and neglects his duty), it is Kirk who brings Spock back to himself, his duties, and their friendship—by inspiring an equally powerful negative emotion: rage at the racially tinged insults Kirk hurls at him. When Spock shows emotion not caused by spores or mating cycles, it happens only in relation to Kirk. (Sex spores and irresistible mating cycles both went on to become long-standing multifandom tropes, still going strong today.)

Fanfiction explorations of this central friendship were not predominantly slash—especially not at first. Hurt/comfort (vulnerability showcased, friendship tested and proved) in the context of a strictly platonic friendship was extremely popular and remains one of the most popular genres in all fandoms. In the early days, in fact, the slash (as in Kirk/Spock, or K/S) that today identifies a sexual relationship only indicated that the relationship was central to the story. Many fics gave both Kirk and Spock female love interests, with erotic encounters at first implied and in later years detailed with specificity. Slash in the contemporary sense did not begin appearing even in zine publication until 1974 (though it was circulated before that), when the Kirk–Spock relationship as a driving interest of fic was already long established.

That zine publication long postdates the underground existence and circulation of slash stories is anecdotally established. And while the heyday of K/S slash was not until the 1980s and 1990s, the idea of Kirk and Spock as potential romantic partners was commonplace enough in 1979 for Gene Roddenberry, the show's creator, to address it himself, in response to the following question:

> There's a great deal of writing in the *Star Trek* movement which compares the relationship between Alexander and Hephaistion to the relationship between Kirk and Spock—focusing on the closeness of the friendship, the feeling that they would die for one another...
>
> [Roddenberry:] Yes, there's certainly some of that—certainly with love overtones. Deep love. The only difference being, the Greek ideal— we never suggested in the series—physical love between the two. But it's the—we certainly had the feeling that the affection was sufficient for that, if that were the particular style of the 23rd century.[34]

Writing as Captain Kirk in the novelization of 1979's *Star Trek: The Motion Picture,* Roddenberry took to the Vulcan language, and a footnote, to coyly comment on the nature of Kirk–Spock:

> Editor's note: The human concept of friend is most nearly duplicated in Vulcan thought by the term *t'hy'la*, which can also mean brother and lover. Spock's recollection (from which this chapter has drawn) is that it was a most difficult moment for him since he did indeed consider Kirk to have become his brother. However, because *t'hy'la* can be used to mean lover, and since Kirk's and Spock's friendship was unusually close, this has led to some speculation over whether they had actually indeed become lovers. At our request, Admiral Kirk supplied the following comment on this subject:
>
> "I was never aware of this lovers rumor, although I have been told that Spock encountered it several times. Apparently he had always dismissed it with his characteristic lifting of his right eyebrow which usually connoted some combination of surprise, disbelief, and/or annoyance. As for myself, although I have no moral or other objections to physical love in any of its many Earthly, alien, and mixed forms, I have always found my best gratification in that creature woman. Also, I would dislike being thought of as so foolish that I would select a love partner who came into sexual heat only once every seven years."[35]

Fan discussion of this passage has been—of course—rather extensive. Paratextual, parasexual, and incredibly noncommittal, the famous footnote displays Roddenberry's excellent qualifications for Federation

diplomacy. It apparently puts an end to a "lovers" rumor without placing any negative judgment on homosexuality, and furthermore makes
such a reasonable interpretation on linguistic grounds as well as a logical
assumption based on the men's unusual closeness. Reading closely—as
fans and English professors tend to, and as the footnote models through
its attention to language and itself—highlights some additional teasing:
that Kirk's "best gratification" has been with women certainly implies a
more varied experience. Spock's reaction is not firsthand, and the fact
that his raised eyebrow "usually connoted" a range of reactions explicitly
leaves the door open to others. That Kirk "would dislike being thought
of" as choosing such a rarely active sex partner speaks to perception rather
than reality. It's cagey, playful. It begs interpretation. It got it. *Star Trek*'s
creators recognized the importance of talking to fans early on, although
these talks did not always go smoothly among all parties (witness Shatner's
mocking of Trekkies on a 1986 episode of *Saturday Night Live*).

The early days of *Star Trek* fandom have been documented in *Star
Trek Lives!*, *Enterprising Women*, *Textual Poachers*, and a host of other
academic and less academic articles and essays. Of course, Trek fandom
is not *just* history. It is alive and well today, with fic still written for
the original series and its many offshoots: *The Next Generation*, *Deep
Space Nine*, *Voyager*, and *Enterprise* all continue to inspire fic, as does,
of course, *The Original Series*. Most recently, J. J. Abrams' original-series
reboot has inspired a whole new generation of fic-writing fans. Older
fans sometimes welcome the new influx of fans each incarnation brings,
but can also treat them with suspicion, even derision. The early *Star
Trek* fandom faced similar rejection by the broader sci-fi fan culture,
as "literary fans" of print-based SF decried the supposed superficiality
of "media fans," who were also dismissed on account of their (often
female) gender.

Patricia Poole, a retired Canadian family law barrister and still-active
fic writer (currently writing for *Sherlock*, her twelfth fandom), offers her
own historical perspective on the evolution of fandom and its gendered
and generational conflicts:

> I'm a *Star Trek* "dinosaur." I saw the show first run on NBC in 1966–69. At
> age 57 I remain committed to fandom, even though fandom has evolved
> beyond recognition. (Or, maybe that's "committed due to fandom." :-))
>
> At the same time as I was "writing for money" at my job, I wrote fanfic
> for the love of it in fanzines of the late 1980s and early 1990s (*Star Trek*,

Quantum Leap, and one pseudo-scholarly piece about literary references within *Beauty and the Beast* episodes).

My father was a comics and science fiction aficionado back in the 1930s when the term "fandom" was coined. He inculcated me with some beliefs almost universally held by fans, but not necessarily by the "mundane" world then: "The future will be better much better than we can imagine." "There are no limits to what one dedicated person can change and accomplish." He made sure I watched *Star Trek* with him. He convinced Mom to bend my bedtime so I could.

I attended my first con on Halloween 1973. StarCon was a Detroit *Star Trek* convention. Attendance was equally split between males and females, but ages skewed far younger than most SF cons of the time. The "Discovery Effect" was in the air that weekend, more seductive than pheromones.

I was one of the many fans who corresponded with Jacqueline Lichtenberg, Sondra Marshak, and Joanie Winston through my friend Carol Frisbie about that "Discovery Effect" and other fannish matters. The resulting book, *Star Trek Lives!* may have been the first book about fandom. I remember being stunned to find things I had written transformed into pages in a real book, albeit uncredited.

In the late 1970s and early 1980s, the rising number of women in science fiction fandom coincided with SF appearing in places other than in books. A schism developed. "Media fans" were interested in SF, but mainly as depicted in TV or film. "Literary fans" maintained true SF was in print.

In these early days, media fans were only 60–75 percent female. But, media fans who wrote *media fanfic* skewed closer to 90 percent female. Literary fans were about 90 percent male.

Here in Michigan and Ontario, with the particular people I knew, and from what I could see on the ground, it looked a whole lot like a Battle of the Sexes to me. Certainly the epithets hurled were along gender lines.

A multitude of further schisms have followed over the decades, like the spreading limbs of a logic tree. Fandom is certainly much more diverse and diffuse than it used to be.

I've participated in about a dozen fandoms. Initially, all of them were SF related. Over the years, the links to SF in my personal interests became tenuous. My latest fandom has nothing to do with SF.

But, I'm still on the email list of a group in which most of the members self-identify as "literary" SF fans. Recently I was involved in a discussion about "Welcoming New Fans." Comments were exchanged bemoaning the dearth of young fans joining the group. Members speculated on why the new cohort has "different interests" and "don't attend cons."

The comments got progressively sillier until I snapped and replied: The 2012 World Science Fiction Convention in Chicago had 5,000 members, much lower than in the past. Yet Dragon*Con 2012 in Atlanta (which describes itself as a "multimedia, popular culture" con) had 52,000 attendees, and 130,000 fans showed up at Comic-Con 2012 in San Diego.

I also pointed out the "literary" club had never traditionally "welcomed" those with "different interests." In fact, some of the current members corresponding on this subject were the same people who "welcomed" me 30 years ago with the words, "Oh, Jesus, not another dumb chick media fan!"

I still self identify as a "media" fan. Yet, both "literary" and "media" are laughably outdated terms. Does anyone outside my generation even know what either means?

Nonetheless, discrimination about race or creed or physical abilities was truly less prevalent than in mundane society of the 70s, 80s and even the 90s. But fen discriminated over and fought about—arguably—some incredibly silly things. They weren't yet called flamewars, but they burned just as hot. Some older fans speculate pre-internet fandoms weren't as negative because of the slower speed of fannish communication back then. Telephones worked just fine to spread nasty whispers.

Fandom is really fandoms, plural—an always diverse and contentious sphere. Mass media representations of fanfiction and fan culture present it at best as a "wacky world," or more typically as a bastion of the physically, socially, and literarily inept. Academic accounts of fandom overcompensate, often presenting overly utopian pictures of sisterly collaboration and feminist critique. Utopias and dystopias, though, are not parallel but rather intersecting universes. This is surely one of the great lessons of *Star Trek*—and of its fandom.

Jacqueline Lichtenberg has been a mover, a shaker, and a fixture in science fiction and science fiction fandom for decades, both as a fan and as a publishing writer. She also acted as an archivist and fandom historian for the original Star Trek *(TOS) fandom—both in zine format and, with Joan Winston and Sondra Marshak, in* Star Trek Lives! *(1975), the first book published on media fandom. Of special note is the way she used early zine fanfiction culture to originate and ultimately administer and collect a multiauthored, multigenre fandom universe, complete with its own distinctive world rules and conventions:* Kraith.

Kraith *remains notable among fan productions for taking a critical look at issues of ethnic and racial tension, imagining how minority races and cultures— primarily the Vulcans, Lichtenberg's focus—would respond to the human- and Earth-centric governance of the Federation as it was portrayed in the series. The* Kraith *universe received mainstream critical attention as early as 1986 (from the* New York Times*) and has been discussed in pioneering books on fandom culture such as Camille Bacon-Smith's* Enterprising Women *(1992) and Henry Jenkins'* Textual Poachers *(1992). While neither sexually explicit (usually) nor driven by a particular pairing,* Kraith *nonetheless portrays intricacies of sexual, reproductive, and gender politics, complete with a guide for those who wished to begin writing within its boundaries. Lichtenberg is also the creator of the Sime~Gen universe, a series of published works (and, soon, a video game) that creates an even more detailed and unusual interspecies exchange system.*

Here, Lichtenberg explains how various influences, from women fantasy writers to zines to science fiction fandom to potlucks, converged as the Star Trek *fandom was bringing fanfiction culture as we know it today—including creating social media in an analog world—into being.*

Recollections of a Collating Party

Jacqueline Lichtenberg

It was a mild, sunny afternoon in a far-flung suburb of Manhattan, on a cul-de-sac lined with maple trees, no sidewalks, unpaved driveways, converted 1920s cottages, unfenced, huge back yards, and swarming bunches of neighborhood kids filling the street, which was lined with parked cars, mostly from my guests.

It was the early 1970s, and *Star Trek* was nowhere to be found in that suburb, except maybe in my tiny living room.

The occasion was called a "collating party." My memory is not clear on what we were collating, but I suspect it was either volume one or volume two of *Kraith Collected*, my *Star Trek* fanfic series; volume one was first published in 1972. Most of the people involved, including Joan Winston, who made the trip from Manhattan by bus, were friends from *Star Trek* fandom. A lot of them, like Joan and like Devra Langsam, children's librarian and editor of the first *Star Trek* fanzine, *Spockanalia*, were members of the first New York *Star Trek* Convention committee. (Various members of that committee, and other members of the Lunarians, who still run one of the first science fiction conventions, Lunacon, showed up at different collating parties, so I don't recall exactly who was at which party, but we always had fun.)

Down in my half-underground basement, where I stored cabinets full of *Star Trek* fanzines, sat Roberta Rogow, one of the soon-to-be stellar lights of Trek historians. Like Devra, Roberta was a children's librarian at the time. She was cataloguing my collection of Trek zines because it contained items she hadn't heard of elsewhere, a real treasure trove of Trekdom. Roberta eventually published her index of *Star Trek* fan stories as a fanzine, and she went on to be a widely published mystery writer. One amazing claim to fame, though, is that very soon after this collating party at my house, Roberta published her slashy/raunchy stories in a fanzine that was called, I think, *GRIP* (a sendup of zines *Grope* and *Grup*), and published many funny stories by subsequently famous slash writers. But all that was still in the future, and at that party, we as yet had no idea of what was to come.

Upstairs everyone was walking round and round a row of folding tables, picking up a page from each stack of printed pages, to collate into a complete zine copy, and handing off stacks to proofers to check that each page was in place, right side up. Then they passed the stacks to staplers, who'd drive in three staples to bind them together and put them back in printer's boxes to be ferried to various conventions from Toronto to San Diego. When you have a couple dozen people to do it, collating a thousand copies of a zine takes only a few hours.

The reason people turned up, other than a free meal, was to talk to each other. This was before Twitter and #scifichat every Friday, before

Facebook, when you used telephones (voice only) or went to conventions to have an intelligent conversation about the rare, hard-to-find literature you loved most, and the guilty pleasure of the TV show you dreamed new stories for.

So while marching round and round the extended table as fast as possible, the voices roared over the *BAM!* from the stapling folks. Every once in a while people would switch jobs to avoid getting dizzy, and juggle several conversations shouted over the growing din in half-sentences. It was a balmy day. The windows were open. The neighbors no doubt thought we were utterly nuts. I wasn't asking them.

As hostess, I didn't do much marching in circles that day. I recall I was running back and forth to the kitchen, wafting the aroma of frying onions and meat through the house, poking baking potatoes, dashing outside to wrangle my two kids, yelling for people to move cars so my husband could get in and out of the 120-foot driveway, and running downstairs to be sure Roberta was finding all the zines tucked into dark corners.

At one point, with dinner nearly ready to serve, I was passing through our house's office, noticed a copy of Marion Zimmer Bradley's *The World Wreckers*, and dragged it in to wave at the crowd yelling at each other across the kitchen table, hoping to settle them down so they'd eat. There had to be at least three different conversations per pair at the table. It was just like watching a Twitter-chat stream, which is why I feel so at home in online chats. It's how a family talks over dinner. I shouted down the yelling group and tried to explain Darkover to them as being Trekkish (since Spock is a telepathic half-breed).

If you haven't read *The World Wreckers*, here's the skinny. Humans shipwrecked on this alien world called Darkover intermarry with the remnants of its intelligent natives, the *chieri*, and produce seven families of telepaths and espers who are only partly human. Many generations later, the last of the *chieri* gets into a sexual relationship with one of those mostly human descendants in which they bond telepathically.

Marion later told me she got the inspiration for *The World Wreckers* from Ursula K. Le Guin's *The Left Hand of Darkness*, in which the natives of the planet Winter can change sexual orientation (though Marion had built shifting sexual physiology into Darkover's *chieri* more than a decade prior to *Left Hand*'s 1969 publication). Le Guin's novel was considered a "literary" intrusion into traditional science fiction and sparked controversy because of it. It won both the Hugo (fan-voted) and Nebula (professional SF writer–voted) Awards not so much because of the odd alien sexuality, but because of the sheer literary power of the writing, which was necessary, in 1969, to make the approach to sexuality forgivable. When Marion read *The Left Hand of Darkness*, her reaction to the sex scene was that Le Guin had done what Marion was trying to teach me not to do—pulled the punch, not followed through on the promise the subtext made to the reader. Marion wrote *The World Wreckers* to illustrate how that sex scene had to go; it was now the 1970s, and things could be said aloud (if only in private) that couldn't have been even a few years before.

After dinner, the conversation wove around and through *The World Wreckers* and, of course, *Star Trek*. The group couldn't stop chattering at each other. My husband put the kids to bed, and we (all women) were clustered in my tiny living room while I deliberately didn't think about the pile of dishes in the sink. Out of the blue, someone mentioned a carbon copy of a *Star Trek* story that had circulated hand to hand. I do believe the story was the famous one titled "The Price of a Handful of Snowflakes." The website 1001 Trek Tales lists the copyright date on "Handful of Snowflakes" as 1979, which may have been its first printing in a bound fanzine. I believe this story was first disseminated as an oral telling, then as clandestine carbon copies, and finally published and just burst on the scene. But it's possible the story now known by this title is not the same as the oral one I heard about at this first encounter.

The story's topic was sexuality, a topic that printed science fiction barely touched on at that time, never delving into its erotic dimensions. Today you can't sell fantasy without a sex scene, preferably twelve or so. With the topic of sexuality broached, the standard trope, the half-breed as presented on *Star Trek,* suddenly opened an issue: how can you have a half-breed without breeding? Well, how exactly did that go? We know it was "the logical thing to do," but what was done and why? And where did that leave Spock? Who would he do it with, and why?

That stray comment in my living room turned into an hours-long, intense conversation about the erotic stories, still largely kept under wraps, that were being created by other *Star Trek* fans. And it was during this discussion that I first heard of the existence of slash fiction, as part of a larger conversation. Much larger.

Star Trek had hit me at just the right time to reignite the enormous frustration I'd grown up suffering—a frustration, it turns out, that a huge percentage of teens suffer. In short, it's "But they're writing it all wrong!"

And, for a narrow percentage of those teens, that frustration results in stories dreamed and/or written down and hidden under their beds, eventually to be burned out of sheer embarrassment of ever having been so young and so naïve. Today, that material is posted on FanFiction.Net.

I had grown up inside science fiction fandom since I was in seventh grade, when I wrote my first letter to the editor, in this case to Fred Pohl, the award-winning science fiction writer and lifelong fan who, as editor at Bantam, eventually bought *Star Trek Lives!* The letter, which was published with my address, lambasted artists for inaccuracies, and brought me myriad letters from other science fiction readers and membership in the National Fantasy Fan Federation (n3f.org). I knew professional writers through fandom and saw them interact with their fans in fanzines.

When *Star Trek* was cancelled (the first time), Devra had the typical science fiction fan's reaction, which I shared: "Oh, yeah? You and what army?"

It was from that flood of outrage, shared with other experienced science fiction fans, that Devra started *Spockanalia*. It was supposed to be a "one shot" and had very little fiction. But demand exploded, people sent her stories, and she produced other issues. I did a typical fan essay for issue four called "Mr. Spock on Logic," and through *Spockanalia* discovered Jean Lorrah, who would become a good friend and cowriter, via a contribution she also had made.

Off in Minneapolis, Ruth Berman almost simultaneously had the same idea as Devra from the same outraged reaction and founded the famous fanzine *T-Negative* (after Spock's blood type). As soon as I heard the title of the fanzine, I wrote a story for it (the first Kraith story)—and yes, at the time I expected it to be a one-shot, a single standalone story in a single standalone fanzine, and that'd be the end of it).

All of this fan outrage stewing and brewing through those years— how dare they cancel *Star Trek!*—had found an outlet: fanzines.

What became my book *Star Trek Lives!* started as a bewildered feeling and a sense of horror deep in my gut: "What if I'm missing a fanzine?!" They were springing up so fast, disappearing, and re-emerging edited by other people—it was confusing and there was no central source of information where you could be sure you weren't missing something.

So, afraid I might miss a zine, I circulated a sign-up sheet by snail mail, asking editors I knew to list zines they knew about that were not listed on the sheet, to mail the sheet to someone who hadn't been on it, and to ask them to add what they knew.

That would never work today, but that's how fandom operated then. Today you find a blog or a wiki. Back then, it was not an innovative method of gathering information, just something I felt driven to do even though it put a lot of wear and tear on my typewriter.

All the new fanzines springing up became interconnected because they published "letters of comment" (LoC for short) with the addresses of fans who wrote them. Fans wrote to each other, both directly and via fanzines' letters columns about comments in previous issues, or about comments or stories published in other fanzines by different groups of people. When people started copying my zine sign-up sheets and looping them through groups I didn't know about, but with my address as the ultimate destination, I found I had an ever-growing file of zines. I couldn't afford to buy that many zines, so I wrote stories for them. Fannish tradition is that zines don't pay for stories. Contribute a story or a letter of comment, you get a free copy. So I wrote a Kraith story or a LoC for every zine I found out about. That's why Roberta was in my basement during that fateful collating party. I had them all.

Having grown up in a journalistic family, I knew I was onto a news story as the number of zines exploded. I knew how to construct a newspaper story. Who. What. When. Where. Why. How many? I knew how many fanzines there were, and I could tally up the contributors, but the readers who bought zines but didn't contribute couldn't be counted. So I circulated (and asked zines to print) a questionnaire asking who/what/when of *Star Trek* fanzine readers. At that time, I just intended to write an article for my local newspaper, and was kind of thinking about taking a shot at the *New York Times* with it, because it seemed I was onto a really hot story. As questionnaires came back and the numbers of zines kept growing, I started to think not newspaper story, but book.

I was still sizzling with the idea of a book about *Star Trek* fandom when I attended the very first *Star Trek* convention and happened across Gene Roddenberry standing in a hallway. I went up to him, stuck out my hand, and announced, "Hi! I'm Jacqueline Lichtenberg." Of course, he didn't know "who" that was, but he was nice anyway. He was probably still floating on the uproarious reception the crowd had given him when he'd spoken earlier.

I told him about my questionnaire-circulating project and the results, and I proposed creating a *Star Trek* Welcommittee and a directory of fanzines. He seemed to think that was a good idea, so, emboldened, I told him that I proposed to collect the whole story of the advent of *Star Trek* fandom into a book, and asked if he'd write the foreword. He said yes. Then he knocked me over by giving me his home phone number. I had to promise not to tell anyone I had it, but he said to call him when I sold the book.

I spent the next few years writing the book, but I also spent a lot of time during that period sitting at Gene Roddenberry's feet (literally, with a tape recorder) in various hotel rooms around the country, interviewing him and various cast members and writers. So when I did call him to let him know we had a publication deal, he was not surprised.

Around the time of that fateful collating party, in addition to writing and marketing short stories to science fiction magazines and anthologies and working on what became *Star Trek Lives!*, I was in the middle of two other projects: my *Star Trek* fanzine series, Kraith, and rewriting and trying to sell my original novel, *House of Zeor*.

In addition to writing my own stories set in the Kraith series, I was also editing/managing fifty or so writers and artists who contributed to the Kraith mythos and issuing official numbers to the Kraith stories so they could be assembled into chronological order by readers who found them scattered among various zines. Rather than being a single author's story, Kraith was a story framework based on *Star Trek* that I created, to which I invited others to add their own stories, having deliberately left defined "holes" to be filled. So organizing all the stories wasn't an easy task. Kraith was published in a plethora of fanzines, often reprinted in other fanzines, and eventually collected by two fans I'd met in New York who lived in Michigan. They retyped (on stencils) everything (or all the stories we then knew about; additional unofficial ones later surfaced in England) from other fanzines or from blurry carbon copies for publication as a single volume, first on mimeo and then, after retyping, on offset press in 1,000- to 1,500-copy print runs.

Kraith was the reason we were all there in my kitchen that day, talking about *Star Trek* and *The World Wreckers* and Kirk/Spock stories that weren't yet known as slash, but that collating party led me to something that affected my life just as much as *Star Trek* had: Marion Zimmer Bradley's home address.

In response to my shouting about adding Darkover to *Star Trek* to get Kraith, that day, Devra summarily waved Darkover aside by saying something about what Marion had said at a Lunacon. I was like, "OH MY GOD, YOU KNOW MARION ZIMMER BRADLEY!!!" And she was like, *shrug*, "Who doesn't?" I knew that via fandom, reader/fans regularly interacted with professional writers, but my legs still went weak. I had been reading Marion since college and my biggest ambition was to become as good a writer as she was.

It was because of that conversation that Devra told Marion about me. Marion wrote me, so I typed a five-page, single-spaced letter analyzing what was "wrong" with *The World Wreckers*, but also what made it such an important book for me: the sexual relationship, and particularly chapter thirteen, where human and alien have alien sex. Only in science fiction fandom does that kind of chutzpah pay off; we started corresponding. Eventually, she asked me to send her the draft of *House of Zeor* I was working on.

In the Sime~Gen universe of *House of Zeor*, humanity has mutated into Sime and Gen (there are no humans like you and me in that universe). Simes need life energy, selyn, from Gens in order to live. Yet just taking selyn often kills the Gens. "Channels" are a submutation of Simes who can take selyn from a Gen without killing him or her, then give it to other Simes. But all channels must engage in an intimate act with a Gen once a month—an act termed Transfer that is even more intimate than sex.

In one scene in *House of Zeor*, in response to one of Marion's notes, I inserted a caveat that there are no gay channels. It was not a world-building element added out of any sort of homophobia. All three mutations, Sime, Gen, and channel, come in male and female, and I'd written all except channels to have about the same percentage of gay people as we have today. In Sime~Gen, being gay is not any sort of stigma or social issue. Also, thanks in large part to that collating party, I was gradually becoming fully aware of the K/S electricity vibrating through *Star Trek* fandom. I wouldn't even have "revealed" the no-gay-channels rule in *House of Zeor*, except that, to make one of the scenes work, the explanation had to be included. But the no-gay-channels rule irked fans no end—which may have been a good thing. Irked fans produce fanfic like irritated oysters produce pearls.

I distinguish Transfer in every detail from sexuality. It makes no difference to the characters if Transfer is male-female, male-male, or female-female. None whatsoever...to the characters. Readers? Another matter. Not everyone understood. But via science fiction fandom, there was a way for reader/fans to interact with professional writers, and so I got questions. After *House of Zeor*, all the Sime~Gen novels were written specifically as answers to the questions fans wrote to me and/or Jean Lorrah, my coauthor on multiple Sime~Gen novels. The first one we cowrote started life as an outline she wrote for a story for Sime~Gen zine *Ambrov Zeor*. She showed it to me at a Trek convention in Michigan, and I told her to work it up into a proposal and I'd try to sell it to Doubleday. She did. I did. A fan becoming my cowriter might seem strange to some, but it wasn't odd to me. From participating in fandom and working on *Star Trek Lives!*, I was already used to thinking about the line between readers and writers as fluid.

I believe this kind of communication with readers and responsiveness to them is what has allowed the Sime~Gen series to continue as long as it has. Today, one of the original Sime~Gen fanzines, *Companion in Zeor,* still accepts fiction for online publication, and there is an active group of RPG players producing fiction online; both are on simegen.com. With the advent of the Sime~Gen videogame, I expect reader input to story direction to become a much larger factor. But an interactive, community-oriented philosophy has long been a part of my vision for the Sime~Gen community, just as it was fundamental to the Kraith universe.

Today, some TV shows provide interactive links you can read with a phone app, which take you to the show's website for further insights, more story, and scenes providing additional background, texture, and depth. That is precisely what I envisioned as *Star Trek* fanzine writers began to fill in the gaps of aired *Trek* episodes, explain incongruities by adding characters, and flat-out contradict what the show's writers intended. It takes more than one medium to tell one story. Each medium has its strength, so use them all. Fanfiction writers doing pastiches of so many TV shows has finally driven that point home for TV producers. I hope I've helped, but in any event this is the world I was born to live in.

Why was I doing all this while raising kids? I had a vision of an interactive world where the writers and creators of TV shows and novels could hear and incorporate what viewers think and feel about the characters, where fiction creators get feedback from fiction consumers and all participate in the creation of the stories. I'm now living that vision and I couldn't be happier with how it's turning out.

The Look of Fic: 1970s

EDITOR'S PREFACE

PEACE AND GREETINGS:

I wish that someone would have told me back in 1972 that photo-stats, however carefully cared for, fade. I would have saved $90, this, the third edition of Kraith Collected volume one, would not exist, and fandom would still be walking around with terminal eye strain. Eleven per cent may not seem like much, but oh the difference on the eyes.

Credit for this volume goes first of all to Detta Penna; without her I might have reprinted yet another set of copies on the faded masters. Hers were the fingers that retyped the whole thing from start to finish. Hers the time and hers the compliments. Praise her with great praise.

To anyone who has never read any of Kraith before, welcome. You may find that you like Kraith. You may find that you hate it. But if the pattern of the last four years holds true, you won't be able to keep a pose of indifference. The people who read Kraith rarely agree on what they like or dislike about Jacqueline's universe, but it is the constant interchange of ideas that makes Kraith such a good ground for the serious Star Trek fan.

Since November of 1972, when the first edition of this volume was published, fandom has changed almost beyond recognition. For the most part it has been a change for the better. In fact, most of Jacqueline's preface no longer holds true. The "Johnny-one-notes" of fandom, who were afraid to change any part of the aired Star Trek universe, afraid to let any of the cast grow or mature, have given way to today's serious Star Trek fan, who, unless they have access to the pre-1972 STrek zines, probably don't even understand that there was a time when the status quo was the preferred state of Strek writing. The fen of today, while they may not agree with the particulars of Jacqueline's changes, are not shocked by her willingness to change the Star Trek universe to suit her own ideas of an alien Vulcan. Before Kraith, hard as it may be to believe today, there were almost no series of Star Trek stories. If Kraith was the catalyst that provided the impetus to a whole new generation of Star Trek writers, I can only be grateful that I, who finds myself wholly unable to write fiction, have had a part in it.

Ten volumes is, still, the tentative projection for a completed Kraith series. The last half of the series remains to be written, so even if you have just discovered Kraith you can look forward with me to many more years of new, original, main series Kraith.

Now is the time to read on, and, this time, you won't even need a magnifying glass.

LIVE LONG AND PROSPER

Carol Lynn
December 1976

P.S. Since I still claim that volume I could not be volume one without it, and since Detta was not obliging enough to leave my past mistakes in the public eye, here it is for all to see and snicker over

DEMONSTARTING

EDITING:C.Lynn & D.Goldstein		Editor's Preface . . . 1
	AUTHOR'S DEDICATION	Author's Preface . . . 2
TYPING: Detta Penna	to	Spock's Affirmation . . 5
	Ruth Berman	Amanda's Mission . . . 27
LAYOUT:Detta Penna, C.Lynn	Ray H. Block	Hope to Be Spared . . 29
Debbie Goldstein		Eyeto 31
ᵗᵗⁿˢᵗᵗᵗᶠᵒᵐᵇ:Linda Hunter	and	Shealku 35
		A Matter of Priority. . 45
TITLES: John Benson	Salomon Lichtenberg	Spock, Guardian of
ARTWORK:		the Tradition . . . 61
Robbie Brown: cover,8,94	may they live long and prosper	Spock's Mission . . . 65
Gordon Carlton:30,56,118,122		Surak's Construct . . 85
D.L. Collin: 5,26		T'Borel 87
Tim Courtney: 135,84	EDITORS' DEDICATION	The Disaffirmed . . . 95
Connie Faddis: 70	to	Won't You Walk a
Mike Kucharski: 45	Suvil	Little Faster? . . .101
Alice LaVelle: 130 (94,109	or Shariel	The Tanya Entry 103
G. Moaven:12,43,65,83,87,92,	(as D.C. Fontana would have it)	Spock's Argument . . .109
Cara Sherman: 24		Acknowledgements . . .136
Joni Wagner: 54,61		KRAITH Chronology.....44

There are absolutely no typos in this zine, only lapses into Vulcanur.

All rights reserved to the authors and artists. Not intended to infringe on copyrights held by Gene Roddenberry or Paramount Corp.

The editor's preface and credits page of *Star Trek* fanfiction collection *Kraith Collected*, volume one. 1976 reprint of 1972 first edition. Individual stories were first printed in other zines.[B]

She'd never allowed anyone into that inner keep, not even the Vulcan therapists who'd rescued her sanity and taught her control. They'd taught her to guard her innermost self; they had not taught her to share it.

And then his voice came, deep as a still lake hidden in some mountain cave; cool as black velvet caressing her nerves. The words were ancient ritual, so old they'd all but lost their meaning, but they held the power to unlock the gates of her fortress and cause her to welcome the speaker. Though she'd never been mated, she had Affirmed the Continuity.

She heard herself answering with the same age-old formula. And then she was welcomed to the innermost hearth that is shared only in the ultimate intimacy. And they became one.

It was not a melding of minds, but a mingling of that indefinable substance which burns, creating the flame of life. It was a touching that did not touch, and yet would always touch.

He withdrew his hand and, instead of the usual, clean separation she'd always associated with the breaking of such a contact, there was a drawing out, as if some rope of connective thought-tissue were elongating. She still felt his living presence within her. The surging dynamics of his life processes, his emotions, were hers to know, always. And she knew he had the same contact with her emotions and that her lack of control could cause him terrible anguish.

They stood poised, within and without one another, for a breathless moment before Spock said, "We must hurry."

As she trailed after the First Officer, she knew his urgency, the tensing for action on which lives might depend. And she surrendered to it because it was the coherent power of a laser beam compared to the chaotic white light of her own near-panic, and emotion was what she must not feel now. Curiously, his steadiness actually flowed through her, damping the rising tide of apprehension, readying her for action. And somehow, she knew this new steadiness would be hers as long as the relationship endured.

Arriving at the transporter room door, Spock paused to let her catch up, then breasted the door as if it were a gigantic wave. Within, they found an ocean in torment. It was exactly what they'd expected, but even Vulcans can hope things won't be as bad as anticipated.

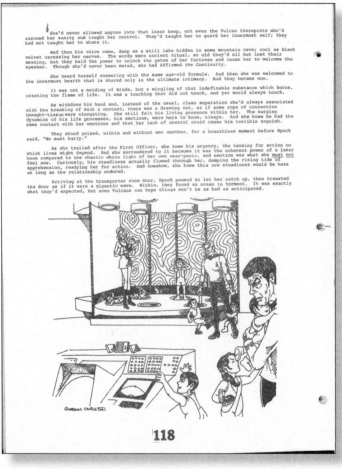

118

A page from *Star Trek* fanfiction "Spock's Argument" by Jacqueline Lichtenberg, from *Kraith Collected*, volume one. Illustration by Gordon Carleton.[C]

Interlude:
Growing Up Fic

FANFICTION AS IT WORKS TODAY is not just stories written about other stories (as has always happened). Fanfiction is stories being written about the same other story, all at the same time. It is sharing these stories with increasing ease and speed and decreasing cost. Zines were the first step in creating this kind of writing culture.

Fanfiction zine culture was taking off as the production costs of television and movies—the works that increasingly inspired fic—skyrocketed. For most fans, participating creatively in these mass media productions was a far less attainable dream than publishing a science fiction story had been for earlier fans. With the creation of the "originals" media fans loved thus firmly in the hands of the official producers, zines nonetheless let fans control the production and dissemination of their own work.

Media fanfiction culture revolved and evolved around zines for a good twenty-five years, with the independent production techniques improving and the number of zines proliferating. As zine-writing cultures grew around large media franchises—*Star Trek,* Star Wars*, Starsky and Hutch,* and *Beauty and the Beast* all had extensive pre-internet fanfiction fandoms—the line between canon and "fanon" was increasingly experienced as one of media. Everyone—those with money and rights and credit and those without—was telling versions of stories and characters; they were just doing it in different ways.

This era also marked the rise of another kind of para-writing linked to these vast media franchises: the tie-in novel. Not just fans but enormous corporations augmented, expanded, and slightly changed stories told on screen with stories told in print. Legally speaking, of course, these stories were sanctioned, commissioned, official. But *creatively* speaking—in the minds of the young people growing up reading them—was there a big difference between a *Star Trek* novelization a corporation put out, and one you might write yourself on your father's Atari?

This era also saw the explosion (on toy store shelves, in backyards using well-placed firecrackers) of the licensed tie-in toy. Every media franchise seemed to beg: play with our stories with these toys. Donny and Marie went to war against Han Solo and Cookie Monster in basements everywhere. What message did this entertainment corporation–generated atmosphere communicate to children as future creators? What did they hope these children would learn? It's at the very least a very mixed message: You play with our stories with toys, which you pay for. Writers play with our stories on paper, which you also pay for. But don't *you* play with our stories on paper, because that would be stealing.

The message corporations were sending was hardly a consistent one, but then, fanfiction is always a story of consequences uncontrolled by rightsholders. The consistent messages that *did* seem to get through? More is better. The more the merrier. Mix and match.

The Empire, of course, eventually struck back. It's not as if rightsholders don't *try* to control fan creativity. For a while Lucasfilm countenanced family-friendly fic, but not anything adult. By the time the internet rolled around, Lucasfilm was targeting independent fansites, doing its best to rein in the consequences its massive marketing had unleashed by focusing all fan activity on its own corporate websites. Cease-and-desist letters were not uncommon. Star Wars as an entity did not want other entities from other universes messing with its toys. George Lucas did not want anyone diluting the power of his original creation with any offensive, ridiculous-sounding creatures from other universes, or unconvincing love stories, or even—God forbid—changing elements of the original stories, distorting character arcs or iconic scenes. Because that would be *awful*. I am pretty sure plenty of Star Wars fans would have been happy to serve anyone who had tried to do any of those things with a cease-and-desist order.

Similarly, late-1980s *Beauty and the Beast* fans, having rallied and campaigned to save the show in the old-fashioned phone and letter campaigns of the pre-internet days, were appalled when their show came back...different. The Powers That Be had killed the love plot—and the heroine. Some fans would have liked to send a cease-and-desist order, too (they didn't have to, the series didn't last long). Instead, they wrote more fic, telling the stories they wanted to hear. Some of them are still writing it. The CW tried to get into the act recently—but fans of the original series are largely not amused. Not all fic is successful, after all.

Certainly, not all future writers and creators who grew up in this era went on to write fanfiction. Some put those toys away for good. Some of them (albeit a distinct minority) grew up to be Joss Whedon. Much like Rex Stout speculating on the parentage of Lord Peter Wimsey, Whedon has spent some time considering the lineage of his own characters with relation to the culture of our youth: "If you are going to tell me that Han Solo isn't the father of Malcolm Reynolds, then I am going to laugh and laugh and laugh...Kirk was also, I would say, Malcolm's weird uncle."

Could I get a fic for that?

As the writer and critic Ron Hogan recounts, growing up in the age of Star Trek: The Original Series, Star Wars, *and their copiously merchandised afterlives gave children many different entry points into the stories that inspired them. Hogan did not go on to become a fiction writer (or hasn't yet), but he did play an instrumental role in introducing literature to the internet by starting Beatrice.com as an author interview website back in 1995 after having seen an article about the early internet browser Netscape. Today, Hogan continues to celebrate "literary" and "genre" fiction in equal measure on the web; his latest project is a series of personalized reading recommendations from authors and booksellers called TheHandsell.com. Here, Hogan explains how a lifetime of unrestrained and unfiltered reading in this "mix and match" era helped shape his future critical projects.*

Literary Playtime

Or, a Childhood Shaped by Fic

Ron Hogan

I.

Star Wars (it was still just *Star Wars* then, no "new hope" attached) came out just before my seventh birthday. It's the first film I remember seeing in the theaters more than once; my parents had just gotten separated, so it was easy enough for my little brother and me to convince first one, then the other, to take us. Maybe their separation—or, rather, an effort to keep us happy during the separation—also made it easier for us to acquire a substantial collection of Kenner action figures from the movie, as well as assorted land vehicles and space fighters and even the cutaway Death Star, with its basement-level "trash compactor" filled with bits of foam.

Whatever the motivation, I seem to remember having a near-complete cast, which we'd frequently use to recreate scenes from the movie—but that would get us only so far. Naturally, we started making up our own scenes: Darth Vader and Luke Skywalker both had those little plastic lightsabers embedded in their right arms, so it made perfect sense to have them fight each other, anticipating the climax of *The Empire Strikes Back* by a couple years. (Admittedly, we didn't see the family angle coming.)

As we got older, and the action figure market expanded, we picked up characters from other franchises; I vaguely remember Killer Kane from *Buck Rogers* becoming Vader's sidekick while Han Solo teamed up with Captain Decker, the Stephen Collins character from *Star Trek: The Motion Picture*. I've long since forgotten what explanation, if any, we came up with for everybody being in the same world. I suspect that after a huge influx from the Fisher Price Adventure People line, we just wound up improvising.[36]

That childhood play is the heart of fic.

II.

A few years into this—1980 or '81, as best I can figure—I discovered James Blish's *Star Trek* adaptations in my public library and promptly set about reading them straight through, in order. I know I was already into Trek by then;[37] I remember owning a *fotonovela* version of the Chicago gangster episode, "A Piece of the Action," when I was in first or second grade, as well as a book where you could fold together paper replicas of phasers and tricorders. But I think I might actually have been into the '70s cartoon more than the original series, most of which I still hadn't seen at that point. (In fact, I never did see "Space Seed" until sometime after its "sequel," *The Wrath of Khan,* came out, but thanks to Blish I at least knew the background to the movie.) In retrospect, those books feel like a turning point, a moment at which I might have subconsciously realized that there was something more to the world of Trek—for that matter, David Gerrold's *The World of Star Trek*, also in that library, was a critical introduction to the notion that the significance of a franchise could extend beyond the content of the original episodes.

Soon after, when I stumbled onto Stephen Goldin's *Trek to Madworld*, it was Gerrold's endorsement on the cover that convinced me to buy it and read it, and that set me down the path of other Star Trek novels. It didn't really register with me that these were "official" Star Trek spinoffs; by this time, I'd read the *New Voyages* anthology, which featured short stories set on the *Enterprise* introduced by members of the cast, and somewhere along the line I'd picked up on the idea that fans of the show had gone off and written stories on their own.

To a pre-adolescent me, it just made sense that "everybody" was off doing their own Star Trek stories, and some of them were getting published.

III.

Skip forward another two or three years. Now fully committed to reading science fiction stories about other people besides the crew of the *Enterprise*, I've worked my way through the entire collection in the public library's children's section, and I've moved on to the main floor. That's where I found Philip José Farmer's *Tarzan Alive*, a "definitive biography of Lord Greystoke." Now, I hadn't actually read any of the Edgar Rice Burroughs stories, but of course I knew who Tarzan was, so I checked it out—whereupon my mind was fully and properly blown by the literary conceit that there was a real person behind the character, and that Farmer had managed to track him down.

But I was most bedazzled by the "Wold Newton family tree," found in an appendix near the very end of the book.[38] Here, Farmer expanded on his initial premise: not only is Tarzan a real historical figure, but so are many of the other legendary characters of nineteenth- and twentieth-century popular literature, from Sherlock Holmes to Doc Savage. Actually, I recollect that I was probably at least halfway on board with the idea that Holmes was real already, as I'd devoured my one-volume complete stories with annotations by W. S. Baring-Gould and—even as I was working my way through the library's science fiction section—I had rifled through the mystery shelves looking for Nicholas Meyer's *The Seven-Per-Cent Solution* and its sequel, *The West End Horror*, along with Michael Hodel's *Enter the Lion*, which was a memoir by Sherlock's older brother, Mycroft.

Maybe I was just an especially susceptible young reader, but I willingly accepted the proposition that Holmes and Watson were real and those who came after Conan Doyle really were passing along newly discovered Watson manuscripts. (Part of the pleasure of the sequels, perhaps, is in the tales the authors concoct to explain how they've come upon the previously unfound documents.) From there, it wasn't much of a leap of faith to assume that other stories were "really real," too, and here was Philip José Farmer, tying them all together into one amazing bundle—and, in the process, handing the adolescent me a list of stories and characters I ought to track down.

I had only middling success finding the other "primary documents" of the Wold Newton family. I had much better luck getting my hands on other books where Farmer borrowed classic characters, from Doc Savage and Phileas Fogg to Glinda the Good Witch, and either told "the story behind the story" or gave them all-new adventures. To this day, I'm still half-convinced that Glinda was behind the death of Warren G. Harding, as suggested in *A Barnstormer in Oz*.

As that last line indicates, I could be particularly gullible when it came to the presence of real-life people in fiction, and Farmer wasn't the only person to divert me with a rather idiosyncratic version of history . . . but that's a story for another essay. For now, the takeaway is that it was impressed upon me early that telling stories with other people's characters, digging into the world of the original stories and giving it your own spin, was—well, maybe it wasn't perfectly ordinary, because I'd read around enough to learn that these Farmer stories were somewhat notorious (as opposed to other Farmer stories that were notorious for their frank sexuality). So, ordinary, not so much, but natural? Yes.

IV.

It can start, as I described earlier, when we treat the stories we grow up with not just as texts to be read, or movies or programs to be watched, but as toys with which we can play. In some cases, that process is facilitated by the existence of actual toys; even without physical objects, though, our imaginations can take hold of the story elements and adjust them to our liking—whether it's a simple tweak here and there or the development of an all-new narrative.

Some of us just move on to another stage, where instead of getting the results of our playful imagination out of our heads by moving figurines around on our bedroom floor or living room coffee table, we set them down in text. That makes them much easier to share, and that raises a complex set of issues—one I'm sure other folks in this book can do a much better job of addressing. Sometimes, though, you get lucky: either the "toys" have become community property, and nobody much minds if you borrow them, or the people who do own the "toys" actually invite you to play with them.

Even if that never happens, though, "playing" with other people's stories is a creative activity I'd liken to others we accept as quite natural for children—and adults—to engage in. Just as you don't need to have serious aspirations of becoming a professional musician to learn how to play "Für Elise" on the piano, and you can carry a sketchbook around without being expected to become a fine artist, we should encourage everyone to create their own Star Trek (or Star Wars, or Harry Potter, or whatever) stories simply as a way to exercise their own imaginations.

For now, I'll leave the practical aspects of protecting creators' economic interests for other contributors to elaborate. What I know, what I can attest to, is that I grew up in a world of fic that spurred me to spend more time deeply engaging the stories that I loved, figuring out the structural elements that made them work. As Michael Ann Dobbs suggests in a post at io9.com, reading fic offers valuable creative writing lessons, including (but not limited to) a healthy respect for all the characters in a story and their underlying motivations.[39]

Reading fic also taught me to look for the threads that bind seemingly disparate stories together, and that's a lesson I've brought to many of my attempts at cultural criticism. When I first read *Lipstick Traces* as a college student, I was prepared for Greil Marcus' chain of connections running from Dada through Situationism to the Sex Pistols, having been thoroughly indoctrinated in the secret history of pulp culture as a teenager. Fifteen years later, as I worked out the central thesis of my study of Hollywood in the 1970s, *The Stewardess Is Flying the Plane!*, there was never any doubt that I'd be putting films like *Empire of the Ants* and *Americathon* on equal footing with *Annie Hall* and *The Deer Hunter*. It made perfect sense to me that they were all part of the same story about American culture; I just had to sort out what that story was.

Fortunately, I had the *Star Wars* section down cold. After all, I'd been finding my way through that material for more than thirty years.

The *X-Files*, *Buffy*, and the Rise of the Internet Fic Fandoms

WITH THE RISE of personal computing in the 1980s and of the internet in the 1990s, fanfiction increasingly has been electronically produced and digitally distributed. The effects of this shift on the community, the literature it produces, and the broader reading and writing public are really only beginning to be understood. With stories such as "The Theory of Narrative Causality," fic writers are bringing this medium shift to bear on their storytelling, and internet fandom's visual and social atmosphere is already worlds away from where it started, on Usenet groups and discussion lists. From these earliest network incarnations, though, one tremendous effect of these changes has remained: speed. Communities, conflicts, and conventions form faster than ever before—probably by orders of magnitude. As my students and I found, genres evolve and spread like lightning—whether within a single canon (post-Reichenbach *Sherlock* or post-finale *Buffy the Vampire Slayer* stories, for example) or across fandoms (coffee shop AU, male pregnancy, the BDSM universe in which gender and sexual orientation are secondary to D/s identities).

In addition to speed, the internet brought anonymity. No more mailing addresses or phone numbers were needed to receive fandom news. At first, emails and IDs (anonymous or pseudonymous) sufficed, and then fanboards sprang up—many requiring no registration. Fanfiction became free, open, public. Readers were free to lurk. Writers remained as anonymous as they wished—even to those who ran the websites. Geekgenre shows—like *Buffy* and *The X-Files*—drew fans who were removed from geek culture and unlikely ever to physically make a zine or attend a convention, but who were happy to read and write on the privacy of their own screens. Revealing someone's "real life" identity and location quickly came to be understood as a sin of great magnitude, whereas in the days of zines, such information was commonly shared.

The option of anonymity led to the possibility of identity play. Plenty of people who would never dream of dressing up as Princess Leia or a Klingon at a fan convention were drawn to create online personae that were themselves a kind of fiction. While in the early days of the internet, the lurid possibilities of such anonymity were used as bogeymen to scare children and their parents, in (virtual) reality they far more often gave people the opportunity to try on new styles, genders, sexualities, and appearances—to live differently, sometimes with more daring, than they did in real life. Today, in female-majority fic communities, a woman writer might take on a male identity to get attention, to experiment with interacting as male, or sometimes to make a political point. A male enthusiast can pass as female and avoid extra attention. People often claim no gender or race or orientation, although many find the same issues and tensions resurfacing in online communities or grow weary of assumptions made about them. Sometimes writers take on sock puppet identities to praise and promote their own work and tear down the work of their rivals. The internet, in other words, has had its plusses and minuses for fic writers, their work, and their communities; as a stern Structuralist tutor once corrected me, "Literature does not evolve; it changes." The internet changed fanfiction. Period.

It has never been only the technology that changes fanfiction, of course. Like any other aspect of culture, fanfiction responds to and shapes other broader cultural shifts. The shift in technology during the 1980s and '90s also coincided with several fic-inspiring genre shows that took an interest in playing with gender and genre conventions—much as fic had been doing. Both The X-Files and Buffy had large, groundbreaking, and long-influential internet fandoms, and each in its own way took established gendered tropes from genre fiction and movies and flipped them, giving central roles to strong, dynamic women characters. The X-Files played on the Sherlock–Watson and Spock–Kirk rationalist-to-intuitivist dynamic but the "doctor" was now the rationalist and the rationalist was a woman—one in no way subordinate in rank to her male partner. In an even more dramatic switch, Buffy the Vampire Slayer took the stock horror movie victim and made her the superhero. These reversals were not restricted to representation, either. While the vast majority of the many screenwriters for The X-Files were men, Buffy creator Joss Whedon went out of his way to hire women writers, among them Marti Noxon and Jane Espenson, each of whom has more writing credits on the show than anyone besides Whedon himself. Noxon eventually went on to become showrunner. Certainly other nongenre shows and even other fanfic-inspiring shows had employed women: D. C. Fontana wrote for both the original Star Trek and The Next Generation, for example, the latter of which employed a number of female writers and also included strong female characters, although both writing staff and starship were headed by men. Xena, which immediately preceded Buffy in the kick-ass female lead department and produced its share of fanfic, employed female writers on a handful of episodes. With *Buffy*, though, women were not only prominent characters but also prominent writer-producers, and what's more, as the internet made such information more readily accessible all around, *Buffy*'s women writers were seen, and heard from, in internet forums in a way that was then new.

Of course, whether a show inspires fic has more to do with relationships on screen than those behind it, and both these shows pushed gender boundaries in that regard. As each series progressed, it increasingly went to edgy places with gender and sexuality. In one *X-Files* episode, another character's talking tattoo (voiced by Jodi Foster) helped inspire Scully to get inked as well, which seemed to lead her to a level of sexual promiscuity out of character for her—but possibly only repressed. Mulder had a porn addiction, and a psychic suggested he'd die of "autoerotic asphyxiation"—the first time, certainly, such a term made its way into a prime-time show. *Buffy* had the first lesbian lovers in prime time; underage sex (that controversially unleashed a supervillian from its hero); and a season-long exploration of dubious consent, rough sex, and BDSM tropes. Both prime-time television and fandom had changed a lot since the early 1970s, when erotic content was relegated to furtive word-of-mouth stories like the ones Jacqueline Lichtenberg described. Erotic fanfiction was already big enough to have exclusively devoted het and slash zines, and all such content was soon to be found online, sorted by kink and by pairing. But with these shows, canon began to follow suit.

Thematically speaking, both *The X-Files* and *Buffy* also had a great deal to say about the power dynamics that play out between renegade, counterinstitutional forces and the institutions they seem to work for and within. As it turned out, these dynamics mirrored the relations between fan communities and corporate copyright holders throughout the early days of internet fandom. Mulder and Scully, *Buffy*'s Scooby Gang, and fan writers and their communities all lived under constant threat of being shut down, or at least of having their work devalued and interfered with if officialdom took too much notice—whether by the FBI or an alien conspiracy (*X-Files*); the world of the Watchers' Council (*Buffy*); high school principals, parents, and police (*Buffy* and fandom); or a cease-and-desist-order-wielding Fox executive (fandom). "The Powers That Be" was a phrase used in fan culture, to refer to a show's official creators and decision makers, and ultimately even adopted by *Buffy* spinoff *Angel* to refer to an evil law firm's lurking supernatural overseers. Fan writers could look to the shows' characters as compatriots in an us v. them world.

The two sides of '90s media fandom, fans and official (paid) creators, had something else in common: both took permissions, precedents, and possibilities from the short-lived, genre-bending series *Twin Peaks* and the broad-based if also short-lived fan culture it created. In the early '90s, "the net was out there," and *Twin Peaks* fans pioneered this new technology's potential for active, collective watching and reacting to television.

Mark Frost and David Lynch's cult show has been credited for paving the way for *The X-Files* creatively as well as in the minds of television executives (and in terms of casting!). Of course, *The X-Files* was a very different show—more procedural, more sci-fi, an episodic/myth-arc hybrid, as opposed to *Twin Peaks'* intensely serialized nature. *Twin Peaks* also embraced its soap opera and paranormal mystery sides equally, while in *The X-Files*, the soap opera—as relationship-centered narrative is often disparagingly termed—was something Chris Carter was insistent (if unsuccessful) about resisting, at least in the early days. Still, taking David Duchovny from FBI agent on the paranormal mystery *Twin Peaks* to FBI agent on the paranormal procedural *The X-Files* helped bring the kindred spirits of alt.tv.twin-peaks fans from Usenet to the new show. (Speaking of going to edgy places with gender and sexuality: David Duchovny's *Twin Peaks* character was a not-at-all-feminized FBI agent who preferred wearing dresses.) The casting of Major Briggs (the father of *Twin Peaks'* Bobby) as Scully's father in the first very Scully-centric episode also helped cement this relationship.

Just as important, the *Twin Peaks* electronic fandom paved the way for the X-Philes. Like the early science fiction zines, the pioneering alt.tv.twin-peaks—active at a time when most people had never heard of something called "the net"—primarily devoted itself to discussion, dissecting *Twin Peaks'* many mysteries, clues, and red herrings rather than rewriting these elements as new fiction. Of course, in obsessing over *Twin Peaks*, the Usenet crowd was just doing online what so many of us were doing in our homes and offices. I obsessed over *Twin Peaks* in a West Village apartment with a group of friends. We weren't writing fic, but we were engaging in "spec"—a direct if unwitting descendant of the Great Game of Sherlockian speculation—pondering the same what-ifs ("Did you see this?" "What do you think this *means*?") that also inspire fanfiction. While researching this book, I've found many a future fandom writer—and more than one contributor to this volume—who was similarly engaged with *Twin Peaks* in those days. I've found the same holds true for nonfandom (that is, official and paid) television writers and producers; our own little group of fanatics included several who would go on to successful careers in television (a producer, a writer, and more than one actor).

It wasn't just us. Today an executive with NBC/Universal, Tom Lieber has been involved with the genre-stretching geek-cred shows *Battlestar Galactica (BSG), Caprica, Warehouse 13,* and, pertinently here, *Psych,* which aired a very fic-like *Twin Peaks* homage episode. Given this last fact, it's unsurprising Lieber is a *Twin Peaks* enthusiast despite what sounds like a somewhat traumatic introduction:

> I was in 5th grade when *Twin Peaks* was on the air, and the only reason it was on my radar was my father forced me to watch an episode, saying he thought I'd really like it. I sat down to watch, and the first episode I viewed was the classic, violent, traumatic episode in which BOB/Leland brutally murders his niece Maddy. I was devastated, sickened, and terrified. But my dad was right: I loved it. I had no idea television could be so visceral and disturbing one minute, and so funny and bizarre the next. The tonal schizophrenia fascinated me, and was probably the watershed moment of my career in wanting to pursue a life in television.[40]

Jane Espenson—who has not only written for *Buffy,* but also for *Angel, Firefly, Dollhouse, BSG,* her own online sitcom *Husbands,* and too many other shows to name—describes her reaction to *Twin Peaks'* mix of tones and genres:

> I was in college when *Twin Peaks* came out. I huddled with my roommates to watch it, which wasn't something we normally did. We were all blown away. The idea of a continuing mystery was compelling and unusual, but it was the sheer darn *quirkiness* of it that really hit me. Agent Cooper and his voice memos and love of cherry pie…the log lady…I'd never seen anything so unapologetically weird. It was a mixture of tones, from macabre tragedy to surreal humor, that kept feeling like it should pull the viewer out of the story, but didn't. In fact, it actually ended up being strangely realistic, because I'm not sure anyone else making TV had quite noticed yet that actual life blends those exact same tones.[41]

The insight here—that "actual life" blends tones in a way that does not lend it to being tidily sorted into genres or bookshelves—may help account for quirky-hokey-tragic-epic *Buffy's* extraordinary emotional resonance, despite the sometimes apparent seams around monster ears and suchlike. *Buffy* creator Joss Whedon has also listed *Twin Peaks* as a favorite, and the idea that quirkiness does not mitigate or interrupt tragedy is surely nowhere more apparent than in Whedon's body of work (on which Espenson remains a frequent collaborator).

This direct and indirect influence on a generation of television professionals notwithstanding, an argument could be made that the *Twin Peaks* Usenet group had an even greater impact on the future of television culture: by taking it from a then largely passive medium to an interactive one. The *Twin Peaks* Usenet group ushered in a new stage in the relationship between the official and fan creators. Alt.tv.twin-peaks captured the attention of network decision makers when it spearheaded a fan campaign to bring back *Twin Peaks*—although the campaign's success was mitigated by the show's perceived decline in quality and audience, and ultimately was not enough to stop cancellation. Fan activism in favor of TV shows was nothing new, of course; memorable campaigns such as those to save *Star Trek* and *Beauty and the Beast* had similarly limited, qualified success. But the online campaign for *Twin Peaks* not only coordinated faxes, letters, and other tangible, real-world activities noticeable to networks, but it also showcased the lightning-fast communication potential of the web. At the time, the net was still very much understood to be the province of geeks, but it would go on to change the fanfiction writing and reading experience, and then the writing and reading experience for all of us, soon enough.

The X-Philes
Giving New Meaning to the Word Ship

> Things are getting strange, I'm starting to worry
> This could be a case for Mulder and Scully
>
> —from the song "Mulder and Scully," by Catatonia
>
> I can't believe you, of all people, are trying to Scully me.
>
> —Buffy, "The Pack" (1–6)

IN MANY WAYS, *The X-Files* and its fandom came of age in tandem with the internet itself. Its premise and casting made *The X-Files* a prime focus of the newly active, electronically connected kind of fan who had gathered on the *Twin Peaks* Usenet group, and many of these fans soon became as obsessed with pursuing the *X-Files'* hidden truths and meanings as the show's main characters were. The Usenet group alt.tv.x-files saw its first activity in December 1993, just eleven episodes into the first season. The fanfiction-friendly group alt.tv.x-files.creative was established in the spring of 1994. Internet fandom as a whole, and especially internet fanfiction, owes a great deal of its apparatus, terminology, customs, and conflicts to the writing and interpreting communities that grew up around *The X-Files*.

For much of *X-Files* fanfiction, it all came down to Mulder and Scully—the noncouple who launched *ship* as a verb meaning something other than the transport of goods. The Mulder-Scully relationship (or MSR—X-Philes, as the show's fans came to be known, love a good acronym) brought into currency rhetoric that meant fans could ship (verb; root for or advocate) a couple or pairing, now also known as a ship (noun). Those who ship ships are shippers. Thank you, X-Philes.

The main tension in *X-Files* fandom was between Shippers (of Mulder and Scully in a romantic relationship) and NoRomos, fans who along with

118

the show's creator Chris Carter actively resisted a romantic relationship between the two leads. Shipper wars—which in many future fandoms would pit fans of one ship against fans of another—instead began among X-Philes as a battle over the question "To Ship or Not to Ship." Fanfiction split along similar lines, with Shipper fic tending (at least according to its critics) to de-emphasize the investigative and paranormal plots in favor of sex and romance and NoRomo fic tending to do the opposite.

It's not as if such conflicts were new. Similar divisions between plot-heavy and relationship-heavy fic, friendship and romance—or het and slash—had been raising hackles among fic writers at least since *Star Trek*. With the internet, however, it became possible for more specific communities of taste to be established with greater ease and speed. The trend toward increasing specialization of both pairing and fanfiction genre (kink, slash, hurt/comfort, etc., each with its attendant acronyms) in the form of dedicated groups and lists and eventually web archives saw its first major iterations in the *X-Files* fandom.

In the early to mid-nineties, fandom culture still largely transpired in zines, at cons, and through conversations among friends and acquaintances. Most fan writing still took place in notebooks or un-networked word processors. Novice fan writers often didn't understand what they were doing as being "fanfiction," as part of a tradition of fan writing; neither were they often aware of any community of like-minded writers. To find zines, you'd almost have to be seeking them out. You'd have to know about fandom, be going to conventions—or at least know people who did and weren't afraid to talk about it. As a schoolgirl in Wales, for example, *X-Files* fanfic writer Bethan Jones—whom we hear from later as a fic writer and an academic—had little opportunity to get online, and even less to come across zines commonly sold at fan conventions or distributed via mailing lists. When she happened to have an *X-Files* fan as a teacher who assigned "writing an X-File" as an assignment, it was synergy, a happy coincidence of taste. But within a few years, it would become common practice for a young (or old) person to type the name of a show or book into a search engine and in seconds find hundreds or thousands of related discussions and stories. *The X-Files* and its fanfiction played a big role in that transition, particularly in its early days.

Although Chris Carter often claimed never to have seen a *Star Trek* episode, Mulder/Scully's parallel to Kirk/Spock helped forge many fans' understanding of intuitive, lone wolf-ish Mulder as the central character (as *Star Trek*'s creators had structured Kirk), with hyper-logical (if almost unfailingly wrong) Scully as the Spock-like second-in-command. As with Kirk/Spock, this dynamic reversed the logical Holmes and intuitive-sidekick Watson dynamic. The gender difference between the two *X-Files* leads offered the added wrinkle of male-female dynamics.

One might imagine that opposite-sex partners would make shipping the leads less controversial, as there was no taboo of homosexuality to over-come. One should guess again. In the *X-Files* fandom, the intensity of the NoRomo position—sanctioned by Chris Carter and other show creators—could make Mulder/Scully romance seem as taboo, and as belittled and frowned upon, as slash was in other areas of fandom. Perhaps even more so. A NoRomo writer, for example, might embrace Skinner/Scully (boss-subordinate), Skinner/Mulder (boss-subordinate slash), or even Mulder/Cancer Man (enemyslash) as long as the central Mulder-Scully relationship remained nonsexual. For NoRomos, the greatest taboo of all was to sexu-alize the show's central, driving heterosexual—or rather, heterosocial—relationship. For these viewers, messing with that partnership and its non-sexual nature threatened the very heart of the series. Reasons given for resisting Mulder/Scully were many—fear of the "*Moonlighting* syndrome" (killing a show by resolving the tension that made it tick); fear of the soap opera (a focus on relationship signals decline in quality or complexity); fear of refocusing (away from critique of government, or from mythologi-cal exploration); fear of political dilution (diminishing the plot line of a professional relationship of equals between a man and a woman).

And as for the Shippers...well, they felt excluded from canon, irritated that pearls dropped for them by the show's writers were never developed. They raised their own questions. Why should a sustained romantic or sex-ual relationship between equals be so devalued? They felt teased, irked, and, as Jacqueline Lichtenberg explains earlier in this book, "irked fans produce fanfic like irritated oysters produce pearls." And then, of course, there were the preferences *within* the shipping community. Did you want Mulder and Scully together only at the end of the show? Did you want them to finally have their baby? Or did you want to banish the baby as a giant turn-off...or perhaps have them engage in a threesome with Skinner? Even within a central pairing—and this is one of the great insights of fan-fiction everywhere—the possibilities and permutations are endless.

On the internet, these pairings and preferences could get their own acro-nyms, contests, and dedicated archives. In the early days of *The X-Files,* some of this transpired in zines, but again, the internet increased access, speed, and specialization. Before the mega archives and FanFiction.Net (which was started by X-Files fans), smaller message boards, email lists, and basic archives began to proliferate. Archives sprung up for ships within ships, kinks within kinks. The work of fic publishing became email list creation, site building and maintenance, award administration, and discussion board moderating. X-Files fans were laying the groundwork for the real-time, near-simultaneous writing, editing, curating, reviewing, and discussing activity that has today become the hallmark of fanfiction. "The Jedi Shipper," who joined X-Files fandom as a teen after the 1998 movie, described fandom life like this:

> In terms of similarity [with her current fandom], the sense of unity is incredible. Everyone in the fandom has a "job." [In the X-Philes], we had the image makers, the site runners (because, again, back then without the Twitter, it was all about message boards and chat rooms), the fanfic writers and the readers. We were this community that needed each other, and we all participated. Since I was a shipper...my crew picked apart every episode for all the intimate touches, the reading between the lines to find the love story. It was a little insane...and awesome.[42]

The Jedi Shipper—still an active writer in other fandoms under the name LyricalKris—is typical of a generation of writers and readers who grew up seeing all these activities as equally valid and necessary to the reading/writing experience. Rather than seeing writing as an isolated activity, she saw it as a part of a collection of related and reciprocal tasks.

Similarly, watching television—long derided as a passive activity despite already being highly participatory for niche groups such as the Star Trek fandom—was on its way to becoming more active, collaborative, and discursive for wider and wider segments of the viewing public. Very active fandoms were still small groups—by today's standards—but they were laying the social, procedural, and cultural groundwork that has influenced every fanwriting fandom since. It became more and more usual to watch something and then jump online to see what everyone was writing about it—or against it, or in it, or around it. Shippers wrote the scenes they felt they should have gotten, feminists wrote the scenes they felt they should have gotten, conspiracy theorists wrote the plots they felt the show might be blocked from writing, and on and on. Archives helped readers find these stories, and the boards helped everyone everywhere argue about it all.

The Shippers, by the way, ultimately won the day. Mulder/Scully became canon. Fic—as it tends to—got there first.

Many of those who study fanfiction also grew up writing and reading it. Bethan Jones is a PhD candidate at Aberystwyth University whose work focuses on how viewers engage with television fiction and its portrayal of gender. Winner of the 2009 X-Files Universe fanfic competition, Bethan has been writing in the fandom for many years. Her work has been published in Participations, Transformative Works and Cultures, *and the edited collection,* The Modern Vampire and Human Identity. *She is currently coediting journal issues on crowdfunding and the transmedia relationship between board games and films, and is also on the board of the Fan Studies Network.*

Bethan's essay takes us through the way some of these gender and sexual politics play out in both heterosexual and femslash X-Files fanfiction.

Mulder/Scully versus the G-Woman and the Fowl One

Hetfic and Femslash in *The X-Files* Fandom

Bethan Jones

When I woke up on the morning of August 9, 2012, the internet was awash with rumors that David Duchovny and Gillian Anderson, stars of the cult TV series *The X-Files*, were a couple. My Facebook feed was full of friends, most of whom I had no idea had even watched the show, talking about it; on Twitter, serious academics whose work I follow were tweeting in delight; even *The Guardian* had a piece about the realization of the "ultimate nerdy Gen-X dream."[43] For a program that went off the air in 2002, and whose 2008 feature film was met with less than enthusiastic reviews, the amount of media attention given to its stars was unusual. Of course, for fans of the show, Mulder and Scully had been together for a long, long time.

I am not, by any stretch of the imagination, a Shipper (someone who wants Mulder and Scully in a relationship), but even I can see the desire to have these two attractive, intelligent lead characters in love.

The chemistry between Mulder and Scully was one of the main reasons I watched the show (that and my childhood desire to become a crypto-zoologist, inspired by my obsession with ghosts, UFOs, Bigfoot, and the Loch Ness Monster), and it's one of the themes that continues to populate fanfic about the series, including my own. But the most lasting appeal for me was its depiction of a strong female character. Although television in the early '90s wasn't known for its portrayal of strong women, *The X-Files* had more than its fair share. As well as Scully the series features major female secondary characters Samantha and Teena Mulder, Monica Reyes, Cassandra Spender, Marita Covarrubias, and Diana Fowley (even if, in comparison to cool, rational Scully, Fowley appears to epitomize the cliché of "ball-busting bitch").

Chris Carter (*The X-Files*' creator) has often talked about his deliber-ate reversal of gender in the series: Mulder is intuitive and empathic, the believer (all traditionally feminine characteristics), while Scully is the scientist, the skeptic, the rational one. Mulder and Scully are not your traditional romantic leads, and this allowed us fanfic writers to play with relationship expectations, even in the context of what appears to be tra-ditional romantic stories or premises: Bad!fic Mulder and Scully attend the annual FBI masquerade ball and eventually leave together because the series never positioned them as characters who would attend such an event; Parent!fic Mulder is a stay-at-home dad while Scully works twelve-hour shifts at a hospital. (This inversion of gender, I'd argue, also got the ball rolling for other non-normative—and in some cases, non-heterosexual—romantic pairings in *X-Files* fandom.)

Of course, fanfiction's embrace of these nontraditional gender roles doesn't mean that there aren't problems with the depiction of gender and sexuality in the series. There are, and fic is one of the ways fans have challenged these problems. A lot of the Mulder/Scully fanfic I read deals with frustrations around the representation of Scully; although Scully has been lauded as a strong female character, the series includes, as academic Emily Regan Wills notes in her essay, "The Political Pos-sibilities of Fandom," "at least three different narratives in which Scully is feminized and rendered powerless: Scully as abductee, as sexually desirable, and as a (potential) mother."[44] Many fans were frustrated, if not downright angry, with Chris Carter when, in seasons eight and nine, the previously strong, capable Scully suddenly ran more often than she fought and spent more time crying over a missing Mulder than she did attempting to find him. But the biggest problem came when

Scully gave the baby she had longed for through much of the series up for adoption. Like many others on my LiveJournal friend list, I've written fic in which Scully and Mulder watch their son from afar while on the run, or in which the family faces the alien invasion together. This type of fic has been one way that fan writers have challenged the depiction of Scully and the way she'd been differently gendered through motherhood.

More recently, however, I've become interested in the series' secondary characters, and in challenging gender representation through them. In the last few years I've started writing about Cancer Man and Teena Mulder, Samantha Mulder, and, most controversially of all, Diana Fowley. Fowley was introduced in season five, with Chris Carter saying that she "was a character you were destined to hate because she was a competitor for Mulder's affection with Scully."[45] Den of Geek ranked Fowley among their ten most disappointing female characters in sci-fi TV.[46] Hating Fowley quickly became a favorite fan pastime. The Diana Fowley Hater's Brigade was created in 1999 and contains links to fanfiction, poems, and songs about Fowley (almost all of them wishing her dead), as well as a mailing list. The Anti Diana Fowley Archive, which lists fanfiction stories relating to Diana Fowley and includes titles such as "Die Fowley Die!" and "Diana Fowley dies!!!" was also set up in 1999. The hate continued even past her death in the show, in which she sacrificed her life to save Mulder's (an act that, as I see it, aligned Fowley with other women of *The X-Files* who have made sacrifices, including Scully).

In their examination of *X-Files* fanfiction in the journal *Communication Studies*, Christine Scodari and Jenna L. Felder suggested that the hate toward Fowley stemmed from Mulder's trust of Fowley in the face of her duplicitous behavior and his refusal to clarify his relationship with her to Scully, causing what Shippers view as a breach in their partnership and developing romance. Many Shippers had noted the hypocrisy in Carter's introduction of Fowley, with one complaining, "Chris [Carter] has droned on and on about his objections to 'soapy' plot devices yet he goes right ahead and uses the soapiest idea of all: the meddling ex-girlfriend that returns from abroad."[47]

Much of the underlying antagonism toward a Mulder/Fowley relationship, Scodari and Felder go on to show, comes from the way Shippers view the (potential) romantic relationship between the two. As one Shipper quoted by Scodari and Felder noted, "I love how [Mulder] loves Scully...with patience and respect and real affection. She's not an easy woman, and he wouldn't want her to be. He likes her mind, her willingness to challenge him..." Another suggested, "This is exactly why I find the M&S relationship so important... I think they are attempting to define the heterosexual romantic relationship for the new century," while a third concurred, "I think that women see that strength of equality and say wow—'that' is a male/female relationship at its best."[48] In contrast, not only would a relationship between Mulder and Fowley draw upon a "soapy" plot device (soaps are traditionally considered a devalued feminine genre), but the existence of a prior relationship between the characters, and Fowley's duplicitous nature, would provide a poor basis on which to develop a romance.

While plenty of fanfiction was written in response to fan frustration with this storyline—Scodari and Felder relate that "Fanfic answer[ed] sixth season chagrin by stating in headers that the objectionable events [were] going to be ignored, or by reconciling the agents and eliminating 'The Fowl One,' often mortally and at Mulder or Scully's hand"[49]—other fans defended Fowley. In her post to the halfamoon LiveJournal community, recommending Fowley-centric fic, wendelah1 wrote that

> Diana Fowley is one of the most neglected, misunderstood, and hated characters in TXF fandom. I guess it's no secret that I love her [...] I like writing her [because] : (1.) she's an intelligent, complicated, middle-aged woman with divided loyalties, and (2.) smart as she is, she's still in love with someone she knows she can't have.[50]

Among the fic wendelah1 recommended was maidenjedi's "Something Strange," which follows Fowley through her return to the United States. Although Fowley is portrayed as disloyal and untrustworthy in the series, in fic her motivations are examined in much greater detail. Through lines such as, "She wasn't sure why she had agreed to come. Someone else could've handled the dirty work. She thought longingly of Saudi heat and sand, of Arabic voices. She'd rather pretend there if she had to at all,"[51] the reader discovers where Fowley has been since leaving America, as well as her state of mind on returning. Fowley's feelings for Mulder are laid bare, and maidenjedi shows us a much more vulnerable woman than the series did:

> A small figure topped with red hair got up from the table and got to Fox first. He dropped his stare down to her as she placed her hand on his arm.

> She whispered to him, he answered her. All his attention was on her, and Diana felt the dread return.[52]

It is this barely hinted vulnerability that I find interesting both as a writer and a reader. Although fans often complain about Chris Carter's predilection for leaving loose ends, these holes allow fic writers to create a backstory for Fowley, and make her a more sympathetic character. Fowley, like Scully, is not an easy woman, and Mulder wouldn't have wanted her to be. He would have liked her mind and her willingness to challenge him, traits that can be developed further in fanfic than they are in the series, and that reveal Fowley to be more than the manipulative shrew as which she is often pegged. This kind of revision or augmentation of received canon, the backbone of fanfiction, can be (and in academic work often is) seen as a form of resistance.[53]

One of the most common ways writers resist original texts, however, is through slash fiction. Of course, other genres can be just as resistive as slash. In fact, as Will Brooker argues in *Using the Force: Creativity, Community and Star Wars Fans*:

> slash fiction plays exactly the same game with the primary texts, on a formal level, as does...its heterosexual counterpart. [Gen] stories that do nothing more than fill in the gaps...expand on [an] evolving relationship...are no less radical than slash in terms of their relationship with the primary texts. Slash relies on the [texts] as much as genfic does; genfic departs from the [texts] as much as slash does.[54]

As a fanfic writer who now spends a lot of time coming up with stories about Fowley, I would argue that fanfic that portrays her in direct contrast to her depiction on *The X-Files* is just as resistive as most slash. But femslash featuring Fowley—fics in which a same-sex relationship is imagined between Fowley and another female character who is canonically heterosexual—is perhaps the most resistive of them all.

While much of the academic work on *X-Files* fanfiction so far has focused on Mulder and Scully, fic that focuses on Fowley, as well as femslash pairing Scully and Fowley, is an important tool that fans use to critique constructions of gender on the show. By drawing on their knowledge of the series to fill out stories with detail, fanfic writers are able to subvert the clichés and stereotypes evident in the series.

One reason slash is appealing as a genre is that an equal relationship between a man and a woman is not possible in the patriarchal society in which we live, and slash between men enables writers to examine relationships between characters who are equals. Whether the same is true for femslash depends on who you ask. Academics Lamb and Veith[55] argue that women are not equals in a patriarchal society, even if they may be equals in a lesbian relationship. Bacon-Smith[56] and Green, Jenkins, and Jenkins[57] argue that femslash has been largely ignored by fic writers because there are not enough strong female characters on television. In Scully and Fowley, *The X-Files* offers two characters who easily qualify. Their roles as FBI special agents place them relatively high up the chain within the male-dominated field of law enforcement and, while arguments can be made about their lack of equality within the institution of the federal government specifically and patriarchal society more generally, nonetheless they are each other's equals.

idella's fic "The Future's So Bright I Gotta Wear Shades" shows Scully and Fowley developing a relationship following Mulder's disappearance in season six. It comprises five "parts," chronological but not continuous, and begins just after Fowley's apparent betrayal of Mulder at the end of season five. Scully is suspicious of her new partner's motivation, both in joining the X-Files division now, and in her former relationship with Mulder. In this way, Scully's thoughts and fears mirror viewers' at the beginning of season six, as well as the fic's readers': that Fowley is not to be trusted, and that her assignment to the X-Files as Scully's partner is further evidence of her role as spy. As the fic progresses, though, Scully's (and thus the reader's) attitude toward Fowley shifts. At one point, Scully notices that Fowley is quieter than usual and wonders if it's because of the remarks made by the (male) law enforcement officers they had encountered in the field. Her concern and compassion for the other woman is evident: "What could she say that Fowley doesn't already know? Fowley could spout the same platitudes at her. Scully slows down for a red light. 'Small towns, you know,' she says. 'Small minds.'"[58]

When Fowley propositions Scully in an airplane bathroom, then, it seems almost inevitable: though neither woman likes the other, each is the only person who knows how the other feels. Scully/Fowley is not just a slash pairing; it is an enemyslash pairing, between two characters who do not like or trust each other. Catherine Tosenberger suggests that the joy of an enemyslash pairing lies in watching the antagonists overcome their differences. She writes that "dislike is recast as sexual tension, and when the characters are both men, part of the pleasure is in seeing their negotiation of expectations of male aggression (rather than friendship) in terms of desire."[59] Scully and Fowley, as strong, nontraditionally female characters, are also able to resort to aggression, however, and in the fic, their feelings of aggression toward one another segue into desire:

> Scully crosses the room in three quick strides and presses her gun to Fowley's head. She doesn't flinch, but she looks like she's paying attention now. Scully takes a step back, keeping her gun trained on her partner. "Who's after you?" she asks. "Are they after both of us?"
>
> [...]
>
> When she opens her eyes, Diana is standing with her head to one side, looking at Scully consideringly. Scully touches her wrist. It's cold and smooth, and Diana leans forward and kisses Scully. The past two months are pressing down, and the weight of them makes her sag against Diana. When she pulls away, she realizes she's still holding her weapon. "You should go," she says.[60]

Fowley is also, thus, repositioned as a stronger and more three-dimensional character than depicted on *The X-Files*.

I'd argue that what is happening in fic like this one is not so different from what occurs in Shipper fanfiction. At least up until season eight, there is no sexual element to the Mulder/Scully relationship. Fans are thus able to find queer pleasure in the text by writing stories in which they are a couple, and by drawing on the gender reversal created by Carter. Fans similarly find "queer" pleasure in the text through writing Mulder/Fowley fic, and Scully/Fowley femslash. Each of these are non-normative pairings, at least within the *X-Files* universe, and each fleshes out the characters' backstories and motivations in an attempt to understand them better. Each also further critiques canon's construction of gender, and the role it plays in romantic relationships.

In fanfiction, Fowley is no longer the soapy plot device but rather becomes a means through which fans can comment on male writers' depictions of ex-girlfriends, competitors for male affection, and post-feminist women whose enemies are no longer men, but other women. The power of fanfiction, then, lies in its ability to reimagine texts and resist the meanings imposed by the creators of those texts. Be it through het, gen, slash, or femslash, fan writers and readers take control of the characters they love and create stories, scenarios, and a world befitting of them.

The Look of Fic: 1995

```
From: shan@nyx10.cs.du.edu (Steven Han)
Newsgroups: alt.tv.x-files.creative
Subject: "The Calamari"
Date: 5 May 1995 21:32:56 -0600

Hi all,

This story is a spoof of, obviously, "The Calusari", but it is also a
bit of a reflection on recent net events.

The following is a story based on "The X-Files," a Chris Carter/Ten-
Thirteen production.  No copyright infringement is intended.

Here follows "The Calamari", 5/95.

-------------------------------------------------------------------


Saturday
3:15 p.m.
Atlanta, Georgia

    "Hmm, this looks interesting," mused Pauline as she clicked on an
icon in her America Online window.  "So this is Usenet -- where the
Internet's hippest and wittiest crowd hangs out.  I'll have to check it
out."
    The little lights on the front of her modem flashed intermittently for
a while, and her computer screen faded to black.  The modem lights then
flashed some more, as Pauline began to wonder what was taking so long.
Eventually, her screen started to brighten back up again, but this time,
a strange image of a person's face slowly appeared.
```

Steven Han's X-Files fanfiction "The Calimari," posted to Usenet (and also set
partly in Usenet)[D]

The Bronze Age
Buffy Meets the Internet

The best texts are incoherent.

—Joss Whedon

BUFFY THE VAMPIRE SLAYER appeared on screens—both television and computer—at a time when home use of the latter was rapidly expanding. By 1997, when *Buffy* debuted, one in three US homes had computers—up from one in five in 1993—but only one in five Americans reported using the internet. This figure nonetheless represented a dramatic rise in usage, with higher percentages reported among teens and young adults. *Buffy*'s home network (the then-new, now-defunct WB) was on a mission to attract younger viewers, and so the show started life with an official website that soon added an interactive comment zone—called The Bronze, after the series' teen club and frequent vampire feeding ground. Fans met in this virtual space to talk about the show, and the show's creators could see what was said. Soon, fans weren't just interacting with each other, but with the show's writers, actors, musicians, composers, stunt coordinators, and anyone else who happened by. Creators could discuss and defend their choices, explain their process, tease future episodes, or just tease fans: "The whole show's going naked and gay; you heard it here first!"; "I think all viewpoints regarding X[ander]/W[illow] are valid, glad to see I could cause some pain and dissention." Eventually, there were "real-life" get-togethers—posting board parties—that the show's cast and crew also attended.

The primary users of The Bronze were, of course, fans. This fan experience has been documented in an hour-length film *IRL (In Real Life)* by Stephanie Tuszynski, and its greatest point of emphasis throughout is the sense of community the board built. But fans also explained how show-creator participation helped legitimize the online activity—in

131

the fans' own minds. Conversations on the boards also forged a sense that fans, Joss and co., and Buffy herself were fighting common (meta-phoric) demons, whether corporate suits or snotty popular kids—or getting dumped, or dealing with the loss of a parent. The overall expe-rience was one of solidarity. When a fan worried that Joss would think Bronzers were losers for hanging around a computer on a Friday night, he replied, "By the by, if being on the site on a friday nite makes you guys losers, what does it make me? Buffy is a show by losers, for losers. Be PROUD. Losers rule."[61]

Another source of cohesion was language: fans' and writers' posts made frequent use of the show's special slang, which provided a common language distinctive enough to be the subject of a book (*Slayer Slang*, from Oxford University Press, by lexicographer and language historian Michael Adams). Fic writers, too, could learn and employ this language, lending an authentic sound to character voice and dialogue—and they did so in droves. *Buffy* almost immediately began inspiring fic, with the tacit and sometimes more explicit support of the show's creator. The Bronze was by no means a fic community—as is the case in fandom gen-erally, many extremely active fans were very anti-fic themselves. Whedon, however, has been consistently pro-fanfic, and while he doesn't discuss individual stories, his Bronze postings as far back as 1998 display an awareness of what was likely to inspire fic: "Well, my computer's been down for a few weeks. Much has happened. We finished ep 9, which I suspect will generate MUCH fanfic (both adult and otherwise)."[62] It was a good call. The episode in question—season three's "The Wish"— isn't far from AU fanfic itself, playing in the kind of "what-if" universe fan writers love: what would have happened if Buffy had never come to Sunnydale to do battle at the Hellmouth? Spoiler alert! Sweet, geeky Willow is a dark, sadistic dominatrix of a vampire. Dorky Xander is her leather-clad, greaser-style mate. Broody, heroic Angel is now kept as Vamp!Willow's "Puppy" and cowers in a cage waiting to be tortured. And to top it all off, cheerleaders are forced to wear drab colors. Welcome to the Wishverse, where new fic is still being posted.

Whedon couldn't resist the pull of the Wishverse either. Following the fic-like logic that "more would be better," "Dopplegängland" brought part of that world back to Sunnydale. This Whedon-penned and -directed episode practically femslashes Vamp!Willow with herself: "That's me as a vampire?" Willow asks after meeting her vampire alter ego. "I'm so evil and...skanky. And I think I'm kinda gay."

In the following season, "kinda gay" Willow loses the qualifier and becomes canon—at which point the Bronze and *Buffy* fandom generally exploded in the kind of controversy that...happens all the time in fic fandoms around slash pairings. But this time, it wasn't just fandom. One of Joss' Bronze posts about this plot development early on ("Willow and Tara's relationship is definitely romantic. Thorny subject; the writers and I have had long topics about how to deal with the subject responsibly, without writing a story that sounds like people spent a long time discussing how to deal with it responsibly"[63]) went very public, much to his dismay: "Well. The posting board. A place for laughs, for romance, for leaking information...You know, I came on last week, chatted a little about the willow/tara dynamic—couple of days later it's in *Entertainment Weekly*."[64] As many a fan writer has also found, it's easy to forget that the intimate-seeming virtual spaces of online fandom are in fact quite public:

> The truth is, I was a little wigged by all the commotion my posting caused. I think the worst thing that could happen would be for the willow/tara storyline to become some kind of publicity stunt. I guess if I type something here, the papers are gonna pick up on it, and there's nothing I can do about it.[65]

Whedon tried to deal with the situation with humor, throwing out some less likely spoilers (everyone on *Buffy* will from now on be naked and gay, etc.), but his genuine frustration was palpable. He was fielding a lot of hate from homophobic fans and resistance from the network (in a show that *could* feature Buffy and her boyfriend going at it for most of an episode, the lesbians were not allowed to so much as kiss), while at the same time seeing posts from teens telling him how big a difference the storyline was making in their lives. Although fic doesn't (or didn't) usually involve the added level of media attention, this mix of reaction and interaction isn't far from the experience of writing fic for an active audience.

Pioneering fanfiction and media scholar Henry Jenkins argues that fic fandom is "born of a balance between fascination and frustration"[66]—but his insight doesn't apply only to fic. As is obvious from a long track record of interviews and fanboard posts, Whedon loves television as a storytelling medium but is perpetually frustrated by its restrictions. At The Bronze, he posted gleefully about what he was able to get past network censors and about being in "hot water" with the WB. He shared viewers' frustrations with broadcasts delayed when episodes were deemed too close to traumatic events (he agreed in the case of "Earshot," a school-shooting-themed episode originally scheduled to be aired in the wake of Columbine; not so much when the season's memorable graduation finale was delayed by months). Whedon registered dissatisfaction with how episodes were cut when rerun, with *TV Guide* and promo-spot spoilers, with foreign broadcast schedules, and sometimes with fan (or professional) critical reaction. The Emmy-nominated "Hush" was inspired in part by the standard praise/criticism of *Buffy* as being strong but dependent on snappy dialogue. Whedon also explains in the DVD commentary that he was concerned about becoming too reliant on the storytelling conventions of television (shot of one person talking, shot of other person talking, shot of two people talking together, etc.). So he had monsters come and steal everyone's speech. Frustrations with critical reaction and the limits of television also inspired *Buffy* fic, especially of the "fill in the gap" or the "I can't wait any longer" variety (fic!Willow/Tara faced no network restrictions). When, after two seasons of witchcraft-as-lesbian-love metaphor, season six burst into song and fans got to hear and see Willow make her girlfriend complete, fic, it goes without saying, had long been exploring the same territory (if not in song).

Speaking of fascination and frustration, Buffy fans added a word to the pan-fandom fanfic lexicon: Jossed. It's what happens when you meticulously plan a storyline over a broadcast hiatus only to have canon contradict it, often violently, when the show returns. *Buffy* fans loved a show created by someone avowedly dedicated to giving them "not what they want but what they *need*"—but it's not as if they always *agreed* with him about what that was. Known for brutally killing off beloved characters (a secondary meaning of "Jossed"), Whedon seemed to revel in making characters and their fans suffer, as in a season three Bronze post on Willow/Xander: "it felt so right—give her what she's always wanted just when it will make her miserable! That's the JossY way. Purr."[67] It does sound like a Whedon mission statement.

Not everyone loved that mission, and the boards weren't always friendly. Many fans (and apparently the lead actress herself) rebelled at the kinky sex-, drug-, and gun-fueled darkness of the show's sixth season. Whedon's response to this fan criticism—on a later, fan-run, post-WB version of the board known as the Bronze Beta—led to a different kind of mission statement: a very serious, theoretical, and obviously genuinely searching meditation on the ethics of representation:

All right, you get the "kept Joss From Sleeping" award. (The ceremony is televised oct 11th). Your question is well put, and it's one I've asked since the only things I was writing were for my own 14 year old self to read. What is my responsibility? How dark should I get, how much should every one of my characters represent an ideal or a reality? How far can you delve into evil before you are actually propagating it? Is propagating a real word? These are questions that must be confronted every time out to bat, and every time the decision is different. We have to delve into uncomfortable and even awful places to find the heart of our stories (especially with the horror). These are fairy tales, not driving manuals. However, I have a mass audience, I have to show them something besides horror, I have to have values...

And so on. The fact is, if you are worried about these issues, you're probably worried enough. Too much of our culture today is controlled by people who don't give a rat's *** about their message, who just churn out crap. I don't like most slasher films because they don't like people— they're just kill fodder. Now there's also people preaching one thing while glorifying another, there's what [film and horror theorist] Robin Wood calls the "Incoherent Text" of so many seventies movies, where peace and understanding may be the underlying desire, but horror and violence is the structure—or the fun...

I guess the point is, the best texts are incoherent. They EMBODY the struggle you describe. Horror is reactionary. I'm liberal. But we get along.[68]

It's clear this was no glib response (and in what is perhaps a nod to the critic discussed here, a central character in the following, final season is named Robin Wood). Whedon's genuine intellectual and creative engagement here seems quite profound. While he hardly panders to fans (lots of characters would be less dead if he did), his Bronze postings show he takes fan response very much to heart and, what is more, engages it intellectually. In an interview for NPR, he explained how his thinking changed on encountering a fan interpretation he hadn't intended:

I became irate. A fan—somebody wrote—because I checked the posting boards all the time back then because, you know, it was a new way to hear from the audience, and it was still very fresh and exciting. And somebody said, oh, there's lesbian subtext. And I just blew up. I was like, you guys see lesbian subtext behind every corner. I mean, you know, when Buffy's mom had a friend over, you're all lesbian subtext. I'm like, guys, you just want to see girls kissing. It's not lesbian subtext, and get over it.

And the person who wrote it said, we would like you to go to our Web site where we have dissected every episode and written our treatise about the lesbian subtext. I went on it, and came back and apologized. It was like, everything you said is true. It's all right there. And you know, it's where I first coined the phrase, BYO subtext, because...I realized that, you know, part of art is going to be people bringing—it's got to touch everybody in a way that's totally personal.[69]

As a writer and director Whedon is famously exacting that his lines be spoken as written to the letter. For all the creative collaboration of television writing, Whedon is the rare writer/director who attained *auteur* status for his television shows. Fans and writing staff alike tend to fall over themselves to give him credit for all the best lines, plot points, and concepts. He hardly has a reputation as an artist with no interest in control. Yet the limits of his creative control seem to feed and fascinate him also—which helps explain his supportive interest in fanfiction.

It's clear that Whedon and the other show writers were fascinated, as well as sometimes frustrated—even angered—by fan reaction. Sometimes they come off as defensive—one reason we see less of this kind of unguarded interaction as the internet has grown up. Joss sniped that "he wasn't aware of the evil/dead lesbian cliché"; fellow writer David Fury demanded that *Angel* viewers recognize that "it's the WRITERS who bring humor to the show" and even pulled rank, telling a fan "when you address the CREATORS, it's MR. Whedon and MR. Greenwalt" and to "show a little respect" (Fury apologized almost immediately). Marti Noxon was clearly stung that fans accused the show of "getting all 'Buffy's Creek'": "You're just now getting bothered by the amount of sex on the show? Guess all that S&M and bondage stuff we did last season flew under your radar." But for all that, the writers *wanted* to know. Time and again, the writers' eagerness for feedback and reaction was palpable: "Speak out, postifers! For or against? (not that this will change anything—I just want to know)."[70]

This kind of give-and-take around serially unfolding stories is the coin-in-trade of fanfiction. In their online reactions, these professionals were not so different from the many unpaid writers unofficially writing for Joss Whedon's characters. As I hope should be clear, I don't mean this as any kind of insult to the *Buffy* writing staff. Today, writers everywhere are *still* adjusting to the mixed blessing of immediate feedback and interaction the internet made available—and if this writing staff were pioneers in that endeavor, fan writers were pioneering right along with them. I recall similar musings about the ethics of representation from, for example, a devout Christian housewife posting Spike/Angel slash stories she believed reflected an ethos of love and acceptance in keeping with her religion, or defending violence or coerciveness in fic and on the show itself because such behavior represented real struggle and had real consequences. Instances of such searching critique and self-reflection in response to reader reaction are everywhere in fic fandom.

One *Buffy* writer from this era at The Bronze has been particularly encouraging to aspiring writers, including, explicitly, fan writers. Jane Espenson was enthusiastic about fic in her Bronze postings: "BTW I love fanfic...not really allowed to read the Buffy fanfic, I do read in other fandoms...there's some great stuff out there. (also some crappy stuff, but people should feel free to read/write that as well)."[71] She explained that reading fic in other fandoms could help her with research: "I love writing both Spike and Giles, although I find that I have exhausted my supply of British slang...I better read more 'Professionals' fanfic, that's where I find the words!"[72] Espenson was the guest of honor at the first Writercon, a gathering of fan writers in 2004, where she made her support of fanfiction and its writers abundantly clear. She has been consistent in offering concrete advice to aspiring writers and sharing about her own process—her Bronze posts on writing, scripts, dialogue, voice, and how to get started in television writing are extensive and detailed.

Notably, *Buffy* fanwriting communities were also full of groups and posting boards devoted to issues of writing, style, fictional devices, scriptwriting, guides to British and American slang—and to Buffyisms. Criticism of language and style could be stringent. Some archives screened for quality. Popular fan writers were recruited to discuss tricks of the trade and their own writing processes on boards; there were complex awards and recognition systems in place. The blogging platform LiveJournal was very active as a forum for posting and discussing fics, fanon, research, and clichés, gently (or not so gently) mocking bad fic, and complaining about bad grammar.

Many Buffy fan writers were not present in the relatively small circle of posters at The Bronze in its heyday. But the show's sense of common cause with the broader culture's disparaged margins—geeks, losers, queers, women, and, yes, fanfic writers—remained long after the Bronze board's demise. Another side effect of this culture was that the show's writers had fans—had online fan clubs, even—and acted genuinely as fans of each other. Television staff writers didn't usually have fanbases, but in the *Buffy* fandom, they were rock stars. Fans paid attention to writing credits, knew and cared who had contributed what, and repeatedly asked after and were educated on the collaborative ways of television writing. *Buffy* left a legacy of mutual fan-creator respect that included fan writers even when other fans derided them. In a 2012 interview, Espenson reflects on parallels between the fic-writing and television-writing processes:

> To get a job as a writer in Hollywood—you write episodes of television shows [someone else has created]. And actually, the eventual job you get in television is writing for characters you didn't create. I write fanfiction every day when I sit down to write something for the characters of *Once Upon a Time* in a way because I'm writing for characters that I didn't create. I'm putting myself in Adam and Eddy's shows and writing in as close to their voice as I can do. And that's the same thing that fanfiction writers do.[73]

Espenson goes on to say that fanfiction is "the best training you could have to be a working professional television writer" and agrees with Whedon that fanfiction is a huge compliment to a writer: "It is a sign that a character has been created that seems to the viewer to have a life beyond the edges of the screen. Nothing could be a bigger compliment to a writer than a character that other people feel that they can write for."

People are still paying that compliment to *Buffy,* but The Bronze is long gone. It's a virtual space from a different virtual era; the online world has changed. Some of that fan–creator interaction has moved on to Twitter, but most television writers know to keep it a little more guarded—or very quickly learn. Most shows now *try* to have fanboards, but The Bronze looks a little like the Wild West compared to what you'd find on officially sanctioned boards today. One of Jane Espenson's sign-offs offers an aptly (in)appropriate epitaph: "All right. We've had our fun. A little history. A little filthy sex talk. A lot of Syphilis." Could be an AU fic prompt.

In the fic world of the early naughties (appropriately enough) NautiBitz was a legend: as fellow fic writer Stultiloquentia describes her on Fanlore, "The queen of smutty comedy. Hot, hilarious, zippy, conspiratorial. Very much 'genre' writing—Spike's idealized—but if you're worried about that, you're a dope." In those days, Nauti was known for writing "gateway fic," the kind that came up near-universally on rec lists and Google and drew people into the fandom. She wrote the fic that other writers wrote fic for. She inspired new writers to start posting: "Nauti[B]itz was the first Spuffy [Spike/Buffy] fanfic I read, and a huge inspiration, so I really wanted this to be the first one i posted, even though I have started writing others" (BloodEnvy, writing in response to a review of her fic posted on the Bloodshedverse, a popular archive).

Buffy's was the first fic community I looked in on, and as I kibbitzed my way around the fandom, NautiBitz came up repeatedly as a gold standard, someone to be learned from. Nauti even participated in communities that gave writing advice and technical help. (There were a number of these, such as slaymesoftly's riters-r-us on LiveJournal, in the Buffy fanfic world.) Like so many writers, readers, artists, and even researchers, NautiBitz saw giving back to the community that helped fuel and teach her as an integral part of her process.

As she explains in her essay, she was learning, too. While other writers (such as myself) have endured or enjoyed (or both) hours of writing workshops with this or that Very Serious Writer, NautiBitz's workshop was the chorus of fans reading her snark-filled sex (or sex-filled snark). Nauti paid close attention to the writing of Joss Whedon, Jane Espenson, and Marti Noxon and, to the best of her ability, transposed those voices into extremely explicit sex scenes. In time, she even discovered...plot.

Fic U: Higher Education through Fanfiction

(Or, How Several Years of Writing Sex Stories about Television Characters Can Be Just as Valuable as—and Way Cheaper than— a College Education)

Jen Zern (NautiBitz)

Fanfiction. When I first heard of it, I thought it was a laughable, shameful expression by the nerdiest of nerds. I was way too cool for something like that—I lived on the Lower East Side! I partied with the art-house crowd! I sang in a band that played CBGBs!

And yet, somehow I ended up writing stories about *Buffy the Vampire Slayer* for the better part of a decade—and as an unforeseen consequence, I earned an (unofficial) education that set me on a career path I'd never before considered.

Let's rewind to November 2000. I was still in a band (and still cool, of course), but my longtime partner and I had tied the knot, rescued a couple of scruffy mutts, and moved to a house in the 'burbs. Every Tuesday night, she and I made sure to stay in, cuddle on the couch, and catch our all-time favorite show, *Buffy*.

We loved everything about *Buffy*: the kickass female lead, the comedy, the pathos, the romance, the supporting cast, and I, in particular, had a soft spot for Spike. Not only because (his lookalike) Billy Idol's video for "Dancing with Myself" may have jump-started my puberty, but also because he was hilarious and charming and had a surprising range of emotions for a sociopathic vampire.

This was no ordinary Tuesday night, however. This episode ended with the twist that would rock my world: a *so-wrong-it's-right* kiss was shared in what turned out to be a dream, and Spike awoke with the horrifying and shocking realization that he was in love with the woman who had been trained to kill him. Bad boy falls for good girl—what a great direction for the show! Of course, Buffy would never give him a chance—she was much too moralistic—but boy, did I want to see it happen! Immediately!

Yes, something broke in me that evening. And the only way to fix it was FANFICTION.

Of course, I didn't know that yet. Sure, I heard fanfiction's distant digital siren call, but surely that path would only lead to disappointment—terrible writing by sex-starved nerds, right? Instead, I tried comics, tie-in novels, everything I could get my suddenly Spuffy-hungry mitts on, but none of it was enough. Eventually, the siren got so loud and so insistent, and I got so desperate, that I succumbed. One morning after walking my dogs, I fired up my laptop, ran a search, and lo and behold, there at my fingertips were not one, not two, but *hundreds* of sexcapades starring Buffy and Spike. People had been writing about them getting together since season *two*! I had three whole seasons' worth of stories to read!

Ignoring everything that wasn't rated NC-17—because I had only one goal, really—I quickly devoured everything there was to read. Several times. I got OCD about it. I downloaded each story, graded it like it was a feature in *Entertainment Weekly*, filed it by grade, and cross-referenced it by author. I even fixed the typos so I could read them without distraction. I was officially insane.

To my surprise, some of the writing was actually pretty great. There were more than a few silly sex scenes, and character actions or clothing choices I didn't agree with, but hey, beggars can't be choosers, right?

Unless...unless the beggar writes her *own* sex story.

People write fanfiction for different reasons. Some want to fix everything they think is wrong with a show. I wanted only to adjust two minor inconveniences: the fact that Buffy refused to give Spike a chance, and the fact that it aired on a PG-rated network. I also wanted to adjust what I thought was wrong with erotic *Buffy* fanfiction at the time: too much of it was generic, as if it could be pasted into any dime-store romance novel. Not enough of it employed the multidimensionality of the show's characters, the witty repartee, and the way the show's writers deftly blended drama with comedy. Thus, strictly for my own enjoyment and satisfaction, I set out to write a sizzling sex scene featuring the characters I knew and loved on the show, acting and talking as much like themselves as possible.

Taking a cue from the tie-in novels that always opened with a good hook of a first line, I settled on this:

Buffy Summers was being baked alive.

She isn't actually being baked alive, of course; she's trying to sleep during a miserable heat wave while having a vivid sex dream about

Spike—the inverse of his dream about her. Because it's a dream, she can let go of her inhibitions, indulge in her darkest fantasies. But then she wakes up, and Actual Spike appears in her room, wondering why she's yelping his name and shuddering from the aftershocks of an orgasm.

I could have ended it there, as a short, steamy one-shot, but the sudden irrepressible Spike voice that had materialized in my brain was extremely curious as to what would happen next, and so was I.

The three months I spent exploring the possibilities were maybe the most fun I'd had with my own imagination. I filled two notebooks with notes, I discussed it with my partner over coffee and pancakes, and wrote tirelessly, day and night. It became a multichaptered erotic romantic comedy I called "In Heat."

Curious about how an immortal male would react to his mortal lover's period, I added a scene where, to Buffy's horror and revulsion, Spike yanks out her tampon, drops it in a mug of human blood (which she'd presented to him to throw him off the scent), and says, "One man's tampon, another man's teabag," before voraciously eating her out. (That specific line was dreamed up over tea at IHOP—and my partner and I laughed and laughed. We're not easily grossed out.)

As a bisexual woman in a deeply affectionate relationship with another woman, I think I offered a unique perspective. I could describe a sense of desire and longing from both male and female points of view. To me, Spike was a lot like a lesbian. The Buffy/Spike relationship was arguably a queer one—their roles were so often reversed, Spike so open with his emotions and Buffy so guarded. She was just as physically strong as he was, if not stronger. Perhaps that's what most attracted me to their dynamic. I constantly drew from my own relationship in the fic I wrote— many of Spike's quotes (often during sex) came directly from my partner; I just adjusted them to be in his voice, not hers.

At last, after several (thousand) revisions, my work was done. I had achieved my goal: the ultimate how-they-get-it-on fic. I could retire! But of course I wouldn't. Once I posted "In Heat," there was no turning back. I was part of a community now. People loved my work and wanted more, and I couldn't help but keep thinking of more to write. I made a website and received glowing reviews and approval from my now-colleagues. Someone even gave me an award! One day, I signed in to a Yahoo! group called "One Good Day" (referring to Spike's comment that he'd get Buffy one day) and everyone squee'd at my arrival. I was famous! A red-carpeted welcome mat was rolled out for me, with long-stemmed roses landing all around it. It was a far better reception than I ever got as a musician. How could I not want to spend all my time there?

Not only were they a complimentary bunch, but most were talented writers as well. I was thrilled to have found myself in the company of so many like-minded individuals. We became fast friends, gave each other writing advice, offered to be "betas," or test audiences/editors for one another's works in progress, bounced ideas around, and generally had a great time. All because we shared a burning desire to read and write smut about two fictional characters.

Fic U: Authoring via Spuffy Fanfiction 101

SYLLABUS:

1) **Write Hot Smut Without Breaking Character**

   A) *If You Wouldn't Hear It in the Show, It Shouldn't Be on the Page.* Don't use florid descriptions or pretentious phrases, unless that's what the characters do. Don't do what I once did early on and end a sexy, tension-filled chapter with a cheesy line like, "And then, fire met ice." (Groan.)

   B) *What Makes Smut Good?* The feeling that you're there, in it, WITH them, or better yet, that you're one of them. Approach the scene from the point of view of one or both of the characters, not as an impartial narrator. Bring in immediacy, emotion, thought, touch, sight, and sound. Make it rhythmic and lyrical, but avoid (A).

   C) *Smut MacGuffins: Easy AND Fun.* Direct routes include: dreams, spells, curses, chains and/or kidnapping, mystical doodads, pheromone demons. Easy AND fun. Harder and less fun routes include: Buffy dies and comes back to life and hates herself and feels dead inside, so why not sleep with Spike? (Just kidding—that's what happened on the show!)

   D) *Use UST.* There is nothing hotter than Unresolved Sexual Tension, so use it. Keep it going. Push it as far as it can possibly go before you can't stand it anymore and have to get them naked. (I once wrote thirty-one chapters of Spuffy UST. It was by far my most popular fic.)

E) *Fuck Outside the Box.* Buffy and Spike are two very strong, acrobatic people. They're superheroes! They probably wouldn't just lie there and take it slow and romantic—at least not at first. (This was confirmed when they made a house fall down in the show.) So what would they do? Think of something outrageous that hasn't been done before, then prove it could happen.

2) **Write Snappy In-Character Dialogue**

A) *Hear Voices.* Watch an episode to refresh the character voices and the cadence of their speech patterns in your mind. If you can hear them talking, you can write their dialogue. Just make sure what they say doesn't stray too far from their personalities or beliefs.

B) *Avoid Catchphrases.* If Spike is using the phrase "bloody hell" in every sentence, he should stop. If Buffy is saying "soooo not ___" or "___ much?" more than once per fic, it's time to think of something else for her to say. I made this mistake a couple of times in my earlier fic. I learned not to as I improved.

C) *Would You Like Sex with That Dialogue?* If you don't whisper hot nothings during sex, or can't imagine people conversing between all the grunts and moans, don't bother with this. I'm an auditory person—I need to hear my characters fucking as well as see them. Of course, they're not gonna say, "Did you buy the groceries today?" because that's not sexy (unless you *really* like grocery shopping). They'll say something breathless, heated—and depending on how they feel, ardent or conflicted or hateful—in a rhythm that echoes the act itself.

Being a part of this community was not only a great social experience, it was like a crash course in learning to write. And over the years, my classroom grew. We all moved from that relatively small Yahoo! group to FanFiction.Net and LiveJournal and created our own websites, all of which invited thousands more into the fray. And while the *BtVS* fandom wasn't the largest, it boasted members who were professional authors, screenwriters, and playwrights, as well as editors, literary agents, and college professors. And everyone, professional or not, was extremely vocal and opinionated. Soon enough, what started out as a drive to fulfil my own desires had evolved into something more serious.

Writing sex and dialogue came relatively easily to me, although I did get better at it through practice. Plot, on the other hand, was another matter. If my stories ever had a plot, they would be built around whatever sexual scenario had popped into my head that week. One of my betas coined a phrase for this type of fic: PDP—porn-driven plot. Another one of my betas, a librarian in Florida, continually challenged me to write a fic with a "real" plot. *Why not?* I thought. And what better way to educate yourself than to try your damnedest and test it out on a built-in audience of thousands?

A year or so earlier, one of my fanfiction heroes, Saber Shadowkitten, had approached me with an offer I couldn't refuse: her one-shot "Humping Like Bunnies" was begging for a part two called "A Bunny in the Oven." She didn't have the time to write it, but she wondered if I did.

Saber's "Humping Like Bunnies" hit all my fic buttons: a lot of antagonistic UST; vampire and slayer united against a common enemy; a spell gone awry (one that turns Spike and Buffy into bunnies unable to resist each other); "waking up" DURING the sex act, horrified/shocked/disgusted, but OMG it feels oh-so-good, can't stop now; and an ending that alludes to a blossoming relationship. That was *so* my jam.

Pregnancy fics, on the other hand, were *not* my jam. They were the opposite of my jam, as I had no interest in ever seeing myself or Buffy in that condition. Saber didn't have to explain what the sequel would be about; it was evident from the title. I took it on as a challenge and was proud of the short and sweet outcome. Readers begged for more, but I wasn't interested in continuing it until my beta set me on a plotting mission. I knew that story had growth potential, wink wink. Not to mention, it gave literal meaning to the fic term "plot bunny."

For the sake of this story—which I wasn't getting paid for, just writing as an exercise—I pored over several books about plot and pregnancy and spent hundreds of hours online researching every aspect and timelining each event. While the finished product, "Heart Don't Lie," was far from perfect, it was an invaluable learning experience.

Fic U: Authoring via Spuffy Fanfiction 201

SYLLABUS:

1) Write a Plot That Doesn't Suck

A) *Keep the Pace—or, Don't Let Smut (or Shmoopy Love Stuff) Grind Your Plot to a Halt.* For "In Heat," I wrote fourteen chapters that were fast and furious, then went back and added a couple of interludes that, I realized much later, derailed the momentum of the story (which was really about the blossoming of their relationship). In "Heart Don't Lie," my solution was to have every sex scene advance either the plot or the direction of their relationship. As long as sex *does* something other than make you wait for the next development, it's good. In one scene that occurs in the thick of the action, they break the bathroom mirror and uncover a hidden tablet that's the key to taking down the Big Bad.

B) *Create Intriguing Original Characters.* While the story's villain, Lilith, wasn't a creation all my own, I did have to give her a personality; the same was true for her henchman. It's difficult for me to write character voices when I can't hear them in my head—so I assigned either accents or actors to them. The more life and depth and sense of humor I gave new characters, the more comfortable I became with creating them.

2) Utilize Audience Feedback

A) *It's Not as Great as They Say It Is.* Fanfiction affords you a vast audience you wouldn't normally have. Use it, and learn from it. If you give people what they're looking for, they'll give you praise, some of it hyperbolic. You're allowed to bask in the love for a while and let it bolster your confidence, but don't get complacent. Be aware that it's all subjective and that audiences are fickle. But praise *is* helpful in that you begin to see what works and what you shouldn't stop doing.

B) *It's Not as Bad as They Say It Is, Either.* Every creative person needs a thick skin. Not everyone will love your work and you're bound to hear about it sooner or later. But it's also important to stay objective and not take it personally, to learn the difference between constructive and useless criticism and to separate the two.

C) *Follow Your Gut.* Pick and choose what you're going to listen to and learn from. Change it only if you really agree. Don't write only for the masses; don't do anything just for praise. I always regretted changing something simply because a beta told me to and I wanted her to like me. In the end, it was my fic, and I needed to believe in it 100 percent.

3) **Avoid Clichés**

A) *... To a Point.* Avoiding clichés was always my biggest concern; it still is. But initially, I was so anti-cliché that in a story about a heat wave, I refused to write a sex scene using ice, even though it would totally make sense. I later learned that people actually *want* those kinds of clichéd scenes. (When writing my fic "Older," I asked for suggestions. Most of them were clichés.) As long as you write them without being lazy, they can still be sexy. Some clichés are unavoidable. Sometimes you don't know they exist, and sometimes, because things progress so quickly on the internet, they become clichés before you know it.

B) *The Cliché You Read May Be Your Own.* Sometimes, *your own* writing becomes a cliché. To wit: every now and then, someone writes a one-shot that is a parody of fanfic clichés. Each time, I've seen something of my own making in these. I say, "What? I wrote a cliché? But I try so hard to avoid them!" and they'll point out that they became clichés after I wrote them. Sometimes it's the dirty talk—Spike saying "perfect fit" became one—but sometimes it's really odd, like, "'Yep,' she said, popping the p." (That somehow ended up all over some Harry Potter fics!)

After *Buffy the Vampire Slayer* ended, followed by its spinoff, *Angel*, I still missed the characters and wished I could change the course of the series somehow. Spike and Buffy's relationship in canon had taken a depressing turn. I'd lost my inspiration. Around then, a new type of fic was gaining popularity in the Spuffy community. It was called "fantasy" or "all-human" AU.

At first it seemed ridiculous—why read something that wasn't about vampire Spike and slayer Buffy? Wasn't that what made them so great? Were these so-called fic writers just trying to get *Buffy* fans to read their unpublished manuscripts by finding and replacing the character names? I held out until I read a fic where someone recast them as high school students trying to make their exes jealous, and they still miraculously sounded and acted like themselves. That was all it took. I was hooked, and immediately started writing my own AU.

I wanted "Crash and Burn" to reference and parallel the show as much as possible so it couldn't be mistaken for some generic work. Buffy had a doomed first love with Angel—not because he was a vampire, but because he was her stepbrother. Buffy was a little more shallow, closer to her personality before she was chosen as a Slayer. She was who she'd be, I thought, without that element present in her life. Spike was a wayward rocker nursing a broken heart who literally crashes into Buffy (in lieu of her town's sign). Naturally, they fall for each other. He even writes a song for her (which I wrote and recorded and posted with the fic).

Eight years later, I still get emails that say it's the only AU some readers have ever cared for, because it's so much like the show. (And recently someone asked me if they could play that song for their first dance at their wedding. /brag)

The popularity of my fic gave me the confidence to write something all my own. That manuscript landed me an agent. I can now officially call myself a Writer. After more than ten years learning (and teaching) at Fic U, I'll take that diploma now.

The Look of Fic: 1999

The homepage of Buffy the Vampire Slayer fansite The Slayer's
Fanfic Archive[E]

There Are No Willows Here

by Mediancat

Joss owns everything and everyone connected in any way with this fanfic, except for the story and the author. Thanks to Arlane, Sam, Danielle, and all the other members of the Watcher's Council for their help with the story. Since the story begins in medias res, I feel a bit of an intro in order: It begins at the end of Dopplegangland, with one little twist added . . . which you'll discover shortly. Enjoy!

Part One

They tried the spell of return three times. The third time, after she, Giles and Angel had gone over everything, they hoped and prayed it would succeed.

It didn't. She opened her eyes and saw her vampiric self still standing there with a petulant look on her face. "Bored!" She whined. "Want to go home and have fun!"

"I don't understand it. This IS the reverse of the spell you cast earlier tonight, isn't it, Willow?" Giles asked.

"Yes! She should be home by now, sucking the blood from innocent victims."

The vampire Willow shifted in place and moved a step towards Willow, smiling. Willow did not like that smile, oh no, no she didn't. The vampire said, "All this talk of blood is making me hungry." Willow took an identical step backwards.

Thankfully, Buffy moved forward. "Back off on the appetite there, Willow de Sade," she said. "You're not attacking anyone here." Giles and Angel were looking intently at the spell."

"Can I attack someone not here?" The vampire asked teasingly. "I'll make it someone you don't like! Promise!" Her eyes narrowed as she scanned the room and saw Anya. "How about her?"

Mediancat's fanfiction on The Slayer's Fanfic Archive[F]

149

Megafandoms: Harry Potter and Twilight

Lesson One: Size Matters

Harry Potter. Its author, J. K. Rowling, the first billionaire from books. A movie franchise that kept several generations of British actors employed for the better part of a decade. An entire imaginative world for the generation of children that grew up reading and writing in it. FanFiction.Net alone hosts over 500,000 Harry Potter stories, and there are many more on other archives, some still active, some gone and never coming back. In addition to the large multifandom archives like FanFiction.Net, Fanlore lists thirty general Harry Potter fanfic websites (including some sites with more varied purposes, such as the influential MuggleNet, which include substantial fanfiction sections) and at least three times that many smaller archives devoted to particular relationships, themes, or characters. The influence of these fansites and the networks, systems, and cultures they help put in place has been enormous—and it isn't likely to fade any time soon.

Twilight. Like Harry Potter, marketed as a children's book series—in the Young Adult (YA) category Harry Potter helped establish. It came home from elementary school via my daughter's book-order form, and I didn't think twice about it. Like Harry Potter, Twilight is a global book and movie franchise that inspired hundreds of thousands of fics and also like Harry Potter, it gathered a fanbase big and passionate enough to transform mass culture and the industries that help produce it in unprecedented ways. But on the question of what *kind* of transformations—the two mass franchises part ways.

Lesson Two: Sex Matters

Harry Potter was in great part responsible for the explosion of YA as a book marketing category. Twilight also helped establish a highly lucrative publishing category (after more firmly entrenching YA literature and paranormal romance in particular as lucrative markets)—but books in the publishing category Twilight helped launch were not going to come home in my daughter's grade-school backpack. These were adult books. Really, really adult. Unlike any other fanfiction fandom, and certainly unlike any children's franchise, Twilight not only inspired an underground erotic romance revolution but took it mainstream. But long before *Fifty Shades of Grey* and other forays into the world of commercial publishing, Twilight fanfiction had become the virtual site for an enormous and sometimes astonishingly frank conversation about sex, stories, and how to go about integrating the two in writing. Such conversations had been going on for a long time in fanfiction circles, as we've seen in the *Star Trek*, *X-Files*, and *Buffy* fandoms, but when it comes to conversations about sex (as opposed to the actual act, where your mileage may vary), size, as it turns out, *does* matter.

Harry Potter spawned no Fifty Shades–style commercial boom in YA-inspired erotica, but make no mistake: its shipper wars—the conflicts about romantic relationships between imaginary magical teenagers—were *epic*. The cultural importance of Harry Potter slash in particular—of which there was plenty—should not be discounted, because in an enormous global fandom, even subcultures are giant. Although the sexual life some fanfiction imagines for Harry Potter's underage characters has long been a source of discomfort for their creator (and for a different set of fans), J. K. Rowling's post-series announcement that beloved wizard Dumbledore was gay fixed in canon the kind of possibility in which fanfiction had long been dwelling. Harry Potter slash helped shape and challenge attitudes toward sexual diversity among the generation that grew up reading it and arguing about it (a lot) online.

Even today, when YA novels and television shows frequently thematize and represent sex between underage characters, much more often than not these stories present cautionary tales. They are stories of What Goes Wrong when you drink at a party, trust a boy, don't use protection, go too far before you're ready. These stories do not represent frank conversations about tastes and preferences and protection, gradations of gender and sexual orientation, or the mechanics of orgasm. Unsurprisingly, teens are eager for that information, and have never really needed adults to tell them that sex exists and that they may find it interesting. Where previous generations may have looked to parental porn stashes and the pages of *Cosmopolitan,* today's teens increasingly find such information in fanfiction. They *write* it in fanfiction—and in some version or another, they always have. They used to write it in notebooks, and now they write it and share it online. Like it or not, this has become normal and public, a part of growing up for *millions*. If Twilight and Harry Potter have taught us anything, it's that authorial intent has nothing to do with the afterlives of characters.

Lesson Three: Age Matters

Growing up reading and writing in online fanfiction communities has become widespread and has helped shape the thinking, reading, and writing habits of a generation of future writers. Many professional writers working today began their careers in fic. Some of these writers are erotica writers, sure. But it would be a mistake to see the cultural or even the economic impact of fanfiction only in terms of the number of published books it has generated directly. This shift to writing as a social, communal activity is already having a profound impact on the economics and production of fiction as well as on the relationships this fiction represents and itself forges and relies on.

When I say "age matters," I mean the age of the fans, the fic writers and readers, but also of the internet itself. Harry Potter helped create the conditions for the Twilight phenomenon, paving its way both in the world of traditional commercial publishing and entertainment and in the online world of fan-generated culture. Not that Twilight fans always acknowledged or even knew of this debt. Although there was some overlap between the two fandoms, and some Twilight fans had participated in other fic fandoms, most—according to my research—had not. This lack of collective knowledge (and acknowledgment) of fan history and custom did not go unnoticed by those who did possess it. The same arguments—"These fans don't know what they're doing!" "And they're doing it wrong!"—have been leveled by older fans against newer fans since literary science fiction fans belittled media fans, since zine producers belittled the internet. Certainly, the same criticisms were leveled against Harry Potter fans, too, but Harry Potter fans were on the front lines of establishing the mechanisms and traditions of online fandom on a massive scale, taking them outside of smaller subcultures to a much broader online audience. By the time Twilight fandom rolled around, internet fandom had set ways and patterns, and while Twilight fans by and large weren't steeped in them, these established online cultures still provided basic models for fanwriting traditions such as awards, beta readers, feedback, disclaimers, and so forth. Twilight fans took these elements even more mainstream. Twifans were not coming from subcultures; they were often not self-identified geeks; and importantly, they were also more likely to be older, professional women with professional-grade skills and resources. By contrast, the people who built Harry Potter fandom were largely older teens and young adults in an era when web skills were still largely new to *everyone*—because the web was still new. By the time the Twilight fandom got going, it really wasn't. In 1997, when *Buffy* premiered and the first Harry Potter book was released, household internet use in the United States was at 18 percent, and all dial-up. By 2007, two years after *Twilight's* publication (but before the films that infused so much energy into the fic fandoms), home internet use was at 62 percent of households, and mostly broadband; by 2011, it was at 72 percent. Age matters.

It wasn't just age, though, and it wasn't just the internet. In terms of fanfiction itself, there were key differences between the two fandoms that had to do with fan writers' attitudes toward their source material. Harry Potter inspired work that, however divergent in terms of the activities of the characters and the worlds they might visit, tended to stay closer to Rowling's characterizations—emphasizing some, deemphasizing others, but remaining largely recognizable. Twilight fanfiction, however, evolved to maintain only the slightest structural connections to its originals and to draw equally if not more from other fics and fandom tropes. (Although this certainly happened in the Harry Potter fandom, it ultimately caused a *lot* of controversy.) In terms of *fanfiction,* then, if not in terms of scale and internet and social media use, Harry Potter operated more or less in keeping with tradition: fans creating works of homage and sometimes parody, but creating them primarily out of love. Twilight fic writers, on the other hand, could be ambivalent about their source. They might love it, but they might hate themselves a little for doing so. Or they might not even love it at all, but love the fiction-writing community, bound by its characters and the actors who play them. Whatever their differences, each megafandom revolutionized fan-based internet culture and market-ing in its own way, each led to commercial and financial gain for a few prominent individuals in fandom, and each generated controversy. A lot.

Lesson Four: Wank Matters—Even Though Everyone Wishes It Didn't

Greater wank hath no fan than to lay down one's fic for one's friends and then pick it up again and make *millions*. It's not that individuals hadn't profited from fanworks before *Fifty Shades of Grey,* or that fan writers hadn't repurposed work or gone pro with other material, but there really wasn't precedent for the scale of what happened with Twilight fanfiction going pro in 2011–2013. There was, however, plenty of precedent for wank big enough for even the biggest size queens.

Or Snowqueens, as the case may be.

As any Twifan could tell you, long before Snowqueens Icedragon changed some names in her popular fic "Master of the Universe" and published it as *Fifty Shades of Grey* by E. L. James, the wank surrounding her, her attitudes, and her relationship to the fandom had already reached epic proportions. And *long* before Snowqueens Icedragon, there was the Harry Potter fandom's Cassandra Claire—now better known as Cassandra Clare of the Mortal Instruments series (which has 7,000-plus fics on Fan-Fiction.Net). Aside from their fandom origins and being lightning rods for controversy as popular authors, these two bestselling writers' fandom histories have little in common. Cassandra Claire was a dedicated and central member of the Harry Potter fandom, participating in all kinds of ways, whereas Snowqueens Icedragon by her own account found the whole thing a little scary and preferred to hold herself a bit apart. The controversies that surrounded them, however, share a common element, and that has to do with ascribing credit—and eventually profit—to individuals for creative work that takes place in a collective culture of circulating texts and people.

In a less explicit way, of course, all creative work takes place in a circulating collective of texts and people. This is why fanfiction is interesting beyond the bounds of its own subculture, and why these controversies have higher stakes than some bruised egos, hurt feelings, or sour grapes.

The fandom dynamics of wank—though I do not believe they show off the best of fanfiction or fan communities—are telling because they often serve as proxy controversies for working out complex but more abstract arguments about the nature of authorship, textual boundaries, individual v. community ownership, and responsibility. Shipper wars—which long seemed incomprehensible to me, because I didn't see how people could get so angry at other people for liking to read about the sex lives of different imaginary people—function in much the same way. For many fans, who you ship, and how you tell that story, stands for what kind of relationship you think is *right*, what fits. In all these fandom dynamics, the central question may be the same: Who gets to tell the story? And whose story is it? Jane Austen—also a popular fanfiction source—makes the stakes clear in *Persuasion*: when the men are the ones telling the story, only certain stories get told. Dramione shippers apparently feel the same way when too much attention is paid to Drarry. Online fan communities evolved to give as much space as possible to *all* the different stories people wanted to tell.

Indicative of the many blurring, shifting roles these enormous franchises and their fandoms create and sustain, Chris Rankin's path within Harry Potter and its worlds took him from fan to movie actor to student of the fandom, writing a university thesis on the Harry Potter fandom. That 2012 thesis is excerpted and adapted here.

An Excerpt from Percy Weasley's University Thesis

Chris Rankin
(Percy Weasley in the Harry Potter film series)

Joli Jenson, in *The Adoring Audience*, describes the preconception of fans: "The fan is consistently characterized (referencing the term's origins) as a potential fanatic. This means that fandom is seen as excessive, bordering on deranged, behaviour."[74] She further suggests that there are two types of fan; the obsessed individual and the hysterical crowd. The interesting thing about the Harry Potter fan community, and something that separates it from the majority of fan communities, is that they are not fans, per se, of J. K. Rowling, Warner Bros., Daniel Radcliffe, or of any other individual. They are fans of a book series, its related subjects. In their hearts, what they connect with is the literature, and the message it sends out.

In 2000, the internet, which had been available for some time, had become massively accessible to users across the globe. With the announcement that Warner Bros. was to cast and produce a film based on J. K. Rowling's first book, *Harry Potter and the Philosopher's Stone,* fans turned to the internet to see what they could find out. The answer, at the time, was very little. The solution was to create the information. From this, the Harry Potter fan community, as we see it today, evolved. What is remarkable, in my opinion, is the way that online social media has changed how our culture views fandom.

Personally, I have been active in the Harry Potter fan community since its early days. I joined a forum no longer in existence called the Unofficial Harry Potter Movie Site (UHPMS), which latterly became Harry Potter Connection, in September 2000. I had recently been cast as Percy Weasley in the first of the film series, and was curious to see what the fan world was speculating about the forthcoming films. I was immediately swept along with the outpourings of love and affection for a book series that had been a large part of my life for the two years prior to my audition. The friends I made through that website are still close to my heart twelve years later. That particular forum sparked long-term relationships, and even marriages.

At the time, Warner Bros. was still very wary of the fan community. Filming was taking place under a veil of secrecy and very little was allowed to be said. I wasn't allowed to announce my role in the franchise for almost six months after I had been cast, in order to stave off press attention. My presence on these particular message boards was relatively anonymous. Initially, I registered under the username iampercyweasley, proclaiming that I had been lucky enough to be cast in the role. I was shot down in flames almost immediately. Thankfully, one of the moderators, Richard Cresswell, contacted me to confirm this claim, before suggesting that I re-register under a more subtle name and continue my participation anonymously, until such time that I could prove, and people would be able to believe, that I was indeed a member of the cast.

For my eighteenth birthday celebrations, I invited members of the forum to a charity screening of *Harry Potter and the Philosopher's Stone,* which had opened the weekend previous. A number of them came to visit from as far away as Toronto and Seattle, and thus began for me a wonderful relationship with the fan community. Today, I am still actively involved with the community and am a regular guest at conventions around the world. I have spoken at length about my views on the fan community and its importance to the continuation of the franchise, and I have taken part in academic discussions about the films and books. I cherish my relationship with the fans, simply because, at heart, I am one of them. I am just very lucky to be involved with the franchise in many different ways.

The Harry Potter fan community is arguably the biggest and most dedicated of them all, and it can be divided into two main camps: book fans and film fans. Of course, these camps often overlap, and others have sprung forth from them: those devoted to creating fanfiction, fanart, etc. This community of fans is special for a number of reasons. Not only have the founding members been dedicated to the cause since the publication of *Harry Potter and the Philosopher's Stone* in June 1997, but they can also be held predominantly responsible for the creation of the first truly global internet-based fan community. Harry Potter fans can find solace in hundreds of websites dedicated to all things Harry Potter. MuggleNet, The Leaky Cauldron, HPANA (The Harry Potter Automatic News Aggregator), Veritaserum, SnitchSeeker, Harry Potter Fan Zone, and others all dedicate their time to providing news and speculation on the books, films, related actors, production teams, and the like, along with hosting forums for the users to share their views, create discussions, share author fanfictions, and share artwork and, generally, everything they love that has anything to do with The Boy Wizard and his friends. This online community spirit has sparked successful ventures into the real world. A company called HPEF, Harry Potter Education Fanon, Inc., is "a US based educational non-profit organization committed to producing academic symposia on the Harry Potter books and cultural phenomenon."[75] Over the past ten years, HPEF has held these conventions in cities across America, including Salem, Massachusetts; San Francisco; Las Vegas; Dallas; and Orlando, Florida, to celebrate the opening of The Wizarding World of Harry Potter at Universal's Islands of Adventure.

The fansites are, however, only the tip of the iceberg. Another huge and more recent development in this fan community is Wizard Rock, known to its fans as Wrock. These are bands who write and perform songs about all things Harry Potter. There are literally hundreds of them, from 142 Staircases, a name dedicated to the number of staircases in Hogwarts Castle, to The Zabini Machine, named for Blaise Zabini, a minor character in the series. Some of these bands have made it to the "big time" in the fan world: their albums are available on iTunes, and they tour the United States, and sometimes even farther afield. At an HPEF convention in Florida in July 2010, the autograph line for the Wizard Rock bands was longer than that for actors in the films.

There are two key figures in the internet culture surrounding Harry Potter: Melissa Anelli, web mistress of The Leaky Cauldron, and Emerson Spartz, webmaster of MuggleNet. These two people are veritable superstars in the fan world. Anelli is a *New York Times* bestselling author with her semiautobiographical account of the history of the Harry Potter phenomenon: *Harry, A History*. Spartz is a successful entrepreneur; he founded MuggleNet at age eleven, and now acts as CEO of several websites. He oversees 120 volunteers and paid staff for MuggleNet alone, which in past years has raked in over $100,000 a year in advertising revenue. Fan musicals have become the latest trend to hit the community, with a group called Starkid Potter leading the way. They describe themselves as "an ensemble of writers, actors, directors, designers, producers, and other goof-offs [who] blend...live performance with the accessibility of the internet...[taking] the long-revered art of parody and fumblingly march[ing] forward with it into the 21st century."[76] Their first show, "A Very Potter Musical," has nearly five million views on YouTube. They followed this with "A Very Potter Sequel." Their brand of spoof has taken the fan world by storm, not only because they are unique, but because their productions are well penned and incredibly witty. Their leading man, Darren Criss, is now starring in *Glee*.

When podcasts became the latest craze in online media, the Harry Potter fan community leapt at the opportunity, with both The Leaky Cauldron and MuggleNet leading the way. Actors from the films started taking part in the early days of Leaky Cauldron's podcast, PotterCast, in September 2005. As of this writing, there have been 265 MuggleCasts; PotterCast is planning to end its regular podcasting soon with its two hundred and fiftieth episode.

Harry Potter's effect on the world of social media has been profound. The franchise began and boomed at the same time as the World Wide Web became widely accessible to users from the comfort of their own homes. Its brand managers soon realized that the internet was going to be a key player in their marketing strategy.

> The team behind the Harry Potter brand...latched on to influencers such as the webmasters of popular fan sites, making them an integral part of the marketing strategies that were critical to the brand's success. By giving influential fan sites sneak peeks and insider information, the online buzz soared, and by listening to what customers were saying...the marketing team could adjust their marketing strategies and tactics to best meet the customer's demands and massage perceptions or messages to meet the needs of the business.[77]

The Leaky Cauldron is at the forefront of the fan community. It describes itself as "an all-purpose site for the Harry Potter enthusiast." The Leaky

Cauldron started life in 2000 as a one-page news blog, constructed and run by Ben "B. K." DeLong, a Harry Potter fan from Massachusetts. Over the years, The Leaky Cauldron has grown into one of the most successful examples of a fansite that you could find. Their brand has spread over the years, and now, in a strange twist of fate, Melissa Anelli and her fellow site leaders are celebrities in their own right.

Naturally, it takes time and money to run The Leaky Cauldron, a site that, according to Anelli, currently sees 20,000 to 30,000 unique visitors per day. "[The] Leaky [Cauldron] makes money on advertising, and takes roughly about what it makes, to run. We pay a small staff of six a few hundred dollars a month each, and the rest gets covered by the considerable cost of bandwidth."[78]

On the back of a decade at the forefront of Harry Potter fandom, Anelli used her training and growing career in journalism to pen an autobiographical look at, as *Harry, A History*'s subtitle puts it, "the true story of a boy wizard, his fans, and life inside the Harry Potter phenomenon." The book has sold over 70,000 copies worldwide. She is currently working on a revised edition that will include the final years of the saga. Over the years as web mistress of The Leaky Cauldron, Anelli developed close relationships with Warner Bros., the film's producers, and with J. K. Rowling and her publishers. This has allowed her site to lead the way with news direct from the source, quashing rumors and confirming castings. Arguably their greatest achievement—a joint venture involving friendly rivals MuggleNet—was being invited to J. K. Rowling's house in Edinburgh to interview the author on the release day of *Harry Potter and the Order of the Phoenix*. Having famously steered clear of the fan community for many years, Rowling at this time showed a tremendous faith in the work that Anelli and Spartz do, as Anelli described: "I think she knows that we really respect her and the franchise, and that the people on Leaky are really loving of it. She knows our interests are hers, where the fans are concerned. And we do a lot for charity—I think she likes that a lot."[79]

Anelli has found fame and fortune through her work with The Leaky Cauldron and her subsequent book release. However, surely there are legal and moral implications to this? Anelli defends her success:

> I don't think I've made a living based on J. K. Rowling's success, per se—I think I've made a living writing a nonfiction book, which is what I am equipped and trained to do...I won't deny that the immense popularity of Harry has helped, but so did spending more than six years reporting on

the phenomenon before writing a word. So, I think it's a mix, and that it's symbiotic: I couldn't have walked off the street and written a successful book on this, I had to have the history. Similarly, I couldn't have written this successful of a book on a phenomenon that wasn't, you know, a phenomenon.[80]

Heidi Tandy, an intellectual property lawyer, sets the record straight on fan-generated content and its ability to make profit:

> If you're writing about the books or films or fandom, you can make money off it. That's why things like Melissa's book...can sell and bring in money for it. The HPEF con[vention]s have also produced and sold compendiums of papers and presentations. For things like [W]rock, I know they have "agreements" with Warner Brothers about how and when they can sell stuff and for how much, but that's based as much on their wanting to have a good relationship with WB.[81]

One of the major contributing factors to the online Harry Potter community is fanfiction. This takes many forms: book fiction, film fiction, actor fiction, romance, horror, continuations from the books, sequels, "ships," and, most alarmingly (for some), "slash" (gay) fiction, incest, or teacher/pupil-based stories. Fanfiction is a remarkable outlet for fans. In an UrbanWire interview, Tandy, a founder of the popular FictionAlley.org, says:

> [F]or a lot of people, it's just another way to discuss the books...People like exploring their creativity in a communal format—you can have that community with fanfic, whereas you don't when you're writing on your own. Fiction Alley is much more than a fanfic site—we have over a million posts discussing the books, the movies, writing, etc.[82]

Tandy's role in the fan community is a very interesting one. By day she is an intellectual property lawyer; in her spare time she writes fanfiction, has chaired the HPEF panel, and continues to report on Potter events. "As a lawyer who works in Intellectual Property, I wanted to research the legalities of fanfic before reviewing/commenting on any, and especially before writing my own. And that's how I started developing a speciality as a 'fandom lawyer.'" This intriguing set of circumstances has led Tandy to become a go-to person for fan communities who need confirmation of their legal standing in respect of intellectual property rights. In her role as an intellectual property lawyer, she represents "a number of authors, websites and literacy, writing and education-focused nonprofits in contractual and intellectual property matters."[83]

The lawyers of Warner Bros. famously embarked on a campaign in 2002–2003 of sending cease-and-desist letters to the owners of Harry Potter fansites they felt were breaching their trademarks and confusing other fans with their unofficial websites.

> WB was very concerned that kids would Google for Harry Potter and find higher-rated fanfic and fan art. They asked our site [fictionalley] to make all slash fic…R-rated and we refused to do so…WB never asked us to do it again, and it didn't seem to hurt our relationship with them, but that's just from my perspective…we did get invited to the premiere for [*Harry Potter and the Prisoner of Azkaban*] the following year. Once Daniel took the lead in *Equus*, there was a significant drop-off in requests that sites "ensure" that kids Googling Harry Potter saw nothing salacious! And when JKR said Dumbledore was gay, that was the end of requests to rate slash differently from mixed-gender relationships.[84]

This is one area of the online community that will undoubtedly survive. As a purely creative medium, fanfiction will continue to allow fans to engage in their own literary talents.

Another new area of fandom can be found in The Harry Potter Alliance. Their mission statement:

> The Harry Potter Alliance (HPA) takes an outside-of-the-box approach to civic engagement by using parallels from the Harry Potter books to educate and mobilize young people across the world toward issues of literacy, equality, and human rights. Our mission is to empower our members to act like the heroes that they love by acting for a better world…We are harnessing the power of popular culture toward making our world a better place.[85]

The Alliance was started by Paul DeGeorge—a founding member of the Wrock community—and Andrew Slack on October 10, 2005, when they decided that they "needed an organization to act as a Dumbledore's Army for our world, full of Harry Potter fans wishing to embody the message of the books to create social change."[86] Their success stories speak for themselves; raising $123,000 in just two weeks, they sent five cargo planes of supplies to the earthquake-stricken Haiti. They have donated more than 55,000 books to locations around the world, including 20,000 to the Mississippi Delta in the wake of the 2010 floods, and 4,000 to Rwanda. This is a very powerful tool; the themes that Rowling discusses throughout her canon of work are reflected in so many ways in "reality." It is promising to know that Slack and his team are using this initiative to collaborate on such important themes. Not only do they promote literacy among young people around the world, but they allow them to actively participate in current affairs and issues.

Heidi Tandy (Heidi8) has been involved with the Harry Potter internet fandom since its earliest days. She began as a moderator (mod) on the discussion group Harry Potter for Grownups, helped found and administer the fanfic website and archive FictionAlley, and wrote for the popular sites The Leaky Cauldron (J. K. Rowling's favorite) and the Harry Potter Automatic News Aggregator (HPANA, now defunct). She's a multifandom vidder, fanfic writer, fanart/gif reblogger, and an intellectual property attorney who has often commented informally on legal issues surrounding fanfiction and long advocated for fanfic as a type of transformative work.

How Harry Potter Fanfic Changed the World (or at Least the Internet)

Heidi Tandy (Heidi8)

I used to be terrified of Warner Bros.

Recently, I asked a friend to re-send to me a cease-and-desist letter that her fansite had received from WB in January of 2003, and when the subject line "C&D" showed up in my inbox, even though I knew it was going to be there, my heart skipped a beat and I had to catch my breath. Even after years of a good working relationship with Warner Bros. and Bloomsbury, J. K. Rowling's agents, Universal, and Scholastic, seeing those letters and that symbol in my inbox sends me right back to 2001 and 2002 and 2003, when we felt like we existed at their sufferance.

That's what fandom taught you, all those years ago. Anne Rice would send a nasty letter to FanFiction.Net and they would delete all the fanfic based on her books, close the section, and bar comments in the forum. Paramount could come into a fan con with Cleveland law enforcement and close the vendor room for three hours, with no warning and no notice, and fans couldn't do anything about it. If someone uploaded the *Sorcerer's Stone* trailer to the Files section on your Yahoo! group, and WB found out about it and complained to Yahoo!, they might delete your entire community and everything in it; they didn't even have to provide

165

a way for you to get in contact with the members of the community. It'd just be gone.

The large-for-that-time Harry Potter for Grownups Yahoo! group, which hosted over 4,500 messages per month at its peak, suffered a few nerve-racking months when a former mod decided to retaliate against the community. Her complaints to Yahoo! resulted in the deletion of one of the group's organizational mailing lists, and forced us to close the files section. Then it got worse. After she unsubscribed herself from the mods' organizational list, the mod claimed complete ownership of the posts she had made, and only stopped her harassment when I successfully argued to Yahoo! that she had granted the group a license to her posts for archival purposes.

If one individual could cause that much unrest, we thought, imagine what Warner Bros. could do if they learned about fandom!

Of course, they already knew. Fandom had already survived the domain name disputes of 2000 and 2001, where Warner Bros. sent Umbridge-esque threatening letters to teens around the world, insisting they hand over domain names that included terms from the Harry Potter series. Children and teens (and their lawyers) had pushed back by pointing out that their usages were noninfringing and noncommercial. But the disputes made it clear that Warner Bros. and J. K. Rowling were aware that fans existed, chatted, and created among themselves.

But was it true that fanfiction writers were bad fans, as journalist Christopher Noxon claimed in a sensationalized article in 2001 (which he rewrote in 2003, causing fans to panic when it was published again)? Was Warner Bros. waiting for a section of fandom to poke its head up so they could lop it off? Was WB "likely to greet Harry Potter slashers with more takedown orders than tolerance"? Were "billable hours...about to start piling up"?[87]

Probably not, as I learned late in 2003 when I made my first visit to the sudios of Warner Bros. in Burbank to meet with members of the Harry Potter team and their intellectual property counsel. At every meeting, they were nice, friendly, and supportive of fans, fandom, and fannish creativity—even slash fanfic. In a way, our discussions were the direct result of a piece on the front page of the *New York Times* in May 2002. The *Times* article opened with a paragraph from a Harry/Draco AU (alternative universe) called "Snitch!" where the boys were gangsters in London circa 2010, then continued with a few quotes from me and others about fanfiction, romantic ships, and storyline predictions.

The day after the article ran, when posts were popping up on Usenet, in Yahoo! groups, and on FictionAlley about the havoc Warner Bros. and J. K. Rowling were surely going to wreak on the Potter fandom and all other fandoms besides, I got an email from the new manager of the recently relaunched WBShop.com site asking if FictionAlley wanted to be an affiliate of their store.

They didn't want to shut us down. We could stay online; we could go on hosting and sharing fanfic and fanart, discussions, debates and all sorts of creativity, regardless of the ships/romances they included—and we didn't have to worry that they'd Expelliarmus our stories or pictures. That kind of contact from The Powers That Be—supportive, interested, and curious—would start to occur more and more frequently as time went on, until an invitation to the Warner Bros. studio was, if not a common occurrence, at least a logical step. But that's the moment when everything changed.

Ten years ago—before LiveJournal, Tumblr, Facebook, the iTunes store, Kindles, midnight book-release parties, YouTube, Google Docs, Kickstarter, or CafePress—*Entertainment Weekly* had to explain Quidditch in their Harry Potter FAQ, Dragon*Con filled only one Atlanta hotel, and Comic-Con didn't sell out at all. I mused about a time in the future when there'd be dozens of Harry Potter fansites.

My prediction was not as accurate as Trelawney's prophecy; by the release of *Harry Potter and the Deathly Hallows*, there were hundreds of thousands.

In those days, TV networks and movie production companies could shut down online communities with a sharply worded letter to Yahoo! or FanFiction.Net, but communications scholars hypothesized that "eventually…there will be a continuum between point-to-point and broadcast communication…"[88]

But even they couldn't predict half of the wizardry Harry Potter fans would do.

The Harry Potter fandom, which began in 1999 and shows no sign of ever ending, arrived in a perfect storm of radical new communication methods and interpersonal relations, which combined with the fantastic creativity of Harry Potter fans—creativity in writing, art, law, social networking, filmmaking, science, animation, humor, and a drive to change the world.

Kids and young adults who wrote Harry Potter fanfic in 2000 and 2002 and 2004 now have novels on *New York Times* bestseller lists.

College students who wrote and performed in fan films now star on TV shows and have created their own production companies for stage and screen.

Authors have teamed up with Wrock bands to raise funds after natural disasters and have brought in hundreds of thousands of dollars to help those in need.

Filmmakers cast Harry Potter fans in major roles and as extras, and cast members write dissertations about the Harry Potter fandom.

Theme parks and museums include fans as consultants and team members to help perfect their rides, showcases, and exhibits.

Fans—with the support of J. K. Rowling and other authors, actors, and celebs—have raised about a million dollars over the years by creating and selling Wrock albums, fanart collections, T-shirts, stickers, wristbands, and fanfic stories, alongside Rowling-signed books, in fundraisers to support marriage equality, victims of earthquakes and tsunamis and hurricanes, kids who want to read, and so much more.

Fan artists who shared their art with friends and fellow fans create games for Electronic Arts and book covers for Scholastic and Random House, and work for Dreamworks.

Site moderators and archivists are librarians and teachers and literary agents.

Quidditch had a place at the 2012 Olympics.

Multinational corporations no longer go to war against fans who want to set up websites, podcasts, vlogs, or Twitter accounts about their favorite books and films and bands and shows. Instead, they give them advance reading copies of books, visits to film sets, and space on the red carpet at movie premieres.

The fandom crowdsourced the grammar on the teaser poster for *Harry Potter and the Order of the Phoenix,* persuading Warner Bros. to add a vital comma; helped an exec at Warner Bros. with an email to the producers about the incorrect date of death of Tom Riddle's father, which was corrected using computer graphics by the time the film came out; participated in the creation of Pottermore; and worked with Universal Orlando as consultants as they created and built The Wizarding World of Harry Potter.

That's not all that's changed, when it comes to the rightsholder/fan relationships, interactions, and magic. In the 2000s, fans felt like they had to cave and kowtow even if the rightsholder overreached and claimed more rights than they were entitled to under US copyright or trademark law. But in the last ten years, in cases utterly unrelated to fan creativity, US courts have expanded the definitions of "fair use" and transformative works. At the same time, the Organization for Transformative Works and their fanfiction archive, archiveofourown.org, have invested in their own servers so as not to worry that some ISP will overreact to a bogus and legally untenable complaint from a copyright holder and delete thousands of person-hours of transformative works.

The Harry Potter fandom is really the first "social network"—possibly the largest, and still one of the strongest. But it's not a monolith, and never was. To some, it's Fluffy, Hagrid's three-headed dog, where some fans focus on fan creativity; others indulge solely in discussions of the book canon; and a third group are fans of the fandom itself. Or perhaps the Harry Potter fandom has split into seven or more parts, like a Horcrux. Or maybe it's a reverse of that, as thousands of souls came together to generate something new, unique, and fascinating.

When I ordered *Harry Potter and the Sorcerer's Stone* from Amazon in December 1998, I was twenty-seven years old, newly pregnant, and already an internet veteran. I'd been online for over six years and had done stints on staff at the *New York Times* Electronic Media Company, modding the Cyberlaw forum on America Online, as the chat room coordinator and freelance writer for TheKnot, as a fill-in moderator at the Crowded House fansite, and as the attorney for Cybergrrls/Webgrrls.

While I'd read scripts for *Twin Peaks* and the original '70s version of *The Tomorrow People* in Gopherspace, posted actively on alt.weddings and, um, extended the Melrose Place Drinking Game, my "fandom" participation was comparatively limited. I didn't read fanfic, or link to fanart, although I knew what they were.

However, thanks to a mailing list run by a grad student at Dartmouth, in September 1994, I became somewhat involved with the fandom for a brand-new TV show called *Friends*. Back then (it sounds almost like I'm discussing something from a hundred years ago; yes, it was the last century, it's nearly 20 years on!) newspaper articles and TV programs regularly warned that if you had "real-life" meetups with people you had come to know online, you'd learn that they were ax murderers or a different gender than they claimed. But most likely, they were an ax murderer.

I had no idea that there was a small, intense, dynamic, and talented mass of writers, artists, debaters, obsessive list makers, analysts, gossips, academics, and technologists creating magic every day. (There were also some trolls, as there are throughout the internet.) But those fanwriting communities had no idea that their below-the-radar subcultures were soon to be flooded by thousands of "feral" fans, be written up on the front page of the *New York Times*, show up on Fox News and MTV, and somehow become part of the mainstream.

In 2001, a fan suggested that people put buttons (we'd call them icons now) on their websites or fics to show how long they'd been part of the Harry Potter fandom. Nobody had been around for more than two years at that point, so even a line of lightning bolts, one per month, wouldn't take up too much space.

Now? It's been half a lifetime for many; for millions of people, there is no "before Harry Potter."

When I joined Harry Potter for Grownups the day before *Goblet of Fire* came out, there were a few hundred people on the list; eight months later, there were over 1,000, and now, over 25,000. When I joined The Leaky Cauldron in the spring of 2001 to post blurbs about new Harry Potter merchandise in WB stores, Harry Potter fans who wanted to create a fansite used Tripod or Geocities to do so, then typed their site name, URL, and summary into the Directory on Yahoo! so someone could manually approve and add it so subsequent fans could find it. During that summer, AOL added House seals and the Hogwarts crest as emoticons in AIM and launched 1-2-3 Publish setups for creating homepages; on most websites, comments from visitors were posted to a guestbook.

There were massive debates among fandomers as to whether the series was for children, whether adults could legitimately read it, and whether fanfic writers were creatively inspired by J. K. Rowling's wizarding world or thieves lurking in Nocturne Alley and The Restricted Section.

Everyone was afraid that Scholastic, Bloomsbury, and/or Warner Bros. would show up within the next hour and shut everything down, but the few lawyers in fandom, including myself, didn't think they'd have a leg to stand on if they tried.

Nearly two years after the release of *Goblet of Fire*, with one Harry Potter film already on DVD and another set for release a few months down the road, fans were getting desperate for new canon. There had been thousands of posts on Yahoo! groups, on ship-specific forums and more general Harry Potter discussion boards, and at small meetups at movie theaters and during DVD releases. While those were awesome and fun, every one of us wanted something more from J. K. Rowling. And if we couldn't get it, we would read something else.

I spoke with a reporter from the *New York Times* about how thousands of fans were passing the time before the release of Book Five (we didn't know the title yet) by writing and reading fanfic, as well as participating in roleplaying projects in communities on LiveJournal. On May 5, 2002, the *Times* ran the front-page article that quoted me, linked to FictionAlley. org's fanfiction/fanart/discussion archive, and reported that fans were writing fanfiction to pass the time before a new book from J. K. Rowling was released. The article mentioned slash fiction; it seems that it was the first time that the *Times* had ever reported on slash.

Some panicked, and even I was nervous. When I checked my email on Monday morning and saw an email from someone at Warner Bros. asking me to give her a call, I downed a Diet Coke for courage before picking up the phone.

She'd seen the article in the *Times*, and thought what we were doing on FictionAlley was very interesting! I took a deep breath, hoping this wasn't going to be the "but you can't continue…" call I'd feared since we'd started the website.

Instead, she asked, "Are you interested in becoming an affiliate of the WBShop? We're about to relaunch the site!"

In other words, it was the complete antithesis of what I'd been expecting. Of course, the article wasn't the first time WB, or Scholastic, or Bloomsbury had read about Harry Potter fandomers and their creative ways of sharing theories, debating ship viability, and proposing possible character arcs. But it was the first time that the Harry Potter Powers That Be had publicly reached out to a fansite in such a positive way—although it wouldn't be the last.

What I, as a newcomer to online fandom, didn't know at the time was that a few fans who'd come to HP from other fandoms thought that the only proper response, if The Powers That Be asked you *anything*, was to shut down your site, pull down your fics and your discussions, and go away—maybe even change your online name, which definitely had no link to your real-world self.

But how could you be a fan of a book that was premised on standing up to evil and saying no to overreaching by The Authorities, and just do that?

A few months later, Warner Bros. asked me (no, they never demanded or even suggested that they would kick us out of the store's affiliate program) to recategorize all fanfic on FictionAlley that included gay characters as "Rated R." I said we wouldn't. I pointed them to our policy on ratings that didn't rate kisses between Sirius Black and Remus Lupin any differently than kisses between Percy Weasley and Penelope Clearwater. (Years later, when J. K. Rowling said that she had always thought of Dumbledore as gay, it made me wonder whether she had ever even been aware of WB's requests, and she reinvigorated my confidence in that 2002 decision.)

Warner Bros. weren't the only ones who were concerned about slash fiction. There have been significant strides in LGBT rights since the early 2000s, but while slash fanfic, gay characters, and gay couples are common in Western media in 2013, ten years ago it wasn't yet part of the mainstream within fandom, or on tv, in films, or even in books. The Harry Potter fandom was no different, as Nimbus–2003, the first Harry Potter fan convention, made clear. In July of 2003, over 600 fans from all around the world converged in Orlando, Florida, years before Universal even thought about placing the Wizarding World amid its palm trees.

To its attendees, the event was a smashing success; dozens of fans and academics presented on aspects of the series, Harry/Hermione and Ron/Hermione shippers debated where the series was going, and the Welcoming Feast turned into a wake for Sirius Black, killed on page 806 of *Order of the Phoenix,* which had come out barely a month before. Judith Krug, Director of the Office for Intellectual Freedom of the American Library Association, spoke about the growing problem of book banning, especially as parents demanded schools and libraries ban the Harry Potter series because it promoted witchcraft (it doesn't).

But two vendors were not happy and clearly hadn't attended Dr. Krug's presentation. They complained to attendees and other vendors that we were hosting a smut-fest, griping about the panel that explained and discussed slash and the sentence uttered by one of the Ron/Hermione proponents to start her debate: "Harry Potter has two best friends— Hermione and Ron. Will he end up with one of them or will they end up with each other?"

In other words, the very idea of two characters in a book being gay offended them deeply; discussion of homosexuality was inherently wrong and should be banned. Just after lunch, we refunded their money and asked them to leave.

But they were outsiders to fandom. What about webmasters and academics and adult fans?

Some of them were anti-slash, too. When I started at The Leaky Cauldron in the spring of 2001, I tried to convince the site's then-webmaster Rames to allow me to create a fanfic section for the site that would accept all Harry Potter fanfic regardless of ship or lead characters. He said that he didn't want to host slash somewhere that kids could read it, even if the characters didn't go beyond kissing. In the mid-2000s, MuggleNet took the same perspective: stories with same-gender relationships shouldn't be easy to access and wouldn't be hosted on MuggleNet's fanfic site.

Fans who wrote slash fanfic were pilloried in articles in papers from Scotland to San Francisco, and Warner Bros. was concerned that kids doing internet searches for Harry Potter (in those pre-widespread-use-of-Google) days would find "problematic" material.

Fanficcers, fan artists, and those who enjoyed fanworks kept their names and their Potter interests hidden from friends and family. Many were worried that if people found out, they'd be called freaks— dangerous freaks—and anonymous trolls stirred the cauldron of concern when they could. Anons would show up a few times a month on forums and mailing lists to condemn mods for hosting fics with gay characters where kids could see them, even if the characters were barely kissing. In 2004, for example, an anonymous user wrote:

> While I understand that the majority of the writers here at fictionalley may be adults, or at least well into their teens, some of the readers may not be. Even if you consider your fic to be PG, with just a bit of kissing or whatever, I think that any level of homosexuality from the main characters would be sufficantly [sic] traumatic for a child that one might want to consider rating all of those fictions R.[89]

And ten years ago, this sentiment wasn't uncommon. As one fan commented back in 2000, "And as to Ron/Harry shippers- let 'em ship. I know that JKR would never screw up a perfectly lovely series like HP because she wanted to make the main characters boyfriends. That would instantly make me set down the book and run screaming."

In 2002 or 2004, it wasn't unusual for a Concerned Netizen to post on a forum or email a site's mods and warn that "making" the beloved Harry Potter characters gay was libelous, confusing, a slap at J. K. Rowling, and, worst of all, noncanonical.

But in 2004, J. K. Rowling gave her first website award to Immeritus, a Sirius Black–centric site that hosted fanfic and fanart as well as discussions and speculation…and in some of those fics and some of that art, Sirius was snogging or shagging Remus Lupin (or occasionally Snape or Lucius Malfoy). Rowling said, "For a while I had a picture of the four marauders drawn by Laura Freeman on my desktop. It is a particularly accurate portrayal of Sirius and Lupin…" There were discussions about what she meant by that, focusing on the characters that comprised one of the most popular ships. Was she okaying it? Was she granting permission to fanart in general, and same-gender, romance-centric fanart in particular?

Three years later, though, when she stated that she had always seen Albus Dumbledore as gay, everything changed, not only for slash readers, writers, and artists, but also for fandomers across the net.

Back on October 19, 2007, thousands of fans posted comments and essays about Dumbledore's sexuality; many if not most comments criticized Jo for celebrating homosexuality, for making it all right to be gay, for "ruining the books" or this favorite character. "Now people are going to call HP fans gay…lol hope it doesn't come to that!!"

By 2010, the world was different, and so was fandom. MuggleNet changed its website in support of Spirit Day, in memory of six young men who killed themselves after being bullied because they were gay. Hundreds of fans posted support for those gay teens, for the inspiration fans had gotten from the Harry Potter books, and their memories of how terrific it felt to hear that J. K. Rowling had always seen Dumbledore as gay.

A decade ago, I was slammed as immoral for letting teenagers discuss whether gay wizards even existed; in 2007, J. K. Rowling told us they did. Kids who were thirteen in 1999 and 2002 and 2004 are in their mid-twenties now, and those who were college students then have kids and nieces and nephews of their own. If you told them that it was immoral to let thirteen-year-olds read YA stories about gay teenage wizards, they would probably laugh and tell you it'd be immoral to ban them from reading those stories.

Or anything else.

The Look of Fic: 2001–2002

The homepage of Harry Potter fanfiction archive FictionAlley, 2001[G]

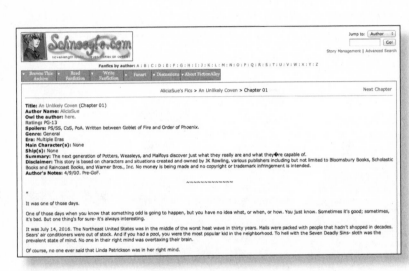

Fanfics by author: A : B : C : D : E : F : G : H : I : J : K : L : M : N : O : P : Q : R : S : T : U : V : W : X : Y : Z

Browse This Archive | Read Fanfiction | Write Fanfiction | Fanart | Discussions | About FictionAlley

AliciaSue's Fics > An Unlikely Coven > **Chapter 01**   Next Chapter

Title: An Unlikely Coven (Chapter 01)
Author Name: AliciaSue
Owl the author: here.
Rating: PG-13
Spoilers: PS/SS, CoS, PoA. Written between Goblet of Fire and Order of Phoenix.
Genre: General
Era: Multiple Eras
Main Character(s): None
Ship(s): None
Summary: The next generation of Potters, Weasleys, and Malfoys discover just what they really are and what they♦re capable of.
Disclaimer: This story is based on characters and situations created and owned by JK Rowling, various publishers including but not limited to Bloomsbury Books, Scholastic Books and Raincoast Books, and Warner Bros., Inc. No money is being made and no copyright or trademark infringement is intended.
Author's Notes: 4/9/00. Pre-GoF.

~~~~~~~~~~~

*

It was one of those days.

One of those days when you know that something odd is going to happen, but you have no idea what, or when, or how. You just know. Sometimes it's good; sometimes, it's bad. But one thing's for sure- It's always interesting.

It was July 14, 2016. The Northeast United States was in the middle of the worst heat wave in thirty years. Malls were packed with people that hadn't shopped in decades. Sears' air conditioners were out of stock. And if you had a pool, you were the most popular kid in the neighborhood. To hell with the Seven Deadly Sins- sloth was the prevalent state of mind. No one in their right mind was overtaxing their brain.

Of course, no one ever said that Linda Patrickson was in her right mind.

Alicia/Sue's Harry Potter fanfiction "An Unlikely Coven," as posted to FictionAlley, 2002[H]

The Twilight Fandom

Mainstream publishing wasn't giving us what we
wanted, so we made it ourselves.

—tby789, author of "The Office"

THE TWILIGHT FANDOM. Maligned and mocked, belittled and ridiculed all over the internet. "The Feral Fandom," people called it. A fandom with zero geek cred, none, no idea what fandom or fanfiction was, how it should work and had worked for years. They were rabid, ridiculous Twihards.

And that's just what they said about each other.

This is what MSNBC said, in a 2009 headline: "Devoted 'Twihards' get their fix online. Many 'Twilight' junkies hit the Web to connect with like-minded devotees."[90] The article elaborated: "Just try prying a Twihard away from the computer screen and a rousing tweet or a lusty blog. You might come away badly wounded." It went on to discuss fanfiction: "Believe it or not, there are Stephenie Meyer wannabes out there who have taken her characters and expanded on them." Conceding that some of these "wannabe" fics are "quite good," the article cites AngstGoddess, whose massively popular "Wide Awake" many fans felt was "better than anything Meyer has churned out."

"Churned out"? I didn't care for Twilight, neither the movies nor the books. Not my cup of tea. Curiously, not even the cup of tea of a lot of Twilight fan writers, or maybe "a cup of tea they would admit to no one" (although "S&M and Bible Studies" could pass muster as a Belle and Sebastian–penned Twific prompt). But "churned out"? This mainstream media coverage—and it's hardly the *least* respectful article out there—clearly characterizes thousands of women as dangerous lustful junkies so devoted to the ridiculous stories of a "churning" hack that they're forced to make their own stories to feed their habit, as if fanfiction were some kind of cut-rate home meth lab.

It's remarkable how poorly this characterization fits the women the article actually quotes. AngstGoddess, for instance, is quoted describing fic-writing not as a desperate bid to get more Twilight or as a way to emulate Stephenie Meyer, but as a learning process: "'It's kind of like training wheels,' she explained, 'to be given the opportunity to explore writing styles and techniques using a template in which the relationships and logistics have already been decided and proven enjoyable to the fandom.'" MSNBC relied on AngstGoddess to explain the various categories or niches most Twific falls into in the Twilight-specific use of terminology: "Canon"—close to Meyer's world; AU—loosely based on Meyer's world; and "'All Human,' the most controversial, which usually consists of original fiction with 'Twilight' names attached bearing little resemblance to the original works" (MSNBC's language, paraphrasing AngstGoddess). The article also has her describe the Twilight fandom's pan-generational appeal: "'I think the most notable aspect is the variety of ages we see,' she said. 'With every generation, you see differing trends in what they enjoy and create with the characters. Niches notwithstanding, this also provides an opportunity for people to find something in common with one another.'" She doesn't *sound* like a rabid junkie. Neither do the women who run LettersToTwilight.com, a fansite that also poked fun at itself, the fandom, and the objects of the fandom's love. The article quotes them, too: "'Twilight' isn't really that great of a movie. The books aren't always written so well. But that doesn't mean it's not great, amazing and captivating. That doesn't mean we don't love it and don't go all fan-girl crazy over it."

Despite the preponderance of self-aware, even self-ironic, professional women in the Twilight fandom, however, Urban Dictionary defines Twihards as "stupid obsessive people (mostly teenage girls) who are in love with fictional characters and wouldn't know a good book if it punched them in the face." Such misconceptions are extremely widespread. It's the fandom even other fandoms love to hate.

It's tempting to parse some of the intra-fandom hatred of Twilight as paralleling the prejudice of (mostly male) science fiction fans against the emerging (more likely to be female) communities of media fans in the late sixties and seventies, but this Twi-hate cuts across gender boundaries. I've seen enormous disdain for anything Twilight related expressed in any number of equally female-dominated fanfiction communities. Some of the most intense Twi-hatred has been expressed by *Buffy* fans, perhaps in reaction to the idea that one vampire-themed teen-based franchise would resemble another. A typical response: "*Twilight* is very bad fiction of the worst kind. On the level of Mary Sue [self-insert] fanfic bad. Not witty, concise, well-plotted, or at all interesting, its themes are generally anti-feminist and the protagonist is the exact opposite of Buffy: largely helpless and whiny. Stephen King put it best when he said, 'the moral of Twilight is how important it is to have a boyfriend.'"[91]

Often, we see other fangirls disdain Twilight and its fandom because they see it as *girly*—not challenging gender stereotypes, but reinforcing them, like a vampire version of the Disney Princess line. It's hardly the case that I can't imagine—or make—a really strong feminist critique of *Twilight*. But frankly, I can do one for *Buffy*, too, and that's a feminist show of which I'm a big, flaily fan. Furthermore, lots of Twilight fanfiction itself explores feminist critique from a variety of different perspectives—including the one that says, "We're grownup women, and our sexual fantasies don't govern our politics. Or the other way around."

I would speculate that a great deal of the stigma surrounding Twilight and its fans—among other fans, even among other fan writers—has to do with internalized gender and genre prejudice. Fanfiction fandoms tend to be genre-based. Romance is a genre, but it's not a *geek* genre like science fiction or fantasy, and not a *cool* genre like mystery or crime drama or horror. The enthusiasm indicated by the preponderance of romance plots and tropes in the fanfiction inspired by these genres doesn't transfer to romance as such. Romance is a *girl* genre. It's not girls doing cool things boys typically do, or girls doing girl things in boy territory. It's just girls doing girl things in the way girls do. Pathetic much?

I didn't think so. I was completely fascinated by the Twilight fanfiction fandom. It took so many of my loves—outrageousness, mashups, women writers, coterie literature, discredited cultural forms—and smooshed them together, serving them over virtual cocktails and flashing GIFs. It was a massive global exchange of porn and recipes and writing advice, all for the fun of it, all for free. These women didn't just write fic; they built an industry—a cashless one, sure, but a sophisticated, large-scale global economy of review and interview websites, promotional and marketing campaigns, credits and rewards, labor exchanges, vast charity drives—by and for women, though open to whatever men wanted to come along.

The downside is, they often hated themselves for doing it. They built this vibrant community industry, and then they tore it—and each other—down. It's the worst and best of women's culture, all the stuff that makes me proud and all the stuff that makes me want to tear my hair out and weep—often in reaction to the same person, within the space of several lines or tweets or seconds.

The story of the Twilight fandom is a story of mostly nonradical women who came together in a radical and original, creative, self-sustaining global community. In a stunning bit of irony, their collective power as I witnessed it was fueled in part by their own belief that they were a community of derivative, amateurish hacks who could lay legitimate claim to nothing. Twilight fans were inspired by a book that they maybe loved, but that many also saw as being derivative and amateurish itself. If their original source wasn't original, for God's sakes, *they* weren't—which spared them from having to worry about it. They simply could write what they wanted and see how far they could go.

For some of these women, had they not believed they were "only writing fanfic," they would never have started writing in the first place. "It's just fic" meant they didn't *need* the confidence to innovate and create because they didn't think of themselves as doing that. They thought of themselves as being silly and having fun, or working through their issues, or giving back to a community. Of course, they *were* doing all those things, but they were *also* being creative and innovative. In some cases, it just took them a while to realize it, and the realization came as a happy surprise. In some cases, they still don't see it that way, and are even offended at the idea. Whatever realizations did or did not come later, the idea of writing "just fanfic" gave a kind of permission. "Just fanfic" made it possible to write for an audience without having to identify as a writer—which can also attract criticisms of arrogance and presumptuousness.

It worked this way for some, but obviously not for everyone. Some Twilight writers had been writing for years, professionally. Some were CFOs and neuroscientists, some were MFAs, some were queer. Some were housewives. Some were queer housewives. Some were even men. I've rarely met more assertive, outspoken women than I have in the Twilight fandom, and some of them (though only some) found their voice there. Some of the writers represented in this volume tell a version of that story. Over the course of years of conversation, I've spoken to many fan writers who have described coming to creativity in this back-door way, because they didn't think they were doing it. But individual writers' journeys were only a part of what they did without exactly meaning to.

The Twilight fandom accidentally made an empire. The fandom's most popular fics—works like "The Office," "Master of the Universe," "Wide Awake," "Emancipation Proclamation," "Art after Five," "The

Submissive," "The University of Edward Masen," and a number of others—had readership that dwarfed most *New York Times* bestsellers. People outside the community began to see this readership and wanted in. It's *hard* to get original fiction read, even for published writers. And the Twilight community offered more than eyeballs—it offered *thousands* of reviews, and publicity, and awards. In time, the Twilight fanfiction community grew to be less about the Twilight books and movies and more about the fanfiction, which in turn *also* became less about the books and movies and more about, well, romance writing in a mix of subgenres.

Aspiring writers began repurposing their original work as Twilight fanfiction, changing the names *to* Edward, Bella, Rosalie, Jacob. Writers with little if any connection to Twilight began writing stories about its characters because they could get attention and feedback and *so many readers* if they played along. Some did this but entered into the spirit of the community, giving interviews and recommendations and reviews, revising Twilight tropes and structures along with everyone else—even if Twilight itself never was their favorite, and the community was what had drawn them in. Others were more cynical, standoffish. However they behaved toward the community, the presence of fan writers who were not actually fans made for a different atmosphere than what we normally find in fan communities: fan reverence for the source was missing.

The Twilight saga stopped functioning as source per se and began functioning as one massive erotic romance prompt. A template. It provided a basic structure, some basic characterizations, and relationship and plot trajectories, but increasingly these elements appeared vampire- and glitter-free. Often in All Human fic, Twilight's characterizations would be reversed, inverted. Switched up, mixed and matched. Sometimes only the vaguest parallels were retained. One character tended to have more power, be more controlling; one tended to be clumsy. They tended to live in the Pacific Northwest or Chicago (where canon Edward was from). Popular fics spawned genres practically overnight, like tby789's "The Office." Others involved high school or BDSM. Genres were often designated by a version of Edward's name: Tattward (more than one tattoo artist fic); Artward (lots of artists); Domward (*Fifty Shades* was hardly the first); Subward (there were a few); Geekward; Drugward; Doucheward; Dadward (DILFward); Jockward. And on. And on. There were hundreds of thousands of stories about Edward and Bella doing practically everything *except* being teen vampires.

Twilight had been eclipsed. There was fic for fic. Readers and writers alike began to forget where canon stopped, where fanon began. Twific had taken over its own world.

I started reading compulsively. What did these people think they were doing? So many stories, the same but different. Variations on a theme, permutations, inverted, reversed, restructured. A fugue of a novel, spun out in different directions. I tried to sustain them in my mind simultaneously, thousands of what-ifs—it was like a new structure of fiction.

My interest in Twilight started with a fanfiction writer called The Black Arrow. She'd read my fic! Which was about a very outdated source, and was not in a fandom, so every early reader was very exciting. (Plus I'd just finished the index of my first book. EVERYTHING that was not my index was exciting.) In any case, my gentle reader mentioned that she'd written a fic for Twilight. I diplomatically said I hadn't read the books. I'd glanced at them, but... again. Not my cuppa. Then The Black Arrow said with her fic, it didn't really matter if you'd read the books or seen the movies.

I didn't believe her. Almost all of the fic I'd read to that point seemed to rely quite heavily on *something* from its original—even if it was just my interest. The Black Arrow liked something I'd written, though. She'd been supportive. I wanted to return the favor. I only ever said constructive things about fan writers, praising what I saw that I liked and leaving out what I didn't. I was sure I'd be able to find something to praise, but I didn't expect to enjoy the story, or even really to be able to follow it.

First impressions were not auspicious. "The Blessing and the Curse" didn't sound like my kind of thing. The prologue (a convention I'm not fond of) talked about soul mates, and I was even more skeptical. But there was something that piqued my interest—this soul mate thing, she made it sound coercive, controlling.

I had no idea.

As the story progressed, I noticed the writing was good and getting better. Not just "good for fanfiction," *very* good. Sexy and heated, but also *creepy*. The writer had created an entire world out of a house and a neighbor—a world that was very clearly layered over *Wuthering Heights,* which also provided the epigraph. It wasn't just that, though. The character Edward was possessive, controlling (Heathcliffian), but he could read Bella's mind. She'd broken free, moved away, but a family illness forced her back. The created space was claustrophobic and strange and I read it all night, fascinated and a little repelled, really the same way I'd been by the Brontës. Yes, there were sex scenes, eventually, and they were very well done—often such scenes seemed formulaic to me even in professionally published commercial fiction. I was deeply immersed despite not being a contemporary romance reader, not being a fan of paranormal fiction, and never having read the story's source. When I went back and read Twilight, I saw the connections, but I didn't need them to read the story. I'm sure the same holds true for its *Wuthering Heights* connection.

If Twilight inspired some amateur writer to do this, I thought, *I'd probably misjudged it.* I made an agreement with my students. We'd take a long weekend. They'd read Flaubert, and I'd read the Twilight series. So I read it—and I didn't think it was nearly as well written as The Black Arrow's fic. There was clearly something there, though: I didn't care about the characters, didn't like them, didn't think much of the plot or the style, and yet I read most of the series in a long weekend (I couldn't get through the final volume).

The primary result of my reading, though, was that I was now *very* impressed by the twists and turns The Black Arrow had taken with Twilight's plot and characters. The biggest was the simplest: Twilight Edward could read everyone's mind *except* Bella's, while "Curseward" could read *only* Bella's. More coercive, sure—but also a huge narrative challenge. If he could know everything, how could the tension be maintained? How could he have anything but total power?

I was impressed, as I said, but also curious. I started reading around in The Black Arrow's favorites on FanFiction.Net, and then in the favorites of *her* favorites. I found parody, and porn, and the point of view of a long-suffering Volvo. A story in which Emmett is trying to turn peaches into vampires (I loved this one). Edward crossed with *Angel* to make an OCD detective-vampire. His fastidious suit closet and secretive habits lead Bella to an erroneous conclusion: he asks Bella to (per *Twilight*) "Say it. Out loud." So she does: "Edward, you're gay."

Then there was "Wide Awake"—a phenomenon in and of itself. Long the biggest fic in fandom—as featured on MSNBC. On Mommy boards. Mentioned at my daughter's soccer games by people with no awareness of my interest in such things. The story that inspired thousands of women—including E. L. James, by her own account—to try their hand at writing. Its author, AngstGoddess, still refuses to earn a penny from it, but even back then, Snowqueens Icedragon (E. L. James) paid over $100 in data fees to download it to her phone (a reminder that *someone's* long been making a buck from fic, just not the people writing it). "Wide

Awake" had its own fan communities—and it had its own hate communities. I wish it had its own recipe book; Bella communicated her emotions
by baking. Mmmm. Cookies.

Like "The Blessing and the Curse" by The Black Arrow, "Wide Awake"
took a detail from Twilight and tweaked it: in Twilight, vampire Edward
doesn't sleep. In "Wide Awake," both characters are terrified to sleep and
bond by helping to keep each other awake to stave off debilitating night-
mares. They both suffered childhood traumas—it became a favorite game
of the Twilight fandom to imagine the kinds of psychological traumas or
mental disorders that would make the canon characters' behaviors make
sense in the real world.

They did this a *lot*. Fansites obligingly provided guides just to keep
them all straight: Darkward, Highward, Curseward, Drunkward, Hock-
eyward, Toonward, Mobward. Many of these popular 'wards went on to
refer not to a single fic but an entire genre. And there are more. Some
even got their own non-'ward names—which in two cases became the
names of bestselling books: Beautiful Bastard (BB) and Fifty.

Of course, there were also fics that exploded the fast evolving genres
and conventions of the fandom, either by taking them on or by violating
every convention in sight. Enter BellaFlan's "Becoming Bella Swan" and
algonquinrt/d0tpark3r's "Mr. Horrible" (we hear from both authors later
in this section). Enter "Gynazole": Edward is a loud-talking pharmacist
at a Target. Bella is a woman with an embarrassing vaginal condition.
"Gynazole's" characters had Twitter accounts—Bella's handle named a
hot-sexy vampire-esque alter ego; Edward's ID was an earnest series of
numbers. These accounts were real and actually tweeted; these tweets
figured into the story and also announced spoilers and updates. The fic's
author showed up as her character's neighbor and started stealing cats
from other fics and holding them for ransom.

As a literature professor, I found both this body of work and way
of reading truly astonishing. Because yes, these 'wards and Bellas were
distinctive characters, but they *were* all riffing on a common source.
Even if the source had not been their initial inspiration, being published on fansites with canon names meant they came asking to be
related to Twilight and also to other fanfictions. They asked readers to
compare and notice where they came together with and departed from
canon—and they departed *a lot*. Still, their stories were commentary on
one another. They were conversations. And, more often than not, they
were conversations the writers didn't have the opportunity to have in

their day-to-day lives—about sex, or rape, or BDSM, or what friendship means. About cookies.

I read fics that commented on and started conversations about middle school and fandoms (a romance between a Harry Potter fan and a Lord of the Rings fan—conflict!). About religion (featuring an invented, Amish-like religious community—where attractive adult virgins were the norm). About class politics. About Washington politics. Elementary school politics. After a lot of research and reading, I still didn't know quite what to make of it—but I *had* to teach it. I did. And my classes decided that Twific was, collectively, kind of brilliant.

It was also *huge,* global, and, as my students and I realized during the summer of 2010, kind of doomed. If Twific had been a bank, it would have been "too big to (commercially) fail," but its implicit contracts were all based on an assumption of noncommercial, nonoriginal collective enterprise. This assumption meant (or so participants believed) that no one individual could take advantage of all the many hours of donated labor everyone was putting in. And so people gave freely—often at the expense of their family life or work life or own profitable enterprises— *many* hours, to promote and share and illustrate and edit and host other people's stories.

But this implied contract didn't exist anywhere, and as it turned out, its assumptions weren't universally shared.

Even when I was teaching it in 2010, this cashless empire had begun to become...less cashless. The popular fanfiction hosting site Twilighted launched the publishing house Omnific, which "specialized in transformative works," changing the character names on popular All Human fanfics such as "Boycotts and Barflies" to publish novels such as...*Boycotts and Barflies.* Omnific went on to publish a popular fanfic from my syllabus, the Dante/Twilight crossover "University of Edward Masen." The Writer's Coffee Shop (TWCS), which published the "original" name-changed *Fifty Shades of Grey,* grew out of another popular Twilight fanfiction hosting archive of the same name. These endeavors and other instances of wank (which is how authors' attempts to take themselves or their work seriously are often categorized) made writers targets of tremendous collective vitriol. After my class was over, a hate website called Twankhard, Twilight's very own, much nastier "fandom wank" site dedicated to bringing down writers who gave themselves airs, was launched—anonymously. It reported on anything its likewise anonymous posters found to be in any way self-aggrandizing, or even other-aggrandizing. It was all *just fic,* and people should know their place and stay in it. In some ways, Twankhard was a case of a lioness's rage at the creature that threatened its young. But the threatening creature was also... its young.

Even this site was really nothing compared to the kind of mutual shaming and hatred that went on around the publishing question— which is complicated enough to deserve (and here gets) its own section. It was not—and is not—always like that, however. The Twilight fandom also encompassed many women working together and finding much to love and support in each other and in themselves.

My students' perspective on fandom, romance, and Twilight fans, and even on women writers, really changed as a result of reading and listening to some of the writers here. Making equal use of prominent Marxist critic Theodor Adorno and *Fic* contributor Kristina Busse, my student Myles Barker theorized that in a mass culture where three-quarters of media jobs go to men, fanfiction introduced a space in which women could assert control and undermine the dominant culture. Barker saw the women of the Twilight fandom as displacing the roles of the publisher, distributor, and author, devising their own systems, and thus giving the lie to Adorno's theory that mass culture leaves no room for imagination or reflection on the part of the audience. Everyone in the class had a theory—that was the requirement. Dai Newman saw fanfiction as a kind of collection: "actively, selectively, and passionately acquiring... things removed from ordinary use," ordinary use here being commercial use but also the way that characters usually interact with trappings of fiction such as plot, pacing, and development, which Newman found less important in fanfiction. Importantly, he relied on Susan Stewart's sense of the collection as unity, not sequential but as synchronous whole—a theory he believed equally applies to Twilight fanfiction taken as a body of work. Cooper Savage saw Twific as the punk rock of fiction; Pace Measom—via Slavoj Zizek and Philip K. Dick—saw fanfiction as "the replicants of the literary world." (All theoretical and fanfic pairings are my students' own, and the complete work can be found on the course website.[92])

The point is, these students began as tremendously skeptical, but by reading the works, interacting with the authors (who were generous with their time), and above all taking these writers seriously enough to read them in conjunction with other writers who took themselves seriously— like, say, Immanuel Kant—the class developed a tremendous respect for the Twific writing community. And whether they liked all the individual stories or not, everyone found something to like they wouldn't otherwise have imagined existed.

To which many of the fic writers responded: "You're so funny, we were just writing smut."

Fic is of necessity a kind of survey-like volume, but this section examines one fandom in a little more depth. I wanted to give a firsthand sense of fic community motivations, dynamics, and experiences—good and bad. Although I haven't known it the longest, I probably know the Twilight fandom the best, as a result of my course and the research that went into developing it, and so it was the natural choice for this more in-depth treatment. It's a good fandom to focus on, though, for reasons independent of my scholarship. Certainly, it's been the most widely represented and *mis*represented in the media since the commercial publication of *Fifty Shades of Grey* and the growing list of Twilight fanfictions that have followed suit. Many of those media articles were very hurriedly researched, and while others were much more thorough, a number of both kinds were quoting me. My perspective on my fifteen minutes as the press' fanfiction professor is just that. It was me. It isn't *them*—the actual contentious, articulate writers in question. So here they are—at least some of them—including some who probably disagree with a lot of what I've just said.

Jolie Fontenot has been tracking trends and motivations in the Twilight fandom as part of an academic study in communication. In her essay, she explains how even Twilight fanfiction that stayed as close as possible to Meyer's series was sometimes written to protest elements of the original people found disappointing or distasteful. She also shows how this kind of anger toward the object of fan love, when combined with cultural negativity about fan culture and (in the case of the Twilight fandom) its beloved object, can both splinter a community and bind it more closely together.

Twilight's True Believers

Jolie Fontenot

I've studied the Twilight fandom for several years. What initially started out as curiosity about fan uproar over the series finale, *Breaking Dawn,* transformed into a long-term study of a community and, more important, how they portrayed themselves and their work.

There is no such thing as "the average Twilight fanfiction writer." I've seen ages from teenagers to senior citizens. College students, stay-at-home moms, husbands, lawyers, medical professionals—I've seen stories written by people who claimed to hold all of those roles. No short essay could describe all of these people and their motivations. But there are a few broad observations we can make about the responses of the community as a whole, especially to *Breaking Dawn.*

While there are those who wrote fanfiction as a way of expressing their love for the Twilight Saga, a considerably vocal element of the Twilight fanfiction community composed stories as a means of expressing discontent with its ending. These works of Twilight fanfiction and the websites that hosted them functioned like counterinstitutional websites— sites started to protest particular organizations. Radio Shack, for example, ran into problems with a website that an irate customer started called RadioShackSucks.com. A counterinstitutional website can act as a lightning rod, offending some, representing the voice of alienated others. In the case of Twilight, the organization to be protested was the final book of the series itself.

Breaking Dawn was released in 2008 to incredible sales—it sold 1.3 million copies in the first twenty-four hours, and over 6 million by year's end—but to poor reviews in the book critic community. Elizabeth Hand, for instance, wrote a review of the 700-plus-page book for *The Washington Post* that called it "frankly, dreadful," citing Bella's passivity, infantilization, and failure as a role model, as well as the book's general "ick factor." Twilight fandom, on the other hand, was split between two very vocal communities—those who loved the book and those who loathed it.

Of the latter group, some readers returned their books. Others took to blogs and message boards to vent their ire. Critics' negative reviews functioned as "evidence" for their hatred of the book. They would post them online in forums or email the articles to like-minded readers. One reader started an online petition asking Meyer to explain the inconsistencies in *Breaking Dawn* that seemed to contradict the universe that she had created;[93] over 2,500 people signed it. Another fan created a Live-Journal titled "Twilight Sucks" to express her discontent. A rather vocal community began posting on the Amazon forum for the *Breaking Dawn* book. They began calling themselves "The Dark Side," because of how they felt they were being painted by Twilight fans who loved the final book. Because of conflict on the Amazon boards, a few members of this group formed their own forum so they could exchange opinions about the story in peace. However, each side felt that they were marginalized and mocked by the other. Others who loved the final book in the series felt they were no longer welcome at the Amazon forum for the final book, and took their discussions over to the Goodreads site.

Emotions were high, and when you throw in the way that the internet had evolved with social media and resources like Twitter, it was a recipe for controversy. When you can use only 140 characters to send a message, the odds of that message being misunderstood rise exponentially. Also, the lack of nonverbal cues, which is a hallmark of email and other electronic communication, occasionally makes it difficult for people to understand one another. Sometimes such incidents sparked nasty exchanges via forums, email, or blogs. For a while, this controversy split the Twilight fandom.

Reader reaction to *Breaking Dawn* represents an especially interesting occurrence from a fanfiction perspective. With the publication of

Breaking Dawn, combined with the news that the first book would be turned into a major motion picture, the popularity of Twilight fanfiction grew. Fanfiction gave all those who mourned the end of the series a way to return to that reimagined universe. They could, in effect, almost go home. But many also turned to fanfiction in an attempt to rid themselves of the bad taste of the book's finale, or because in fanfiction, they found stories that reminded them of the reasons they fell in love with the series in the first place. One FanFiction.Net reader, who self-identified as a teacher named Kelly Hardy, posted the following comment about the story "Sacrifices" by Enthralled:

> I honestly think I enjoyed reading your chapters as much (if not a little bit more) than Stephanie's. Mainly because yours were full of emotion that evoked tears from me. I missed that in Stephanie's books. Although I did still cry through her Twilight series, reading yours made me feel so intuned with them, Edward and Bella.[94]

Others wanted to read the story minus elements that they disliked. A reviewer of the story "Waiting for Dawn" by Alice laughed wrote:

> Did I read somewhere that you wrote this before Breaking Dawn? If so, you're psychic. It followed the storyline so well without including Renesmee. Actually, it was exactly what I was expecting of the book, and I didn't even factor in a half species baby.
>
> If you wrote this after the book was published, again, it was great how you made the story your own. Whether or not you wrote the story before or after, you stuck so well to the characters. Everything they did, every little decision they made, was believable. There was not one moment where I thought that something was out of character. That's a momentous thing to achieve and I congratulate you on that immensely.[95]

In fanfiction, then, as well as on message boards and protest sites, Meyer's fans resisted the changes that she had made to her own canon. Sometimes called "true believers," these readers, acting like fundamentalists, believed they and they alone understood the original canon of the series, insisting that Meyer be held accountable to *their* perception of her canon universe and protesting that the franchise had gone in a different direction. One vociferous group opposed the inclusion of a child in the story, because they perceived that Meyer had established vampires as sterile. Many felt she changed the rules in order to complete her story. A close reading of Meyer's letters posted on the site Twilight Lexicon, however, as well as comments she made in interviews, indicates that she intended to include the baby from the very beginning. This did not stop many fans from referring to the baby as "venom spawn." Others posted on their profiles that as far as they were concerned, the Twilight Saga was only three books. One way of organizing Twilight fanfiction so that fans can find the stories they like is by connecting the events to a particular book. The anger became so great in some sectors that authors of stories that retold or took place during *Breaking Dawn* wanted to reclassify their stories—removing the *Breaking Dawn* categorization from them—because of a perceived boycott by readers of "pro" *Breaking Dawn* stories. Many also observed that, ironically, once they removed that classification to the story, their readership increased remarkably.

Some of this anger and negativity was fueled by factors such as the stories' online medium, the perceived anonymity of the writers, and even the stigma often applied to writers of Twilight fanfiction, which many, in turn, internalized. Because of the way the franchise was mocked by some, as well as the general stigma of writing fanfiction, many writers worked hard to keep their Real Lives separate from their pen names and online identities. In some cases, this backfired, as there were several cases in which writers felt forced to leave the fandom when the attention became too intrusive, such as when their family members stumbled upon their stories—especially if they contained content that contradicted the author's religious norms. There were rumors of a few writers, members of the Mormon Church, who had to tear down their stories out of fear of religious reprisals from people in their real lives. Several women also claimed they had to give up writing because their husbands resented the time that they devoted to it. Other people felt threatened because the criticism directed at their stories was interpersonally hurtful. I've worked with authors who received hate mail when their story took a direction that reader(s) objected to. I've interviewed authors who were so upset by the "drama" that they sought medication and counseling, or took breaks from participating in the fandom. The anonymity of fandom and the negative feelings produced by both internal pressures and external stigma—the frequent belittling of both fanfiction and Twilight fans—only fed and fueled this negativity further.

This phenomenon also led to the close ties that many of the fandom felt to other members: a fortress mentality, if you will. They felt that only other Twilight fans could appreciate the lengths they went to in writing fanfiction for a book series they loved (even when it made them mad). In addition to attending national conferences like San Diego Comic-Con, the fandom threw several get-togethers where authors and readers could mingle with one another face to face. I'd see cases on forums or Twitter where writers would mention having lunch with one another, or calling each other's cell phones, or attending premieres of movies together. This community developed into something that went beyond an online phenomenon and became an interpersonal one. In this way, fandom became a safe place for members. Importantly, my research has shown that for some writers, posting fanfiction offered a means for dealing with painful and traumatic issues. I read the work of several writers who composed stories about sexual assault and/or physical and emotional abuse. Almost all claimed that telling the story served a therapeutic purpose.

It's this kind of positive experience, perhaps, that is responsible for the continuation of Twilight fandom among both *Breaking Dawn* fans and detractors; despite the widespread fan discontent and the controversy, the fan community and its fic writers still appear to be going strong. Even the 2012 movie adaptation of the last half of *Breaking Dawn* was a success, which may seem surprising in light of how the book was initially received. (It is ironic to note that many individuals in online communities such as A Different Forest insisted they would boycott the *Breaking Dawn* movies; if they did, Twilight's other fans more than made up for them, with the film earning $240 million in the United States and $577 million internationally in its first two weeks.) Times may have changed, but the effect of counterinstitutional websites appears to have retained a hold in the Twilight fandom, and perhaps made it even stronger.

Twilight fic writers, as many of them will tell you, came out of reading the Twilight Saga with an itch to scratch. Some scratched by reading; others, like LolaShoes, by writing. And writing. And writing.

Now better known as the Lauren Billings half of the Christina Lauren writing partnership, LolaShoes—by day a neuroscientist with a serious research program—wrote enormous canon-verse sagas detailing Bella and Edward's relationship as it matured, emotionally and sexually. For LolaShoes, as for many adult fic writers, writing erotica marked a return to an adolescent pastime once enjoyed behind locked doors and in the privacy of hidden notebooks. Sharing it online turned it not only public, but communal. It also introduced her to the possibilities of collaborative writing with her coauthor tby789 (Christina Hobbs)—possibilities they've pursued to the bestseller list and a movie deal.

A Million Words

Lauren Billings (LolaShoes)

When I left for college, I packed up some clothes, drove across the country, and completely forgot about the stack of notebooks full of "stories" I had left in the drawer under my bed.

Of course I remembered them a few months later when my mom mentioned cleaning out my room and getting rid of my bed. I went into immediate, full-on, fight-or-flight mode with adrenaline flooding my system so fast I actually sat down on my dorm room floor because I was so shaky. OMG DID MY MOM FIND THE PORN I STARTED WRITING WHEN I WAS FOURTEEN?

DID SHE *READ* IT?

She totally would have, that stinker. She loves me so much she would want to read anything I wrote unless I'd explicitly written DO NOT READ. Which I hadn't, of course. Sweet Baby Jesus, my poor mother probably laughed herself unconscious.

I mean, it was horrible. I don't remember much, other than the main character was Kayla (hello, it was the eighties! PATCH AND KAYLA

4EVA). I'm guessing Kayla and her boyfriend basically went from place to place, kissing with a lot of tongue and then having passionate humping sex that made her scream his name and him shout hers. I'd actually love to see it now. I'm sure it was totally lulzy.

Sadly, when I started writing smut just into my thirties, the porn was only marginally better. This isn't to knock anyone who liked it, but let's be honest, you guys: I used the words *bottom* (ass), *center* (vagina), *core* (ditto), *hardness* (erection), and *anus*. Just let the sexiness of that last one sink in for a minute. I'll be over here cringing.

Not only did I write smut, but I wrote fanfic smut based on the YA novel *Twilight*. It's a fantastic story, actually: I'd just finished *Jane Eyre*, which I'd hated in high school and decided to give another shot. And I fell in mad, obsessed love with Edward Rochester. I had a Rochangover, as it were. I needed something fluffy to get my mind off the fact that we never got to see the epic Rochester/Jane bangfest. (Oh the irony. If only I'd known about fanfic then.)

So I picked up *Twilight* as my distraction. I won't lie: I judged myself a little.

After I finished the first book, my dad came home from the hospital, and I went up to Berkeley to help Mom with his transition. The Berkeley part is significant because have you ever been to an independent bookstore there and asked for "the next book in the Twilight series"? I swear the look I got would have melted the skin off my face if I'd cared enough to be deterred from my *New Moon* mission. I glared back, and he stroked his gross beard, sighed, and told me to try Barnes & Noble. That was even better, because at B&N there were handwritten letters lining the Twilight shelf, written by some adorable baby goth begging vampire lovers everywhere not to buy this series. I made an "awwww, so cute" noise, then moved the letter aside and bought the rest of the series. No shame.

But then: *Breaking Dawn*. Like most, I got to the honeymoon and had to check to make sure pages in my book weren't missing. I put it down and walked away and counted to ten. He carried her to deeper water? REALLY STEPHENIE? As I established, I'm a total piglet so even though the book is YA I was like, "Why isn't there any *bottom* or *core* or *hardness* in here? We've read four books on how hard Edward is, let's see it! Clearly I must write it."

So I did. I sat down after my kid was asleep and wrote *really* smutty fanfic about a YA novel.

The best part is how naïve I was. I wasn't on Twitter. I didn't read blogs. I was a total internet virgin, and it's a miracle I managed to figure out how to upload my story to FanFiction.Net. Beta readers? What's that? I didn't really think anyone would read the first chapter. I just had this thing inside me, clawing its way out. For some people that *thing* is a need to understand the neutrino, or solve the global warming mess. So glad those people exist, because for me, that thing was describing the moment Edward took Bella into deeper water. AND THEN WHAT? Type type type. Bottom, core, center, hardness. Again, no shame.

But I wrote like the wind, putting out all 68,000 words of "Let Your Light Shine" in twenty-one days. There were more that followed, and people actually read them. Early 2009 was an insane time; the fanfic world exploded. We were *all* becoming obsessed with two teen characters getting together, smooching, having escapades, and (yes, sometimes) having sex.

It sounds weird. I know it does. Even though we're writing legal teens doing legal things, we did get our fair share of shit for being "TwiMoms" writing "TwiPorn." Um, yep, happy to admit it.

As I mentioned, I've always been a fan of the smut. Some kids like horror and gore, some like mysteries on trains, and others like military crap. I like nekkid bodies and kissing and when your heart does that little twisty-pirouette thing in the swoony parts. THAT IS THE BEST.

And what's a better time in our lives for swooning than when we are teens? There are so many firsts: first kisses, and first relationships, and sometimes first times having sex. I had a lot of boyfriends in high school; apparently I liked those "firsts" a lot. And my parents were very progressive about sexuality and our bodies, which if I'm being honest is *really fucking healthy*. Why society embraces violence over sexuality boggles, but it strikes me as obvious why so many teens and women flock to Twilight and Harry Potter fanfic smut. We are at our most open to experience, most beautiful, most sweetly innocent as older teens.

I'm way too lazy to look up how many pages were in The Saga, but Steph basically gave us forty bajillion pages of teenage angst and weird obsessed stalker love and foreplay, and then buttoned up Edward's pants because he almost killed Bella with his monster hardness. In the words of one fanfic, WHERT? The fade-to-black was so epic, one of the best fanfic tropes became the Edward/Bella cockblock. I'd love for someone else to make a list of all the thousands of ways Edward and Bella have now experienced coitus interruptus.

Don't worry, there's no cockblocking in my fic. Or...I don't think there is. I was a woman possessed, writing over a million words in a year.

I wrote one of the better-known alternate universe vampfics, but Twilight fanfic quickly morphed into its own beast. It became more than finding what we didn't get from *Breaking Dawn* or wanting to imagine Rob naked. The writing in the fandom was *good*. "The Blessing and the Curse." "Tropic of Virgo." "The Office." "The Submissive." "Scotch Gin and the New Girl." "Wide Awake." Holy hell, those stories had me up all night, slowly going blind from reading on my phone.

It wasn't just that the smut was good (but damn... "Tropic of Virgo"'s "Hello, Spark"? The moment Curseward says, "I'll suck on you until you dissolve" in "The Blessing and the Curse"? Yes, sir!), it was that the *writing* was good. Not every story had sex, and certainly most stories didn't have as much as mine did. But the creativity, and risk-taking, and the sheer investment in writing something amazing was—and still is—there.

There's something fascinating about the way a community decides what stories to promote. There isn't an editor or a team of editors reading a book and choosing to put it out there. Instead, it's a collection of people—mostly women—who pick up a fic and decide they love it. Sure, there is an element of the hive mind to fandom, but there is plenty of room to have a different opinion. People share links to a story and it either takes off or it doesn't, and it isn't always dependent on some standard literary value, such as breathtaking prose or creative erotica. Many editors wouldn't have given *Fifty Shades of Grey* a second look. And yet look how many people worldwide who didn't give a crap about Edward and Bella wanted to read that book because it introduced them to something they'd never seen before: (relatively tame) BDSM. That's what fic does; you're obsessed with the characters or the world and so you're willing to go to new places just to read more. In the process, you end up learning about an entire subculture to which you never really paid much attention before.

I wasn't *reading* much fic when I started writing it—again, I just had that fade-to-black I needed to exorcise from my brain—but as I grew aware of the sheer size of the community, my obsession expanded to reading all of these stories. All Human, canon vamp, crossover. Slash, poly, BDSM. Angst, fluff, you name it. And here's the thing about fandom: you get to know everyone—online or even in person. You meet your favorite writers, and they become your peers. It's nothing like being a movie or television buff in that respect: you might love them, but you'll never meet and interact daily with Joss Whedon or Nathan Fillion (and if you do, shut up, I hate you). In ways other fan activities don't, fanfiction communities blur lines: author, fan, reader—everyone plays the same roles. While it's true that some people can really get ridiculous egos when they have a popular story (what Cyndy Aleo calls the "whale in the toilet bowl" phenomenon), for the most part, fic fandom is a really safe place to fangirl other people and just . . . share.

When I looked past my own desktop and realized how many other people were out there doing Twific, it felt like the Twilight fandom was already huge, but in hindsight the 2009 fandom was still really in such toddler years. In my early days the fandom hadn't yet been split over issues such as pulling to publish, pulling fics without/before ending them, or online hate directed at an author. In 2009, the fandom was still sweet, and sincerely wonderful. People pimped stories they loved. When "The Submissive" updated on Tuesdays, Twitter would literally go SILENT because we were all reading it in the bathroom at work. There was a shared excitement over the whole thing that is hard to describe. It's a little like going to a rave: you get so caught up in the screaming and the jumping and the hugging and the pounding music that you forget yourself and don't think to ask until later, "Was I being completely ridiculous?"

The answer is probably yes, but especially in the case of the fandom, everyone else was being just as absurd, so go with it. No one cares.

I gained readers, and a few kindly offered to beta (edit) my stories. I mean, I had improved in the smut department a little between the ages of fourteen and *mumble*thirty*mumble*, but I still abused semicolons and adverbs (my friend DeviKalika liked to call "Let Your Light Shine" "Slowly Porn"), dialogue tags, and HEY, let's not forget *anus*. The fandom made me want to be better. I learned to write. I learned to love to read again. I realized how much more I loved reading erotica than watching it.

I definitely took some heat in real life for writing porny YA fic, and when Christina Hobbs and I first signed with our agent, we didn't even tell her we used to write fic because we worried that she would laugh quietly and then rescind her offer of representation (she didn't). I mean, I get it, I really do. There are a couple of issues here. One, writing smut about teen characters is a clear gray area. When is it OK? When Bella is eighteen? If so, are we going to ignore the pesky detail that Edward is always going to be seventeen?

The second issue is one that I hear a lot: "If you like writing so much, why not just write your own stuff?" Well, I don't know . . . maybe because

I'm not very good yet? Maybe I just want to play around a little? Out in the real world, writing fic is judged, as if it's somehow silly (it can be), or frivolous (it can be), or a waste of time (it never is). Writing is *hard*. Character development is the stuff of gray hairs and wine consumption. Fanfic is a way to have fun, to learn to do something, to create something new from something beloved. AIN'T NO SHAME, PEOPLE!

I believe true fanfic is work that is derived from the same world as the original characters, commonly called "alternate universe" or "canon." [*Book author's note*: This meaning of "alternate universe" to mean alternate storylines, same world and rules, is usual to this fandom.] I see the place for All Human fic in the Twilight community, but I don't really think those stories are about Twilight as much as they are about Rob, or writing, or wanting to jump into a community and make some words. Writing alternate universe is like walking into a movie set and taking over the directing role. Everything in my stories was how Stephenie initially set them up, but then I just…well, mostly I just took their clothes off.

I did that with my Barbies, too.

When I explained to people that I wrote Twilight fanfic—which I did, because I never hid it in my real life—for the most part they understood. Who wasn't a tangled mass of bottled-up hormones between thirteen and twenty?

The best part in my opinion is that some of us never change. If you're a "hoor," you're my people. I still have notebooks under my bed, and I bet my mom will be proud to know they're still filled with smut.

An Interview with tby789 (Christina Hobbs)

WHEN TBY789 (CHRISTINA HOBBS) STARTED reading Twilight fanfiction in 2008—relatively early in Twilight fandom fic-years—most (though not all) stories still featured sparkly vampires and took place in Forks, Washington. Review counts were still comparable to those in most other fandoms. A multichapter fic might have fifty reviews. Reviews were not yet widely acknowledged as a mass currency by which stories could be found and read. "Fic diving"—browsing around for new stories on FanFiction.Net as opposed to following a trail of awards, reviews, and recommendations—was not yet understood as an adventure activity, evidence of one's commitment to democratic values, or an anarchic poke in the eye of fandom hierarchy. It was just the way you found new stuff to read.

Then she found the website Twilighted, and saw that the fic world there was very different.

Strange things were afoot in the Twilight fandom, and tby789 and her fic "The Office" were a big part of what would be a transformation in the way fanfiction was read and received, both by other fic writers and ultimately in the world at large. In part, this change had to do with the way Twilight fics began to understand their relationship to their source material: very loose, sometimes barely tangential, in fact—increasingly, Twilight fanfics were more "inspired by" than set in or even based on Stephenie Meyer's books and their world. As Jolie Fontenot notes, and some of the other contributors in this section illustrate, many Twilight fan writers were more irritated by the books than enamored of them, or if they were enamored, they were irritated at themselves for this preference. tby789 did not fall into this category—she was an unabashed fan of the series—but her fic was still worlds apart from Meyer's style and sensibility.

More similar to the typical Twilight fic writer than her clumsy, virginal teen precedent, "The Office"'s adult Bella was assertive, potty-mouthed, and professional—when she wasn't riding her "beautiful bastard" boss all over the office...and the elevator...and the stairwell...and the parking garage...(That behavior had little in common with the actual lives of fandom women, but a great deal in common with their fantasies about "Robward.")

By many accounts, the "smut revolution" in All Human Twific came about with "The Office." Now, that's not to say it was the first to do sex. There was, and always has been, a lot of sex in fanfiction. But even more than the influential BDSM story "The Submissive" that Lauren Billings' essay mentioned as silencing Twitter once a week, "The Office" put sex front and center and kept it there. "The Office" was also, immediately and tenaciously, front and center in the fandom. It was aggressive and raunchy, but its volunteer marketing was very smooth. It was up for only nine months and got millions of hits. And inspired more than one tattoo.

I've argued that part of the change "The Office" wrought was to help inspire the rise of Porn *as* Plot (as opposed Porn *without* Plot), a narrative that really told a story almost entirely through sex. Obviously, that turned out to be a big deal. TO, as the story became known, was hardly the first fic to use a lot of sex in a story (see, for example, all the other fandoms, ever, at least since *Star Trek*—and, in a closer Twific precedent, the million-plus words of canon smut written by tby789's future writing partner, LolaShoes/Lauren Billings). Nonetheless, "The Office" and its often quite shy author had an *enormous* impact on the history of Twilight fanfiction and thus, ultimately, on the history of fanfiction, and even of publishing.

The real (cash) economic effects of the evolution from fanfiction "filling in" or "continuing" Twilight, to fiction "based on" Twilight, to fanfiction "inspired by" Twilight only made themselves known later, when it emerged that Twilight-generated presses Omnific and TWCS could publish repurposed All Human fics with very little revision and face no legal challenges. But this change in the *writing* culture of the Twilight fandom accounts for only part of the community's transformation into what amounted to a big business based on a currency of credit (review counts, shout-outs, recs) rather than cash. The complex, innovative, often professional-grade marketing of these (as yet) noncommercial products is an equally important part of the story.

To be clear, other fandoms had also employed marketing strategies for their fanworks. But the Twilight fandom operated largely in isolation from other fandoms, so in some sense, they really *were* inventing the wheel, despite wheels that already existed elsewhere. And so they were free to go straight to the most recent technologies currently available, rather than starting from older web protocols and customs. The look of web design (like the technologies and programming languages that create it) changes incredibly fast, and in this way, a new, naïve fandom had the advantage of *not* having to wade through old archives and websites and skill sets on its path to innovation.

In another unintended advantage of their status as newcomers to fandom culture, Twilight fans hadn't come of age with the same threat of cease-and-desist orders, fanworks purges, or police shutdowns of fan conventions, and so did not suffer from the chilling effect such experiences had on other, earlier fandoms—even, as we've seen, on Twilight's close precedent and contemporary, Harry Potter. Furthermore, many of the most popular authors, designers, and webmasters in the Twilight fanfic fandom were professionals, former professionals currently at home with children, or university students studying to become professionals. Their involvement in internet fandom notwithstanding, many had tastes and lifestyles that ran to the commercial and mainstream rather than to the cult or geek.

I asked tby789 and her fandom "director of marketing," Moijojojo, about this time of transition, and how it was that "The Office" became such a game-changing phenomenon.

When did you first notice things changing in the way fic was presented?

tby789: When I came in to the fandom in 2008, [the fic archive and discussion site] Twilighted was already doing things a little differently. Authors could have forums there, and the avis [avatars, or icons associated with online personae] were more personalized. It also had a more commercial feel; visitors were asked to donate to keep the site going, and then their avatars could display a little "I donated" button.

Plus it was all black and red, which annoyed a lot of people, but it was a distinctive look.

Then came the signatures—people could include little displays, like advertisements or brands, under their names. Readers who liked a story would make them—it was a way of giving back to writers. So on Twilighted, signatures became a way for readers to identify their tastes and market their favorite stories.

What were your own early graphics like?

> tby789: "The Office" "blinkie" (a little sign that blinks through several different images) read: On the conference table, in the stairwell, in the elevator. Then you'd see a coffeepot flash onscreen, then a stapler, then La Perla panties. Followed by, "Get yer panties ripped at The Office." That was Moijojojo/Eddiescherry. She did all the initial "Office" graphics.
>
> So much of [the signatures' design] was ridiculous, there were so many manips of Rob in...a fireman's hat or whatever "character" fit that particular story. And there wasn't supposed to be nudity or porn in the signatures—but there were so many animated GIFs that were...very explicit.

My students talked a lot about the marketing of fic in the Twilight fandom—how much of it seemed commercial, like branding, even though there was no money changing hands. How did that come about?

> tby789: We definitely had an "Office" "brand." And the visuals were a big part of the package. I didn't want garish; I wanted everything in black-and-white images. Classy smut. We used to joke that it needs to look like money. And they did. There were avis, blinkies, banners, videos, and I liked them to have a look. But it wasn't just the visuals; we wanted readers to feel like they were a part of something. So we started calling readers "interns" and giving them titles (usually Moi, whose title was "research and development," handled this part). As the author, I was CEO, and I chatted with people on the Twilighted thread—about the story, but also about underwear or clothes, even our children to some extent. It was like a giant twenty-four-hour chat room that went on for tens of thousands of pages. Sometimes the discussions moved so quickly that after being away for hours, even I had no idea what was going on.
>
> I didn't do all that on my own—no one did. There was a system.

Moi, tell me about your role in marketing "The Office." What were your ideas, and how did you come up with them? And why, in the first place, did you devote all this time and energy to marketing someone else's fic?

Moijojojo: I read the first chapter of TO before it was posted, and told Christina there was no way it wouldn't be a huge success. It was a perfect storm of sorts; the premise was new and fresh, her transmutation of the canon characters was completely different than anything that had been done in fic before, and the lemons [sex scenes] were smoking hot. I think the fandom had unknowingly been waiting for something just like it, and when it hit, the reaction was nothing short of explosive.

Passionate word of mouth fueled the early readership, but blog features exposed TO to an even wider audience. Banners, GIFs, and badges had been a part of fic promotion for a while at that point, but we wanted to take it to the next level. It seemed clear that TO ought to be branded in a way that unmistakably represented Christina and her work.

Iconic, classy, and a little bit sassy were the touchpoints we agreed on, and a bold theme of black and white with a pop of red worked well on a visceral level. The first banner was a black-and-white composite manipulation of Robert Pattinson and Kristen Stewart. The next two were character banners, featuring a shot of Pattinson from a *GQ* article, and then one of Stewart from an *ELLE* pictorial—both solid representations of TO. American Typewriter was a perfect font for the title and author names, with Zapfino providing a calligraphic flourish for the personalized banners.

Once a TO board was created in the Twilighted forums, a community of readers quickly began to form. I created an "Office Intern" badge that anyone could grab, then titled versions for top members, like, "VP/Sales" or "Quality Control." Announcements were made via company memorandum. The GIFs were simple, with an ever-present thread of insider humor, and easy to spot in busy forum-signature blocks.

These various graphics served not only as an inclusive connection to TO, but also as a solid promotional item. Whether large or small they were instantly recognizable, and readers *wanted* to use them. You love the fic, the banners and GIFs are cool, the author's a doll, the forum's fun… you're part of all that! Readers wanted everyone to know that they loved TO, and we gave them a lot of tools to make that happen easily.

It wasn't just individual authors and readers who did the marketing. What else got your story noticed?

tby789: There were the rec sites, they did a lot. When the Perv Pack Smut Shack featured "The Office" after the second chapter, that was a big deal. They had a lot of influence. But—you can guess their interests from their name, probably. It was more of a surprise when The Lazy Yet Discerning Ficster mentioned it, because they liked "smart fics," and mine would have fallen into the category of "smut fic." But ManyAFandom liked it; she mentioned a sex scene in the parking garage and she liked how it advanced the plot. She said basically, if you want to put smut in your fic, this is how to do it, and that rec helped draw in a different set of readers, I think. It made my smut seem smarter.

The Look of Fic: 2009–2010

Much of Twilight fanfiction appeared on FanFiction.Net and the archive Twilighted, where signatures and icons displayed reader tastes and story support. Some authors had elaborate websites with character interviews, playlists for chapters, and even character outfits and other consumer goods featured in the stories (most of these sites from the 2009–2010 heyday have been scrubbed or are missing too many images to reproduce). A variety of other websites supported the massive fic fandom: rec and review sites, podcasts, and award sites.[1]

A banner from tby789's Twilight fanfiction "The Office," 2009

, tby789's "The Office CEO" button, 2009

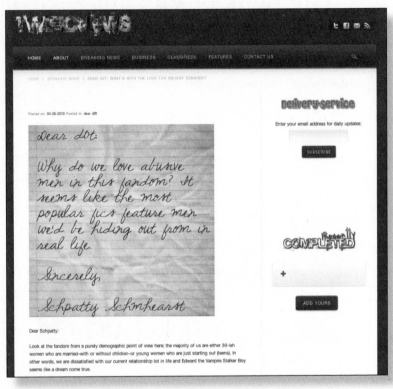

Posted on: 04-26-2010 Posted in: dear d0t

Dear d0t:

Why do we love abusive men in this fandom? It seems like the most popular fics feature men we'd be hiding out from in real life.

Sincerely,

Schpatty Schmhearst

Delivery-service

Enter your email address for daily updates:

SUBSCRIBE

COMPLETED

+

ADD YOURS

Dear Schpatty:

Look at the fandom from a purely demographic point of view here; the majority of us are either 30-ish women who are married–with or without children–or young women who are just starting out (teens). In other words, we are dissatisfied with our current relationship lot in life and Edward the Vampire Stalker Boy seems like a dream come true.

Twificnews was an elaborate online newspaper complete with fic recs, news, glossaries, guides, and columns. Pictured here is the "Dear D0t" advice column.[J] *algonquinrt/d0tpark3r was a beloved figure in the Twilight fandom, and she was also kind of a ranter. For a while she had a "Dear Dot" column in a fandom newspaper, where she'd answer questions on fic and editing and professional publishing. Unlike many Twilight writers, she had experiences with other fandoms and often found herself irked at the "feral" ways of Twilight. d0tpark3r also broke a cardinal rule of self-respecting fic writers everywhere: she wrote a Mary Sue. It was epic.*

On Writing—and Being—a Mary Sue

Cyndy Aleo (algonquinrt/d0tpark3r)

My story starts with a drag queen and various versions of the Christian Messiah on carbohydrate-based foods.

I was mid-divorce, experiencing about the most hellish two years of my life, and addicted to writing Twilight fanfiction that no one ever read. On a dare from another author in the fandom, I sat down one night, cranked out 5,000 words of the most crass comedy I could—the opposite of the dark, angsty things I was writing—and sent it out into the world.

Unbelievably, it was a hit.

Fanfiction, for me, is inextricably tied to my divorce. While I began reading it in other fandoms before and have continued to read in other fandoms since, my time in the Twilight fandom can be traced on a timeline to dovetail neatly with the end of my marriage and its inexorable drag through the divorce courts.

Christ on a crudité, indeed.

With the trend of popular Twilight fanfictions being turned into bestselling novels, I've been asked more than once why I never shopped mine, why I never tried to get it published, why I pulled my fic and vanished into obscurity.

The answer is both simple and complicated.

Publishing it was never an option, from the beginning. While most people viewed my fanfiction as what's called "all human, alternate universe" and felt it deviated so far from the original text as to be original fiction, they'd be dead wrong. The writing itself was often slapdash and not something I'd be particularly proud to publish, but the content was tied so closely to the original work and to fandom dynamics that to separate them would render the text unreadable.

If you want a cultural snapshot of the Twilight fandom circa 2009, look no further than "Mr. Horrible."

The first general rule of writing fanfiction is to not make your main character a Mary Sue, but what do you do when the original text's heroine is a Mary Sue? You make her bigger and badder. I invested in my Bella all my own insecurities: about working (she was a temp, a job I loved and wish I could return to, because it requires no commitment), about writing (she wrote fanfiction herself, and was afraid to send her work out into the world), about relationships (Hello? I was in the middle of an ugly divorce). Bella was the Mary Sue to end all Mary Sues, complete with my trucker mouth and penchant for taking the Lord's name in vain, left to me after sixteen years of Catholic School Rebellion.

In other words, take the most hyperbolic caricature of me, merge it with the biggest Mary Sue in YA literature history, and you have comedy.

Giving Bella a fanfiction hobby allowed me to poke at the fandom at my leisure. While I was never sure if readers would laugh along or take offense, there were many references to the tropes of fanfiction. Perfect example? The tendency of fanfiction authors (and a lot of romance and erotica authors as well) to compare the tastes experienced during oral sex to sweet-tasting foods. A few months of this, and you're rolling your eyes. Now put a Mary Sue character—a virgin, naturally—into a position where this is all she's ever read, and have her experience the reality of semen in her mouth: "But...but...everything I read says that the spunk-cipient just swallows it like it's no big deal. That was like nasty rancid tapioca that never set up right..." When everyone else was comparing it to candy or milk or god only knows what, my Bella was telling it like it was. Bluntly.

I was also all about taking the stereotypes of fanfiction and annihilating them wherever I could. Edward was always a filthy rich CEO/doctor/lawyer. Sure, mine was still the rich CEO, but he was a socially stilted Mark Zuckerberg clone running an online site. He was unable to communicate, vomited in desk drawers, and let everyone else run his life.

The minor characters, however, were where I had the most fun.

Even a nascent fandom will begin to develop its own tropes. You could see it, for instance, in the popular Sterek pairing in the *Teen Wolf* fandom as it took off. Language is often repeated from one fic to another. Occupations become accepted as fanon. In *Teen Wolf* fic, shirts are often "rucked"; incorrect usage, such as "chock" for "choke," appears in one fic after another, and Sheriff Stilinski, who so far has no canon first name, has been unofficially baptized "John" by the fandom. After a while, it becomes difficult to separate what came from the original canon material and what has developed as part of the community growth.

Which is where the drag queens came into play.

That doesn't sound like a logical jump, but it really is. In Twilight fanfiction, the character of James is usually some type of criminal. A rapist, a murderer, a rapist/murderer... but again, I was in the middle of a divorce. Thinking of all the things I'd ever done wrong in my life. And naturally, thinking about The One Who Got Away.

Like my Bella, back then I had a gay best friend I spent a (probably unhealthy) amount of time with. And when I got dumped, that was one of the reasons cited in the dumping.

Now, whether that was reason number one or not, I'll obviously never know, but again, I was going for shock value and a complete reversal of fanon. So James became Bella's gay best friend and a drag queen: Jamie/Victoria Secret. It let me combine two minor characters into one, and mine a bit of a blighted NaNoWriMo novel that had been sitting on my hard drive.

The character was based on no one person, but rather an amalgam of friends I'd had at the clubs back in the early nineties. I took a little bit of this and a little bit of that until I had the most outrageous bitch I could come up with: a selfish slut queen who was possessive, distrustful, but underneath loved his bestie to death.

Next, into this entire hot mess of a poke at the fandom in general, add some audience participation.

Early on in the fic, I'd started adding cultural allusions to nerd things: classic horror literature, cult movies, and so on. It didn't take long for fans of the story to begin sending things to me as either a challenge or a request to include. "Christ on a bicycle," quotes from *Fear and Loathing in Las Vegas*, a reference to Frank Herbert's *Dune* series: all came from reader suggestions or challenges. I'd estimate that at least two-thirds of the chapters had one or more of these offerings from fans.

Now tell me, after all this, how this fanfiction would qualify as original fiction.

Sure, there are some authors who have done similar things. Piers Anthony, for one, with his Xanth series, took countless reader suggestions, poked fun at traditional mythology, and included even more puerile humor than I think I managed, coinage of the term *spunkcipient* to the contrary. Michael R. Underwood, in his 2012 book *Geekomancy*—as well as similar books of this genre—uses countless pop culture allusions with an urban fantasy twist.

The difference, however, is that for me to consider "Mr. Horrible" original fiction, I would have to overlook its ties to source material as well as to the fandom. If it were merely parody of Twilight and the Twilight fandom? That's one issue. If I were to strip all the user suggestions, which were offered under the assumption that they were being used for a fanfiction that was written to be freely available for fans? That's a second.

Beyond the slapdash writing and the ties to the original text and the fandom and the user contributions, I have such a strong mental association between "Mr. Horrible" and my divorce that I'm not sure I'd like to see it on bookshelves in perpetuity.

Approximately halfway through writing this fan fiction, I received a counterfiling from my now ex-husband. On the very first page of the filing, entered into the New York State Family Court records, was a link to where my fanfiction resided and a description of what I wrote.

The argument was twofold. First, what I was writing was inappropriate as the mother of four; the fanfiction did contain several sex scenes, as did other fics I wrote. Second, I was writing it for no pay, when—according to my now-ex—I should have been job searching, which I was certainly doing at the time after losing my nearly full-time freelance client that March.

First reaction: general tears and hysteria.

Second reaction: Fuck. Him.

I talked to my attorney. Explained terms like *fanfiction* and *slash* and *smut*, and after she pointed out that his attorney very likely billed him his usual hourly rate to read my fic, we left it alone.

I changed usernames, got a new Twitter account, and kept going.

The judge, as it turned out, didn't much care what all I was doing with my spare time.

The second time the now-ex found my account and quoted things back to me, however, was when I gave up. I quit writing, quit posting on Twitter, and exited the Twilight fandom about as quietly as I'd arrived approximately two years prior.

I had accomplished what I wanted to by writing fanfiction: honed my writing, learned that I often lean too far into angst, and discovered I may have a flair for comedy writing. While I knew there were fans who were disappointed—I still get occasional emails when I check my old accounts from people wondering if the fics will ever reappear or, in some cases, be finished—it was no longer worth the constant struggle of staying anonymous.

Do I miss it on occasion? Certainly. Writers write in solitude. Fanfiction writers write with an entire cheer squad behind them. Each chapter is met with immediate response. You know where to take the story based on reactions. It's an entirely different writing process when you are relying on a couple of betas and then hoping an agent will love it, instead of posting a single chapter and having hundreds of reviews telling you how much they loved what you wrote.

For me, though, it was also like when you have a child on a bicycle with training wheels. At some point, you take those off and it's harder to balance, and you may fall more, but you can go a lot farther with them off.

I removed my fanfiction from FanFiction.Net the day that I spoke to the website Dear Author about the issue of pulling fanfiction for publication and officially tied my real name to my fanfiction names.

Non, je ne regrette rien: No, I do not regret anything.

I spent two years with instant access to an online support system that probably had no idea it was supporting me.

I practiced my writing.

I made friends who chipped in and got me a secondhand laptop when mine died, which enabled me to apply for (and get) a new job.

I sold my first story—under a pen name, of course—and I could never have done that without what I learned in the fandom, and without three of the four pre-readers I met there.

I can't rule out anything at this point: ever writing comedy again, or ever writing a character who does drag again. But like a lot of people I met during my two years in the Twilight fandom, it stays compartmentalized in a little "Remember when?" box.

Like d0tpark3r, BellaFlan messed with the notion of the taboo self-insert, and like d0tpark3r, BellaFlan—whose real-world alter ego holds a degree in creative writing and works in a publishing context—was a fantastic teach. Assigned as our representative postmodern or experimental Twific, "Becoming Bella Swan" and its author were very popular with my English major students. BellaFlan's biggest fans saw her writing as a kind of innovative literary criticism, a brash brand of postmodern reader-response erotica. By breaking most of the rules of traditional narrative fiction and fanfiction, BellaFlan fractured character and relationship—the driving forces of so much fic—and left the most important relationships to rage within rather than between characters. Mary Sue took on Mary Sue Prime. The result is filthy, funny, serious, and broken.

Becoming Bella Swan

An Experiment in Subversion and Perversion

Randi Flanagan (BellaFlan)

> Hey, you created me. I didn't create some loser alter ego to make myself feel better. Take some responsibility!
>
> —Tyler Durden, *Fight Club*

Part One—Lost in Meyer

No story is an island. That is to say, the act of reading a novel affects it—every reader is a participant in the story, whether she imagines herself in place of the protagonist or she's taking a voyeuristic approach. When a story stays with you, when you think about it and dream of what happens after the final page, you are writing a fanfiction. When you apply critical thought to a text, you are participating in the novel.

In fanfiction, a Mary Sue is a self-insertion into the world of your source material. Example: the BBC miniseries *Lost in Austen* drops an OC, or other character, into the universe of *Pride and Prejudice*. Amanda is dissatisfied with her life and uses Austen's world as a form of escapism.

She wreaks havoc in the world, but does her best to set things straight, having an obsession with the canon text.

But what if we insert an OC or Mary Sue who doesn't want things to stay true to canon?

In 2008, Bella Swan stared at me—all dishwater brown—through the pages of *Twilight*, and I wanted to grab her by her lackluster hair and smack her several times. "You're a coward!" I screamed at her. "A selfish bitch thrown into a world of magic and terror and...really hot men! Do something other than brood and trip over your own feet." There was nothing about this weak, selfish girl that interested me, yet I couldn't put the book down. In fact, I read the entire series several times.

Clearly, Bella Swan needed to be replaced.

For all of its faults, I was drawn into the fantasy world that is *Twilight*. I wanted to live in that world, to play in it, and to imagine what I would do if I were Bella. Yes, I wanted to become Bella Swan. And this is how I discovered fanfiction, because as it turns out, an active community of at least 50,000 readers and writers also wants to be her to some degree.

Fanfiction in the Twilight fandom is often reactive rather than written as tribute to canon. We tear apart Meyer's universe and rebuild it at our whim. As a reader of fanfiction, I want to experience what is missing from canon: genitalia. As a writer of fanfiction, I wanted to have a very stern conversation with our heroine, Bella Swan, and by extension, her creator.

So I did what any rational person would do, of course: I took Stephenie Meyer's characters hostage. My experimental fanfiction "Becoming Bella Swan" was an exercise in critique by self-insertion. My protagonist was essentially my id setting fire to the Twilight universe and playing in the ashes. And no Swan rose from Phoenix, Arizona, in this particular fanfiction; a thirty-something, broken woman woke up in a mental institution in Tacoma, Washington, faced with the task of *becoming* Bella Swan. Isabella Flanagan, my alter ego, gave Bella Swan a voice to scream with.

Part Two—Fucking in Twilight

So here's a personal question every woman needs to answer for herself: if you could fuck your way through the Twilight universe without any consequences, what would you do?

No, I'm serious! Imagine a universe without consequences, where you can revisit themes the author neglected to resolve, and you can give

Edward and Jacob their cocks, since Meyer seemed to have forgotten men have them.

Fanfiction makes us God in a world that doesn't belong to us—it lets us break through the proverbial fourth wall.

And while we're there, oh God, do we want to fuck Edward Cullen. But why?

A profound power shift occurs as a woman leaves her teens and twenties and ventures on toward middle age—one that renders her both impotent and aggressive. As a teenager, I noticed girls seemed to own the sexual power in a relationship, whereas boys were the pursuers. (This hunter/prey metaphor persists in *Twilight*, with an interesting twist: Bella can't be certain if Edward craves her body or her blood.) While boys reach their sexual peak at eighteen, it doesn't happen for women until thirty. Thus the shift in sexual power—the hunter becomes the prey. It can be inferred that the women who fell for Edward's charms both enjoyed the fantasy of being pursued—and craved so desperately that said pursuer didn't just want to fuck her, he wanted to eat her, too—but they were also free to lust after a grown man in the body of a teenage boy.

Of course, if you ask "Becoming Bella Swan" protagonist Isabella Flanagan, she'd say: we're all horny bitches who want to transform Edward into the fuck-beast that he's capable of being. We want him to live up to his potential. We want him to fuck us. We want him to dominate us, and sometimes, we want him to take it up the ass.

Isabella Flanagan can speak to Meyer's characters in a way that Bella Swan couldn't. While Bella Swan blushes and hides her face, begging for Edward to make love to her, to give her the only human experience she actually craves, Flanagan simply shoves her hands in her underwear and forces him to watch her masturbate:

> On my hands and knees I crawled the length of the bed to my virginal centenarian vampire lover. I kissed him very softly on his unyielding mouth and said, "So you want to see my pussy?" . . . Part of me felt guilty, like I was defiling Jane Austen's Mr. Darcy or some shit. Whatever, though . . . everybody fucks. Sex is the great equalizer.

T. S. Eliot wrote, "That is not what I meant at all," in "The Love Song of J. Alfred Prufrock" when he speaks of Lazarus returning from the dead. That line always echoes in my mind when I'm interpreting an author's meaning. And, as Flanagan deconstructs Meyer's world, I have psychotic flashes of Meyer screaming that line at me, shaking her fist.

In "Becoming Bella Swan," the sex is extreme, sometimes even violent, but the heroine—this ménage of Swan/Flanagan/me—is always in control and owns the sexual power in almost every situation. She has no power over her own identity, but the Edward and Jacob archetypes are completely at her mercy.

But the "Becoming Bella Swan" universe isn't all candy and roses. Flanagan chases the White Rabbit down the rabbit hole, not just to live in the fantasy but to escape something sinister that pursues her, lurking out of reach from her conscious mind. In canon Twilight, Edward leaves Bella in the woods and she wanders, disoriented and vulnerable. In my fic, Flanagan also faces monsters in the woods, but not of the fairy-tale variety:

> "Hey, darling." A voice materialized from behind me. I pulled myself off the ground but got kicked back down onto my knees. "Get on all fours, pretty thing."

> No fucking way. No fucking way was this asshole going to fuck with me.

> "What do you want?" I tried to speak calmly but had trouble controlling the hysterical timbre in my voice.

> "Ah, shit, baby. Don't be like that." He flashed something metal in my peripheral and my hysteria was replaced with terrorized shock. My limbs went completely numb with fear and my breathing quickened beyond my ability to catch up.

> Fight or flight. Fight or flight.

> I never thought I'd be the damsel in distress. I always imagined that if I was ever attacked, I would somehow be brave and kick ass. I knew the rules: never beg for one's life.

> "Please?" I begged.

And so, both Bellas are victimized, leaving the reader wondering which Bella is using the other's identity to work through her trauma.

Is Swan using Flanagan's strength to confront Edward?

Is Flanagan using Swan's traumatic experience in the woods to suppress her own?

Did I create Flanagan to work through my own issues?

The answer to all three questions is yes, because it's not the truth that matters in this story but the journey—the opportunity to deconstruct the book by becoming a part of it.

Part Three—Mass Hysteria

I've read so much Twilight fanfiction that I have difficulty distinguishing canon from fanwriting at times. All of the stories seem to happen simultaneously in parallel worlds.

> "Isabella...you're expecting me to entertain the possibility of multiple universes?"

> "Why not? I believe in vampires. How's it a stretch?"

> "I see. So, how is this a metaphysical question?" I couldn't read Carlisle's expression. He had an excellent poker face.

> "Well, because I'm questioning standard beliefs about existence. How do we know something exists, what's real and what's fantasy? And, by that same token, can fantasy become reality if enough people believe in it?"

Flanagan explains to a room of people (with a tenuous grip on reality) that if enough people believe a pink elephant is in the room, the elephant will materialize. Belief affecting reality is a central theme in "Becoming Bella Swan," and it's one that is an allegory for the Twilight fandom.

Participating in social media is part of the fandom experience for many readers and writers, and the pink elephant phenomenon can be witnessed daily in this forum. We adapt and amplify popular opinion, spreading information like wildfire.

As participants in this community, we worship the idols of Edward Cullen and Bella Swan to such an extreme degree that we impose their personalities onto the actors who portray them in the movies.

Particularly of interest is what happens when the fantasy is destroyed. When Kristen Stewart cheated on Robert Pattinson last

July, there was a broad sense of disillusionment in the fandom, and you could witness participants exhibit the Kübler-Ross model stages of grief via social media.

Part Four—Becoming BellaFlan

Who the fuck am I? If you asked me that three years ago, the answer would have been simple. Now? Not so much.

In the process of adopting Isabella Flanagan's narrative voice, an unexpected by-product was created—one that took the form of my avatar, BellaFlan.

BellaFlan is better than me. She's louder and funnier and more interesting. She's the person I thought I'd be when I grew up. She's that snarky voice inside my head that screams over my own voice of reason.

And as I type this, trying to be mature and eloquent, BellaFlan is goading me to have several shots of vodka so that she can take over. She has such loose fingers, whereas mine are rigid. She pounds the keyboard when she writes while I squeak along, clicking my mouse, moving the cursor over her cursing. Delete! Oh, for the love of fuck, delete!

No, BellaFlan says. *Shit just got interesting.*

The first time BellaFlan appeared was in my author's notes. I had a bit of a Jekyll and Hyde reaction to an unkind review:

> Why do people flame? Any ideas? I call it random acts of unkindness. Fuck, if you don't like a fanfic, then don't read it. No one is holding a gun to your head. And if they are, include it in your review. I'll call the fucking police for you.
>
> Lot's of love and stuff.

BellaFlan became more brash and egotistical as the story garnered more readers and reviews:

> Hello. If I didn't reply to your review, then I'm a shit eating monkey cock. Let me know.

She then started a nasty rumor that she masturbated to her reviews via a buzzing iPhone:

> Okay, so I'm putting my pretty iPhone in my pocket. All I need are a few
> buzzes to take me home. I could go all night, baby.

As I communicated with readers and writers in the fandom, I found
myself adopting the BellaFlan persona more and more.

Was becoming BellaFlan a natural evolution? I think so. Not just
because I created a character with dissociative personality disorder. I
mean, I'm pretty sure I'm not insane. I can't be certain since insane people
don't realize they're unwell, but no one has tried to institutionalize me so
one can only assume...

We all create avatars online—these elevated, "epic" versions of ourselves. We don them like masks. I've met people in the fandom who self-
identify as evil cats, cock-loving whores, zombies, pundits, squirrels,
and cupcakes. It's part of the fandom experience—the opportunity to
not only lose ourselves to the fantasy world of Twilight, but to become
someone else.

I'm a pink elephant. None of us are really who we seem to be.

As anyone who knows anything about fandom generally could tell you, fans have a long tradition of raising money for charity. But as we've seen, the *Twilight* fandom by and large didn't know anything about fandom generally. d0tpark3r (as she explained in her essay here) and others like her would express their frustration with *Twilight* fandom reinventing the wheel and calling it new. This lack of familiarity with general fandom history and tradition, however, meant they could do things their own way. They did it huge.

The Fandom Gives Back auction, the focus here, was by far the biggest charity undertaking, but even smaller scale, in *Twilight* terms, meant big numbers. The Twifans for Haiti drive, organized quickly in response to the devastating 2010 earthquake, raised over $85,000 in the space of just two weeks. The drive organizer, Ms Kathy, explains that immediately following the January 12 disaster, stories were solicited, donated, compiled in a PDF collection (labor donated by manyafandom), and emailed to donors, all between January 13 and January 25. The collection is sitting on my hard drive, 1,800-plus pages by 260 authors. A huge amount of work—and a huge amount of money raised in very little time.

The Fandom Gives Back was much more complicated. Authors auctioned off story chapters, alternative POVs, and made-to-order fics. But it wasn't all fic; artists, crafters, and web designers got involved, as did celebrity fansites and bloggers. It was a fandom-wide effort. Some of the most popular Big Name Authors were intensely involved not just as contributors but as organizers. tby789 and LolaShoes (Christina Hobbs and Lauren Billings, aka Christina Lauren), both of whom we've heard from individually about their experiences as fandom authors, were instrumental in this enormous campaign, with the fandom writer Ninapolitan being the other major organizer. AngstGoddess did the website. Each of these women donated hundreds and hundreds of hours to the cause.

Since the Fandom Gives Back: Eclipse auction was going on during my 2010 course, I joined "teams"—collective bids to receive outtakes—for fics we were reading in class, including "Master of the Universe" (now the Fifty Shades trilogy), "The University of Edward Masen" (now Gabriel's Inferno), and "An Introduction to Swirl and Daisy" (PG-rated, middle-school Harry Potter fan Bella v. Lord of the Rings fan Edward). My students followed along with the auction as part of our look at the nonprofit economics of Twilight. It's my recollection that these three teams alone raised over $50,000 for childhood cancer research.

Fandom Gives Back was created as a charity and inspired an enormous collective outpouring of fandom pride and generosity that far surpassed the expectations of the organizers, as we learn below. But this auction also played a leading role in the story of unintended consequences in the Twilight fandom. The creation of teams and the large sums of money they were able to raise also had the result of translating the economics of online fandom (e.g., review counts, hits) into actual financial numbers that people outside the fandom could understand. If a single alternate-point-of-view outtake of a single fanfiction could raise $30,000, as the "Edward Point-of-View" chapter of "Master of the Universe" did, then there was obviously actual money to be made. Furthermore, this fic, written as a charity donation, was repackaged and resold as part of the record-smashing trilogy. From my perspective as observer, it was obvious that this enormously successful nonprofit charity event was an important step in demonstrating the cash—as opposed to cashless—economic potential of fanfiction.

Here, Fandom Gives Back organizers tby789 and LolaShoes describe the time, effort, and excitement that went into planning and administrating this vast event.

The Fandom Gives Back

Christina Lauren (Christina Hobbs/tby789 and
Lauren Billings/LolaShoes)

While huddled together in line at San Diego Comic-Con, we (Christina and Lauren, along with our fellow FGB organizer Ninapolitan/Nina Cello) saw a pair of young volunteers pushing a cart full of lemonade, selling each one for a dollar. It started a conversation: What would happen if each person there—or each person in the *fandom*—donated a buck to charity? It could make a huge difference. Too often, Twilight fans are portrayed in the media as screaming teenagers or overzealous cougars. We're not. We're strong women, even some men, who were inspired and impassioned by a story and a group of characters. We may have come together because of Twilight, but we stayed because we found friendship, community, encouragement, and sometimes even love that stretched across the globe.

But where to start?

We went through a group of charities, stopping when the name Alex's Lemonade Stand Foundation—a cause Nina was already heavily involved in—was brought up. ALSF emerged from an actual front-yard lemonade stand of then four-year-old cancer patient Alexandra Scott. Although she lost her battle with cancer in 2004 at the age of eight, her goal of raising money to fund pediatric cancer research lives on through volunteers and virtual stands all over the world. We had four small children between us, and we talked about our love for them and the unfathomable devastation we would feel should one of them fall seriously ill. Within an hour, we'd named our cause and formed the basic structure of The Fandom Gives Back (FGB).

It was our hope to harness the frenzy surrounding the *The Twilight Saga: New Moon,* so we chose the week leading up to the film's release as the time for our event. Organizing the virtual stand was one of the biggest challenges we'd ever faced, and with only a month to go before *New Moon* hit theaters, it would be a massive undertaking in a very short amount of time. Thankfully, we were surrounded by a community that was not only willing but thrilled by the opportunity to donate their time and talents to support the cause.

We bought the domain and started a Twitter account, and within hours word had already begun to spread. By the end of that first week we had over two hundred affiliates, ranging from fanfiction and LiveJournal communities to sites dedicated to Twilight and the upcoming movies. The original plan was for fic authors to offer outtakes or even multichaptered stories written specifically for the auction. But soon, people were donating voice work, site design, and podcast interviews; compiling a cookbook of fandom recipes; and offering cast-autographed merchandise and books, graphics, gift baskets, craft items, and much more.

We used a free forum and spent the next few weeks, together with volunteers, both planning the event and moderating the actual auction. And since all donations were made directly through the ALSF virtual stand, no funds were ever dealt with by any FGB organizer or volunteer.

Organized in just eighteen days, the first FGB event was a rousing success. With an initial goal of $10,000, we were left speechless as we watched the total raised grow with each passing hour. Fandom Gives Back: New Moon ran from November 15 to 20, 2009, and raised $87,640 for ALSF.

In 2010 we wanted to do more. The fandom had grown and FGB hoped to, as well, with all proceeds again to benefit ALSF. The Twilight community rose to the occasion. We bought hosting and enlisted the help of AngstyG (AngstGoddess003), a fandom writer and web designer who volunteered hundreds of hours building a beautiful custom site, which included a landing page for information pertaining to FGB and ALSF; a live auction board; and even a forum. More volunteers were needed to run and moderate the sites, and many stepped forward to do their part.

I remember there being worry that with the number of hits we'd experienced with FGB: New Moon, and with the sheer number of items being offered for auction this time around, there was no way the server could handle the traffic. We had several test runs, asking thousands of people on Twitter to click the test site at once, and—surprising no one more than our webmaster—it worked perfectly.

Bloggers from several fandoms beyond Twilight's, including those focusing on Harry Potter and Beautiful Creatures, heard about our project and encouraged their readers to participate and spread the word. Fic writers noted in their updates that they would be participating and offered outtakes or entire stories for auction. In addition to more of the same items offered for the first FGB, published writers outside of the Twilight fandom donated signed books and merchandise, even blogging or tweeting to promote the cause. You couldn't go on Twitter in the weeks leading up to the auction without seeing the hashtags #fandomgivesback or #vivalafandom all over your timeline.

The number of people participating this time around meant that organization was key. Online spreadsheets were made available for the many writers, artisans, and graphic designers to register their offerings, and something that had caused only slight controversy in the first FGB— the formation of teams—became an even bigger force.

During FGB: New Moon, teams allowed a group of readers who wanted a particular POV or outtake to pool their donations and ensure a winning bid—but in FGB: Eclipse, they took on a life of their own. Entire websites and Twitter handles were created and dedicated to keeping team members informed of current totals or relevant news. Listings offered by some of the most popular authors in the fandom at that time resulted in tens of thousands of dollars' worth of donations raised by their teams alone. Not everyone was a fan of the team effort. Some of the larger teams were huge and consisted of hundreds of people, making it a daunting task for lesser-known authors to compete in terms of fund-raising; of course the largest amount raised would be by the most popular authors, since they had the largest teams. There were some ruffled feathers, yes, but the point of the auction was to raise as much money for ALSF as possible, and nobody could deny that the formation of teams did result in a far greater amount being raised.

With an initial goal of $50,000, FGB: Eclipse ran from June 26 to July 3, 2010. We worried at the outset that we'd overestimated, and were certain we'd never surpass the previous amount. But the Twilight fandom did it again, and we were floored when the final donation tally came in at $147,537. All in less than a week.

There were tears on Skype that night. All of us—the organizers and volunteers—were exhausted but ecstatic to have witnessed such an outpouring of love and generosity. The love and pride we felt as a fandom was palpable across the internet that day, but the sense of community fostered during FGB lasted for much, much longer.

FGB continues to run, though on a smaller scale, and embraces several fandoms outside of Twilight. To date it has raised over a quarter of a million dollars for ALSF and pediatric cancer research, along with other causes such as autism awareness and natural disaster relief.

Snowqueens Icedragon (E. L. James) and Sebastien Robichaud (Sylvain Reynard): A Fandom Exchange

SNOWQUEENS ICEDRAGON (E. L. James) and Sebastien Robichaud (Sylvain Reynard/SR) are the first fanfiction writers to receive seven-figure contracts from mainstream publishers—and the only ones I know of to have done so. Both posted fics online, and both first published minimally edited commercial versions of them with small presses (The Writer's Coffee Shop and Omnific) that had grown out of Twilight fanfiction archives. As E. L. James notes in the acknowledgments of *Fifty Shades of Grey,* SR "went first," pulling his fic, renaming it *Gabriel's Inferno,* and publishing with Omnific, as a number of popular fanfic writers had already done. The popularity of their stories and the fact that the two are friends led them to be associated with each other, but their personae inside and outside of fandom are as different as their fic. *Fifty Shades of Grey* contains far fewer musings on medieval conceptions of love as derived from classical models. *Gabriel's Inferno* includes fewer orgasms. While their publishing contracts are in no way representative of fanfic, the authors' differing attitudes toward writing, sources, and community do reflect some basic divides in fanwriting today.

Although she has not hidden it, James has tended to downplay her role in fandom—a role that was initially revealed to the general public on *The Today Show* in March 2012, when viewers wrote in on the show's website in to suggest "the book everyone was talking about" had been plagiarized from a well-known fanfiction. James clarified—the fanfiction was hers. As the *Fifty Shades* story grew, James increasingly acknowledged her debt to Stephenie Meyer, and eventually praised the interaction and response she got from the "smart, warm, witty" women she met in fandom.[96] But overall, she does not dwell on the fanfiction community as a source of inspiration.

Her author website clarifies the trilogy's source at the bottom of a FAQ:

> *Fifty Shades of Grey, Fifty Shades Darker,* and *Fifty Shades Freed* were never self-published as these novels. An earlier version of this story began as Twilight fanfiction which was posted on the internet. The trilogy was picked up by an Australian publisher, The Writer's Coffee Shop, who released them as e-books and print-on-demand paperbacks.

None of the above is untrue, but it is misleading. While as a literary critic I continue to be surprised at how simply swapping out a few names can change a reading experience, a few cosmetic changes of this nature don't really constitute a substantially different version. (When compared on the anti-plagiarism website Turnitin.com—useful for content comparison despite the fact James wrote both versions—*Fifty Shades of Grey* came in with a 89 percent similarity index to "Master of the Universe" [MOTU].) James' author website advises beginning writers that they should write, and it speaks in broad terms about her writing process (she likes "geography," by which she means the arrangement of objects in rooms), but nowhere on the site does she talk about the interactive, multiply sourced (or multiply "inspired") process by which she wrote and posted "Master of the Universe."

While extremely close-lipped about his identity, Reynard has been more forthcoming than James about his connection to the Twilight fandom, nodding to his fandom identity in his recognizably connected professional pen name and openly expressing his debt of gratitude in interviews. Both writers were vocal participants in fandom while they were posting their stories, engaging their readers, their suggestions, and even their vitriol (Robichaud once suggested he went so far as to write an angry fan into his novel as a kind of vengeance). Both benefited directly and tangibly from the feedback, encouragement, interaction, and publicity their readership offered—as they used to frequently acknowledge in shout-outs and notes in their posted chapters.

In one such instance of fandom engagement, Sebastien Robichaud and Snowqueens Icedragon interviewed each other for a popular fansite. My students and I read this interview when we were studying their stories and the Twilight fanfiction community overall, and I linked to it on our class blog. Some time after the publication of *Gabriel's Inferno,* the interview was taken down, but like much of fandom history, it's been privately archived. The following excerpts give a sense of these writers' lives and personalities, friendship, and writing processes, and the way Twilight and its community helped inspire and promote their work.

In response to questions from Sebastien Robichaud (SR in the excerpts, as he's still known), Snowqueens Icedragon (Icy, as she was often called) details her discovery of fanfiction via AngstGoddess' story "Wide Awake"—the "gateway fic" for her as for so many other fanfic readers and writers. The path to fic Icy describes is typical enough of this fandom—"Wide Awake" was discussed in all kinds of non-fic contexts):

SR: How did you learn about Fan Fiction?

Icy: Christmas 2008 NEW (my hubs and beta) bought me the Twilight saga—I'd seen the film in November 08—and I sat down and read them in 5 days, non-stop, and fell in love with Edward Cullen & the boy [Robert Pattinson]...I used to stalk internet sites about the boy. It was on Rpattz Daily on Live Journal that I saw two people chatting about Wide Awake—I was on holiday in Spain at the time [...] I found Wide Awake and couldn't stop reading it. I spent £60 on mobile phone bills downloading it. I read it on Live Journal – and after that discovered Twilighted and Fan Fiction.

As the conversation turns to James' inspiration, she suggests the initial impetus for her story came more from Twilight fanfiction than Twilight itself.

What inspired you to pen MOTU?

I read some BDSM [Twilight fanfiction] stories and wanted to know why people got into it and actually see the paperwork. So I started researching. It was always my aim to publish a contract pertaining to a BDSM relationship—so I went from there. I didn't set out to write a BDSM story...I know nothing about BDSM other than what I have learnt on FF and the research I've had to do for this story (some of which has been great fun, let me tell you...sorry TMI—but then I told you I suffered from that)—Fundamentally I set out to write a love story—because that's what interests me with BDSM as a back-drop.

BDSM stories were popular in the fandom after Tara Sue Me's "The Submissive" (now published by Penguin) and "Master of the Universe"/*Fifty*

Shades obviously riffs on that story as well as on other popular Twifics. In 2010, I included MOTU on the fanfic syllabus as representative of several then-popular genres within Twilight fanfiction, among them BDSM. The other major genre it represented was the one that grew up in the wake of tby789's "The Office"—CEOward stories, as I sometimes thought of them. Like BDSM, the corporate setting was a popular way of literalizing the power differential between canon's immortal ageless vampire Edward and clumsy mortal teen Bella.

From inspiration and process, the interview moves on to a possible endgame: publication.

Do you have any plans to publish and if so, what?

I'd like to. MOTU is the 4th novel I've written in a year. After my Twilight and the boy [Robert Pattinson] obsession, I sat down and just wrote a novel—I'd always wanted to do it and the time was right. I was exceptionally miserable at work so I escaped into my first novel [....] Looking back it was a fan fic—but I didn't know fan fiction existed at the time. I plan to publish it on FF when I finish MOTU—I think—but it will needs to be re-written. It's quite a hard thing to pull off...and interestingly it's written from two POVs...so I am going to have to think about that. My second novel isn't finished...that's the one I have high hopes for and I would like to re-write. NEW has a literary agent, and the field that I work in puts me in touch with many agents—so...who knows?

James, clearly buoyed by her success in fic, has publishing on her horizon, but it's also clear how porous and fluid her sense of fanfiction is. She wrote a novel unaware that it was fanfiction—and announces plans to publish it (she never did, or hasn't yet). Perhaps she felt that with MOTU, she wrote a fanfiction unaware it was an original novel. She uses *publish* as the verb that applies to FanFiction.Net. The answer shows a blurring or confusion of categories that for many other fan writers are absolutely distinct. (The implied but nowhere explicit contracts of fanfiction were another facet that originally drew my attention to MOTU—in which, early on, a contract is produced, discussed, but ultimately not signed. It's a point of tension in MOTU's story—and in that of its author.)

SR asks about James' nonfandom beta, or editor/pre-reader (ultimately revealed to be television writer Niall Leonard), and his take on fanfiction: "it's an amazing resource and a wellspring of hidden creativity. He thinks it's the way the Web should go. It's the future of the internet where people come together to create and enjoy stories." Icy explains how she spends her time—all of it, apparently—devoted to engaging fans and writing her story: "all I do these days is fritter (my new word for this ridiculous social networking tool that I have unfortunately become addicted to) and write MOTU and occasionally try and catch up with the daunting MOTU thread..." The thread in question was the comment thread on the Twilighted forum where her story was also posted.

The fic's comment threads on Twilighted were enormous: readers spent hours discussing her story, their reactions to it, their hopes, speculations, and expectations of characters and plot. Often, Icy joined in— early on asking for a banner for her story, asking for technical advice, eventually asking for other kinds of input. She sometimes responded to reader concerns in the fic: "I actually put Edward's comment in because a few people had been asking in reviews what did Edward see in her...and that's some of the answer there...I think you're take on it is very interesting...I shall go away and think about that."[97] She often repeated how much she enjoyed thinking about reader comments, how she loved seeing all the theories about her story.

The interview turned to the author of "The University of Edward Masen," and Icy asked SR about *his* inspiration and process. He credits a fanwork with his initial inspiration, while making explicit his intention to rewrite Twilight:

How did you come up with your storyline?

It dropped almost fully formed into my head after I got over the disappointment of learning that my favourite FF "In the land of Milk and Honey" was unceremoniously (but perhaps justifiably?) pulled.

I love how you weave canon into your narrative. Is this deliberate or do you find your fans pointing out things that you never intended and their interpretation is that you are following canon? (Happens to me a lot – sometimes I am... and maybe sometimes I'm doing it on an unconscious level)

My story deliberately includes canon, especially for the characters. This is so because UOEM ["The University of Edward Masen"] is my intentional re-writing of the Twilight narrative for an adult audience in a human universe.

Some fanfic writers incorporate suggestions more than others. SR claims not to have changed the overall shape of his story, but to have considered reader suggestions for smaller details, again reflecting the community feedback—often understood to be given in exchange for free stories—from which fan writers benefit. And the more popular the story, the more feedback it gets.

> **Has the path you've chosen for your characters changed at all from the feedback and reviews you've been getting?**
>
> No. The major plot points are fixed. Minor things could be changed if someone gave me a good suggestion. So for example, Miss JAustenlover suggested I include Edward's lecture. I balked at this initially, for I thought no one would care to read it. I have been surprised and pleased at how many people wrote to me to say how much they enjoyed it. Who knew?

This scene remains in the published version.

In the interview, SR admits that he also has publishing dreams, in response to a question about "using his own characters" next time and trying to get published: "Truthfully, [I] would love to have a literary agent and write fiction professionally and be published, while still enjoying my anonymity and living in my hobbit hole." Unlike James on her website, in this interview SR does recommend writing fanfiction as a path for aspiring writers:

> Just write. Write what you know or what you don't, but write and then have a trusted friend read. Let them give you suggestions for improvement. Correct your work, and then put your work out there. FF is a great venue. I've never shared my fiction with anyone since the last writing contest I ended. So this venue is very encouraging and very easy to enter.

Even for these two highly successful fan writers, however, the fanfiction scene is not without its negatives and potential consequences. SR reveals in his interview with James that he protects his identity because like many fan writers, he fears for his job if his identity were to become known:

do you enjoy your work?

I enjoy my work very much, which is why I'm trying to protect it.

I have a sense that you keep your real life very much separate from your FF life—are you afraid your colleagues will find about your fan fiction fetish?

Yes.

What would they say?

"You're fired."

The interview turns to the negative side of reader feedback and interaction:

How do you handle negative reviews/blog postings ?

Not well. Anonymous nasty reviews I just delete and it gives me an extraordinary amount of pleasure to do so. I have to learn to avoid blog postings, but I am a masochist at heart so I do look. I was reading one recently and I was astounded at the kicking the fic got from people who have never read it...which is rude quite frankly. They seemed to be especially peeved at the review count—according to someone on that blog, '1000 is the new 100 everyone!' What upset me more was that an author whom I really respected dissed it—though she's never read it...I have to say she's slipped hugely in my estimation since then.

She's clearly upset, as the unnamed commentator was AngstGoddess— the author of the £60 download fic that was E. L. James' initial inspiration to enter the fic community.

In the comments section of the page on which the interview was published, AngstGoddess responded:

AngstGoddess003 Feb 5, 2010 05:16 AM [...] SnowQueen...I know you are referring to EdwardVille [a Twilight fandom community] and I feel your comment about dissing was somewhat directed at me, since I'd made a comment on how I hadn't read, but I assure you, my comment was certainly no dis. I simply stated a non-preference for BDSM-related fic. Sorry if that offended you. I actually defended your story's epic review count, so I was a little confused as to the animosity there...? Edwardville is fairly tame and the members go to great lengths to express their criticisms with respect. And the mods go to great lengths to enforce that. It is a very lovely place, and both of your storis have plenty of fans there.

(AngstGoddess and Snowqueens Icedragon would have more adventures together—spoiler alert—the very public outing of which left the fandom in turmoil. We'll get to this shortly.)

The point I want to make here is simple: fanfiction communities are writing communities, and interaction drives them as much as stories do. Whether the individual writer is more or less community oriented, whether he or she actively incorporates fan suggestion or not, reader response feeds and sustains—and sometimes angers—the writing community. Snowqueens Icedragon and Sebastien Robichaud were no different. Novelists writing in a vacuum, even in a vacuum that includes some trusted friends, cannot know their story has the power to cause rage *or* joy. The way review communities such as Goodreads function may have some parallels, but the situation is not the same. The stories Goodreads reviewers read are fixed. The reviews there are for other reviewers, and authors respond to them typically at their peril. They aren't offered in a system of exchange; readers are consumers, not participants. It's this system of free exchange that many in the fic community fear commercialization may end.

An Anatomy of a Flame War

It happens sometimes. Fandoms just explode. Natural causes.

—*Repo Man/Fic* mashup

SOMETIMES FANDOMS EXPLODE by growing exponentially and becoming large enough to change culture and drive wide-ranging economic growth. And sometimes these same fandoms explode in conflict.

The causes really are natural.

As we saw with Snowqueens Icedragon and Sebastian Robichaud, even close friends in fandom communities have very different approaches to and feelings about the communities. Sometimes these differences even end such friendships. And as for writers who *aren't* close friends? Snowqueens Icedragon and AngstGoddess were never going to be besties. As we just saw (in "A Fandom Exchange" between E. L. James and Sylvain Reynard), even their first interactions betray a certain tension.

Fanfiction makes for a lot of strange bedfellows. It's known for that, right? But so do fanfiction communities—where *bed* should be understood to mean both the vast, rumpled playground of a common source everyone has been rolling in, and also the thing that, once made, you must lie in. The thing that, if you were a dog, instinct would tell you not to foul.

What's "fouling it" to you, though, is "feathering the nest" to someone else. Both feel like instinct. Both are defended as such.

In these communities, where rules are taken to be self-evident but are not written down (or are written down but routinely ignored, until suddenly they are not, as has sometimes been the case with FanFiction.Net) the misunderstandings that arise are colossal. They hurt. People leave. People are *damaged,* and damage others.

I began this book with a discussion of a fic set in the middle of a fandom conflict for a reason. These conflicts—flame wars, wanks, kerfuffles—can be as important as they are depressing and aggravating for all concerned. What sometimes seems like squabbling over petty issues is almost always a proxy for large, unresolved, and perhaps unresolvable concerns. Here I want to look at two of the best-known conflicts in the biggest fandoms. Each involves a now-famous bestselling writer; each turns on a combination of interpersonal difference and real disagreement about the nature of fanfiction, intellectual property, authorship, and community.

The Cassandra Claire Chronicles

Before she was Cassandra Clare, author of the internationally bestselling Mortal Instruments series, Cassie Claire was a Big Name Fan in the Harry Potter fandom—by most accounts, the very biggest name of all. Beginning in 2000 with "Draco Dormiens," Claire wrote and posted The Draco Trilogy, which ultimately amounted to nearly a million words of fic. The Trilogy was enormously popular and served—like NautiBitz's stories for *Buffy* and AngstGoddess' "Wide Awake" for Twilight—as a gateway fic for many, many readers and writers.

While not slash itself, the Trilogy contained enough homoerotic subtext between the Draco and Harry characters to stir up controversy (as well as to inspire a very popular "leather pants Draco" trope). Claire's story transformed the fanfiction afterlife of Draco Malfoy, making him into a more sympathetic, and much sexier, leather-clad bad boy quite distinct from Rowling's depiction. Claire's Draco became fanon, a widely accepted and often preferred alternate to official book or movie canon.

Readers of both this fanfiction trilogy and Claire's (or rather, Clare's) professionally published, bestselling Mortal Instruments series have noted parallels between the two, but such commonalities are not the major source of the Cassie Claire "scandal." The controversy surrounding Claire began much earlier, and initially involved FanFiction.Net. In 2001, Claire's Draco series was pulled from the site for violating its posted guidelines. The charge: plagiarism.

A reader brought to FanFiction.Net's attention that a chapter of Claire's fic incorporated elements of a scene from an out-of-print novel by Pamela Dean—reproducing both the scene's structure and several verbatim or minimally altered passages. The reader, whose screen name was Avocado, felt the attribution given in the fic was incomplete and did not acknowledge the extent of Claire's debt to its source. Avocado has elsewhere self-identified as a member of the professional organization Romance Writers

of America, a detail suggesting a sense of common cause with rightsholders over amateur fic writers. Avocado also listed the Dean novel in question, *The Hidden Land*, as a great favorite. Pairing passages from Claire's
fic with passages from Dean's novel, as Avocado has done, indeed reveals
direct quotes, paraphrases, and similar scene structures.

For many of Claire's readers, this was not new information. The issue
of quotation and attribution, both generally and with specific reference
to Dean, had already been discussed publicly in Claire's Yahoo! comment
thread, where the fic was also posted. Claire credited Dean's work, but
vaguely, initially without the author's name but later more fully. She often
quoted from the works of others and did so openly, explaining her practice in her author's notes. She later suggested that in the case of the Dean
passage, she'd gotten confused on the pages of a notebook and hadn't
realized that some of what was written there—in proximity to some of
her reactions to the Dean novel—was quotation rather than her own
writing.

Avocado's report to ff.net, then, was less a case of discovery than
"alerting the authorities," who agreed Claire's use of Dean's material was
a problem. They removed Claire's work without warning, and despite
being one of the most popular authors on the site, she was also banned.
FanFiction.Net's terms of service explicitly prohibit copyright infringement and warn that any content proven to infringe can be taken down
without notice.

But wait. Doesn't the whole site infringe? Well, no, probably not. Each
case is different; some fic is clearly fair use, some parodic, some wildly
transformative. Still, doesn't a lot of it? Probably. Who knows? It's never
been tested. Copyright is a thorny, widely misunderstood, variously interpreted code that ultimately comes down to case-by-case instances of use,
and people don't (yet) litigate about fanfiction because there hasn't been
much profit. Rightly or wrongly, fanfiction's not-for-profit status has been
widely understood as the cornerstone of its toleration by the rightsholders at whose pleasure fanfiction is often (and often erroneously) understood to exist. This belief is so firmly entrenched, however, that anyone
threatening the uneasy détente between rightsholders and fan writers
attracts the ire of other fans, who believe the survival of the fanfiction
community to be at stake. For this reason, fans can sometimes police
the bounds of copyright and intellectual property (as they understand it)
much more stringently than those with an actual legal stake in the property in question. Similarly, many—like, perhaps, Avocado—did not want

to see fanfiction challenge the copyright status quo because they saw themselves aligned with rightsholders on principle—again, regardless of any position the rightsholders in question may or may not have taken.

The science fiction writer and industry blogger John Scalzi took up this fanfic controversy after Claire received a publishing contract for what would become her Mortal Instruments series. His response and that of others in the comment thread underscored the disconnect between the world of conventional professional publishing and fanfiction. Despite his dismissive, damning, yet tolerant attitude toward fanfiction, his reaction to the controversy aligns more closely with Claire's than with her detractors'. In a 2006 post entitled "Crimes of Fanfic," Scalzi explains that he's received a number of emails asking him his opinions on "a long-running kerfuffle in the Harry Potter fandom about a particular fanfic author who allegedly plagiarized other works in the construction of her own fanfic story." He reacts with a shrug: "I'm not feeling a whole bunch of outrage here." He doesn't see how a fanfic writer's actions could affect anything outside of fanfic, and also doesn't agree that "this fanfic writer needs to be punished or humiliated prior to their formal publication." Scalzi doesn't care about what happens in fanfic because "almost all of it is entirely illegal to begin with"; ethics within the fanfiction community can only be "honor among thieves." After all, he argues, "If you're *already* wantonly violating copyright, what's a little *plagiarism* to go along with it? Honestly. In for a penny, in for a pound."

He suggests in a mildly threatening vein, however, and in keeping with those who are nervous about disturbing the détente of the status quo, that if people are going to ask him to comment on plagiarism in fanfiction, he's going to need to weigh in on the "appropriation of copyrighted character and settings." In other words, let sleeping dogs lie. Don't wake the grown-ups. He adds:

> On the other portion of the issue, should what an author does within the confines of the fanfic sandbox have any effect on what happens when they start to do original fiction? I think not, personally. What happens in fanfic, stays in fanfic. I'm perfectly content to think of fanfic as a sort of free play area where anything goes and what goes on has no bearing in the real world of writing.

All condescension aside, this attitude also confirms fic writers' sense that all is well as long as they keep their world separate, don't talk about it, and don't consider it as applying to the "real world of writing." My research suggests these factors played a role in some reactions to Claire's practice, but attracting unfriendly attention from rightsholders did not seem to be the main issue in the Cassandra Claire controversy. And as for Scalzi, he clearly wants to avoid appearing to legitimize some fanfic practices by condemning others.

For the record, Scalzi's views appear to have evolved over time. In 2007 he said it's fine with him to fic his work but claimed all rights and cautioned against trying to profit; in 2010 he agreed with critics that his *Fuzzy Nation* "reboot" of H. Piper Beam's universe was (licensed) fanfic, and he also hosted a Lupus Foundation fund-raiser inviting readers to fic a picture of Wil Wheaton riding a kitten unicorn and wielding a spear against a John Scalzi!orc. Most recently, he also wrote thoughtfully about Amazon's Kindle Worlds.[98] Many people's opinions on fanfic have evolved in the past few years; the comment threads as well as Scalzi's own posts provide historical snapshots of how attitudes played out—in the science fiction community, at least—at different times.

In complex, opinionated communities, there are always complex motivations, and plenty of Claire's detractors were already angry for other reasons. Many disagreed with her position on various relationship pairings, both het and slash. Some were unhappy because she was a Big Name Fan whom they believed had undue influence. Others felt slighted, excluded. The dynamics surrounding Big Name Fans are a constant in fandom, and the attention they attract can be both positive and very, very negative. Sometimes this negative attention is targeted at real-life identities, with threats to professional and, in some extreme cases, to physical lives as well—as in Claire's case, according to her agent, Barry Goldblatt, who weighs in on the comment thread of Scalzi's post (Claire's accuser Avocado is there as well). The anger and complaints of "small name fans" are often dismissed as jealousy, but like most fandom conflicts, these feelings usually turn on disagreements over big issues: the nature of fandom, fanfiction, community, originality, and relationships.

Community dynamics shape individual reactions in any fandom, and this controversy was no exception. Courtney Hilden was thirteen at the time the Claire scandal erupted, and in her words, it "unleashed chaos on the fandom." Hilden had been reading the Draco Trilogy when it was removed, and so was happy when it found a new home at the Harry Potter fanfic archive FictionAlley, a site formed (or at least hurried along a bit) by trouble with FanFiction.Net. Hilden said she understood the controversy at the time to be about the misattribution of a single quotation, but she later came to believe it was more extensive. Today a graduate student in English, Hilden now recognizes how fandom social dynamics shaped her opinions of individuals and stories. She remembers the allure of fitting in with the people who seemed to "run the show":

> At the time of the scandal, I would have put Claire as a BNF, and I'm at a loss to find anyone else in the fandom who ever came close to the level of notoriety that Claire had. Even though I didn't know the term BNF, part of the fascination for me was these fans who seemed to hold so much sway over other fans. I think at the time I thought of it in terms of popularity, like one would think of a popularity contest in high school. And like most narratives about high school popularity, I wanted to be one of these popular fans, so I followed them around, like a lackey. Interestingly enough, I was never much a lackey in my actual high school, because I didn't like any of the popular girls enough to care what they were up to. I don't even remember their names.[99]

While some fans respond to that kind of hierarchy and aspire only to be included, others react very, very resentfully, having had enough of what they see as bullying or controlling behavior in high school. These dynamics certainly contributed to the overall sense of controversy surrounding Claire, but they don't fully explain the strong feelings involved.

The fact is, some people saw Claire as a plagiarist, and were angry— even though none of those angry people appeared to be the writer Pamela Dean herself.

Incidentally, about homage: Claire's incompletely attributed Dean quotation was not an isolated incident. Cassandra Claire openly and frequently incorporated passages of dialogue—and sometimes ideas and rough outlines of scenes—from popular sources such as *Buffy, Black Adder,* and *Stargate*—often without attribution. She mentioned that she did so in her author's notes, inviting readers to play "find the quotation." Other fandom writers did the same thing; it was a fandom game, at least in some circles. Nonetheless, other readers—perhaps less plugged-in, less active participants in the community, or at least in that part of it— were shocked to hear of this practice. Some of these readers were very young, and some may simply not have known the sources or recognized them out of context. Others (who did know, who had recognized, who liked the game and participated) felt it was impossible that anyone could *not* know. Claire was open about it. The game was a nod to a common pop culture language—but of course, not everyone speaks the same language, ever.

To further complicate matters, the various pop culture sources that generate this language are *also* full of homage. Just recently, there was a *Twin Peaks* episode of *Psych* and a *Castle* homage to *Rear Window*; more contemporaneous with the Claire controversy, there was the *X-Files'* *Frankenstein* episode, "The Post-modern Prometheus"; *Buffy's* calling the Slayer's best friends "the Scooby Gang"; *Moulin Rouge,* with its "jukebox musical" take on the Orpheus myth, as sung to '80s pop music and set in nineteenth-century Montmartre. In my field, postmodernism itself has been defined (both positively and negatively) in terms of such mix-and-match pastiche. A later section of this volume takes up these issues as they pertain to nonfanfiction writing contexts, but suffice it to say, quotation and appropriation are very, very common. While rights and use are only sometimes negotiated or litigated, terms of such negotiations are rarely visible to casual viewers.

There doesn't seem to be any question that Claire *was* incorporating passages from other writers and doing so quite openly, if not always specifically citing them. The question—the controversy—had to do with how readers interpreted this act, whether they felt they were part of a game or were duped. The reactions of all sides beg a variety of questions. Why was *this* act—mixing other sources in—different from the whole fanfiction enterprise to begin with? For some readers, a whole set of unwritten rules seemed to have been violated. For others, it was business as usual—a sense that remix culture what was fanfiction *did*, that it was *all* noncommercial—and they were shocked that anyone could think they were doing anything wrong.

Looking back at the Harry Potter blogs and archives, what I see is a lot of people who felt the need to draw a firm line about what is and what is not OK, with little agreement on where and how such a line should be drawn. Even so, there's a sense from the tone of these discussions that the line should be obvious to *everyone.*

It isn't.

It might be logical to assume that a writer like Claire, who rose to fandom prominence on a story that made frequent and sometimes unattributed use of existing creative content, would hold a liberal view of similar use of her own fanfiction (and she's encouraging to fanfiction based on her published work). It might be logical to assume that in a fandom where tropes are exchanged, and characterizations and storylines are *by definition* shared among thousands, writers would recognize a certain amount of sprawl in ideas as natural and inevitable, or be flattered by any imitation or reworking. Some of the writers in this volume have expressed just such sentiments.

Cassandra Claire—in her fandom incarnation, at any rate—didn't always take this position. When another writer began posting a fic Claire felt was too close to one of her own, she requested it be taken down. The writer complied initially (the two were friends), but then reposted it when the friendship fell apart, and Claire was unhappy with this decision. I can't pass judgment on the specifics of that situation—I wasn't there, haven't read the works, have no comment. But it's a good example of how fanfiction does indeed confuse and destabilize notions of authorship and ownership in ways fanfic authors themselves are not always consistent or clear on.

From the perspective of both reader and fan, I understand the anxiety around a fan writer presenting another fan writer's work as their own. Credit is the only currency most fan writers will ever receive in exchange for their work. Paying homage to work that has already been published, from which an author has already reaped rewards, and giving full credit to that work may seem different than sharing credit with another fan writer in an all-credit, cashless economy. Similarly, to many people, lifting actual expression (words or sequencing) feels different from borrowing story, ideas, or inspiration—and the law marks a difference here as well. On the other hand, there are different conventions for fair use, transformative use, and critical use. Today in fandom, remix challenges that (openly, avowedly) rewrite other people's fic are quite common—a sign of respect. Context matters. In my profession, incompletely citing my *own* work would be seriously frowned on, and could even lead to charges of academic fraud. In political speeches, on the other hand, lifting material from other politicians' speeches seems fairly widespread (ask Joe Biden).

One constant in all of this, and it doesn't just apply to fanfiction writers: you may be clear on your rules, on when *you* feel it's OK to use the work, ideas, or words of another writer and when it isn't; but to another writer, *that* act, the one you thought was totally fine, is beyond the pale.

A Tale of Angst and Ice

Some say the world will end in fire,
Some say in ice.
From what I've tasted of desire
I hold with those who favor fire.
But if it had to perish twice,
I think I know enough of hate
To say that for destruction ice
Is also great
And would suffice.
—Robert Frost

You might think the epigraph is a little over the top, but from where I'm sitting, it reflects the sense of elemental differences and high stakes that divided the Twilight fandom into what sometimes felt very much like armed camps poised to do apocalyptic battle—and with no miraculous hybrid vampire child to step in and magically charm them to peace. It got ugly—in private, anonymously, and eventually in public.

AngstGoddess and Snowqueens Icedragon represent opposite and starkly opposed views of fanfiction and its community. One of these authors has gone on to earn multiple millions from her fanfiction; the other flat-out refuses to earn a penny. Each had enormous influence—both constructive and destructive—on the Twilight fanfic community, by extension on fanfic and fandom overall, and ultimately even on the publishing industry. Many—among them *Time* magazine—blame or credit Icy with the dramatic change that has led to a drive to commercialize or "monetize" fanfiction. E. L. James tends to support this single-author view of herself and her influence, but had she been a traditional author shopping a manuscript, *Fifty Shades* would never have happened; *Fifty Shades* was first published by a small press started *from a fanfic website*. Its editor there was a fellow writer of BDSM Twilight fanfiction (Tish Beaty, whose essay follows this one). It was cashing in on a popular genre within a hugely popular fandom. Clearly *Fifty Shades* struck a chord with the much (much) wider reading public, but it was not a one-woman phenomenon. As the long-suffering source (Austen) of James' source (Meyer) puts it, James deserves "neither such praise nor such censure."

While Snowqueens Icedragon/James' influence on the relationship between fanfiction and the publishing industry has certainly been more direct, AngstGoddess' influence was also powerful and varied, ranging from the creative to the critical to the very mechanisms and infrastructure of the fic fandom. With regard to the commercialization of fanfiction, Angstgoddess is the poster child for unintended consequences. She didn't just write the gateway fic—she helped build the gate. And helped open it. And nothing she could do, try as she might (and she certainly tried), could close that gate again.

AngstGoddess wrote "Wide Awake"—the one Twilight fic that everyone read. She also reviewed, recced, and ranted. She helped administer and judge influential contests, and won them as well. She was on the 2009 fanfic panel at San Diego Comic-Con. She was intensely involved with The Lazy, Yet Discerning Ficster, a highly influential review blog active in the heyday of Twilight fandom. She was interviewed by the mass media, to whom she spoke intelligently and cogently about fic. She helped run the massive charity auction The Fandom Gives Back; she contributed highly skilled web design and expertise (under her web design brand name, AngstyG) to many fandom writers, including Snowqueens Icedragon. The site where Icy hosted "Master of the Universe" after she'd pulled it from FanFiction.Net, but before it sold 70 million copies as *Fifty Shades of Grey*, was an AngstyG site. In short, AngstGoddess helped bring about the developments in fic she most hates. Then she flounced the fandom in what she referred to as a "gentleblaze," the implied "glory" absent and self-consciously ironic.

The conflict between these two figures illustrates diametrically opposed views of fanfiction and also underscores what may be the biggest lesson the Twilight fandom teaches us about authorship: authorial intent has *nothing* to do with the effect stories may have. AngstGoddess would no more have helped Snowqueens Icedragon introduce massive profit to fanfiction than Stephenie Meyer would have helped her launch an erotica empire. And yet, here we are. The key difference: unlike E. L. James or Stephenie Meyer, not only will AngstGoddess never see any share of the millions her work helped create, she believes it would be ethically repugnant for her to do so.

At first, the conflict simmered behind the scenes. In the spring of 2010, AngstGoddess agreed to design a blog for Snowqueens Icedragon, who was so well pleased with the work that she paid double for it. In the course of this project, the two chatted online on a range of topics from fandom authorship to publication to community ethics. When news of publication plans for what would become *Fifty Shades of Grey* hit, Angst-Goddess tweeted excerpts from these conversations. Snowqueens Ice-dragon responded by posting more complete excerpts and "providing context" and some editorial comment. The tone of this comment suggests just how far this relationship had already soured:

> I just want to reassure you that [AngstGoddess] has taken these private conversations, selected quotations, distorted them and tweeted them out of context. I don't want to editorialise about her motives — I think we can all guess what they are.
>
> For those of you with the time and inclination I have published these private chats so you can see for yourself just how dishonest and petty AG's distortions are. I normally ignore this sort of stuff, and didn't really want to engage with a woman who clearly has issues but I couldn't sit by and let her slander me again. Neither did I want to get into a slanging match with the Queen of Fan Fiction but I don't see I have much choice. We all know she's a bully, but IMHO she's crossed the line this time.

Icy provided longer excerpts of these chats and gives her version of the events. The complete posts of both have long been archived on my course blog (some of these conversations between authors we were studying even occurred during our course). Icy explains that, in July 2010, Angst-Goddess had emailed her about an idea for website that would host original fiction and charge a small fee per chapter, and invited Icy to participate. Icy had previously suggested she'd be interested in investing in something similar, but at the time AngstGoddess had been less than enthusiastic. Apparently this discussion is the context for Snowqueens Icedragon's comment, as tweeted by AngstGoddess:

> Well don't tell anyone – I have visions of being interviewed by Time Magazine for revolutionizing publishing…

This strangely prophetic comment dates back to a longer conversation on web-based models for publishing original fiction that, as posted by Icy, seems generative and cordial. When the topic of publishing *fanfiction* comes up, though, a clear conflict emerges. AngstGoddess is very against the practice. The conversation turns to Omnific, the house started by the fanfic site Twilighted, which first published Sebastien Robichaud's *Gabriel's Inferno* and many other novels with fic origins. The house was still in its early days in 2010, and its creation was extremely controversial.

(*Note*: The following excerpts are reproduced as Snowqueens Icedragon posted them, with typos, etc., intact for the sake of accuracy.)

SAM [**AngstGoddess**]: i do. look at omnific's creation. that is a huge black scar.

ME [**Snowqueens Icedragon**]: Why?

SAM: because okay, think about the fandom in terms of SM [Stephenie Meyer] gave us this thing and we're making fics off her concept however loosely doesnt matter its a community of free give and take we have already given and we have already taken and now we want to milk it further and use the fandom to fill our pockets for something they could have had for free something that admittedly wihtout SM would not have gotten a second blink

ME: Well... it's not like we're robbing her. And you'll have to forgive me – but I'm still relatively new to this fandom

SAM: no, but we're robbing the CONCEPT of FF

yeah i know

ME: I don't think so...

SAM: thats why i like to kinda show you the other side im just not certain you've seen this other, more logical side of the fandom

ME: I just don't feel as passionately about the fandom as you do.

Frankly it scares the living daylights out of me

SAM: i think you've seen a lot of your own reviewers, which is great, but they are only one side, and they want to support you. and you have to consider that there's another side to the coin

ME: Why?

SAM: but the fandom made motu popular. you made it good, fandom made
it popular

ME: True

And they've been able to read it in its entirety

And I even did the FGB thing..

which isn't really for me cos I never, ever wanted to do the EPVO [Edward
Point of View]

EPOV even. I was bullied into it...though having said that...I have
enjoyed writing it. So pushed my boundaries.. And it's earned a few bob
for ALS But I think you and I are poles apart on this.

The two authors really couldn't be further apart—on publishing fic and
on the fanfiction process. AngstGoddess had donated enormous quanti-
ties of time and expertise to the Fandom Gives Back campaign, while
Snowqueens Icedragon was apparently a very reluctant participant. AngstGoddess saw fanfiction as a collective endeavor; Icy saw herself as an
author with readers.

In an April 2010 conversation, AngstGoddess tried to explain her
opposition to publishing fanfic, and her misgivings about her own popular story, which she considers to be her "poorest form of writing":

ME: So if harper collins came to you and said we would like to publish WA
["Wide Awake"] would you say no

SAM: i would say fuck no

ME: hmmm – I'm not sure if I would have that resolve...unlikely to happen though but as a calling card... hey...

SAM: well WA is...progressively, my poorest form of writing. and its Twilight FF. i don't want any aspirations to succeed based of something so
silly.

ME: I wasnt silly!!!

SAM: i mean, i get your mindset. ive been there, honestly. but time in the community will change that

ME: I paid £60 downloading it on to my phone … in spain!!!

SAM: writing twilight smut is a little silly…. at least i consider it silly for myself. but that's okay, because most hobbies are a little silly

So, part of what we see in AngstGoddess' response is the sense—deeply ingrained in many fic writers—that it's somehow wrong to take fanfiction seriously. It's fine for a hobby, but to succeed on the basis of a devalued or silly hobbyist form would be of less value. However, despite placing a low value on her own story, AngstGoddess places a very high value on the community.

Snowqueens Icedragon, in contrast, is uncertain about the value of the community and her part in it: "I'm not sure I feel part of the community…I'm nervous of it…" In response, AngstGoddess tried to explain its value—a system of egalitarian exchange, an alternative economy:

SAM: and you have to read and review. nothing frustrates the community more than an author who is only willin to take reviews and never give…i think in cases like ours, the community has given us so much, and we just have to remember that the relationship was meant to be symbiotic a lot of newly popular authors forget that i did once

ME: I don't know what you mean…??? explain please…I am fascinated

SAM: like…a reader means just as much as an author. we're offering something. readers offer feedback, and authors offer free literature…it's all equal in that sense no one is entitled

ME: Yes I can see that…

SAM: so they give and we take, and we give and they take but only being an author who takes makes it seem very imbalanced even though you give updates, you could also be contibuting to the fandom's form of currency in recs and reviews which cultivates it

ME: I see … I just don't have time to read more.. If I do read—I review.. but only if I like—if I dont like I stop reading … Since I have started writing— if I do read I'll review … but I just dont have the time …

SAM: yeah i know how that is, totally

This conversation is best understood as representative of divides in fandom that are much more widespread and see many gradations. In fact, investments in the community side of fanfic vary as much as opinions on any other topic regarding fic—that is to say, a great deal. However, for people who *are* invested in community, an individualistic attitude toward fandom writing can be hurtful and frustrating:

SAM: i just get the feeling that you dont really … care about the fandom as a community whole. which is your choice, totally. and if that's the case, and you arent really concerned with the foundation of this place we've all been able to visit and grow and learn, then yeah. publishing motu is totally what you wanna do. the only reason not to, aside from the fact that it has major legal issues, is that you have a respect for the community that made motu into what it is, you know? but if you dont really feel that then no one can make you feel it

ME: Like I said…it freaks me out more than anything. I do respect and love my readers What I don't like is the negativity…So I find my horizons getting smaller and smaller so I can avoid it

SAM: well negativity exists everywhere. even when you publish it on amazon, theres still gonna be negativity

ME: true … but I'm sure it's easier to take with a big fat paycheck LOL.

SAM: and negativity has its place. it's what stops us all from monopolizing on ideas that arent totally ours

The notion that "negativity has its place" as a check on ego, individualism, or bad behavior is a very fandom notion. It's what drives wank and anti-fandom sites. It even, as we've seen, drives fic, as in, "I hate the way they did that. I can do it better."

These exchanges also underscore the extent to which misconceptions about copyright law are repeated with authority within fandom and in fact provide the foundation for the kinds of implied contracts fanfic fandoms run on, such as, "I'm OK donating my labor to your work because none of us can profit." These misconceptions—that a work such as *Fifty Shades of Grey* could not be published because it once had character names and a few plot structures in common with a copyrighted work, or because it was written and posted in a fandom context—were taken as gospel by many. I have seen a number of highly respected fandom authors who had always been quite reverent about Stephenie Meyer announce they'd lost all respect for her because she failed to sue Omnific or E. L. James. In fact, as we've seen, the traditional gift ethos of fandom originated in part from fear of persecution and even prosecution by rightsholders, but the understanding of these traditions has changed over time. People have been *quietly* "filing off the serial numbers" of much less popular fic since— well, we saw the practice encouraged by Arthur Conan Doyle. But many writers never considered publishing their fanfic because they believed that trying to do so would harm the community, that introducing profit would break working fandom systems based on trust and free exchange. On the one hand, these implicit fandom contracts, derived from beliefs about copyright, constitute a classic "chilling effect"—one that kept all the profits out of the hands of fans. On the other hand, these beliefs fed creative, collaborative solutions as fans built their own community structures and economies.

All these structures, traditions, and implied contracts, however, were based on voluntary participation and spontaneous community understanding. When it comes to writing and posting fanfiction, there are no posted rules that say only community-minded people need apply—and if there were, how would such rules be enforced? In the early days of both zine and internet fandom, as we saw, everyone had a hand in aspects of production and distribution, but these days, those mechanisms are already in place—in some cases (such as Wattpad, a "social reading" site that hosts both fanfiction and original work) they have been put in place by an explicitly commercial enterprise. All you need to do is take a minute to get an account and you can post fic to your heart's content. Paths to fic differ: having already tried her hand at writing novels, and enamored of a book that inspired her, James found other stories like the ones she wanted to write online. So she wrote one, and then another.

Nothing demanded or required that she join an organization or donate labor in addition to her writing. And just as in the Harry Potter fandom when Cassandra Claire used unattributed quotations, different expectations and presuppositions in the Twilight fandom created enormous controversy:

ME: Look I am not saying I will publish it…or pull it or anything.. I have to say I do not feel as passionately as you do about the fandom…

SAM: that saddens me i think fandom has been a really great place for you a lot of your supporters are here

ME: My readers have been a great place for me… I have some wonderful, wonderful readers and they are fabulous and I am beyond honoured

SAM: but your readers are the fandom

ME: but I see them like that… part of the fandom it's like the old groucho marx joke which I cant remember about not wanting to belong to a club that you're a member of…and I don't think I'm being arrogant… I am just this one middle aged woman.. who wrote a reasonably interesting fic That turned out to be very popular… why I don't know…and I can react to the readers on that level… as readers…

SAM: you just have to get in there. read what people are saying and reacting. make yourself more reltable [relatable]. show them theres a person behind the penname and not just some lady sitting on a perch

ME: I like my perch…

SAM: the hate will be less

ME: its safe

SAM: yeah, but you dont wanna seem as though you think you're above the community, you know?

ME: I think anyone who tweets with me regularly wouldnt think that..

SAM: i'd just be careful if i were you keeping business away from motu

thats really the only thing you have to be concerned about

ME: I don't feel about motu the way you felt about wa [Wide Awake]…I have done it as a sort of exercise.. to see if I could … and I think I have proven to myself that I can…

I now want to capitalize on it..

I am not a spring chicken like you.. I am in my 40s… so I want to try and do something before its too late – lol

I have only found out what I love to do – and it's taken this long!!!

And life aint no dress rehearsal etc

Life may not be a dress rehearsal, but it seems in some ways that this chat was, as E. L. James has used this same line in countless interviews. While Snowqueens Icedragon may have gone into writing her fanfiction "Master of the Universe" "as a sort of exercise" to prove to herself that she could do it, she quickly decided to repackage the dress rehearsal as the main event. As also emerges from the extended conversation, James—that is, Erika Leonard, the television producer—was not only no spring chicken, she was also no stranger to finance and the world of writing for profit. Her husband was a successful television screenwriter; as a producer, she had business acumen of her own. For her, writing was, from the beginning, a for-profit enterprise. That was her world. She was a confident professional who learned her newly discovered skill could have value, and she decided to sell it. Her readers had proven her own marketability—the Twilight fandom had become, in effect, a test market.

AngstGoddess first published heavily edited excerpts of these chats; Snowqueens Icedragon retaliated by posting more complete context. She closed her post by trying to clarify her respect for the fandom that made her:

I want you guys to know that to the people that have supported me I am grateful. Really grateful. I have met some amazing, talented, witty, wonderful women in this fandom. I do not consider myself above any of them—they are my peers. I know some of you will be disappointed that I have stooped to AG's level, and part of me is too — but really, I've had enough of her negativity. I'd like to put this ugly mess behind me.

That's all I am going to say, except finally – because I have an inner bitch too – here's a certain someone saying they would like to publish their fic.

[Picture of AngstGoddess at the 2009 San Diego Comic-Con]

In the "gentleblaze" LiveJournal post with which AngstGoddess left the Twilight fandom, she explained some of her motivations for taking the conflict so public: "SQID displayed continual classism toward me. When I was asked if I'd consider publishing my own popular fanfiction "Wide Awake," I said no, and she wondered why this would be, since I'm *so poor*." AngstGoddess also explains her conviction that the large sum of money the "Master of the Universe" outtake auctioned for the Fandom Gives Back auction was instrumental in making that publication a reality:

> I know she's going to publish MotU eventually, and I'm 100% certain that seeing her outtake raise $28,000 for pediatric cancer research had more than a little to do with that. I'm not extremely active in fandom anymore, and the auction website was my last mention-worthy contribution, so I have no problem ultimately revealing these chats.

The ramifications of this conflict didn't end or begin with this public outing of private chats. Before they became public but considerably after they occurred, a new player arrived in the Twilight fandom: Twankhard, the center of the kind of negativity James mentioned in her chat post. On this Big Name Author–hate website, all posters were anonymous; its targets weren't. Speculation about its administrators and posters were rampant, but when the truth was revealed, it shocked the community. One of them wasn't just an insider. It was *the* insider. AngstGoddess. Her stated motivation? Rage at Snowqueens Icedragon and the "pull-to-publish" phenomenon. That same "gentleblaze" post explained Twankhard, its motivations, and her own motivations for joining it:

Twankhard, created in late September of 2010, was an anon-meme'ish blog that I had some involvement in. It's hosted on Wordpress.com, and posts made there were usually related to authors publishing, archives converting themselves into vanity-presses, reviewer bashing, ego wank, etc etc. All mods, admins, and commenters were forced to anonymity. No high horse'ing allowed.

[. . .]

When I was approached about doing the Twankhard blog, my reaction was this:

THAT IS AN AWFUL AWFUL IDEA AND WILL PISS OFF THE ENTIRE UNIVERSE (when can we start?)

[. . .]

The general mission of Twankhard was to highlight various wanks in the fandom and cultivate an anon-based discussion on them. As stated continually, it wasn't meant to be serious. We only wanted to mock others' egos and inform the community of which stories were being pulled to get published. The blog posts themselves often smacked of mockery, while the real discussion happened in the comments.

Like most things, I was too flaky to offer any really significant involvement, but I will say I did the technical work, wrote a little (less than I should have), and was in charge of answering emails.

What was the immediate catalyst for AngstGoddess tweeting edited excerpts from private chats? She is very clear on that:

The morning I found out about MotU being published, I tweeted to my 6,500+ followers, *"I'm possibly about to commit fandom social suicide, but I just want you all to know, it's totally worth it."*

Her final tweet was as follows:

/blaze of glory. I'm out. Stop perpetuating arrogance. Give your kindness to people who won't take advantage of it.

AngstGoddess did not leave Twilight circles permanently, though she has stopped posting fic in this fandom. They did not end up being her last words, but at the time she chose these words to go out on:

> I did learn a lot (this was my first fandom), and I'm able to reflect on my wanks with equal amounts humility and amusement. I know where I've gone wrong, and I know where I've gone right.
>
> Grudgewank? *Wrong.*
>
> Charity? *Right.*
>
> So I'm not entirely deluded. I give myself a firm C-, I'm only human after all, and let's face it, I can change my screenname and move on to my next fandom without issue.

Tish Beaty is a romance writer and editor. She used to write BDSM Twilight fanfiction and also edited another BDSM Twilight fanfiction, MOTU, in advance of its first presentation to the world as Fifty Shades of Grey. Here, Tish recounts her experience with the Twilight fandom, and explains her involvement with "that book" and with The Writer's Coffee Shop, the independent publishing house she helped build from the fanfic website of the same name. Like Omnific, this publishing venture was very controversial within the Twilight fandom.

Bittersweet

Tish Beaty (his_tweet)

The only fandom I'd heard of prior to 2009 was the Star Trek films' fandom—the Trekkies. I was introduced to the Twilight fandom in November 2008 by a good friend of mine. It was unlike anything I had ever experienced: moms, daughter, sisters, and friends who were so passionate about the Twilight Saga that they stood in line for hours waiting for a movie and developed online communities to follow said books and movies. I thought they were kind of crazy—until January 2009, when I read all four books in five days. I was hooked.

I joined the online community NewMoonMovie.org, where I met a great group of ladies who would eventually turn me on to fanfiction. "Wide Awake," by AngstGoddess, popped my fanfic cherry. "Wide Awake" took the innocence of Twilight and twisted it into something mature, raw, and passionate. I read as many fics as I could on FanFiction. Net for several months. What drew me to fanfictions like "Wide Awake," "Emancipation Proclamation," "Clipped Wings and Inked Armor," and "The Hunter & The Hunted" was actually the differences between the fics and their characters compared to Twilight. I liked reading Edward and Bella on a mature level, with more substance, and in somewhat more realistic conflicts. After opening a Twitter account as a NewMoonMovie. org moderator, I found many of the fic authors also had Twitter accounts, and I began following them. Twitter is what lead me to other fic communities like Twilighted.net and LiveJournal.

It was on the other sites that I discovered just how dog-eat-dog and ugly the fandom could be. It was like high school, with cliques of authors and their followers. Should you cross one or the other on a board or in a review, you would almost certainly be run off. Excommunicated. For example, the group known as the Bunker Babes—James' most devoted cheerleaders while she was writing "Master of the Universe" (aka *Fifty Shades of Grey*)—were quick to pick up on negative reviewers and block them from the MOTU thread at Twilighted. I heard of one instance where a reader wasn't allowed back on the Twilighted site at all after calling James' knowledge of BDSM into question. I wasn't a fan of this kind of behavior, but it didn't affect me directly. I didn't get involved in fandom drama, and while I didn't like it, it wasn't enough to turn me off from the fandom entirely. I even began writing my own fic.

"The Submissive," by Tara Sue Me, was the first BDSM fic I read. It piqued my interest in the BDSM lifestyle, and ultimately led me to an alternative-lifestyle site. The alternative-lifestyle site introduced me to people in the BDSM community I bonded with and grew to love. These relationships inspired me to write my story "Nilla Days and Bound Nights."

I wasn't shooting for a Twilight-inspired story when I began writing "Nilla Days." I considered the story an original creation, with characteristics of real people in my life woven into it, as well as real experiences with which I took creative liberties. BDSM was increasing in popularity on the fic sites, and I felt Twilight fic readers would be a good community to write for and learn from—a sounding board of sorts for a story I wanted to eventually publish. (I knew nothing about the stigma of pull-to-publish when I first began writing my fic.)

You can't be a fic author and expect your story to do well without becoming involved with others in the fandom. So, once I started posting my story, I began interacting more and more with the fanfic community. It was through these interactions that I first heard of the "Literate Union" (LU).

Founded by a FanFiction.Net user from the UK, the Literate Union had members spanning the globe—many from countries other than the United States. They proclaim themselves as the "killer of dreams, destroyer of love, and ripper of stories." The following guidelines are from their thread entitled "Critique/Flame Request":

> Seen a shit!fic? Read a poorly written story that made you want to use bleach to clean your brain and eyes? Then post the link here and we shall look on to the story...Add a short description telling us why it should be reviewed/reported...It will save people time and you're more likely to succeed in your mission.

They seek out stories, cross-fandom, that they deem unworthy of posting and/or reading. An author can expect to be flamed in chapter reviews until he or she changes whatever it is the LU finds offensive—or until she takes the story down. In their "House Rules and Newbies Guide," they actually state their members should "sign every LU review with 'LU' at the bottom. This will spread around the word of the LU, and possibly irritate those we are reviewing in the process." The group seems to thrive on turmoil and confrontation.

In late 2009, as the Saga's worldwide popularity grew, the Literate Union homed in on the Twilight fandom. Members of the forum agreed that Stephenie Meyer was a "talentless hack" and that the fandom consisted of a bunch of "lemmings," and the assault on Twific began. The first fics targeted were the ones breaking ff.net's ratings guidelines: "Fan-Fiction does not accept explicit content, Fiction Rating: MA, and the rating is only presented for reference." Mature or "M" is supposed to be the highest rating that ff.net accepts: "not suitable for children or teens below the age of sixteen with non-explicit suggestive adult themes, references to some violence, or coarse language. Fiction M can contain adult language, themes and suggestions. Detailed descriptions of physical interaction of sexual or violent nature is considered Fiction MA."

I'm not sure how many ff.net authors actually follow this rule. The majority of the fics I read on the site were MA in content, and MA fics can still be found there in abundance today. Regardless, ff.net administrators started sending out warnings to the authors who were turned in for posting MA content. These authors were given the choice to remove the content or be pulled from the site. More often than not, the stories targeted were the ones with high numbers of reviews and/or hits.

Around this time, fics started disappearing from the site, either because the authors didn't want to change the content and so moved their fic elsewhere, or because FanFiction.Net had forced them off the site. I started posting on Twilighted.net to protect "Nilla Days and Bound Nights" because it, like so many other Twifics, contained MA material. But I found the process at Twilighted.net exclusionary and irritating. The use of "validation beta" readers to preapprove chapters reminded me of what the LU was doing at ff.net—the beta readers were deciding whether or not a story and/ or its author were worthy of being part of the site. And while my story was approved for posting, I was bothered by the need for preapproval as well as the tight circles of readers that formed on some of the story threads.

The tumult messed with my creativity, and I sought out another forum for my story. A friend suggested a new fic community called The Writer's Coffee Shop (TWCS). One of the founders of the site had been targeted on ff.net for noncompliance due to explicit MA content, so a group of ladies from the United States and Australia decided to start their own place where fans could discuss books, authors, blogs, and more. In January 2010, TWCS Library was opened to allow writers to post original works as well as fanfiction without having to jump through the hoops that other sites required.

After visiting the community and library, I moved my story over to TWCS. In my opinion, the site was the best available to fic authors at the time. TWCS had feature stories, used cute little coffee cups for readers to rate the works they read, held writing challenges, and posted top ten lists. "Nilla Days and Bound Nights" was welcomed with open arms by the readers and admin on the site, and it remained a top ten story for several months. It didn't take long for me to become friends with Amanda Hayward, one of the original founders of TWCS. After a few weeks I was made a site administrator. I spread the word to my readers on ff.net and followers on Twitter that TWCS was the place to be.

Amanda and I chatted a lot about our love of all things literary, as well as our desire to see some of the talented writers on TWCS Library published. She had been thinking about opening an online publishing house and felt TWCS would be the perfect platform to do so. I agreed because I believed in what the site stood for: a place for people all over the world to meet and become friends; a place where authors could post their fic or original stories and not be limited by cliques or groups like the LU; a place where I felt welcome and wanted.

A major topic of the discussions between Amanda and me was the creation of Omnific, an e-publisher that got its start by turning popular Twilight fics into publishable books. These fics ranged from contemporary to paranormal romance and were published after minor editing and changing the Twilight characters' names. Their first "edited" fic, *Boycotts and Barflies*, was released in January 2010. The vision for TWCS Publishing House was to encourage writers of the fic community to spread their wings and write original works that could be published while helping them grow as authors. A publishing house that catered to the needs of aspiring authors. Although TWCS Publishing House would go on to publish some reworked fics, unlike Omnific it was not started as a place to publish popular fanfic.

From February to May 2010, we researched the ins and outs of book publishing. I worked during the day, so I spent my evenings and weekends looking up contract law, writing contracts and formulating information packets for editors and authors, contacting printers across the globe for run prices, and discussing with Amanda how the publishing house should be set up and run. I signed several authors while I was with TWCS Publishing House and helped bring in new editors as well. In the summer of 2010, TWCS Library hosted a contest for original works in which two or three participants would be offered a contract with the publishing house. Miya Kressin's *The Changeling's Champion* and JD Watt's *The Children of Creation: Convergence* were both chosen and given to me as my first edits.

From the beginning, I was given the title of managing and acquisitions editor. It was my understanding that I'd be brought in as a 20 percent partner in the publishing house as a form of compensation for all of the work I was doing, because there was limited cash flow prelaunch and probably would be for the first year or two. Then, after my first few months of work, I was told it would work out better for me if, rather than receiving any stake in the partnership, I were paid more per book than the other editors as compensation for all of the administrative work I'd done and continued to do. I had no reason to doubt that I would be compensated fairly for helping in the acquisition of authors as well as the development of the publishing house. After all, Amanda and I had formed what I thought was a close working relationship as well as friendship, frequently signing our emails or ending our chats with "Love Ya."

I had the honor of working with several wonderful authors during my time with TWCS. I edited five amazing women—including the world-renowned E. L. James. The decision to publish *Fifty* was an easy one for TWCS. James had an established fic fanbase that spanned the globe. Her series was exactly what our company needed to put it on the map as a bona fide publisher while generating revenue for the business. Up to that point, the only fics TWCS had published had been heavily edited and reworked, and while I can't say I fully embraced the idea of pulling fics to publish, I knew that TWCS needed a boost if I was going to begin working solely for the publishing house. After being told I was "the only one for the job," I agreed to work with James as the editor of *Fifty*.

My main purpose, according to TWCS, was to make sure the content was changed enough that we wouldn't have any copyright-infringement issues. I was asked to handle *Fifty Shades of Grey* and James with kid gloves to maintain the peace and keep her happy. Looking back, would I have handled the edits of *Fifty* differently? Sure I would. I'd have gone with my gut instinct and made the changes I felt were necessary to the manuscript. Not doing so made me TWCS' scapegoat when James became unhappy about the lack of a copy edit on *Fifty Shades* (there was no copy editor on staff when I edited *Fifty*). It also lost me the chance to edit books two and three, and kept me from being compensated properly for editing the book and from recouping any compensation for the work I did to develop TWCS as a publishing house.

I was phased out of the house over a nine-month period—just around the time that deals were being brokered in New York for *Fifty* to be sold to Random House. TWCS replaced its offer for me to become managing editor over the erotica division with one for a position over TWCS Library, which didn't pay enough for me to quit my day job. I have been blacklisted by many in Twilight fandom for working on the book at all. I have been unfollowed and not spoken to on social media by authors I once considered friends; fandom friends turned a blind eye when TWCS let me go—even though I was told over and over again that what happened was unprofessional and wrong. I am now known as the editor of the book that needed editing: the *New York Times* number-one, mega-millions-selling novel *Fifty Shades of Grey*.

My experience has been bittersweet. I have seen sides of the fandom, fic, and publishing worlds that most people don't—the good, the bad, the fabulous, and the ugly. I worked with authors who became close friends and who have gone beyond TWCS Publishing House in their publishing endeavors. I've seen a few of my favorite fics be transformed into works worthy of publishing and actually get published. While my opportunity to work full time for TWCS vanished long ago, I am now represented by Louise Fury, a fabulous agent with the L. Perkins Agency. I have my own novel in the works, and for the first time in a couple of years, I'm looking forward to what the world of publishing has to offer.

part three

FIC AND PUBLISHING

THERE'S A WRITING COMMUNITY—well, many nested or overlapping or strangely parallel communities—based almost entirely on exchange, praise, mutual respect, and critique. The works produced in this community, almost by definition, have no monetary value. In at least some circles of this community, producing work for money is frowned upon, even derided, as selling out. A few may make money from the sale of their works, and these few are the best known to those outside the community, but they are mocked by true believers.

Of course I'm talking about poetry.

It wasn't always this way. In a different time, two young men wanted to raise money for a trip to Europe. They thought, *Hey! Let's write a book of experimental poetry!* While William Wordsworth and Samuel Taylor Coleridge could hardly have retired on the proceeds from *Lyrical Ballads* (although they certainly amassed an impressive amount of cultural capital), the idea of raising money through poetry sales was not as absurd in the late eighteenth century as it seems today. (Admittedly, *Lyrical Ballads* did not sell nearly as well as *Fifty Shades of Grey*.) The fact is, attitudes and expectations about writing change all the time. The systems of value—whether financial or cultural—that apply to different kinds of writing change as well.

Financial and cultural values are sometimes seen as antithetical. The cultural critic Theodor Adorno argued that any form of mass, popular, commercial culture—anything that participated in "the culture industry," as he termed it—was not art but rather art's enemy. In an entirely distinct cultural milieu, *Fic* contributor Rachel Caine remembers getting the cold shoulder at a fan convention because she was commercially published—*real* writers, she was told, wrote only for love. In other circles (the Science Fiction & Fantasy Writers of America, for instance), only paid writers need apply; membership is open only to those with paid publications in approved markets. From yet another perspective, it's also where you publish that counts, but in a different way: some serious, professional, publishing writers of literary and experimental fiction consider any association with the major commercial publishing houses to be destructive to literary aims and values, tantamount to consorting with the enemy.

Ultimately, cultural and financial systems of value are very different, and should probably be understood as distinct. Instead, they are endlessly and perhaps unavoidably confused.

This confusion has certainly been apparent in the tangled world of fan-fiction. Some of it stems from fear of legal consequences, some from an exaggerated sense of the originality of the source material as opposed to the fanworks it inspires, and some from taking pride in "fic for fic's sake" and the ethos of the gift economy. The fan culture tenet that "thou shalt not profit from fanworks" has been, depending on who you talk to, an almost sacred and inviolate, wholly necessary founding principle of fandom. To others within the same community, it's only been a necessary evil.

Part of the confusion about publishing fanworks stems from the fact that *fanfiction* does not name any one thing. It is a blanket term for works identified by their authors as relating to a particular cultural product or public figure, but the term itself makes no actual assertion about how closely related a given fanwork is to its purported source. Sometimes departures from the original are intentional (Holmes and Watson are Trojan women in ancient Greece!), and sometimes they are completely unintentional—the fan writer is trying, but the style, tone, and nature of the story would be unrecognizable as remotely related to its source were it not for character names, identifying tags, and the website where it appears ("OMG Homes, I cant even said Jon LOL Wastin U R so dumb that was homes said that"). So there's more than one reason that for most fan writers publishing for profit will not become an issue.

Many fan writers are surprised to learn that there's a long history of adapting fanworks for commercial use—in the case of Sherlock Holmes, as we've seen, at the suggestion of Sir Arthur Conan Doyle himself: "Dear Sir, I read your story. It is not bad and I don't see why you should not change the names and try to get it published yourself." Of course, fandom history is not necessarily cumulative in the minds and experiences of any given generation of fans. Today's fan writers know nothing of Conan Doyle's letter, nor of the open, accepted practice of transposing new names onto Sherlock Holmes pastiches and publishing them commercially. Similarly, the new generation of readers and writers today who are growing up sharing original and fanworks on a single platform, as we see them doing on Wattpad and online writing community Movellas, may not experience the sharing of original and fanworks as different in kind. And as for the small number of writers who have gained recognition and even commercial contracts on those sites, I've seen no outcry.

Of course we will never know how many novels began as works of fanfiction that were never publicly shared, the writer realizing at some point in the process that the work had veered off into independent territory and could be pursued as such. Even for work that *has* been shared as fanfiction, "filing off the serial numbers," as repurposing derivative or transformative work is often termed, isn't even a little bit new. What *is* new is that the practice has now come fully and loudly out of the closet—so much so that what *Newsweek*, *Time*, and *Publisher's Weekly* singled out as last year's bold new fashion trend is old hat this year. But it's a hat that still seems to get plenty of wear. Fanfics that get publishing contracts don't make headlines anymore, but as long as fics amass millions of reads online, they will continue to receive publishing contracts—until a sufficient number of them tank precipitously enough that publishing an author with a record of tens of thousands of readers seems riskier than investing in an unknown debut novelist. For now, it's the hugely, wildly successful fanfics that are getting contracts—those whose hits number in the multiple millions—not the undiscovered gems, or the gems discovered only by a few hundred or a few thousand readers.

As I hope this section will make clear, though, filing off the serial numbers is by no means the only relationship fanfiction has had to commercial publishing. The far more common story is one of apprenticeship, of new or novice writers building skills and confidence within fanwriting communities before launching their own publishing careers. These fanfic origins used to be hidden, but these former fic authors *also* are increasingly coming out of the closet.

It's not always a one-way street, either. There are instances of long-successful professional novelists who write fanfic on the side, for fun. S. E. Hinton is perhaps the best known, although she, like many others, is less public about her fanfic pen name than she is about the fact of writing fic. Anonymity is a key benefit. Fanfic offers professionals the same things it offers amateurs: honest critique, the play (which can also be discipline!) of assuming other voices, other styles and story lines. The freedom to experiment without risking your reputation or the investments of your publishers. Nonfiction writers—and professors!—get to take off our mantles of authority and all the positive and negative baggage that comes with them. If only J. K. Rowling had published her mystery novel as fic, she could have gotten much of the benefit (the honest, unbiased, Potter-free response to her work) she sought.

The writers in this section all have different experiences of fanfiction and how it has related to their publishing careers. With new fic licensing schemes, corporate-sponsored fanfic-like projects, and the integration of fanfic and original amateur stories on sites such as Wattpad and Movellas, we're likely to see an even greater variety of these experiences in the future.

An Interview with Eurydice
(Vivien Dean)

I KNEW I'D WANT TO CONTACT a fan writer named Eurydice for this book, because she wrote the first fanfiction I ever read all the way through. I was in the hospital. I was hurt—I wanted comfort. Wait...I had heard...wasn't there was a whole genre for that? I'd been collecting fanfic links for when I was brave enough to read it (several times already, I'd had the same experience most people have when they randomly click on some fanfic link: horror—in my case, not at anything that's going on in the fic, but at the grammar and punctuation. Professional hazard). What I finally settled on was a long (I wanted long, it was going to be a long night) "between-the-scenes" or episode insert, a classic hurt/comfort fic called "The Promise of Frost." Buffy and Spike got stuck in a cabin in winter and...stayed.

Eurydice was a writer who seemed very in control of her style, and while she could be more romance-y in spots than I myself preferred, many readers singled out those same passages as favorites. As I researched her, I found that she had published original work since writing "Frost." Today, she's moved back and forth between fanwriting and professional romance writing for most of her career. At one point, Eurydice significantly revised a work she'd posted as fanfiction and published it as a novel, leaving the fanfiction version up online. It was all very open.

I asked Eurydice how she experiences the differences between fanwriting and original romance; about changes she's observed in fanwriting culture, including the relationship between fanfiction and publication; and about what, as a writer, keeps her coming back to fic.

How do you see the difference between your original work and your fanwork? Are the processes different for you? Which seems more free, which has more rules or constraints?

> The processes are very different for me, actually. I was always driven to write fanfiction because of my love of the characters, and so I mostly wrote stories specifically to make the characters happy.

My [fic] readers had one expectation most of the time: to see the pair they love get together. I could bend or ignore a lot of rules on the road to getting them there. It's not the same in original romance. There are genre expectations that typically need to be met. Depending on the audience (I write m/m as well as het original work, and the audiences don't always have overlapping needs), I might have to specifically choose to limit secondary characters, for instance, or stick to monogamous relationships even if they're not committed. I actually began writing in a new fandom the past couple of years specifically because I was in search of something with more freedom.

As a writer, what do you get out of fic that you don't get from your professional writing? Many people—including fic writers themselves— view fic as practice, something to be moved on from, but I know a number of pro writers who still write fic—or who started after successful publishing careers. Speaking only for yourself, why do you enjoy both?

Writing fic allows me to wallow in characters I adore. There are only so many shows out there, a finite number of experiences for me to have with these people. Fic, both writing and reading, gives me the opportunity to spend time with them when I couldn't otherwise. But I get bored pretty easily, to be honest. I don't want the same thing over and over again. So writing both gives me the best of both worlds.

I know you reworked [your *Buffy* fanfiction] "Rhapsody in Oil" as original, removing the vampire elements. Did you feel you needed to change much about the characterizations, or had that Spike and that Buffy—in the painting world—become so distinct they felt like your own?

I actually reworked "Rhapsody" quite extensively. Many plot points are different, some relationships are different, the ending is different, and more than 70 percent of the prose is rewritten. What I ended up taking from it was the basic premise, the initial antagonistic relationship between the hero and the heroine, and certain scenes. Because I had to create completely new backstories for them, they took on a life of their own that felt separate enough from Buffy and Spike for me to be comfortable calling them their own people. Of course, they share similarities. Cash is British, quick-witted, slightly dangerous, and sexy as hell, for instance. It actually took me as long to rework it as it did to write it in the first place, because of all the changes/rewriting.

I was taken by the open way you announced the publication of "Rhapsody" on your LiveJournal, and I notice that the fic version is still up online. It all seemed low-key. Are you aware of the controversy in other fandoms over "pulling to publish," or "filing off the serial numbers"? From what I saw in the Buffyverse, fandom seemed encouraging of writers going pro with their fic. Did I miss a lot of wank?

In *Buffy* fandom, not so much. I have heard mention of it in a few other fandoms, but not witnessed it firsthand. I've seen more wank in the original [writing] world by readers and other authors who have blown up when it's been revealed that fanfic has been reworked for publication. I get it [the fandom controversy], actually. One of the primary beliefs in fandom is that you never profit from it. I think part of it might depend also on how popular writers are when they announce they're pulling fic. Writers with a large support group, people they consider friends, don't seem to get as much flak for it.

Do you have any idea how widespread that publishing practice was, in this or in other fandoms you were in?

Other than what I knew of my *Buffy* friends, I only know what I see in the original romance market, mostly in the m/m niche. Opinions seem to be divided. On the one hand, the writers who know how much work goes into fanfic seem not to be too bothered by the practice (and certainly some publishers don't care where it comes from as long as it makes them money). On the other hand, I've seen readers feel cheated that they paid for something that was once free, and writers angered because they don't understand fandoms and fic writing.

Did you have any idea of readership numbers in the *Buffy* fandom for popular stories like yours? There seemed to be so many different archives, LiveJournals, and award sites, and at least when I was there,

the fandom had largely migrated from ff.net. I don't remember anyone talking about review counts. I wasn't sure if that was just a difference in culture, in the scope of the community, or a lack of tracking (review and hit counts on sites like FanFiction.Net and Wattpad are now sometimes used as evidence of "platform").

> I only knew about hits to my site, but I'll be honest, I never bothered paying attention to any of it. Popularity has never been my goal (I'd probably sell more original if I wanted to cater to broader, public needs, LOL). But caring about review counts, monitoring hits...that's at the core of what drives blogging mentality these days, so it doesn't surprise me at all that it's deemed so important in certain communities.

Was there ever any wank/drama about being a Big Name Fan or Big Name Author in any of the fandoms you were involved with? This was a big deal in the Twilight fandom, and there were sites dedicated specifically to bringing down fans that seemed "too big for their breeches."

> I never saw it, no. The closest thing I can remember in my corner of the Buffy fandom was a popular Spuffy author who wanted to write full time. She offered to write fic for people who "donated" to her, I'm sure thinking it would be like patronage during the Renaissance, and she immediately got slammed/torn down for daring to want to make money off her fic. She disappeared from the fandom very quickly after that. I have no idea whatever happened to her.

I remember Linden Bay Romance as being an online publisher who published a lot of fan authors, sometimes their original works, sometimes their repurposed fics. Was this an open practice of theirs? Did they discuss it, do you know? Linden Bay was bought by Samhain Publishing; was Samhain aware, and do they still support fan writers?

> Two of the original Linden Bay owners were popular Spuffy authors, so they immediately approached a lot of us about writing for them. I was asked to rewrite something and I refused, mostly because I didn't believe it was right to shave off the serial numbers and call it good like I knew some authors chose to do. I ended up writing an original romance novel instead. The practice didn't get discussed in the

romance community, only behind closed doors and within the fandom community from which they got their authors. I only ended up rewriting "Rhapsody" after three years of writing original fic, both with Linden Bay and elsewhere. I felt at that point I'd learned enough about the market and was comfortable enough about how much to significantly change to make it original.

When Samhain bought Linden Bay, they didn't automatically assume the entire catalog. Most of the books were released from their contracts. Of the three I had out with Linden Bay, they accepted one. It just happened to be the rewrite of "Rhapsody," but even then, I was asked to make even more significant changes to it (including rewriting the entire third act/ending for the second time, LOL). I don't think my editor was ever aware that it began its life as a Buffy/Spike fanfic, though, and certainly, the practice of reworking fanworks was never encouraged.

Andrew Shaffer is a writer, critic, and publishing observer who tends to attract the label "gadfly." He is remarkable for having more alter egos than your average fic writer, among them Evil Wylie, Emperor Franzen, and Fanny Merkin, the acclaimed author of the parody Fifty Shames of Earl Grey. *Here, he reflects on the phenomenon of publishing fanfiction and his own role of parodist.*

Fifty Shades of Gold

Andrew Shaffer

When James W. Marshall discovered gold at Sutter's Mill in Coloma, California, on January 24, 1848, he inadvertently triggered a mass influx of settlers that came to be known as the California Gold Rush. Similarly, when Random House signed E. L. James to a seven-figure, multibook deal for her Fifty Shades series in March 2012, it was the shot heard 'round the publishing world. Not only had fanfiction become fair game as a writing farm system, it was now a lucrative vein of ore just sitting there waiting to be mined. By the end of the day that Publishers Marketplace announced the Fifty Shades deal, half the agents and editors in New York were busy panning for gold on FanFiction.Net—while the other half assigned the task to their interns.

By now, the story of Fifty Shades is familiar and tired: forty-something mother of two becomes a worldwide sensation by writing Twilight fanfiction under the pen name "Snowqueens Icedragon." After changing the characters' names and restructuring her work as a trilogy, she releases the books through a small Australian press. And fans can't get enough. Within a year, the press sells a combined 100,000 print and ebook copies of the trilogy. When a *New York Post* reporter catches wind of the racy books making the rounds of wealthy mothers in the Hamptons and publishes a subsequent exposé, the books *blow up*. Not just explode: they actually *blow the fuck up*. They top the Amazon ebook charts for weeks on end; bookstores can't keep the $30 print-on-demand editions in stock. Dr. Drew is talking about them on *The Today Show*. And then Random House buys the trilogy and republishes them with minimal edits in order to get them in stores as quickly as possible. It turns out they didn't need to worry about the fever dying down: the rereleased Fifty Shades trilogy spends an unprecedented six months on top of the *New York Times* and Amazon bestseller charts, dominating the national and international consciousness in a way no other book has in quite some time.

Not since Twilight, of course.

Which brings up a question, one that was in the minds of every publishing industry professional (including those scouring fanfiction websites in search of the next Fifty Shades): Isn't there something *wrong* with this? Isn't there something wrong with co-opting a living author's work and fanbase?

Copycats are not a new phenomenon; blockbusters had been spawning them forever ("If you liked X, you'll love Y!"). But this was different. Random House was not publishing a vampire novel because Twilight had proven there to be a market for paranormal romance; Random House was publishing a series that copied another book character by character (Edward = Christian, Bella = Anastasia, Jacob = José). This wasn't so much marketing a similar work to a fanbase as it was using Meyer's characters and fans as a springboard.

New York Times bestselling author Jodi Picoult was one of many authors to speak out about the shady origins of Fifty Shades. "If u like [erotica], read erotica," Picoult tweeted. "But read authors who create their own characters and don't steal a fan base another author worked hard for. [James'] readers wanted more of Meyer's characters, & tuned in. If she hadn't started as fanfic would she have been as popular?" Still, she acknowledged there were shades of gray when dealing with the ethics of publishing fanfiction. "Interesting to ask where to draw line: is [*Pride and Prejudice and Zombies*] suspect too?" she tweeted, questioning Quirk Books' "mashup" of the public domain Jane Austen classic.

I was also a vocal critic of the pull-to-pub trend (pulling fanfiction offline and publishing it for profit, also called "removing the serial numbers" when changing the names to avoid legal complications). In fact, I announced on Twitter that I would write fanfiction of *Fifty Shades of Grey* and put vampires back *into* the story. I started writing a parody, titled *Fifty-one Shades* (because it was "one better than *Fifty Shades of Grey*, an oblique reference to one of my favorite satirical films, *This Is Spinal Tap*), and serialized it on my blog for free, posting a few paragraphs a day. I joked that as soon as I had a chance to "cash out" with a publisher, I would change the title and character names à la E. L. James.

After just three days, the unthinkable happened: I received the first of several inquiries from publishers. My agent asked me how quickly I could finish the book; I said I thought I could have it completed within a week. One case of Red Bull and seven days later, I emailed the rough draft to my agent; a week later, I had a book deal with Da Capo Press. Da Capo rushed production to get the ebook and print editions out as quickly as possible (although I spent two months revising the manuscript with my editor, to ensure we were putting out the best book we were capable of producing). And, true to my word, I changed the title (to *Fifty Shames of Earl Grey*) and changed the characters' names.

Despite my jokes, it wasn't "fanfiction of fanfiction," but instead a parody that poked fun at *Fifty Shades of Grey*, erotic romance, and the media's coverage of the whole affair. Still, I dropped hints throughout *Fifty Shames of Earl Grey* that the hero, Earl Grey, was secretly a vampire. In the acknowledgments, I also thanked Stephenie Meyer—who, in an ironic twist, was not thanked by E. L. James in the Fifty Shades books' acknowledgments. I felt like I had righted a wrong in the universe. But had I? An irate Fifty Shades fan approached me at a literary convention and told me my parody was offensive and that I should be ashamed. "It's wrong to piggyback off someone else's success," the fan said, apparently unaware of the irony.

Parodies are legally protected in the United States and Canada. By mocking and questioning pop culture, they serve a critical function in society. Fanfiction, by contrast, doesn't (at first) appear to serve any function other than to let fans get their rocks off. But isn't some fanfiction just as transformative as parody? Especially alternate universe fanfics, where the characters are changed from vampires to kinky businessmen. Had I been too swift in my judgment of *Fifty Shades of Grey*? Were E. L. James and her publishers just as entitled to their profits as I was to mine?

For many writers and artists born into the pop-culture-saturated twentieth and twenty-first centuries, fanfiction is an important stepping stone in their creative evolution. My first experience with fanfiction was in the third grade. I was a huge Teenage Mutant Ninja Turtles fan: I had the comic books, I played the Nintendo video game, I watched the cartoons. Hell, I even tried to learn to skateboard because that's how the Turtles rolled. I wrote and illustrated my own TMNT comics in college-ruled notebooks. Somehow, one of my teachers must have caught me drawing in class instead of paying attention, and, to her eternal credit, she didn't scold me. No. Instead, she asked me to contribute a monthly four-panel TMNT comic strip to the grade-school newsletter sent to every home in the school district. I think I drew only three "episodes," though, since we were close to the end of the school year, so—horrors!—my big debut in the comic book world ended on a cliffhanger. (There are probably old classmates still waiting for me to finish my saga, to which I can only say: keep waiting.) But even at the time, I, a third grader, *knew* that it was somehow "wrong" to use the Eastman and Laird characters without permission. The school was letting me do it, though, so what did I care?

That was sort of the publishing industry's informal response: what did it matter if we're now in the pull-to-pub game? Stephenie Meyer didn't seem to mind that *Fifty Shades* had begun life as a facsimile of her work. "I haven't read it," she told *MTV News*. "That's really not my genre. Good on her—she's doing well. That's great!" Everyone kept waiting for the other shoe to drop, for some nasty litigation from Meyer or her publisher now that millions of dollars were changing hands...but nothing happened. And so the publishing world descended on the fanfiction forums in a feeding frenzy...

Penguin's Berkley imprint picked up Sylvain Reynard's *Gabriel's Inferno* and *Gabriel's Rapture* in a "substantial seven-figure," two-book deal in August 2012. *Gabriel's Inferno* began life as the Twilight fanfiction "The University of Edward Masen," under the pen name Sebastien Robichaud. Once the fanfiction was complete, Reynard pulled it offline and published it under the new title—with the characters' names changed, of course. Reynard made the decision at the urging of his readers, he explained. "I was listening to the thousands of messages sent to me by readers who wanted the story to be published," he wrote in a blog post that April. "So of course I didn't expect a backlash at the publication's announcement. In fact, the [negative] reaction of some, including those I called friends, has greatly surprised me." A few months later, Simon & Schuster's Gallery Books imprint bought the rights to Christina Hobbs and Lauren Billings' *Beautiful Bastard*, a reworking of the Twilight fanfiction hit "The Office." The deal was reported, again, as "substantial"—meaning major publishers were plunking down serious money, all in the hopes of tapping into the same success that E. L. James found with *Fifty Shades*.

The "angry" fans to whom Reynard alluded have voiced their displeasure with this new phenomenon on forums and in Goodreads and Amazon reviews. One anonymous reviewer, using the name "VanessaLovesBooks," left this one-star review on Amazon for Tara Sue Me's "The Submissive," another former Twilight fanfic: "Save your money, this is another fanfiction story, THAT WAS FREE, in which now the author is using Stephenie Meyer's fans to sell their books." Australian blogger Bianca wrote on her blog WriterlingWorks about the trend, "Can't *anybody* come up with anything original anymore? Or are we just going to exhaust this thing ad nauseam just for a few extra dollars? The snake is eating itself!"

The controversy over pull-to-publish and "filing the serial numbers off" has so far been limited to online fanfiction communities, and has not negatively impacted the commercial prospects of any of the novels that were originally fanfiction. The general public simply doesn't seem to care about the ethical questions surrounding the publication of fanfiction. All most readers are looking for is a good story; if that story resembles another story they liked, then all the better (which probably goes double for Hollywood executives in charge of greenlighting movies). And while many authors such as Picoult have spoken out against the trend of publishing fanfiction for profit, it's (probably) not illegal. It's difficult to imagine a court of law reading *Twilight* and any one of the reworked fanfics and finding any infringement—in fact, that may be one of the reasons Stephenie Meyer hasn't tried to sue James or any of her other imitators. (Only Meyer and her lawyer know for sure.) Even if Meyer or another author takes a fanfiction author to court, it's far from certain that it would set a precedent.

All indications are that the trend will continue until the FanFiction. Net archives are exhausted. (They'll be replenished, but possibly not fast enough for speculators.) Thankfully, the next gold rush has already been identified: self-published ebooks, not derived from fanfiction. Self-published authors such as Tracey Garvis Graves and Bella Andre have already signed seven-figure deals; Sylvia Day signed an *eight*-figure contract for books four and five of the formerly self-published Crossfire series. Self-publishing is experiencing something of a golden age, as a publishing industry shaken up by the Great Recession and the rise of ebooks struggles to adapt.

But when the fanfiction and self-publishing wells temporarily run dry, what then? Editors and agents may need to return to panning the slush-piles for gold—a grim prospect indeed. It's no surprise that publishers and authors have begun to circle the wagons and hunker down to protect their intellectual property. In perhaps the ultimate irony, James' French publisher sent a "warning letter" in November 2012 to publishers it felt were infringing on the copyright of *Fifty Shades of Grey* by publishing books such as *50 Ways to Play: BDSM for Nice People* and *Fifty Shades of Pleasure: A Bedside Companion*. "Some of these titles, which pick up on elements of the book, are clearly parasitical," an editorial director for James' publisher told *The Telegraph*.

James' lawyers have also busied themselves by clamping down on everything from *Fifty Shades*–themed lingerie parties to bootleg T-shirts. Her agent, Valerie Hoskins, defended the crackdown. "You can't just hijack something someone else owns," Hoskins told the *Mirror*. However, if the success of Fifty Shades and other Twilight fanfics is any indication, you *can* hijack something someone else owns—and make money at it. So, for now, the gold rush continues...

The Briar Patch
Fic Writers on Publishing Fanfic

RECENT PUBLISHING TRENDS have demonstrated there is money to be made on fanfiction. Publishing houses (Omnific and The Writer's Coffee Shop) have sprung from popular fic archives; the sale of self-published repurposed fics has become quite common; fanfiction contests have offered gift cards or other rewards; and, most recently, Amazon's authorized "fanfiction" licensing scheme Kindle Worlds has begun offering royalties for works that obey set conditions and rules. The most prominent (though least common) instances of former fic going pro have entailed the Big ~~Six~~ Five publishers taking on reworked fanfiction as "original" novels: *Fifty Shades of Grey, Beautiful Bastard, Gabriel's Inferno, The Submissive, Wallbanger, Sempre,* and *Loving the Band.*

I've used scare quotes around the word "original" not to suggest that fanworks can't deserve the term, but rather to highlight the term as contestable—and much contested. In publishing, it often seems to mean "original enough" (not to be sued), and it seems to have meant that for a *long* time—not just since *Fifty Shades.* To lay readers, the meaning ranges from "unique" to "the product of my own labor" to "I think I can make a buck from this" to "the completely autonomous expressive content of my soul." "Original" means different things to different people in different circles—much like the word "fanfiction" itself. "Fanfiction" is often used synonymously with "derivative work," a phrase with copyright implications. Yet fanfiction is often better described as transformative, parodic, critical, and, yes, "original," in any of the senses above. And, while such distinctions may be the stuff of literary debate (is this really parody? Or is it just bad imitation? Isn't all work derivative of something? Does any piece of writing really "stand alone"?), these slippery terms are often used to distinguish the legal difference between "okay to profit from" and "infringing."

The recent explosion in published fanfiction has occurred because *publishing companies* came to realize—very publicly, and on a large scale—that "fanfiction" was not a synonym for "derivative." It turns out that the publishing world and fanfiction communities had long been operating on assumptions about copyright law as it pertains to fanworks that were even *more* restrictive than copyright law itself.

Fic contributor and intellectual property attorney Heidi Tandy offers a perspective on how and why at least some of this profit has been legal:

> One of the fundamentals of U.S. copyright law is that an author/creator can only protect the "expression" of an idea. Usually, that means the word-for-word text in a song, movie, or book. Since the 1950s it's also been possible to copyright a character, but the protection for characters is very limited; a character is only copyrightable when she's especially distinctive, or so central to the story that the character is essentially the "story being told." Young, dark-haired boy wizards with scars and owls are not copyrightable; if they were, Neil Gaiman's Tim Hunter (in *The Books of Magic*) would have made impossible the existence of the Harry Potter we all know. But as Gaiman said in 1998:
>
> > It's not the ideas, it's what you do with them that matters.
> >
> > Genre fiction, as Terry Pratchett has pointed out, is a stew. You take stuff out of the pot, you put stuff back. The stew bubbles on.[100]
>
> Tropes, oft-used character elements, character flaws, Mary Sues and Gary Stus—even when an author uses a lot of those elements all together, it doesn't make the character copyrightable, and therefore, if someone else uses those elements to tell a different story using different words (and different character names, because using the same names could be a trademark issue) the second author isn't automatically engaging in copyright infringement. The expression of the ideas—the specific words—aren't the same.

Legal opinions, of course, vary on *every* subject, and *Fic* is not handing out legal advice. But the idea of copyright described above is very far from the one many fan writers understood. Fan writers often believe their writing lives exist at the pleasure of rightsholders, and while that may not be true, few fan writers have the resources to fight a legal challenge from a large corporation, and no case has ever been fought in court. Most fans take work down when asked. Many oppose attracting attention to fanworks in *any* way—let alone commercially, as *Fifty Shades of Grey* and its cohorts have—and this has been especially true of those fans who remember the "bad old days" of multiple cease-and-desist orders.

Legality aside, however, I think the general awareness that people *can* sometimes publish fanfiction has led to some misconceptions about how fan writers see themselves and their work. Outsiders often assume fan writers must be ecstatic over the new potential for profiting from their works, and many fan writers *are* pleased to have new opportunities. But not all of them have been pining for profit, and some find the practice terribly unethical. While many fans express nothing but love and support for fan writers who have found commercial success with their fic, others view it with tremendous scorn and anger. Some reacted with outrage initially, but have accepted the change; some judge on a case-by-case basis (greater transformation of the fanwork makes selling it more acceptable, while minimal or superficial editing is "just cheesy"); some hope their turn may also come. Some simply shrug and go on writing for fun and love—I've often been told by fan writers that if they'd wanted to profit, they would have written something different, but that what another writer wants to do with his or her work doesn't affect them.

Many others, however, remain intensely, passionately opposed to the practice of publishing fic—most vocally, perhaps, among the ranks of the Twilight fandom that itself helped launch the current trend. The most vehement opponents to publishing fanworks quickly investigate and label any new publication on Goodreads lists and on Amazon, posting damning one-star reviews noting the publication's fic origins. One such comment on Tara Sue Me's *The Submissive* reads, "A lot of people want to give this woman a pass (and are coming up with hilarious bullshit to excuse it—pathetic hypocrisy at its finest) because they like her. She's no different than any of the other morally bankrupt people engaging in this unethical, repugnant practice." Another simply reviews the self-published *Wake,* a reworking of a popular fic in which cancer patient Edward struggles to come to terms with his ailing body's sexuality, with the tags: "cheap-ploys-to-make-a-buck, rewritten-fanfiction, dont-even-bother, gonna-be-sick, no-just-no, not-cool, not-if-i-were-dying, severe-side-eyes, shouldn-t-be-published, wtf-is-this." Even by the standards of Twitter and Tumblr (highly expressive rhetorical climates), exchanges on this issue stand out. Close friendships and working partnerships years in the making have ended, bitterly.

One of the most prominent, vocal, and vigilant critics in the Twilight fandom has been einfach mich, who early on wrote an influential blog post:

> Sad fact is that not every situation can be a compromise. Especially when the actions of a greedy few insults the foundation of what we do.
>
> You may not care where the stories come from. You may think you're supporting a friend to live their dream (god knows I did), but in the end using fan fiction and someone else's fandom to launch your own writing career will eventually harm all fan fiction writers and readers. Either by threatening fan fiction writers['] ... ability to do what we do without threat of being shut down or by convincing other fan fiction writers that their work is not legitimate unless they attempt to sell it.
>
> If you do not see fan fiction as a legit art form do not write it.[101]

In this view, fandom is not and can never be about money; it's about equality, open discourse, a near utopia of free exchange. Money threatens it, cheapens it, sullies both fan writers and source.

Of course, very few fan writers have received large publishing contracts: ~~seven~~ eight with major houses at the time of writing, but even ten times that number would represent only the tiniest fraction of the almost 4 million fanfics posted to Wattpad alone—just one archive, and a new one at that. Also, community mores vary by platform, fandom, and generation. In some fandoms, it's acceptable to (quietly) pass around a kind of electronic tip jar or even to pay authors for commissioned fanworks. What is and is not acceptable within fanfiction communities changes all the time.

Some fans, though, are still wondering how any of this was possible. As Aja Romano, longtime fangirl and now commentator for The Daily Dot and other venues, explains:

> For decades, the golden rule of fanfiction has been *Thou shalt not profit.* This is a twofold protection: it protects the original copyright holder from having their work infringed upon for profit, and it protects the fanfic author from claims of infringement.
>
> But attitudes about fic for profit have changed so rapidly and so drastically that within the space of a few years, we've moved from the illicit,

tacit practice of "filing off the serial numbers" to *Fifty Shades of Grey* openly owning its published-fanfic status.

And now, of course, we have Kindle Worlds, whose approach to fanwork as a kind of free-enterprise franchise tie-in may be an inevitable growing pain along the way to corporations reaching a more equitable permanent relationship with their fandoms.

But what does it mean to "profit"? At what point does one start profiting from fandom? Is it profit when someone loves your fanfic enough to draw fanart for it? When you have your way paid to a convention? When you get a job because of fandom connections, or when you capitalize upon your fan following to launch a successful Kickstarter, like *Fight Like a Girl*, the largely fandom-funded campaign that saw my literary fiction debut in 2013?

The road from "Thou shalt not profit" to "If thou profit, for heaven's sake don't admit it" to "Screw this, thou canst profit if thou wants to" is not a simple trajectory. It doesn't track the course of early outliers like Cassandra Clare and Naomi Novik, who each directly tied their successful publishing careers to their successful fandom followings—Clare by retaining her familiar fan handle as her publishing pseudonym, Novik by treating her *publishing identity* as the "open secret" known only to her well-established fandom following. Neither of them were profiting from fanfiction—at least, not directly. But did writing fanfic allow them each to build a strong personal fanbase, make industry connections, and help them become disciplined, polished writers? Absolutely.

Some fan writers are just as critical of these dynamics as they are of writing fic for profit. For example, einfach mich's previously quoted Tumblr post decries the practice of glorifying some fan writers over others, and of making fanfiction fandom about fic writers and fics rather than about enthusiasm for and adherence to the original source stories. She complains that new readers came to find stories about Stephenie Meyer's Edward and Bella and found stories about strangers—a variation on complaints that AU fic "ruins" or "isn't really" fanfic that date as far back as responses to Jacqueline Lichtenberg's Kraith universe in the 1970s.

einfach mich also reiterates the dearly held and oft repeated points that "fanfiction is meant to be a gift to other fans" and that "fans don't turn other fans into customers." The wholly egalitarian fandom she imagines may not be the norm—Big Name Fans seem to have been a fact of fandom life from the get-go—but certainly the introduction of money to a nonmonetary economy complicates the relationships and implicit agreements that underlie its functioning.

Take beta readers. Beta readers act as pre-readers, sounding boards, and editors for fic writers. All their labor is volunteer, and it is real labor. They lavish time and attention on work on short notice, and because many do not write themselves, they won't receive the same service in kind. Critique groups or writing partners, of course, fulfill a similar role in the broader writing community, but unlike a critique partner in a writing group, where the community understands that publication for profit is a likely and desired end result toward which the group is all working, fanfic betas volunteer under the assumption that no commercial gain will come from their labor. One beta reader who wishes to remain anonymous likened the feeling of having beta-read work sold outside the community to donating labor or crafts to a nonprofit that then turns around and says, "We decided to sell your stuff and keep the money because YOLO."

Active fan writer Ms Kathy was the beta reader for Tara Sue Me's "The Submissive" and its fanfic sequels, now available from Penguin. She was also temporarily the Twilighted.net validation beta for Snowqueens Icedragon's "Master of the Universe" (Twilighted.net required its authors to go through this extra level of editing, although Snowqueens Icedragon's popularity meant that she had more leeway to ignore suggestions). Ms Kathy doesn't approve of profiting from fanworks, and has long expressed her concern that this practice has harmed the fic community and will continue to do so. Despite this stance, her volunteered time and energy has arguably contributed to the commercial success of the fanfics she worked on. (While making her position known, Ms Kathy has not been among the more angry public voices and seems unwilling to let even fundamental disagreements destroy what had been productive friendships: "I appreciate everyone's ability to choose for themselves and I'm deeply grateful to the authors for trusting me with their words when their projects were fic. I am grateful they allow me to speak out and say that while I always support them, it's not something I myself would do or support with my money. Differing opinions will always happen in life, and I like it when we can all be respectful grownups."[102])

This idealization of fandom as a profit-free, noncapitalist space is also not strictly accurate. Visit the exhibition floor at Comic-Con and you will see enormous corporate booths and smaller, independent crafters and vendors, all selling to fans. Some of these works are authorized by right-sholders, some not. But there is rarely any outcry from fans towards selling fandom-related crafts to other fans, even those that clearly infringe on trademark (although corporate C&D orders do go out on such works all the time). Fans historically have turned other fans into customers in all sorts of small-scale ways. Part of the difference in opinions toward repurposed fic may be explained by the difference in scale, but even so it does seem that there's a special rage reserved for profiting from fan *writing*. (Why? Writing's easy mass reproducibility? The romanticization of originality and authorship? I don't know.)

The Organization of Transformative Works (OTW), the parent organization behind Archive of Our Own (AO3), is a proponent and supporter of a noncommercial, nonexploitative space for fanworks. Its website explains its position on publishing, profit, and their nonprofit site in their FAQ, under the heading "Does the OTW support the commercialization of fanfic?":

> The mission of the OTW is first and foremost to protect the fan creators who work purely for love and share their works for free within the fannish gift economy, who are looking to be part of a community and connect to other fans and to celebrate and to respond to the media works that they enjoy...
>
> While some transformative works legitimately circulate in the for-profit marketplace—parodies such as *The Wind Done Gone* (the retelling of *Gone with the Wind* from the perspective of a slave), critical analyses that quote extensively from an original, "unauthorized guides," etc.—that really isn't what fanfic writers and fan creators in general are doing, or looking to do. We just want to enjoy our hobby and our communities, and to share our creative work, without the constant threat hanging overhead that an over-zealous lawyer at some corporation will start sending out cease & desist notices, relying not on legal merit, but on the disproportionate weight of money on their side.[103]

Archive of Our Own is a nonprofit space, by fans, for fans, with its parameters and expectations clearly laid out. This already distinguishes it from much of fanspace, which as we've seen tends to hold to the notion of a common ground of self-evident truths that is neither as common nor as self-evident as it seems. It *is* common for fanfic hosting sites' Terms of Service and author disclaimers alike to specify that works are not posted for commercial purposes, but also to specify that fan writers retain the rights to original material in their stories. Yet I have often seen and heard the opinion that posting a version of a story as fic constitutes a promise never to adapt it for profit later. I asked *Fic* contributor and OTW cofounder Francesca Coppa to comment:

> I personally don't think that publishing a story as fanfiction is a promise not to commercialize it later, and there's nothing in the AO3 TOS to stop people pulling their fic and selling it professionally, or even rewriting a fic that's archived with us and selling it professionally, though we would not allow a fan to use the AO3 to promote or link to that published work. You also can't, for instance, post the first chapter of your work, fan or original, to the AO3 and then say, you know, "Buy the rest here"—that's a violation of our TOS. But again, this is mostly hypothetical: most fanfiction isn't suitable for the market (that's the joy of it!) and as I've noted in the media a lot recently, to me *Fifty Shades* is primarily distinguished by how traditional it is (heterosexual paranormal erotic romance is already a huge publishing category).[104]

What constitutes market "unsuitability" is subject to change, and it's been changing pretty rapidly recently. Whatever the given value for what is marketable, however, there's a vast amount of potential fiction that falls outside of it, and the knowledge that there's a space and audience available to that work (if one without monetary reward) is one of the biggest values fanfiction offers literature. As Coppa points out, the works of fanfiction that have received big publishing contracts do not begin to reflect the diversity of stories out there.

The most obvious example: All of the major publishing contracts for repurposed fic have gone to heterosexual romances, despite the fact that even a little research can unearth slash writers who also command "read" or "hit" counts in the millions. But consider the case of fan author Kryptaria's *Sherlock* fic "Northwest Passage," now forthcoming (very substantially revised) as *The Longest Night* (Sourcebooks, July 2014). As the author (publishing under the name of Kara Braden) explains on her Tumblr post about the process of "filing off the serial numbers," one of the first things she decided when planning to adapt her fic for publication was to change the central relationship from M/M to heterosexual.

In fact, she'd begun the revision process and made the choice before she was contacted by a publisher about reworking the story. When the press' editor asked her if she'd be willing to reimagine the story as heterosexual, she had her answer ready:

> Part of wanting to be a writer is that I want to be a professional, published author. Full-time. This means I need to make money off writing, which means reaching the largest audience possible. There's a much bigger audience for het romance than for m/m. I don't necessarily like it. In my opinion, Northwest Passage, as it was originally written, is a gorgeous romance that goes beyond "OMG GAY SEX" and speaks to the heart in a way that might well be obscured by assigning gender roles to the characters.[105]

This post helps illustrate how the market intervenes to shape what appears on shelves in a way it does not shape fic. "The market" that does this, though, is a projection—a set of assumptions about how one book will fare based on generalized trends or perceptions about trends. "Northwest Passage" was a popular story, but despite a proven track record with readers and the growing presence of a lucrative (if less mainstream) market in M/M erotic romance, assumptions about the market led to its reinvention as a more mainstream, more normative story. In the culture at large, this kind of intervention happens in editorial, studio, or network executive notes—and before that, in authors' minds. It happens *before* stories get onto our shelves or screens. Even repurposed, though, internet fanfiction leaves a track record: the finished non- (or less) normative story as originally conceived, realized, and engaged with by readers.

Part of the important—even crucial—social, literary, and political function of fanfiction is that people actually tell the stories they want to tell, without pre-censorship or preconceived notions about what will sell. Writers can do that at any time, of course, but fanfiction gets these stories to readers for whom such stories resonate, even if these readers do not constitute a valuable marketing demographic. It's *this* value that is threatened by the commercialization of fic.

Another concern voiced by opponents of publishing fic is that individual profit threatens the way creativity works in fanfiction communities: the free exchange of ideas—story concepts, premises, prompts, tropes—that occurs in many fic fandoms. There's a sense that fic is a collective enterprise, and that removing a work and laying exclusive claim to it steals community property. This sounds very much like the argument that property is theft, a fencing off of a commons. But that's not a fic argument, that's an anarchy argument. That's Pierre-Joseph Proudhon (*Property is Theft!*) or the Marquis de Sade: "Tracing the right of property back to its source, one infallibly arrives at usurpation. However, theft is only punished because it violates the right of property; but this right is itself nothing in origin but theft."[106] By this logic, E. L. James stole from fic, which stole from Stephenie Meyer, who stole from Shakespeare, who stole from...someone who stole something first, and that first theft is ownership. Whatever the communitarian values of fanfiction, however, and whatever the popularity of BDSM-themed stories, fanfiction communities are not populated by a majority of Sadeans, anarchists, or socialists. The anti-profit position seems better summed up as, "There's an infinite amount of private property—but not for us," as Franz Kafka, who has inspired a lot of fic we call literary fiction, might have put it. Or to put it another way, if the model is "fans don't turn other fans into customers," doesn't that lead to a one-way flow of capital from fans to corporations?

At this point, I want to be quite clear about where I come down on all of this, and what my role has been. I have been quoted fairly often in the media, talking about fanfiction and publication and also talking about well-known fanfics, some of which got large publishing contracts.

Of the ~~six~~ seven Twilight fanfics that have so far gotten contracts, four are by writers I either taught or discussed in the media. And that may have helped draw attention to them, it is true—but these fics got big contracts because they could demonstrate millions of hits. I taught them or discussed them because they were influential and popular—not the other way around. If my mention could draw millions of hits, Victorian women's poetry would top the bestseller lists. (J. K. Rowling did take her mystery book title *The Cuckoo's Calling* from a Christina Rossetti poem. Maybe it *is* catching on.)

My statements to the media have been construed as both very opposed to and very much in favor of publishing fanfic, but the truth is my feelings are mixed and always have been. I worry about threats to the free exchange of ideas. I worry about it with traditional copyright, too. I worry about it in academia. I don't think that market forces and intellectual freedom are necessarily friends. I also have literary concerns about publishing fanfics as traditional novels: to me, fics are simply richer and more interesting in context, in a community of mutually commenting texts. *That* is the form I found exciting and new: fanfiction as organism. While the plot structure and writing often gets tighter through editing, I don't find the publishing process necessarily improves my reading experience. Your mileage may vary, however. Those who dislike the interventions of serialization, commentary, reviews, and other fic-related interruptions—those looking for a smooth popular commercial novel, in other words—will likely prefer the published fics. Those who are expecting the result to have a traditionally novelistic structure, however, may be disappointed even in these, as fics are usually not structured as novels and, even edited, can come off like stringing together episodes of a soap opera and expecting them to make a well-shaped feature film.

Literary stakes, though, aren't the only stakes I care about. I care about opportunities for writers—opportunities of all kinds for writers of all kinds. Fanfic is disproportionately written by women, queers, and others who are underrepresented in or excluded from economies of financial *and* cultural capital. Fanfic can be empowering for these excluded and marginalized groups: they find a voice, they use the voice they have, they reach others. For many readers and writers, this is enough, this is *more* than enough, and I don't want to see that nonfinancial opportunity and reward threatened by the intervention of the same commercial culture that marginalized them in the first place.

But. For many of these fandom writers the mass media universe isn't the only economy in which they are marginalized or excluded. Although some do pursue successful careers in all kinds of fields (and hence may closely guard their fic identities), many successful fan writers *don't* enjoy financial success or economic stability. If a writer, with the help and support of a community, manages to do that incredibly unusual thing—come up with a story that connects with tens or even hundreds of thousands of readers—and then can legally profit from it...I do not believe that writer—or any writer—should be shamed for pursuing that opportunity. It is true that many of the first wave of highly publicized and highly profitable published fics were written by gainfully employed professionals. It makes sense to me that this was the case; successful professionals are in a good position to be informed about copyright law, to have confidence in their own abilities, and to be used to asking for and receiving excellent compensation for their work. This background is not shared by *all* these newly successful writers, though, and *certainly* not by all fic writers. Many are struggling, unemployed or underemployed. It is not reasonable (nor tenable) to demand that all writers who have written fanfic put fanfiction above their own economic interests.

Kara Braden—the *Sherlock* writer who revised her slash as heterosexual romance—explains her decision to make changes to her fic to make it more marketable in very straightforward terms:

> right now, I have a mortgage to pay, food to buy, and dogs and cats to keep in fish and chicken. My husband has been supporting my unemployed butt for two and a half years now. I want to contribute my fair share.[107]

In the face of the potential for profit, noncommercial communities must be communities of choice, not coercion, and I hope and believe fanfiction will continue to flourish as a noncommercial or extra-commercial enterprise. As a writer and scholar, I have benefited from and enjoyed that system immensely. But I also I find the public shaming and humiliation of (mostly) women by other (mostly) women for wanting to benefit financially from their own creative labor to be deeply upsetting. From my perspective as a scholar of women writers and women's history, I see this trend playing into a long tradition of shaming women for wanting compensation for work that social norms dictate should be done only out of love. Domestic work, including childcare. Teaching. Even sex work. So much of the rhetoric employed by the most strident opponents of profiting from fic recalls the rhetoric around an earlier era's "fallen women": publishing opponents speak of "moral repugnance," of a "taint" that can spread moral contagion. I've seen those who sell fic called whores and worse—and by women who would vehemently oppose that kind of rhetoric actually being leveled at prostitutes or sexually active women.

Some of the anger is simply that the fic writer is taking the "easy way" to publication. The argument is often raised that if an author can write such a good fic, she can write an even better "original" story. Maybe so—great!—but the ability to write that story doesn't mean she can sell it. There is no guarantee that just because a writer can write one story that appeals to hundreds of thousands or even millions, he or she can write another. J. K. Rowling is the most successful novelist, economically, in history—but the book she wrote under another name (before being outed) sold a modest 1,500 copies despite strong reviews in important venues.

In some ways, however, all this is a moot point. As soon as my 2010 class and I began to understand the scale of the Twilight fanfiction community and the multiple millions of hits its popular stories received, it was clear to all of us that *someone* was going to find a way to make money from this world. Our question was whether the actual fan creators would see any of the profit. Or would fans be exploited but "allowed" to drive website traffic and enhance brands and maybe even pay for the privilege? Would they give up all rights to the (often) highly original content they were sharing for free so that others would profit?

The internet seems free, but someone's always profiting. Take, for example, Archive of Our Own, a true nonprofit organization. They don't earn, but they have costs: they pay for server space and other necessities; their users pay for internet access; and so forth. *Someone* profits. And what of other free-to-use but *not* nonprofit sites—who profits there? Access providers? Site owners who get advertising revenues or sell the site analytics? For many sites, we don't yet know; we're still in the "early Facebook" era, in which the idea is first to get the millions of users, then to figure out how to profit from them.

That's currently Wattpad's business plan. Wattpad is a rapidly growing site for sharing and discussing original fiction and fanfiction. A little income comes in via banner advertising, but, they say, they'd rather not use a lot of that kind of advertising, as it's annoying, invasive, and "not native." Their ambition is to make an entirely "native digital," nonanalog reading and writing environment. Once they are an integral part of a transformed sense of reading and writing, they'll find ways to profit. That's the plan. And currently, as part of building up that user base, they are very much interested in fanfiction, a real growth area for them. Their site already hosts over 3 million works of fic.

On Wattpad, it's free to download and upload stories, original works, and fanworks. All the content on the site is user generated. Writers retain all ownership rights to "User Submissions"; Wattpad claims a nonexclusive right of distribution, but does not sell the fiction posted to their site, and its terms of service say the site itself is not to be used for contributor's own commercial purposes. Even so, right now the site is averaging 15 million unique views per month. As of July 2013, they have 22 million uploads of user content and around $20 million in venture capital. Their plan for profit is to wait and see; they seem writer- and reader-friendly and well-intentioned. My plan on judging Wattpad's eventual methods for profiting from their site is to wait and see right along with them. They may find paths to profit that add value to reader- and writer-experience and that seem less exploitative than some other schemes that have raised fan ire. In all circumstances, though, I do think fan writers should be careful and informed about who *does* profit from their work, and how.

Also in the category of wait and see—for the moment—is Kindle Worlds. While the current verdict seems to be that this plan is more a crowdsourced licensing scheme than true fanfic (too many rules), it's a sign of the times that here, fic is a brand, an attraction that "spin-offs" or "tie-ins" aren't. Again, jury's out. John Scalzi made an early but very influential post about Kindle Worlds. He quotes the Amazon terms he finds problematic and then responds:

> "We will also give the World Licensor a license to use your new elements and incorporate them into other works without further compensation to you."

> i.e., that really cool creative idea you put in your story, or that awesome new character you made? If Alloy Entertainment likes it, they can take it and use it for their own purposes without paying you—which is to say they make money off your idea, *lots of money*, even, and all you get is the knowledge they liked your idea.[108]

Scalzi worries that Kindle Worlds creates a cut-rate idea mine that rightsholders can simply exploit without further investment in or compensation to writers. Scalzi's perspective is, of course, from the professional side of the equation. Most fan writers have been much more concerned about Kindle Worlds' potential impact on fanfic more broadly. Will this platform simply introduce the same normative corporate control against which many have turned to fic as a form of resistance? Will it give rightsholders increased desire or incentive to stamp out free fanfic? Heidi Tandy isn't worried from a legal perspective:

> Does the existence of Kindle Worlds and similar publisher/IP rightsholder projects impact those who write and share fanfic for free, even if they do so on sites that have ads, Amazon or Apple Associate links, and other small income-producing elements?

> I don't think it's realistic to be concerned that the existence of Kindle Worlds will mean that TV show/film/book creators will stamp out all freely given fics. At this point, for all existing fandoms, the longstanding laches issue that protects fics posted elsewhere and given away will still impact what The Powers That Be can and cannot do. Laches means that if a fanficcer relies on the fact that a copyright holder has allowed creative

fans to share their fics, art, vids, and films, they cannot later be barred from sharing what they create, especially if it starts out as noncommercial and stays that way.

However, it does mean that people who write in the fandoms covered by Kindle Worlds and who *sell* ebooks of those stories outside of the Kindle license may find themselves dealing with cease and desist letters. But there was always a chance they might because of the commercial aspect of that action.

Kindle Worlds and the commercialization of some fanfics may bring questions on issues other than legality that will impact the fan-created gift culture, mainstreaming of fannishness, commissions, fundraising for charity, or even the ability of pro writers to write in other universes, and those are questions we cannot answer in the summer of 2013. But there's certainly a lot of people who are interested in the discussion.

By the time this volume is published, the verdict on Kindle Worlds that is very much still out may well be in; it may peter out, or there may be more ventures trying to license fic, to harness—or to rein in—fanfiction's energy. But I don't believe publishing fanworks will end fanfiction, even as the fanwriting community continues to change, as it always has. The fact is, there are many more people who enjoy writing and sharing stories than will ever be able to make a living from it, or want to. There are more kinds of stories than will ever be mass marketable. Fanfiction enables these stories to find readers, and readers to find stories. Even for professional writers, fanfiction allows freedoms (of length, format, and content) that the market simply doesn't. Sharing versions of beloved stories and characters creates common ground that fosters conversation, creativity, and community. It's a system that works, and despite new challenges, fic seems only to be gaining steam.

Tiffany Reisz is author of the Original Sinners series of BDSM-themed erotic romances published by Harlequin. A seminary dropout, she discovered her passion for writing about passion when she tried her hand at fanfiction on a dare.

Just Change the Names

Tiffany Reisz

My name is Tiffany Reisz, and that is my real name. It's the name I live under, and the name I write under because they are one and the same to me. But once upon a time, I had a different name. While a student at a conservative Southern seminary, working on dual master's in theology and biblical studies, I found my creativity and personality being stifled by my evangelical classmates and their narrow worldview. I didn't want to quit school, but I had to find an outlet for the real Tiffany, the one with the weird, erotic imagination who was slowly going mad while listening to people who called themselves Christians talk about why they supported low taxes on the rich and sending poor kids to foreign wars.

Salvation came in the form of an email from a friend of mine. The email contained a link and that link led to a story. It was a work of erotic fanfiction. The story—I don't even remember the name—centered on the villainous Colonel Tavington from the film *The Patriot*. I read the story with pleasure. Who wouldn't enjoy an erotic romp with a randy redcoat? Especially one as devastatingly handsome as Jason Isaacs, the Oscar-nominated British actor who played him. I had one simple complaint with the story—the writing. I told my friend I adored the erotic images in the story, but I could write better smut than that with my eyes closed. She dared me to try.

Never dare me to do anything. I will do it.

While on spring break from seminary, I sat down at my mother's two-ton HP desktop computer and pounded out the first 9,000 words of a novella about Colonel Tavington and his seduction of a virginal loyal-ist whose house (and body) he'd commandeered. My irritation with the story my friend had sent me was how un-Tavington-like the Tavington character was. The author made him rather sweet and sentimental, an old softie behind all that murdering and church burning he did in the movie. Nonsense. I loved him for his unapologetic villainy, not in spite of it. I did my best to capture his terse, intelligent sarcasm, his sneering seductiveness. I made the sex scenes rougher and more violent while being less explicit, less pornographic. Erotica should make a girl want to shove her hand down her panties, not shove the book in the trash can. So no "creaming pussies" or "throbbing staffs of manhood" in my story. If I was going to write erotica about a borderline sociopath ravishing an innocent who'd do anything to protect her household, including submitting to sex with a monster, I was going to be classy about it.

Once I completed the story, I posted it on the same forum as the short I'd read that inspired this whole nonsense. As a seminary student, I could have been heavily disciplined for engaging in the distribution of pornographic works. Adult students weren't allowed to have sexual intercourse outside of marriage without risking expulsion. I was under a vow of celibacy and didn't like it one bit. If I was going to write and post smut online, I'd have to be sneaky about it.

One of my favorite books as a child was Michael Ende's *The Neverending Story*. My favorite character was the old bookshop owner, Mr. Coreander. I co-opted the name and posted the story as "Corriander." Up the story went, and I didn't think much of it until comments and compliments and cries for more began to pour in. A professional journalist and fellow Jason Isaacs fan emailed me to tell me I wrote the best dialogue she'd ever read. Those 9,000 words garnered me more attention, adulation, and self-confidence than anything I'd ever done in my entire life.

Soon homework fell by the wayside as I poured myself into finishing the story. I wrote a chapter a week and posted them over the next month and a half. In two months I'd completed an 80,000-word novel. And I couldn't stop writing. I had to write more. Jason Isaacs' other hugely famous role was that of Lucius Malfoy in the Harry Potter movies. I couldn't deny I found his sinister powers and long blond hair alluring. Fans begged me for a Lucius story. How could I tell them no?

Writing a Harry Potter story freed me considerably from the constraints of historical fiction. I knew almost nothing of the American Revolution, but Harry Potter took place in the nineties, in a world we very much recognized as our own, where I could reference popular culture and make jokes. I conceived of a feisty teenager heroine who would get roped into this magical world and would mock it at every corner. I thought of the poem "Leda and the Swan," by William Butler Yeats. A powerful wizard seducing a normal teenage girl summoned the image of the god Zeus descending onto the mortal Leda. I named my story *Leda* and filled it with sex and jokes and even David Bowie references (there's a running gag in *Leda* that David Bowie is actually a wizard, because, let's face it, he probably is).

At the time there was no hotter fandom in the world than Harry Potter. Those seven books had spawned thousands of works of fanfiction, mostly short stories and novellas but also a few sprawling novels like mine. Every chapter of *Leda* I posted online began racking up dozens of comments. I was nominated for fanfiction awards. Readers started naming their pets after my characters. A few even begged for my real name and address so they could send me gifts. People translated the story into their native languages. I even recall popping into a chat room and having someone ask me, "Are you THE Corriander?" Yes, I guess I was. And over and over again I received the same comment:

This story is so good you could just change the names and get it published for real.

High praise indeed but a truly ludicrous suggestion. Who would do that? Who would steal another writer's world and sell it as if it were their own? I adored J. K. Rowling, admired her. She had built a beautiful playground in her books and had graciously allowed her fans to come play on it. Changing the names and selling the story would be a slap in the face to this world I so loved, this author I so admired.

Plus I knew I had worlds of my own waiting inside me. I didn't need her characters. I didn't need her world. Writing a Harry Potter novel of my own was like learning to ride a bike with training wheels on. I didn't have to bother with the messy task of world building. She'd already built the house; I only had to decorate it in my own style. I could focus on learning the art of suspense, of creating mystery and mood, of developing sexual tension, of using humor to humanize a character. I learned to write fast and leave damn good cliffhangers at the end of each chapter to keep the readers begging for more. If I was going to do this, though, become a real writer, I would do it on my own. J. K. Rowling put in all that hard work to create her world. I wasn't about to skip any steps or ride on anyone else's coattails. And I sure as hell didn't want to spend the rest of my life labeled as a rip-off artist who didn't have the talent to come up with her own story.

I knew I didn't need anyone else's world or stories since I could find inspiration anywhere. I returned to my favorite muse: Jason Isaacs. He'd said in an interview that while he loved the baddies he played, just once he'd like to play a part more like himself—a neurotic Jewish British man. Could I do that, I wondered? Could I create an erotica character who was intelligent, overeducated, British, Jewish, and a bit neurotic? I could. Definitely. But he couldn't carry the whole book. My buttoned-up Brit would need a foil, a wild child to help him loosen up. Maybe a writer like me, but a writer who lived a life far stranger than her fiction. Maybe she wasn't just a writer either. Maybe she had another job, too. I'd always thought Jason Isaacs would look gorgeous in a black silk blindfold with his hands tied behind his back. What sort of woman would tie up a man for sex? A Dominatrix would. That would be fun, wouldn't it? Maybe this stuffy Brit was a book editor who had to help this wild American Dominatrix with her new novel. He'd loathe her in the beginning, of course. But she wouldn't mind. She was tough, strong, unbreakable. Maybe she had an ex-lover who'd made her that way, made her so strong. Wonder who he was...I had to find out. Yes, my Dominatrix writer would drive my stuffy Brit batty with her flirting and her fearlessness. He hated pain and she doled it out on purpose for money. What an odd couple. It would be like *My Fair Lady* but with sex. A neurotic, gorgeous, type A British editor foiled by a guttersnipe erotica writer. Perfect. I could write this novel. I *would* write this novel.

So I quit seminary. I moved into a friend's closet. I got a full-time job at a bookstore. I started writing.

On May 1, 2012, *The Siren,* book one in the Original Sinners series by Tiffany Reisz/Corriander, was published to the best reviews that Harlequin MIRA, the publisher's women's fiction imprint, had seen in years. It's the first in a series of BDSM novels featuring a quirky and beautiful Dominatrix, her various lovers (including a Catholic priest), and her wealthy and powerful clients.

And all because of a dare.

Rachel Caine is a New York Times *and* USA Today *bestselling author of forty books, including the fanfiction-inspiring Morganville Vampire series. A published writer since 1991, Caine is living proof that fanfiction can have benefits for writers—even those who have already launched their professional careers.*

*Prey*ing for More

Rachel Caine

My writing career was probably saved by my love of fanfiction and especially a particular TV show back in the late 1990s.

Bold statement, I know. And I will explain.

You know how fandoms typically become energized, then creative, then cliquish, then self-destructive? (If you didn't, you do now.) Well, there's one fandom that managed to stop at the "creative" point, and just...stay there, for a very long time. It was awesome, and to this day I'm still in touch with many of the fanfic writers who flourished there.

And you've probably never heard of the fandom.

The show is called *Prey*, and its thirteen (and only) episodes aired on ABC in 1998. Although it had an all-around excellent cast, including Adam Storke, Frankie Faison, Vincent Ventresca, and Larry Drake, it's probably best known as the show Debra Messing appeared in before she was launched to fame in *Will & Grace*.

The show itself had an interesting premise: What if we came to know that serial killers had an evolutionary explanation? What if there were a whole separate species of human out there, with DNA significantly divergent from *Homo sapiens,* who were interested only in ensuring their own survival? What if they had an entire civilization and structure hiding among us in everyday life? It was...fabulous, actually. The whole premise was endlessly fascinating—especially when you factor in an epic Romeo/Juliet love story between a trying-to-reform assassin for the other side and the lovely (human) doctor who accidentally discovers the new species' existence.

293

Unfortunately, TV viewers in general didn't agree, and *Prey* was yanked. Dead. Gone.

But in this post-internet world, it isn't that easy to get rid of fans...no, sir. We just won't go away, will we? Granted, TV studios in particular have developed resistance against fan campaigns—all the cute stuffed animals in the world deluging their offices won't move the cold, hard numbers—but in those relatively young and innocent days, well, we believed that anything was possible. Fans with a passion had the internet, a new method to keep connected and engaged and to conduct save-the-show campaigns, and it also helped distribute an old method of continuing a lost show: fanfic.

The *Prey* fandom was creatively prolific—which in some fandoms means "writing lots of really crappy stories." That's not what it meant among the Preymates. It meant writing really good stories, and lots of them. And participating in the process: editing, providing feedback and encouragement, and giving back—not just to others in the group, but to the world—with charity fund-raisers.

What's even more remarkable is that these fans still communicate, and—even though there are no official DVDs of the show's episodes—still write stories.

I should know, because I was one of those fic writers. And I still am.

A little background first. I had modest success as a professional author (writing as Roxanne Longstreet) from 1991 to about 1996, when suddenly I discovered that my sales weren't all that a publisher could ask for, and I was (very nicely) asked to seek other venues. No problem...I'd gotten married, and I was able to get two more books published, as Roxanne Conrad. But right around 1998, things got complicated, because those two additional books didn't do so well, and by 1999 I was coasting along with no publisher, no prospects, and no inspiration.

Enter *Prey*. Well, actually, enter *Buffy*, *Angel*, *The Pretender*, and a ton of other shows that became fun motivators for me, but my love affair with *Prey* was probably the most consistent and most productive of those lean three years. I didn't start to write fic about the show until it was off the air—mainly because the thirteenth-episode cliffhanger was maddening, and there was just...no more. So I wrote a story called "Bound," which essentially finished off the series. Just for my own satisfaction. And then, greatly daring, I posted it on my website, because...well. Because. And then I wrote a follow-up, "Extinction Event." And then I thought of another direction the cliffhanger could have gone, so I started an entirely second track of stories, starting with "Flashfire."

And I suddenly had *Prey* friends. They were great. They were creative, fun, energized, excited people...mostly adult women, mostly very good writers in their own right who brought considerable skills to the effort. We had a fantastic run of stories...individual stories, cowritten stories, round-robin stories. A virtual second season of the show. More stories. Novels. It just kept going and going, for years. The only thing I can liken it to is *Firefly* fandom, but unlike the Browncoats, the *Prey* fans never had the success of other, related shows to buoy and validate their good taste. Although *Prey*'s showrunners, producers, and writers were excellent, they didn't have Joss Whedon's unifying star power to galvanize their fans.

By 1999, I was ready to quit professional writing. Quit, completely and utterly. I was still doing the occasional short story (for kindly friends—looking at you, P. N. Elrod!) and essays (like the run of Smart Pop essays I did for BenBella Books, which also helped keep me engaged and excited about the whole idea of the power of words and imagination). During this time I wrote another novel, *Exile, Texas*, a straight mystery/thriller; but although it was published, it also sold in not-fantastic numbers.

But mostly? Mostly it was the fic that kept me writing, from the sheer joy of creating stories in a world that I loved to inhabit. I also loved the challenge of working in a world that had clearly defined rules and characters. Unlike most fanfic writers, I didn't want to write outside the lines; the highest compliment I could be offered was when readers confused one of my stories for an actual episode of the show (which luckily happened fairly often).

Prey is also one of the few fandoms I've ever been part of that didn't collapse under the weight of "crazy." There weren't angry words exchanged about preferring one romantic pairing over another; there weren't *I wish this character would die* rants and feuds. We all just...loved the show. It was peaceful, and positive, and fun. I wish more fandoms could exist that way.

So, *Prey* kept me working. It was my lifeboat. The feedback from my fellow *Prey* fanatics and fanfic writers kept me at the keyboard when it seemed like there was nothing for me there on the pro side...and motivated me through a total of ten short stories of considerable length, plus an entire 100,000-word novel.

In about 2001, fairly soon after I'd finished that *Prey* novel (*Chrysalis*, if you're interested), I had an idea for another novel I thought could be fun. Did it have anything to do with *Prey*? No. But *Prey* had fired my mind in creative new ways, and what came out of it was a book later called *Ill Wind*, which was published in 2003 by Penguin Books under my shiny new pseudonym of Rachel Caine. It was the beginning of the Weather Warden series.

Since 2003, I've published nine books in the Weather Warden series, four in the Outcast Season series, two in the Red Letter Days series, one for the Athena Force shared-world series, a whopping fifteen novels in the Morganville Vampires series, and dozens of short stories in anthologies. I've been published in nineteen different languages, and sold somewhere approaching 3 million copies of my books. I'm a *New York Times* and *USA Today* bestseller. I've been number one in the UK and Australia.

My point is that it never would have happened without the fic. Without *Prey* fanfic in particular, I'd have likely given up during those lean years. Without *Prey*, I never would have found such a supportive and enthusiastic group of friends and fans (who later helped me promote *Ill Wind*, by the way, as did my lovely friends in the *Stargate SG-1* community).

I owe you, *Prey* writers, showrunners, actors, and fans. I am grateful for the inspiration and the love and the friendship.

I'll occasionally hear other writers say that fanfic is bad, that there are no professionals out there who write/wrote fanfic who will own up to it, and to that I just simply say, bullshit. I know of four NYT bestselling authors who got their start in the fic world and freely admit it, and more who have dabbled in the fic pool while also working on their own stuff.

And there's just no reason to fear it or be ashamed of it. It's just writing. At its best, it's a hybrid of screenwriting and novel writing—the same structure you get in a shared world anthology, or when you cowrite with another author. It can also provide a safe space in which to experiment and try new things with your writing—things you might not be able to do in original fiction. It isn't bad, and it isn't bad for you. *Writing is writing.*

The important thing is to do your best, regardless of what you're writing.

Having said that, fanfic is obviously not meant for profit. It is derivative work, and it's important to understand and acknowledge that. Can you file the serial numbers off and achieve stunning success? Why, in the name of *Fifty Shades of Grey*, yes, you can. But I don't advise it. It's risky. Instead, take what you learn from fanfic to your original work.

What fanfic can do for you as a writer is to teach you about character development. It can teach you discipline and how to think in highly visual terms. And if you're diligent, it will help you with pacing and dialogue and all those other things that seem insurmountable in an original work when you begin. When you watch a story told in the visual medium, you instinctively learn "beats"—the building blocks of pacing. You train your ear to evaluate dialogue (and to tell good dialogue from bad). Then it's a matter of internalizing it and applying it to your characters and situations.

So how much did I love *Prey*? The final word count of what I wrote in *Prey* fanfiction: approximately 220,000 words. That's a lot of love. And you know what? If I had the time, I'd write more. Because it's an idea that deserved—and still deserves—all the exploration it can get.

But here's a stunning statistic for you, if you think fanfic held me back in any way: How much have I written in original fiction since then? Rough estimate: *5 million words*. And I'm writing at least half a million more, every year.

Anybody with me? Ready? Now write what inspires you.

Hey, it worked for me.

part four

FANWRITING TODAY

ALL THE FANFIC writing communities this book has discussed so far are still active. I've been talking about their activity during particular historical moments, but none has gone away. In putting together this book, I chose fandoms and moments I felt to be transformative but also representative of similar developments happening in other fandoms. Doing so meant sacrificing a more realistic account of simultaneous multiplicity for something closer to a coherent narrative.

That was kind of an anti-fic move, but it's the kind of move books still by and large need to make.

By contrast, this section possibly sacrifices the coherence of narrative for some simultaneous multiplicity. Or at least that's the plan.

By the time anyone reads this, the section would be best called Fanfiction Yesterday, or Fanfiction as It Was Several Months Ago—but that's not so catchy. One of the primary differences between the digital and analog paper worlds, however, is time, and it's a difference worth noticing. Fic communities can change and adapt and rewrite at a speed traditional publishing just can't match. There's a section of this book that deals with the relationship between publishing and fanfiction, though, and this isn't it. Here, the focus is on what fanfiction communities are talking about. The publishing-fanfiction relationship recently pushed fan writing into the public eye, but profit has never been the fic community's primary concern.

As of right now, there *is* no primary concern of the fic community—mostly because there is no unified fic community that could have a single primary concern. There are many communities, and they're only proliferating.

Fic has looked at communities that arise around books, movies, and television shows. Within these communities, we've seen other, smaller communities come together around certain sexual relationships between characters—or the desire to see no sexual relationship. Fan communities organize themselves in other ways, too. There are communities that coalesce around real-life identities (gender, sexual, ethnic) and geography. There are communities that arise around particular tastes and kinks. There are even communities that arise out of opposition to other communities.

In all of these, there are people young and old who find worlds and characters that spark their imaginations, and people want to join in the fun. There are people like a former teacher of mine who recently told me he'd posted his first fic. (Hercule Poirot fic! It's awesome!) There's a boy I know who writes imaginary soccer games. (Wait! Now he's also a publishing poet! He's fifteen!) There's *so* much more going on than could fit in a book, than ever *will* fit in any book. This is just a very, *very* small taste.

Francesca Coppa is a professor of English and film studies who has written extensively on fanfiction and fan video. She has also been active in fanfiction fandom since the zines and cons of the early 1980s and the early internet fandoms of the 1990s, and so has firsthand knowledge of the mutual distrust that can exist between media corporations and the creative fan communities their properties inspire. A founder of the Organization for Transformative Works, Francesca explains how concerns about content control and fan creator rights led to the establishment of this nonprofit, fan-run organization and its fanworks archive.

An Archive of Our Own
Fanfiction Writers Unite!

Francesca Coppa

> [W]e're still left with this problem: we are sitting quietly by the fireside, creating piles and piles of content around us, and other people are going to look at that and see an opportunity. And they are going to end up creating the front doors that new fanfic writers walk through, unless we stand up and build our OWN front door.

—Astolat, 2007

The way I remember it, being a fan on the internet in 2007 felt a little like waking up surrounded by hyenas. After the 2004 O'Reilly technology conference, lots of people started talking about "Web 2.0" and "social media" and "user-generated content," which sounded an awful lot like what fans just did naturally, except we called it "talking to each other" and "doing meta" and "making stuff." But overnight, the creative activity of fandom had become part of somebody's *business model*. Fans were quick to realize the threat and started organizing well over a year

302

before some wag on Bash.com memorably summarized the new, exploitative economics of Web 2.0 as "You make all the content. They keep all the revenue."

Social media? For fans, media was *always* social; it was something to be discussed, dissected, analyzed, and talked through. In fandom, culture was always read/write: fans are not passive consumers of media, whether textual, analog, or digital. Before the internet, fans organized literary pilgrimages, went to conventions, planned viewing parties, contributed analysis to letter pages, and wrote fanfiction—*lots* and *lots* of fanfiction—for zines. But fans have also always been early adopters of technology, and so have communicated with each other via every conceivable platform: Usenet, Internet Relay Chat, forums, BBS (bulletin board systems), mailing lists, web rings, blogs, archives, wikis, Twitter, Tumblr, you name it. The rise of Web 2.0–style social media software certainly made it easier to participate in fandom: now anyone could create a web page just by signing up on a network, whereas before this had required skill, as well as server space. On the other hand, fans were understandably wary of being exploited by internet entrepreneurs, many of whom seemed to want to capitalize on our productivity and vast creativity without having any particular understanding of, or sympathy with, fans or fan culture.

If Web 2.0 was about platforms in search of content—well, we fans had us some content! Fans are prolific authors and always have been, whether writing Sherlock Holmes pastiches 100 years ago or BBC *Sherlock* episode tags today. Moreover, fans had already built "social networking sites" for sharing "user-generated content"—only we called them "fanfiction archives." In the days before Web 2.0 made creating web pages easy, fans worked together to build communal sites, using people power to compensate for technological limitations. So for instance, most fanfiction archives of the early to mid-1990s were run by archive "elves": fans who would personally format and upload your story to the web. You would email your story to one of these elves, who would hand-code it into.txt or .html format, upload it to a website (that someone—typically another fan who was a professional sysadmin or technical person—was paying for), and create a link to it. Fan labor substituted for a technologically advanced web interface, and fan generosity substituted for a business model.

Despite the labor-intensive nature of the process, thousands upon thousands of fanfiction stories were archived on the web during the

1990s, on sites like Gossamer (*The X-Files*), the Due South Archive (*Due South*), and Seventh Heaven (*Highlander*). Once fans developed automated archiving software (*X-Files* fans wrote scripts to move stories directly from alt.tv.x-files.creative into the Gossamer archive; Naomi Novik's Automated Archive software was first deployed in 1998; Rebecca Smallwood developed "efiction" software in 2003), the number of archived fanfiction stories climbed into the hundreds of thousands. After the Harry Potter fandom exploded, the number of fanfiction stories online soared into the millions and then the tens of millions. FanFiction. Net, a site developed by programmer Xing Li while he was a student at UCLA, rapidly grew beyond anyone's wildest expectations.

You can see how this sort of productivity would attract attention. Web 2.0 entrepreneurs were eager to develop platforms and networks that would attract users (whom they saw as eyeballs for advertisers), and fanfiction sites attracted vast number of fans, both as readers and writers. So perhaps it was no surprise that people were registering domains like fandom.com and fans.com, forming companies like Fandom, Inc. and Fandom Entertainment LLC, but the trend was unnerving to long-term fans.

There were strangers in town, setting up shop.

The defining event was the debut of FanLib.com in 2007. Fanlib was a for-profit, multifandom fanfiction archive that billed itself as providing "the world's greatest fan fiction by popular demand." An employee of the company emailed many of the more visible fanfiction writers of the time, praising their stories and asking them to consider using the new site. When fans investigated, they didn't like what they saw. Fanlib's press release asserted that the "launch of FanLib.com represents the coming of age of fan fiction" (a claim that made longtime fans twitch) and that the site would give fans "a space to share what they've created" (fans had been making such spaces for themselves for years). Worse yet were the materials that the company provided to its investors and sponsors, which made clear that FanLib was not putting fans first; rather, the site would be "managed and moderated to the max" with fan activity taking place "in a customized environment that YOU"—the corporate sponsor—"control." These materials made clear that FanLib. com was "a great marketing idea!" that would "create remarkable value for business" by establishing "one-to-one customer relationships with a massive database" and "extensive sponsor integration opportunities," whatever those were.

FanLib wasn't trying to help fans create and share fanworks. It was *packaging* fans for corporations.

Companies like FanLib were threatening to us because they were highly visible and well funded. What was to stop FanLib from becoming the public face of fanfic-writing fandom to the outside world, or worse yet, to newbie fans? Would companies like FanLib stand up for fans if copyright holders (read: their real customers) issued unfair takedowns or cease-and-desist letters? Or what if worse came to worst and fanfiction writers got involved in an actual legal battle? Copyright holders—often referred to by fans as The Powers That Be—were by and large uninterested in fanfiction because there was no money involved, but FanLib.com was a for-profit venture. It was *designed* to make money. Would FanLib's desire to profit from fanfiction put fans at risk, and if so, would it defend them? Would it stand up and argue that fanfiction was fair use and a legitimate and valuable form of culture?

It was in this context that the blueprints were drawn for the Archive of Our Own (AO3). In the midst of the FanLib debacle, a number of fans (I was one of them) began to have a conversation on LiveJournal about not just resisting the commercialization of fan culture, but about creating a positive alternative: a large, visible, nonprofit fanfiction archive run by and for fans.

Longtime fan Astolat declared in a post on May 17, 2007, "We need a central archive of our own...Something that would NOT hide from [G]oogle or any public mention, and would clearly state our case for the legality of our hobby up front." She further elaborated:

I think the necessary features would include:

- run BY fanfic readers FOR fanfic readers
- with no ads and solely donation-supported
- with a simple and highly searchable interface and browsable quick-search pages
- allowing ANYTHING—het, slash, RPF, chan, kink, highly adult—with a registration process for reading adult-rated stories where once you register, you don't have to keep clicking through warnings every time you want to read
- allowing the poster to control her stories (ie, upload, delete, edit, tagging)

- allowing users to leave comments with the poster able to delete and ban particular users/IPs but not edit comment content (ie, lj [LiveJournal] style)
- code-wise able to support a huge archive of possibly millions of stories
- giving explicit credit to the original creators while clearly disclaiming any official status

The idea caught fire. Hundreds of fans commented on Astolat's post, brainstorming and offering to help. It became clear almost immediately that an archive on the scale we were imagining (not just for multifandom fanfiction, but designed to eventually host fanart and video) could not be run by elves on a donated server. We would have to found a nonprofit corporation, both to raise funds and to have a legal entity that was capable of doing business and signing contracts.

Thus was born the idea of the Organization for Transformative Works (OTW), an all-volunteer nonprofit dedicated to providing access to and preserving the history of fanworks and fan culture. The name was chosen to signal our stance on the legitimacy and legality of fanworks, broadly conceived. People who thought that fanworks like fanfiction infringed on copyright had argued that fanworks were *derivative* works, and therefore under the control of the author or rightsholder. But it's the OTW's position that fanfiction is *transformative*—an important legal distinction—and therefore not only legitimate but also legally protected by fair use, at least in the United States. Transformative works say new things, often in ways that wouldn't be acceptable or desirable in the marketplace (which is sadly unlikely to publish your epic Harry/Draco slashfic, at least at the moment). Much as literary criticism does, fanfiction analyzes characters (as with the queer reading of Harry and Draco in your epic slashfic) and constructs explanations of fictional universes. Fanfiction is one of the ways that fans share their ideas about and interpretations of a story. While some fans might write an essay to explain, say, how wand magic works, or how indispensable Hermione Granger is to the war against the Dark Lord, others might write a fanfiction story to *show* how wand magic works or how awesome Hermione is. Fanfiction, like fanart, vids, and other fanworks, is a form of creative conversation.

The OTW immediately began to work on creating the Archive of Our Own. That name was chosen carefully, too, as an allusion to Virginia Woolf's famous essay, "A Room of One's Own" in which she notes that "a woman must have money and a room of her own if she is to write fiction." The "Archive of Our Own" therefore evokes the importance of owning space—albeit virtual space today, *server space*—for women writers in particular, and also serves as a reminder that fanfiction was (and still is) written overwhelmingly by women.

The OTW worked fast; by June 2007 a board of directors had been assembled. I was one of them, as were longtime fans like fantasy author Naomi Novik and Georgetown law professor and intellectual property specialist Rebecca Tushnet. Committees were being formed to work on various projects, not only the AO3, but also a legal assistance and advocacy team, an academic journal devoted to fan culture (*Transformative Works and Cultures*), and a fan culture wiki (Fanlore). The OTW also needed people to organize membership drives, recruit volunteers, develop policies, and manage our finances. We got all that help and more: FanLib might have had $3 million, but fandom has a strong network of people with all sorts of skills. Fandom is positively *overflowing* with talent: we have lawyers, accountants, public relations people, development officers, coders, sysadmins, webmasters, professors, librarians, HR and management specialists, and writers—*lots and lots* of writers. All these and more joined the OTW in its early days; now, six years on, the OTW has more than 400 active volunteers and volunteer-staff running eighteen committees and seven workgroups.

The Archive of Our Own, the dream of fanfiction writers yearning to stay free, has as of this writing over 172,000 registered members, while others are still waiting for an invitation. (Because the site is still in beta, with its software still under development and features continually being added, the AO3 is currently controlling its growth by means of an invite system so that it doesn't get overwhelmed.) These registered members, however, are only a fraction of the number of people who actually use the site. While you need to have an AO3 account to post fanfiction to the archive (or to embed art or vids; the site will eventually expand to hosting other kinds of fanworks), you don't need one to read fanfiction or to comment on it, as millions of fans already have: in November 2012, the AO3 had visits from 2.3 million unique IP addresses. And the Archive of Our Own, like all the OTW's other projects, is free for anyone to use: like National Public Radio or PBS, we are member supported (please donate!).

So that is the story of how a few fans (a few hundred, a few thousand, a few hundred thousand, and someday millions!) came together to resist being commodified by the culture of Web 2.0. Even as I write this, Amazon has debuted a program called Kindle Worlds: yet another attempt to commercialize fanfiction that shows no particular understanding of fans or fan culture. But I'm not worried: we've been here before. The story of the OTW and the AO3 is the history of a community, and of the triumph of fannish organization over the power of venture capital. It is also an argument in favor of fanfiction as an important grassroots cultural activity, because it's probably no accident that so many of the OTW's founders were fanfiction writers. It may be that writing fanfiction gave us the courage to tell our own, nonmainstream version of the story and to write our own happy ending. Or as the OTW's first annual report put it:

- What if the hundreds of thousands of fan-created stories, videos and images were celebrated, instead of half-hidden?
- What if fans had access to an online archive that wouldn't back down at the merest hint of a lawsuit or change policies at the whim of an advertiser?
- What if there were no advertisers?
- What if, instead of letting false assumptions about copyright go unchallenged, there was a group that spoke up for the legality of transformative works?
- And what if, instead of letting four decades of cultural history be rewritten, fannish creators and consumers celebrated their past and shared it with the wider community?

Fanfiction writers, more than most people, know how to tell a story that begins, "What if...?"

Jules Wilkinson is an epic fangirl, best known for running the Supernatural *Wiki, which documents both the show's canon and fandom. She writes fanfic and has also contributed to several books about* Supernatural *and its fans. In this essay, Jules discusses how* Supernatural's *relationship to its highly active fandom is a testament to the ways that boundaries between creators and fans—and between canon and fanon—are increasingly porous, up-ending the traditional relationship between a TV show and its viewers.*

The Epic Love Story of *Supernatural* and Fanfic

Jules Wilkinson (missyjack)

The first rule of fandom is: You do not talk about fanfic.

The second rule of fandom—or of *Supernatural* fandom, at least—is that fandom has no rules.

Supernatural first aired on September 13, 2005, and was a show made for fanfic. It had two attractive leads, drawn into an intense codependent relationship in the confines of a '67 Impala, spiced up with childhood trauma and liberally sprinkled with daddy issues. Toss in a rich mythology that drew on everything from urban legends to religion, and fandom needed no encouragement to hop on board.

What we had no inkling of at the time was that this show we loved and wrote about with such passion would see what we were doing and love us right back.

It is a truth universally acknowledged that whenever there are two hot men in a TV show they must be slashed, and such was the case with *Supernatural*. There was one little kink, so to speak, in the arrangement this time: the two main characters—Sam and Dean Winchester—were brothers.

The *Supernatural* fandom wasn't going to let a little thing like incest get in the way of our creative (and other) urges, and in fact the first fanfic appeared online for the fandom was a slash story featuring Sam and Dean, posted the day after the pilot episode aired.[109] In true fandom form, the pairing had a mashup name—Wincest—within a few weeks.

Fanfic in any fandom is strongly shaped not only by the subject matter on which it's based, but also by its more popular writers and those who run fanfic communities in the fandom's early life. While some *Supernatural* fan websites made it clear from the start that slash featuring the brothers was unwelcome, on LiveJournal—the early creative heart of *Supernatural* fandom—the popular writers wrote across a variety of genres, including slash, Gen, and *even* stories featuring heterosexual pairings.

Slash fiction written during the first three seasons of *Supernatural* was almost exclusively stories featuring the brothers Sam and Dean. Of course some fans were not comfortable writing or reading stories that centered on an incestuous relationship, and so they turned to Real Person Slash, or RPS.

Ironically, at that time RPS, which features characters based on the actors, was considered rather ethically dubious by many fans, which led to the coining of the sarcastic phrase "*Supernatural*—where RPF is the moral high ground."

RPS grew to be a large part of the fandom's fic for this reason, as well as the fact that there was already a well-established fandom around fanfic based on actors from The WB Network (and later The CW Network), particularly *Buffy* and *Angel*, and later *Smallville*, on which Jensen Ackles, the actor playing Dean in *Supernatural*, had also appeared.

Other fans were happy to explore Sam and Dean's relationship without sex, in Gen fic. *Supernatural* fandom has a high proportion of Gen fic—it has been consistently around 20 to 25 percent of stories posted on LiveJournal.[110] It is notable that Gen fic and slash in *Supernatural* fandom often share the same focus on the intense emotional relationship between the main characters, which is of course at the core of the show. Back in 2007, *Supernatural* scriptwriter and later showrunner Sera Gamble jokingly called the show "The Epic Love Story of Sam and Dean." In fact, aside from the sex, Gen and Wincest fics can be almost indistinguishable, leading to the coining of the terms "Gencest" and also "hard Gen."

It's difficult to estimate how many tens of thousands of *Supernatural* fanfic stories have been written. There are over 80,000 *Supernatural* stories on FanFiction.Net,[111] and over 43,000 on the Archive of Our Own.[112] The number of stories posted on LiveJournal is impossible to estimate, but a project that catalogued all the stories posted on the "*Supernatural*

Newsletter" on LiveJournal between October 2006 and March 2010 found links to nearly 40,000 fics.[113]

Supernatural fandom has been hugely productive and creative in its writing and other fanworks over the more than eight years of the show, from niche communities featuring stories around a single minor character such as angel Anna Milton,[114] or stories where one of the Winchester men is pregnant,[115] through to multigenre communities and challenges. You would be hard pressed to find a topic or genre or sexual kink not covered by our writing, and when we run out of established tropes we invent our own. *Supernatural* fandom is credited, for example, with popularizing "knotting" fanfics, in which people take on the social and sexual characteristics of dogs.[116]

Nothing sums up the collaborative and communal nature of fanfiction better than the SPN J2 Big Bang challenge.[117] This challenge has become a much-anticipated annual fandom event, pairing artists with writers and involving many other fans as sounding boards, betas, and of course readers. From 2007 to 2012, it has seen over 1,000 stories, each averaging 40,000 words in length, with accompanying artwork produced. That's over 40 million words written in one challenge in one fandom. There are now fifteen other *Supernatural*-centric Big Bang challenges in existence, each focusing on specific characters or genres.[118]

Two events that had a huge impact on fandom and fanfic occurred during *Supernatural*'s fourth season. As the season started in September 2008, we saw the arrival of the character Castiel the angel, who was embraced by fandom. Fans adored his "profound bond" with Dean, and the pairing (known in true mashup form as "Destiel") become hugely popular; it now outranks Wincest as the most popular slash pairing.

The other significant event in season four was that slash fanfic became canon.

Back in 2005, the prohibition against sharing fanworks with those involved in the show was much stronger than it is today—especially when said works involved incestuous gay porn. Despite this, and despite fandom's first rule, fanfic has never been a secret from the people involved in making *Supernatural*. In May 2007 in England, at the first convention where Jensen Ackles appeared, he was asked whether he knew about fanfiction. He had:

> One of my favorites is, uh, Wincest...I only hope that my grandmother
> never reads those. Jared [Padalecki, who plays Sam] and I had a good

laugh about that one. It was only brought to our attention because [*Super-natural* producer] Kim Manners posted it.

Fans have raised the topic of fanfiction at nearly every *Super-natural* convention. When asked about what he thought of Wincest at the EyeCon convention in Florida in April 2008, Jared Padalecki managed to validate transformative works while avoiding the tricky incest issue:

> With fanfiction and RPGs,...everyone's taking a part in *Supernatural* and they're not just watching it...and they're really passionate about the show, and especially the fans of *Supernatural*. It's a great learning tool, and exploring tool, to explore this world. So I'm supportive.

Jim Beaver (who plays Bobby Singer) was the first actor to tease fans with his knowledge of fan culture when he wore a T-shirt proclaiming "I read John/Bobby" (referring to slash fanfic featuring his character and Sam and Dean's father) to the 2008 EyeCon. He even once sent a complimentary email to the author of a fanfic piece that created a backstory for Bobby (note: it didn't contain any Bobby/John slash).

Misha Collins in particular has shown a great curiosity and willingness to talk about fanfic, which still discomforts some fans, as Misha noted in an interview in 2009:

> You can sense the whole audience tensing up, like they don't want you to talk about this slash fiction weird pervy stuff that they get into. So I do like to bring it up for that reason.[119]

Even the media asks Misha about fanfic. In a 2012 interview by Huffington Post TV critic Maureen Ryan, she commented that his character Castiel and Dean Winchester were "a continual source of speculation, fanfiction, pornography..." In response Misha said: "Yep. I'm just always gratified that I'm in some small way contributing to any kind of pornography. It warms the cockles of my heart. Words chosen carefully."[120]

From the beginning, our fanfic was clearly no secret, and yet that still didn't prepare us for the aptly named season four episode, "The Monster at the End of This Book." In this episode, Sam and Dean discover a series of novels called *Supernatural* by author Chuck Shurley, which appear to be based on the Winchesters' lives. The episode also introduces Sam and

Dean to fandom, and fandom into the canon of the show, when the brothers discover a message board about the books:

> DEAN: There's Sam girls and Dean girls and…What's a slash fan?
> SAM: As in "Sam slash Dean," together.
> DEAN: Like together, together? They do know we're brothers, right?
> SAM: Doesn't seem to matter.
> DEAN: Well, that's just sick!

Some of us were delighted to be included in the meta commentary alongside the show's own writers. Other fans were uncomfortable about the (literal) airing of what they saw as "fandom business." Some fans saw it as the writers' support of Wincest, others as their condemnation.

In "Sympathy for the Devil," season five's premiere episode, written by Eric Kripke, we were introduced to ourselves, in the form of fangirl Becky Rosen. An avid fan of the *Supernatural* books, Becky runs a website called morethanbrothers.net. We first meet her as she works on her latest fanfic, which reads in part:

> The brothers huddled together in the dark as the sound of the rain drumming on the roof eased their fears of pursuit. Despite the cold outside and the demons who, even now, must be approaching, the warmth of their embrace comforted them.
>
> And then Sam caressed Dean's clavicle.
>
> "This is wrong," said Dean.
>
> "Then I don't want to be right," replied Sam, in a husky voice.

Thus the creator of the show that inspired Wincest wrote Wincest. Of course, Kripke left this "fanfiction" unfinished, but on September 13, 2009, only three days after the episode's airing, a LiveJournal member using Becky's online handle—Samlicker81—posted a completed version of the story called "Burning Desires" to a Wincest fanfic community.[121] This is so postmodern it almost hurts.

"Sympathy for the Devil" was actually not the first time Kripke had written fanfic. In November 2008, the last issue of "Rising Son," the second series of *Supernatural* comics, included a six-page standalone story called "The Beast with Two Backs," written by Eric Kripke and producer Peter Johnston.

The beast of the title is revealed to be a chimera of Jared Padalecki and Jensen Ackles, a beautiful two-headed creature who kills fangirls because it cannot bear to let anyone prettier than itself live. The title is a reference to the phrase "to make the beast with two backs," which is a slang term for having sex, most famously used in Shakespeare's *Othello* and James Joyce's *Ulysses*. Kripke, it seems, ships his stars—or at least is well aware that we do.

The integration of fandom and the stories we make into the text of *Supernatural* fits with a show that has always been interested in the role of storytelling in the world. On an individual level it has looked at the stories we use to construct our own identities, and it has explored modern morality tales (in the form of urban legends) and ancient ones (from folklore), and the epic stories of society—the ones we call religion.

The storytelling of pop culture has been examined in episodes featuring movies ("Hollywood Babylon"), TV ("Changing Channels"), and celebrity culture ("Fallen Idols" and "Season Seven, Time for a Wedding"). "The French Mistake" is a notable episode in that it portrays the making of a TV show called *Supernatural,* and many of the behind-the-scenes crew and the actors are portrayed as parody versions of themselves.

The episode "The Monster at the End of the Book" uses the meta-fictional device of the Winchester novels to comment on the process of writing in general and on *Supernatural* and its writers in particular. The character of author Chuck Shurley stands in for show creator Eric Kripke and is used to explore the role of the author.[122] By the end of season five, the viewer is left with the impression that the author may, in Chuck's case literally, be God.

In season eight, an angel called Metratron is revealed as Heaven's scribe. He is an ardent collector of stories and can be seen to represent both the show's and fandom's writers when he says, "When you create stories, you become gods, of tiny, intricate dimensions unto themselves." Notably, he is later revealed to be a twisted, vengeful character.

Geek and fan culture in particular have been represented by a number of *Supernatural* characters and in episodes such as "The Real Ghostbusters," "The Girl with the Dungeon and Dragon Tattoo," and "LARP and the Real Girl." In addition to fanfic-writing fangirl Becky, other fannish characters include roleplaying fanboys Demian and Barnes and lesbian fangirl hacker Charlie Bradbury.

The show itself has always been overtly fannish. Dean Winchester was established from the beginning as a fan of horror and sci-fi movies and classic rock, and we find out he has a big fanboy crush on the eponymous star of a TV drama called *Dr. Sexy, M.D.* Sam Winchester was revealed to be a Harry Potter fan, and even crusty old Bobby Singer revealed himself as a fan of *Deep Space Nine* (a shout-out to actor Jim Beaver's late wife, who appeared in the series). It is left to the angel Castiel to represent the nonfan, as he comments more than once, "I do not understand that reference."

The show has also deployed a number of tropes popular in fanfiction, many of which had been explored in *Supernatural* fanfiction long before they appeared on the show. Acafan Henry Jenkins, upon viewing the show back in season one, also noticed its fanfic similarity, calling it "one long hurt/comfort story."[123] General fanfic tropes that have appeared include alternate universes, time travel, time loops, body swaps, evil doppelgängers, and post-apocalypse scenarios. Some have been specific to the *Supernatural*-verse—fandom was exploring the possibility of evil Sam and vampire Dean long before the show did. Fandom even has a term for when a fanfic story is validated or replicated in canon—"Kripked."

TV writing, of all artistic pursuits, can be seen as most analogous to fanfic. From script to screen it's a collaborative effort, in which writers, artists, crew, and actors work within a shared universe to produce a story each week. Perhaps those involved in making TV are best able to understand what we do, because it is a version of what they do themselves. It came as no surprise to fans when *Supernatural* writers Robbie Thompson and Adam Glass joined Twitter and immediately started to encourage fans to write fanfic about *them*, even inventing the mashup pairing name Robdam for themselves.[124]

While *Supernatural* is not the first show to mention fanfiction, it is certainly the first to specifically reference its own fandom and have incestuous gay fanfic discussed by the characters about whom it is written. It is a sign of a broader, changed relationship that goes beyond breaking the fourth wall, to an open acknowledgment of the epic love affair between fans and creators.

Coeditor of the groundbreaking volume Fan Fiction and Fan Communities in the Age of the Internet, *Kristina Busse is an important voice in the
field of fan studies. Her work has appeared in numerous journals, and she
coedits the fan studies journal* Transformative Works and Cultures. *Her
essay here considers one legacy of the* Star Trek *slash fandom, showing
how some of its edgier tropes now boldly go where, well, no one ever even
thought of going before—and then maybe go a little bit further. Much of
this book has focused on the development of fic communities within specific fandoms, but this essay illustrates how in internet fandom, tropes and
storylines can cross-pollinate faster than sex spores, generating multifandom universes. Even more than your average pop song mashup, these
multiverses remix species and cross biological boundaries—and they're
very popular.*

Pon Farr, Mpreg, Bonds, and the Rise of the Omegaverse

Kristina Busse

When I started reading fanfiction nearly fifteen years ago, I was immediately fascinated by the huge amounts of sex and, more interestingly,
the huge amounts of kinky sex. Every sex act I'd ever imagined—and
some I hadn't—were easily accessible and, even better, labeled. Thanks
to headers and the then still-rudimentary search engines on fandom-
specific archives, I could search and read all the stories of a particular
scenario, whether it was driven by sex, plot, or character. Angel turning
human and getting back together with Buffy in all its hundreds of variations; Mulder as Krycek's hostage, and vice versa; Kirk, Spock, and Bones
threesomes—it was there for me to search and read. "Infinite diversity in
infinite combinations" might be the central Vulcan philosophical statement, but it is also the motto of media fans.

Your Kink Is OK; It's Just Not My Kink

One of the things I like best about fanfiction is that there is a clear sense of writing to specific kinks. Ellen Fremedon describes this as the Id Vortex: "In fandom, we've all got this agreement to just suspend shame...We all know right where the Id Vortex is, and we have this agreement to approach it with caution, but without any shame at all." Branding and bestiality, water sports and mind control, tentacles and voyeurism, but also domesticity and telepathy, amnesia and hurt/comfort, slavery and time travel—all of these are tropes that may get us to read a story; they may even turn us on and get us off.

Favorite tropes, of course, are different for everyone. But fandom is big enough that we can find someone who wants to read what we write and, if we're really lucky, who writes what we want to read. More than that, fanfic gives us that specific story many times over with exactly the characters and the scenarios we want to see. Heck, if we participate in a challenge or have good friends, they might write one to our detailed specifications! Also, fandom as a community is open-minded enough that most fans tend to accept tropes that don't appeal to them personally as Just Not My Kink, rather than as bad or wrong.

Alpha Males and the Fannish Hive Mind

But even with the seeming loss of taboos and a general acceptance of all kinks, there are still some kinks that tend to be considered a bit kinkier than others. One particularly trendy trope at the moment is Alpha/Beta/Omega (A/B/O) stories, which are popular across various fandoms, including *Supernatural, Sherlock*, and *Teen Wolf*. Many A/B/O stories posit societies where biological imperatives divide people based on wolf pack hierarchies into sexual dominants (alphas), sexual submissives (omegas), and everyone else (betas). Beyond the biologically determined hierarchy, these wolf-like humans often have other wolf-like traits: they may scent their partners or imprint on first sight, and often mate for life. Sometimes the alphas and omegas are rare, sometimes they are only males, sometimes they have altered sex organs. Often omegas go into heat and release pheromones that drive alphas wild.

Animal terminology, such as *heat, mating cycles, claiming, mounting, breeding,* and the ever-popular *knot* (a swelling at the base of the penis found in canines after ejaculation that forces the penis to stay inside to ensure impregnation), tends to be popular in A/B/O stories. While fandom has always had its share of animal transformations and bestiality kinks, A/B/O stories also seem to draw from other tropes, including mating and heat cycles, breeding, and male pregnancy (mpreg), as well as imprinting and soul bonds. In fact, it is difficult to make any generalization about the collections of tropes shorthanded as A/B/O or "omegaverse" (while the two terms can be used interchangeably, the latter tends to be reserved for ideological world building rather than the simple sexual dynamics). Rather than attempting to define A/B/O and its multiple fandom-specific subvariants, I want to explore where the trope came from and how it has evolved, using that discussion to illustrate how tropes cross-pollinate, change, and mutate in and across fandoms.

Pon Farr as Ur-Trope

The biological imperative of mating cycles appears in Star Trek canon and subsequently has been embraced across many fandoms. The original *Star Trek* is viewed by many as the first modern media fandom: in the late sixties, fans started to meet up at fan cons and began writing, editing, mimeographing, and mailing the first fanzines. Fans who have never heard of the episode "Amok Time," in which Spock goes into pon farr, may know the term *pon farr.* And even if they haven't, they probably will have read stories where a character's biology forces him to have sex—sometimes with their partner, other times with anyone willing and able.

In *Star Trek*, pon farr describes the Vulcan mating cycle, during which Vulcans must have sex or suffer excruciating pain, insanity, and potential death. But fans are nothing if not creative! This particular moment in the original *Star Trek* series became the basis of a host of pon farr stories where Spock is slowly going insane—and Kirk is his only option. The same scenario also moved into other fandoms where there is no canonical support for pon farr: the justification can be magical, supernatural, or alien, but even in realistic cop shows like *CSI* or *Bones*, we still find myriad versions of this fuck-or-die scenario.

The Animal in All of Us

Animals and animal transformations feature in a lot of fanfiction. A lot of media that inspires fanfiction include animal transformation as canon: *Buffy the Vampire Slayer*, Harry Potter, Twilight, and *Teen Wolf*, for example, all feature werewolves. Other fandoms often create shapeshifter alternate universes to explore ideas of identity and transformation, of monstrosity and otherness. While bestiality seems not to be that prevalent in fandom, it does exist—whether as a subset of shapeshifter-verses or otherwise. In fact, Harry Potter popularized bestiality kinks, often pairing human characters sexually with Remus in his werewolf form or Sirius in his Padfoot dog form. But it was the *Supernatural* RPF fandom, J2 (named for the first names of show leads Jared Padalecki and Jensen Ackles) and its kink memes that large-scale introduced bestiality into non-magical fandoms.

It thus may not be coincidental that *Supernatural* and J2 fandom more than likely originated A/B/O. In her primer, fan writer Nora Bombay describes A/B/O as "something that appears to have been spontaneously created when J2 mpreg and J2 werewolves combined, had a soul bond, and created an idea that was perfect to spread out across all fandom." Nor may it be coincidental that Jensen Ackles' first fannish show, *Dark Angel*, featured him as a genetically engineered soldier with feline DNA. While *Dark Angel* only features heat cycles in female characters, fandom—especially slash fandom—of course responded with males in heat as well.

In fact, the focus on fertility and mating cycles in many fanfictions with male protagonists is certainly interesting when considering that a large majority of the slashers, and thus the writers who use this trope, are women. Whether it is a way to engage issues of enforced sex or to think through biology-based societal constraints, in many of these stories, the male characters in heat are forced to play out traditional female roles, victims of biology. In fact, when putting the man into the position of needing to be fucked, fan writers often alter male biology to include self-lubing asses.

Ass Babies and Boy Baby Bumps

As if the desperate need to be fucked were not enough, the ultimate purpose of heat is, of course, impregnation. Male pregnancy (mpreg) is a popular trope across fandoms, sometimes explained within the logic of the source show's universe through magic or science, but more often just occurring spontaneously. Whether Alex Krycek switches genders, Severus Snape creates a pregnancy-inducing potion, John Sheppard activates an ancient artifact, or Brian Kinney wakes up one morning pregnant for no reason whatsoever, a corner of fandom relishes impregnating its male heroes. And while Kirk and Spock's love child only ever existed in fanfiction, the 2001 prequel series, *Star Trek: Enterprise*, did give us canonical mpreg when engineer Trip Tucker became pregnant during an encounter with a female alien.

Mpregs come in all shapes and sizes and, as a result, can fulfill a vast variety of fan desires: a romantic need to create a love child between male lovers, an interest in pregnancy's emotional and physical fallout on a partnership, or even a fascination with the horrors of forced breeding. Even more than the heat trope, mpreg allows a female writer to play out themes of female bodies, concerns of gender in relationships, and issues of reproduction. And she can interrogate all these ideas in a setting that allows for a certain emotional distance by divorcing the pregnancy from the female body. At the same time, one of the criticisms of mpreg is that it often replicates rather than critiques the portrayal of women by embracing stereotypical gender roles.

Wolves Mate for Life

In fact, given how many mpreg stories feature unexpected, if not initially unwanted, births, the amount that depict happy families in which the child cements their love and lifelong bond is staggering. Then again, fandom generally seems to prefer happy over unhappy and soul mates over one-night stands. So while the fannish desire for intense bonds may not have any canon basis, source texts that celebrate bonding certainly don't hurt.

A/B/O may have transcended its name-giving wolf source, but the role of imprinting, mating, and bonding remains powerful. *Twilight*, for example, features not only intense bonds but gives us canonical imprinting when Jacob first meets Bella's baby. The imprinting trope effectively offers a biological determinism that mandates that the pair belong together. In fanfiction, where we write thousands of scenarios to get our beloved pair together, through space and time and alternate universes, imprinting is a satisfying and effective conceit.

My Mind to Your Mind

Meanwhile, in Star Trek, the Vulcan mind meld, which guarantees "my mind to your mind," has generated a wealth of stories about deep and permanent mind bonds. Given that a lot of fanfiction and particularly slash is about strong emotional bonds and eternal ties—about the love between partners—the predominance of bonding fic isn't a surprise. A marriage vow may only be as good as the participants who utter it, but a bond is forever.

Mind and soul bonds are simply the most extreme form of a trope that habitually collapses the physical and the emotional. It presents readers with a couple whose love is not only unlimited and forever but trustworthy: both partners can be sure of it, since they can feel the other's every thought and emotion. This trope then uses bodies, uses physicality, uses sex to signify emotional intimacy. Partners in these fics read each other's bodies, read thoughts from each other's eyes, know each other's state of mind from their posture, can sense their loved ones by sound or smell. Often their biology allows them—nay, forces them—to seek out the other person and know them in all their parts. All of these things may indeed be horrifying in reality, but if their popularity is anything to go by, as fictional metaphors they have immense emotional appeal.

Omegaverse: The Perfect Storm

This brings us back to A/B/O, where all of these tropes come together in a seemingly perfect storm, often with a heavy helping of raunchy sex: huge, knotted dicks; an enormous amount of fertile alpha semen; and wet, open omega assholes. Still, just as important as the kinky aspects of the omegaverse are the emotional ones: the forcefulness of heat cycles and impulsive desire, the inevitability of imprinting and bonds, the joys and horrors of mpreg.

In the end, then, there can't be only one explanation for why fans enjoy Alpha/Beta/Omega fic, or even one description that encompasses all the stories. Some stories play with the primacy of the senses and the ability to smell one's mate. Some stories engage in dub-con scenarios where one or both partners are out of their minds with heat lust and lose all reasoning and inhibitions. Some stories create near-slave cultures where biology determines all aspects of society and sexuality is the central force of domination. Some stories play with the world building, while others just want the filthy, kinky sex; many do both.

And then there are those stories that play with the tropes only to subvert them: Tony Stark all but loses his company because investors don't trust alphas; Erik and Charles have an illicit alpha/alpha relationship; Sherlock hides his real scent with various chemical pheromones because he doesn't want to be prey to biological prejudices; Mike hides his omega status by remaining close to Harvey. All these stories use A/B/O tropes to interrogate gender and sexuality as well as sexual orientation and cultural assumptions. And when successful, these stories are not only hot and allow our beloved sex objects to get and stay together in bonded bliss but they also interrogate some of the issues and prejudices of our day.

V. Arrow is a fan studies scholar and writer of fanfiction. She is the author of Smart Pop's Panem Companion *and has published nonfiction in a variety of venues. She writes fic in the realms of YA literature and "real person" musicians—including One Direction, her topic here.*

As Arrow explains, Real Person Fic—RPF—is today the subject of much controversy and disdain in the broader fic community, a subculture considered beyond the pale even by writers who have few boundaries regarding what they're willing to read versions of fictional characters get up to. There's a general sense that RPF is a contemporary decadence of some kind—but it's hardly new to fic. J. M. Barrie's parody for his friend and collaborator Arthur Conan Doyle featured both these "real life" authors interacting with Doyle's characters Holmes and Watson, and the 1950s zine-published Fables of the Irish Fandom *stories were RPF by fans about fans. In V.'s essay, we explore the world of band- or musician-fic from the point of view of RPF fan writers today.*

Real Person(a) Fiction

V. Arrow (aimmyarrowshigh)

Real Person Fic, or RPF, is a world in some ways completely apart from the rest of fanfiction subculture. While all of fanfiction suffers from a stigma in the mainstream, RPF is something even other fanfiction writers often mock and deride as "creepy" and often "juvenile."

Why? RPF, as its name suggests, is fanfiction written about "real people"—celebrities. Written, almost solely, about—well, cute boys. And nothing but cute boys, essentially—despite the pervasive idea among other fans that RPF readers and writers want to imagine themselves with their favorite stars, RPF thrives on fans imagining their favorite cute boys with other cute boys.

Almost all RPF is slash, with the notable exceptions of Robert Pattinson/Kristen Stewart (which generated an enormous boom of material from 2008–2010 but has largely, or maybe completely, fallen off now) and David Henrie/Selena Gomez from the Disney Channel show *Wizards of*

Waverly Place. While some RPF has become an ingrained, central part of media-based fic fandoms, notably J2 RPF (Jared Padalecki/Jensen Ackles) in *Supernatural's* fandom or Andrew Garfield/Jesse Eisenberg spinoffs in *The Social Network* fandom, it is generally seen as an entity entirely its own, with little writer or reader crossover between it and the fanfiction about the media canon on which its cast works. And rightfully so: it is its own entity. There is a large contingent that writes Chris Pine/Zachary Quinto completely separate from their basal pairing of Kirk/Spock; the pairing of Robert Downey Jr./Jude Law, which originated in their roles as Sherlock Holmes and John Watson, is written as distinct from their roles as the great detective and his assistant—despite "Johnlock" being a hugely popular slash ship unto itself, no matter the adaptation.

However, most RPF actually revolves around pairings in fandoms that have no ties to fiction. There is fanfiction for actors, there is fanfiction for politicians, and there is fanfiction for historical figures, but the majority of RPF is for musicians. Virtually every mainstream band of the last fifty years that includes at least two men has had a slash RPF fandom, from John Frusciante/Anthony Kiedis of the Red Hot Chili Peppers to Brendon Urie/Ryan Ross of Panic! at the Disco; Nick Jonas/Joe Jonas of the Jonas Brothers (yes, even that line is not sacred in the world of fanfiction— very angsty) to, most notably and *hugely* right now, the members of One Direction with . . . *every* other member of One Direction.

One Direction, of course, is a boy band: a prefabricated harmonic vocal group designed to align with certain archetypes rather than to produce music; fortunately, One Direction does both well. Formed in 2010 (after appearing on the British TV talent competition *The X Factor*) as a business venture of notorious music mogul Simon Cowell, One Direction is made up of five boys, born between 1991 and 1994, from different parts of the UK and Ireland. They align, as all boy bands do, very neatly into their distinct, publicity-driven personae, something that lends itself incredibly well to both writing fanfiction and, its intended purpose, courting the admiration of fans. Niall Horan, the Chill One; Zayn Malik, the Sensitive One; Liam Payne, the Mature One; Louis Tomlinson, the Funny One; and Harry Styles, the Cute One. They've been received with broad critical acclaim and financial success; One Direction was among Barbara Walters' "Most Fascinating People of 2012," won a coveted BRIT Award (the British equivalent to a Grammy) for "BRITs Global Success" in 2013, snagged two VMAs, performed at the 2012 Olympics closing ceremony, and are a favorite of the Obama girls.

Despite this acclaim, One Direction suffers the same pitfalls as most boy bands in terms of "respectability." RPF, as noted, carries a stigma within the larger fanfiction community. But even within RPF, there is a hierarchy of respectability, and One Direction, along with other boy bands—due to the poppy style of their music, their prefab start, and the perception of their audience as teenage girls—is at the bottom. Compared to the muddy festival circuit and close-knit inter-band connections of "bandom," and the pop-punk royalty of the Fueled by Ramen and Decaydance labels, One Direction and its fans are seen as immature, and their fic as underdeveloped fantasy. As music writer Natalie Zina Walschots pointed out in the *Toronto Standard*, "If men approve of an album, if they think it's...sophisticated enough, then that opinion has value and weight...On the other hand, [the] love of female teen fans is seen as something reductive and dangerous."[125]

The way an RPF fandom is viewed is frequently connected to the way its source material is seen by the rest of the world—in other words, whether or not it is based on people seen as legitimate "artists," or at least connected to a legitimate narrative. *The Social Network* (*TSN*) RPF is an excellent example. *The Social Network*, of course, is RPF itself, about Mark Zuckerberg's relationship with Eduardo Saverin, making fanfiction of the film a sort of second cousin of RPF; fanfiction about its stars, then, is RPF about people acting out RPF—an incredibly cool, meta kind of fiction.

Since TSN itself is legitimate art, it's a short step from there to considering fanfiction about the actors playing those roles to be legitimate as well. As TSN was so lauded by film critics and mainstream media, its fandom, including the RPF offshoots like Jesse Eisenberg/Andrew Garfield, is not only well-respected but also assumed to be made up of older fans writing carefully constructed slash. In contrast, because the members of One Direction are young, cute, and bubblegum pop, and are subject to derision by Serious Music Critics, it's assumed that their fans are young and doodle their fanfiction while dreamily staring up at posters of the boys they will one day polyamorously marry.

This misconception of RPF by nonparticipating fans/fandoms comes down to the idea that RPF, because it tends to occur in fandoms seen as being predicated on the good looks of their celebrities, must be a delusional attempt by younger fans to do one of three things: to feel their devotion to those celebrities is validated, and is about more than just their appearance; to "prove" in some way that they "know" a star better than other fans (and therefore deserve his love); or—and this is often RPF detractors' biggest bone of contention—to seek to legitimize the "lesser" form of media of which the star is a part.

By "lesser," they usually mean, as even teenaged fans in other fandoms will snort, the domain of Teenage Girls. Of course, this is not actually true. In a survey performed in the fall of 2012 of over 1,550 One Direction fans who wrote or read RPF, a whopping 83 percent were over sixteen, and 35 percent were over twenty.[126] While teenage girls do comprise the base of One Direction's fans, this survey suggests that the majority of the community that participates whole-handedly in fandom, especially reading and writing RPF, is on an age spectrum comparable to fandom in general—or at least matches many fans' perception of such. What is really being said when the term "teenage girl" is used by other fans as a smear against RPF or, particularly, a fandom like One Direction's, is: *I don't think what you like has as much cultural value as what I like, and I think less of you because you like it.* In a fandomsphere that both glorifies and objectifies men while often demonizing—or wholesale ignoring the existence of—women, this internalized rejection of femaleness is damning.

The implication of criticisms of pop music RPF is that because you like "crap" media, you must naturally produce crap fanworks. The conversations in real-person fandoms couldn't possibly have the nuance of conversations about fictional personae. What could there possibly be to write about besides stripping off One Direction's painted-on red trousers and letting them—to quote their own song lyrics—"be the first to take it all the way like this"?

A look around any One Direction fanfiction community, however, reveals the polar opposite. Of course, as with most RPF, it is largely oriented around slash—98 percent of surveyed fans read slash, while only 15 percent read het fic (and of those, 18 percent will *only* read gender-swap/sexswap het, wherein the girl is "really" one of the One Direction boys in an intra-band pairing). In fact, 66 percent of RPF reader-writers surveyed within the One Direction fandom don't even consider self-insert, wish-fulfillment fanfiction *to be fanfiction.*

"Self-insert, to me, is like writing a more sophisticated diary entry about your daydreams or telling your friends (and the entire internet) of them," says Colazitron, a twenty-four-year-old One Direction writer.

"I do, however, have absolutely nothing against self-insert on principle. We're allowed to fantasize and we're allowed to share those fantasies with friends/the internet, if we wish. I do think it is a companion of RPF, although there is a difference." (Colazitron writes het fic about Louis Tomlinson/Eleanor Calder and Harry Styles/Caroline Flack, in addition to slash fic about Harry/Louis, Harry/Ed Sheeran, and other pairings, and used to write slash fic about the German boy band Tokio Hotel.[127])

Lucy Jones, a twenty-one-year-old One Direction slash writer, takes a semantic view on the subject: "I do consider [self-insert] to be a different genre from traditional RPF. The whole point of RPF is that it's fiction: your characterization is fictional, the setting is fictional, the plot is fictional... [Self-insert is] no longer completely fiction, because the person writing it isn't fictional, even if they are placed in a fictional environment."[128]

"Me personally, and I know this is a probably unpopular opinion to most of the fandom... I do not want to get to know [the members of One Direction] just as much as I do not want to get to know my new neighbors," says eighteen-year-old slash writer Elle. "I believe in the fourth wall, strictly, and I write about them not to get closer to these people, but because they are attractive and entertaining and are fun to write about... To write about them I need a certain amount of distance."[129]

So what kind of fic are One Direction fans reading and writing, if there's such a preponderance of slash and no self-insert? A whopping 94 percent of One Direction fic, as of the 2012 survey, is written about the pairing of Harry Styles/Louis Tomlinson, although other pairings have healthy showings, too: 74 percent of fans read Liam Payne/Zayn Malik, for example, and since the original survey was taken in 2012, Niall Horan/Zayn Malik (then 58%), has seen a massive upsurge in popularity.

As in other fandoms, a lot of the content is smut-driven: 98 percent of surveyed fans read NC-17-rated material, but that is rarely the purpose behind the story; PWP (Porn without Plot; or Plot, What Plot?) is rare in One Direction fandom. While most stories do include (or revolve around) sexual content, the dynamics of the band or pairings are what drive the story, since it is the boys' real-life interactions that tempt fans into fandom in the first place. Far more than their looks (although that's obviously one root of their popularity), it is the way they behave around each other, or the ways they might behave around each other because of inherent similarities and differences, that intrigues fans. While boy band members like those of One Direction come neatly prepackaged in their archetypes, devout fans are the first and loudest to interject that none of them *really fits* the role they're being paid to play. Instead, they find the nuances of behavior that set them apart from their color-coded trousers and use that to create virtually new characters who wear One Direction boys' faces.

A vast, vast majority of the stories are AU, or set in an alternate universe, where the members of One Direction are not members of the band at all. They feature Zayn and Niall as high school marching band drum majors; Harry and Louis as accidental parents; Liam and Zayn caught in a tragic love affair during World War II; Harry as a bartender and Louis as a burlesque dancer; Zayn as an art student and Liam as a barista; Niall as a leprechaun; and on and on. Louis as the Doctor and Harry as Amy Pond. Harry as Mark Zuckerberg with Zayn his long-suffering Eduardo against the nefarious presence of Nick Grimshaw as Sean Parker. Although I didn't count this statistic, there are probably more intense AU fics per capita for One Direction than there are canon-based fics (based on fic repositories and rec lists on LiveJournal, Tumblr, and AO3).

Then again, "canon"—official or sanctioned "reality" as defined by the source material—means something different in regard to RPF, because of course there is no such thing as a canon-based RPF. Not really. There's only the tiny portion of manufactured "reality" that fans can observe. It's a different kind of manufactured reality than fictional canons, where all choices were made deliberately by an author or showrunner, because the observable moments of RPF are a random jumble of marketing ploys and happenstance, crafted constructs and slips of actual personality, about which fandom at large comes to a consensus.

The key difference between RPF and traditional fanfiction is that RPF stems from what Kayley Thomas, a master's candidate at the University of Florida studying folklore and fanfiction, calls remediation:[130] a process of globally creating a common narrative from unrelated real-world events for the purpose of forging a canon or fanon (a common fan consensus not based on observable or textual "truth") understanding of real people as characters.

What Thomas is essentially arguing is that celebrities (or their publicists, at least) create an intentional character through all of their public material, but it varies and changes through time and circumstance. Like any other living person, the celebrity whose actions create his or her "canon" grows, changes, and reacts to situations organically—unlike a fictional character. Watching that organic growth, RPF readers and writers attempt to construct and keep running a cogent, singular narrative of the celebrity's life. However, real lives do not have singular narratives. They're messy. And they're not narratives at all.

Thomas suggests that since interviews with major media sources are often meant to stand on their own for uninitiated viewers (which is why interviews with celebrities tend to be so redundant), each piece of celebrity media should instead be taken as an individual, unique canon, not part of a larger whole.

In the reality of fandom, though, that is not the case. Fans instead take the loose information provided through that material—interviews, Twitter, photos, and so on—and reincorporate it into a unified fanon, or "whole" picture of the celebrity. Because celebrities are often aware of how their fans perceive them, especially in today's age of instant and continuous Twitter interaction, the celebrities sometimes then take fanon into account—consciously or subconsciously—in further creating their personae's canons.

Ramona, a twenty-one-year-old writer in many RPF fandoms, explains that the process of writing RPF is "a lot like [being] an actor preparing for a role, looking over the script time and time again and forming [your] own idea of the character in [your] head. It probably won't be exactly the same idea as the person who wrote the script, but I think that's what I like about fic and movies in general. You're never going to come across two people who characterize [other] people the exact same way...It happens with everything, even people you meet at work or at school. You may've only talked to someone one time, but you already assume a lot about that person's personality based on whatever conversation you've had."[131]

These constructed "characters" are also necessarily simplified, reducing real, complex people into more marketable stereotypes (the Chill One, the Sensitive One, etc.). In this context, even the most "in-character" Liam Payne of fanfiction—the Liam who appears to adhere most closely to the public "canon"—is still deeply, deeply OOC, or out of character, compared to the real person. Zayn Malik himself has stated that although he is seen as the "quiet, moody, mysterious bad boy," he loves a joke and playing pranks; enjoys staying in with his girlfriend, Perrie Edwards of Little Mix; and sees his persona/role as "misunderstood." Louis Tomlinson, financially responsible for his family and a deeply invested booster of his hometown (even helming their local football team—a true badge of patriotism in the UK), is painted in official and fan media alike as inanely immature and self-absorbed, although that is visibly untrue.

"When I read and write RPF, I keep a distinct line in my head, one that separates the real people from their fictional characterizations," says eighteen-year-old reader-writer Shrew.[132] "Personally, I do not believe that any of the relationships that I write (het, slash or otherwise) are real. I tend to feel that I am writing about personae rather than people themselves—I understand that there is a difference between what someone presents to others/to the public as a celebrity, and what they actually are like." Shrew writes both het and slash, with pairings ranging from canon—in this case, real, confirmed relationships—to fanon and crack (pairings that can in no way be construed as canonical, such as real person/fictional character or characters who have never met or interacted). All are based on stock characterizations that she has crafted from assumptions she's made while viewing official material, which she calls "headcanon."

All the same, assumptions based on headcanon are built on the materials available to the fandom during its initial stages (as was the overwhelming popularity of Harry/Louis as the OTP, the One True Pairing, of choice). The difficulty—and the fun, and the challenge, and the beauty—of RPF comes from the ever-changing nature of the materials available for creating canon as the people who generate it grow, change, and react to experiences in new ways. What was considered an "accurate" assumption in 2010 may be seen as wildly unrealistic in 2013. Kayley Thomas' process of remediation (the construction, by RPF writers, of a coherent reality from the available bits and pieces of media) then becomes the creation of a through-line, from who these people "were" at the outset of fandom to who they "are" now, via a cogent narrative—essentially rendering the "real people" being written about into fully fictional characters that happen to have real faces (just like any character portrayed by a live-action actor).

"I'd say the main difference for me with RPF is the accessibility of source material, and the fact that the fandom is constantly moving with new information and events…," says Cat, a twenty-five-year-old writer who has participated in both RPF and traditional fanfiction for nearly a decade.[133] "I use as much material as I can get my hands on in order to form characterization. In no way do I think this means I am getting an accurate characterization, but it does make me feel like I am offering a story appropriate to the particular fandom rather than just a story about two hot guys (or whatever)."

"I try to keep the events and characterization as close to what I think their lives are like as possible [based on the available information], but there's no way to know," says Darcie, a twenty-four-year-old One Direction slash writer. "I try to be as respectful as possible, too."[134]

Therein lies the biggest difference between what RPF is and what detractors tend to think RPF is: the readers and writers of RPF want their work not only to be respectful of its subjects but also to find or create an inner truth about them, rather than sensationalize or shame them. Society at large treats celebrity pairings as public commodities meant for the consumption of all, exploring and poking at the cracks in their relationships until the guts of Why They're Together or Not fall out for us to feast on.

After all, every issue of *People* magazine in the last ten years has featured suppositions about celebrities' home lives, "Are They/Aren't They?" photo essays about alleged couples, and self-reflection reassurances that "Stars Are Just Like You!" The breathless speculation required to ship, say, Harry Styles/Louis Tomlinson or Niall Horan/Demi Lovato or Zayn Malik/Perrie Edwards is a cue taken and a behavior learned from that same media coverage. But it's also more than that. In a way, writers of RPF are attempting to humanize celebrities, rather than *de*humanize them. Instead of *saying* that Celebrities Are Just Like You!, RPF aims to *show* it.

RPF has existed for as long as there have been celebrities. Any media "based on a true story!" is RPF. Any historical fiction narrative that co-opts a real person or real group is RPF. Shakespeare's *Julius Caesar* is RPF, and reflects reality just as accurately as the better and more lovingly, carefully written internet RPF today: virtually not at all. The names remain—Julius Caesar, Mark Antony—as do certain simplified traits, the archetypal roles they play. In lieu of Actual Julius Caesar and Actual Mark Antony, we get AU!Caesar and an AU!Antony in a simpler, more dramatic narrative.

An increasingly connected world—particularly via Twitter—has changed the lens through which "real" history, and real people, are viewed. Historians work by interweaving primary documents to create their version of the truth—historiography being, essentially, a larger framework of Humanity Fanon—and RPF writers do the same. With every new piece of evidence, every day, every interview, every tweet, the canon evolves and changes. Most fans can and will find a workaround for any and every new primary document to fit it into their preferred fanon. In some cases, this requires Steven Moffat–esque levels of plot twists and conspiracy theories, which is often one of the main causes of discord within RPF fandoms (particularly One Direction). This process of remediation is not in itself a bad thing, but when people forget that they are, in fact, creating their canon themselves, they are failing RPF's most basic tenet…

That it is Real Person *Fiction*.

There is no way to know, or even pretend, that RPF is reality. There is no guarantee—or even any desire for one on the part of most reader-writers—that the contents of an RPF fic are any closer to "canon" than a traditional fanfiction about something that happened off page in *The Hunger Games* between characters Katniss never even named. Instead, RPF seeks, like all other fanfiction, to pose hypothetical answers to questions posed by their media.

What happens when a band walks offstage?

What is Niall Horan like at home?

Would Harry Styles and Louis Tomlinson be happy together, and just how messy was their apartment after that New Year's Eve party?

Who is Zayn Malik when nobody is watching? Is Liam Payne really a grown man afraid of spoons?

And how exactly did One Direction decide that playing Real Life Fruit Ninja on a moving bus was a good idea?

Brad Bell is today best known as "Cheeks," the internet persona that also inspired his character on Husbands, *the gay-marriage sitcom he cocreated and cowrites with Jane Espenson. Before Brad was a cheeky fictional husband, however, he was a boyfriend in real life who also (along with his then-partner, Adam) had a flair for the theatrical. Together, they created a kind of portmanteau performance of coupledom, known in the party scene as "Bradam." Neither one was famous—yet. Long after they'd broken up, when one became far better known and, suddenly, so did their relationship, the kind of campy photo ops they'd once loved were now splashed all over major media outlets and threatened to drag down a career. Then, fanfic found and embraced this relationship—as fan writers do—from a variety of angles.*

Brad here reflects on stories told about his life—by himself, by the media, and by fans—and considers the different meanings each has found in telling them.

#BradamForever

Brad Bell

In one sense, the mashing up of two names is simply a manifestation of humanity's timeless admiration of partnership. However, the celebration of Bradam, both pre- and post-fame, wasn't just about a title. Bradam was born because two men fell in love, not just with each other but with the notion that, as a unit, they could conquer the world. As is often the case, that didn't come to fruition. For that very reason it makes perfect sense for Bradam to live on in fiction rather than reality. Bradam continues because people are drawn to the magic of a charismatic couple of men fearlessly showing the world that they're madly in love. This is the nonfic story of how Bradam went from IRL to RLF...

February 2005: Brad closed the door behind him and flopped onto the bed next to Adam. They'd been a solid item for just two months, so sharing even the most mundane details at the end of their day still seemed funny and wonderful. After a few minutes of talking about nothing in particular, Brad propped his head on his hand and looked at Adam.

"You know," Brad said with a gleeful grin, "when we're famous, our celebrity couple nickname'll be 'Bradam.'"

Adam was lying on his back, looking up at the ceiling, when his face lit up with a smile. "Ha! Bradam!"

Adam's reaction was a bit of a relief for Brad, as he was unsure if assigning a celebrity couple nickname, no matter how playfully, would be too...much...this early in their relationship.

"Know what I like about it?" Adam began.

Brad offered, "That it's got both our full names?"

"Exactly! Brad. Adam. Bradam." Adam let out another hearty laugh and looked at Brad. "I love it."

As two months became two years, the name became favored among Brad and Adam's circle of friends. Party-hopping hipsters would cheerfully proclaim, "Bradam wins best dressed again tonight!" Text message invites to parties inquired about "Bradam's availability for a cameo this evening." It was a cheeky label, in the spirit of glamorous whimsy. Neither Brad nor Adam realized the name's future significance at the time.

The summer of 2007 found the couple in Lake Tahoe, decompressing after a week at Burning Man. They hadn't anticipated the cluster of college kids who had invaded the lake, with no other intent than to get rowdy. At first, the chaos of teenage beachgoers was difficult to drown out, but before long, the frat boys in board shorts who had clotted the shoreline disappeared, and the two lovers could see only each other.

Until, that is, a high-pitched "OHMIGOD!" pulled Brad and Adam back to the beachside beer-fest taking place around them. They looked to see two girls, maybe sixteen, eyes wide in awe. "Are you guys, like...boyfriends?" the girls asked excitedly.

Brad and Adam exchanged a glance. Had the two girls seemed disdainful or disgusted, it would've been a more familiar scenario; judgment from the general public was nothing new. Instead, Brad and Adam sensed these were admirers, apparently fascinated by such an exotic sighting.

Brad responded, "Um...yeah."

Piercing squeals cut through the air, drawing eyes from even the most distracted partiers nearby.

"Would you guys, like...kiss?" said the other girl, her hands clasped in front of her chest with giddy anticipation.

"Um...okay." The boys shared a brief, chaste peck, which conjured a long, "Awwwwww!"

"You guys are *so* cute! Thank you!" With that, the girls were off, stealing a few last looks as they walked away.

Brad looked to Adam. "That's a first."

Adam slid his arm around Brad's waist. "We have fans!"

As time progressed, both men had grown more and more into themselves, which also meant they'd become less and less compatible with each other. Their parting was painful, like any breakup, but by the end of 2008, they'd found their footing as lifelong friends. Along with their relationship, the reality of their individual lives had also taken a venture into the surreal. Adam's participation in America's top singing competition made him a household name—let's call him an idol—overnight. Brad had begun producing satire in a promising start to a career as a writer and performer. Both were dating other people and, though they supported each other with great affection and loyalty, Bradam was only a memory. Then, in March 2009, Bradam was resurrected in a way neither one of them could've ever imagined.

"It's finally happened" was how Adam's voicemail to Brad began. "We're the *Velvet Goldmine*."

When Brad called Adam back, he got the details. "Apparently, every tongue-sucking shot ever taken of us has been discovered and picked up by the blogs. They're everywhere." At the time, "everywhere" meant gossip columns. Within weeks, "everywhere" became late-night talk shows, Bill O'Reilly, *Rolling Stone*, *US Weekly*, and Oprah Winfrey. There were false accusations that Brad had leaked the photos in search of his own fifteen minutes of fame. That stung, but Brad was never one to dwell on what others thought of him. This attitude also came in handy whenever strangers would look at Brad sympathetically, assuming he interpreted Adam's success to mean that Brad had somehow failed. It was frustrating, but fleeting. What was most upsetting for Brad was that some of the happiest moments of his life were being portrayed as sins. Their proud, photographic declarations of love for each other were being depicted as shameful transgressions. What was a time of blithe romance had been mangled into a colossal headache that threatened the potential of Adam's future...into a scandal that would be best forgotten.

That is, until a Google Alert brought a new world to Brad's attention: fanfiction. Entertained by the Bradam fics that were popping up online, many of Brad's friends would ask, "Isn't it creepy? These people don't know you and they're...I mean, like, you're a real person." Statements like this are still common.

However, Brad didn't find the fanfic creepy. Bradam fic meant that the cherished time he had spent with Adam wouldn't remain a scarlet letter. Bradam had taken on a new incarnation, resurrected by people who connected to the freedom, boldness, and adventure their union represented.

What began as a lighthearted fantasy between lovers had evolved into the exact reality it had pretended to be: the celebration of first love, of being alive and young, of turning your world into an enchanted realm of whimsy. Because of the authors and fans who give Bradam a place to live in their hearts, that celebration will continue forever.

Peter Berg is a writer, blogger, and high school student. He is also a "brony"— a fan of the children's television program My Little Pony: Friendship Is Magic. *From its first airing in 2010, the show surprised its parent company Hasbro and the world by attracting a large and largely male fanbase of adults and older teens. As the media has puzzled over the phenomenon, trying to understand these fans as rebels against gender stereotypes or proponents of a new era of internet sincerity, bronies have been busy creating a truly impressive array of pony-related art, video (including the "Friendship Is Witchcraft" fandub series by the brony known as "Sherclop Pones"), music, and, of course, stories. Peter Berg has created an enormous crossover universe with these ponies and part four of* Gulliver's Travels, *among other sources. Here, he reflects on his motivations, experiences, and the role this online fandom has played in his writing life.*

Hobbyhorsing

Peter Berg (Homfrog)

Let me start off with a bold declaration: I have far too many ideas for my own good. My brain runs over with great big chocolate fountains of creativity and I can never turn it off, not ever. One might think, "What's so bad about never-ending chocolate?" In all honesty it's not all that bad on a slow day, a day when I'm too focused on other, more mundane things to pay heed to the gushing idea fondue.

But on a fast day, a day when close to 100 percent of my attention is in my own head, too much of a good thing can be overwhelming. Ideas pour into my mind all hours of my waking life, bubbling and frothing like coffee percolators and spewing like geysers. Ideas, to me, are a very liquid thing. They are capable of dribbling, dripping, flowing, running, crashing, streaming, boiling, and freezing. In this regard, and especially in regard to the *My Little Pony: Friendship Is Magic* fandom, I have chocolate on the brain.

Here's a little backstory. I have been writing ever since I could read. I first started reading at age three and a half, and by my estimate it was only months later that I tried to write something. I believe I was trying to communicate my feelings on the ghosts that lived in the scary spruce tree in our backyard; either that or something about one of my stuffed animals. The first complete story I wrote was a short tale about dragons titled "My Dragon Book." It included descriptions of their feeding habits, family structures, mating rituals (as well as I understood such a concept at five years old—I knew it involved butts), and a cover decorated with stickers of the planets, because everyone knows dragons are associated with outer space. Surprisingly, it managed to have a semblance of a plotline. It followed one dragon, an unnamed character who I remember was colored blue, from birth to death. I hand-drew several pictures of dragons for the book and pasted them in with the purple glue stick all schoolchildren have. When finished, the book was about ten pages long, bound with staples, and covered in black construction paper titled with white crayon. It was, to my young eyes, the best compendium of dragon biology and culture that existed, probably the best book that took a scientific approach to mythology in the history of the universe. I was so proud, and from that moment forth, I loved writing. That was the day the ideas started trickling in.

Writing and reading, in my experience at least, behave in a nearly symbiotic biological relationship. Each one benefits and relies on the other for its continued existence, and they react with each other like complex chemical systems. In my case, reading lets me take in more ideas than my body can hold, and writing lets me drain myself of those ideas and relieve some of the pressure that builds up. I am an idea pressure cooker; what leaves my body through hand and mouth is far tastier and more succulent than the raw vegetables that have entered through eye and ear.

I currently have a document of *My Little Pony* story ideas that is, at the time of this writing, over 250 pages in length. It consists of over 400 premises for stories categorized with more than thirty-five different color-coded tags, a timeline of events spanning over 400,000 years and fourteen pages, over 49,000 words of headcanon, and forty-one original characters. Out of the myriad story premises, only nine have been completed, and thirty-two are in the process of being written. My sheer creative output, if channeled effectively and with entirely original content, might have the capacity to earn me some serious dosh. But instead

I choose to write stories about ponies using characters who I didn't even create. "Why is this?" one might ask. "Why would such a prolific writer choose to write fanfiction instead of original, potentially moneymaking masterpieces?"

The simple answer is, I didn't choose the pony life; the pony life chose me. What made my life become so intertwined with the *My Little Pony* writing experience was a combination of factors from within and without. I honestly don't even remember how I got into this fandom, or at what point I said to myself, "I'm a brony now." However, I think the first thing that really appealed to me about this show was the world building. Ohhh, the world building, so grand, so ancient, so in-depth for a children's show. Equestria is such a large kingdom; so much of it remains unexplored by the viewing audience, and yet we get a sense that we almost know what's around every corner. Over a thousand years of history were put into the show's backstory, and I'm willing to bet that there is a lot more we haven't seen yet. Much of the fanfiction I write, and the headcanon I create, concerns the history of Equestria. I've detailed many eras, with five calendar systems, the gradual change of languages and governments, and factoring magic-assisted evolution into it as well, given the scale of time across which I work. I start the march of time before the Big Bang and finish it after the Big Whimper, so to speak. I've quite literally (and literarily) created a universe.

In *My Little Pony: Friendship Is Magic*, there are mythological creatures and their kin at all points: cockatrices, dragons, griffons, hydras, changelings, chimerae, trickster gods, hippocampi, living constellations, plant-animal hybrids, insectoid tribbles—the list goes on. The mythology that the show simultaneously incorporates and produces really attracted me, particularly the races and species of beings that make Equestria and the lands beyond it their homes. Its rich and complicated universe makes my brain resonate with a multitude of symphonic ideas. So I do my duty as a devoted fan and build on that myself.

I have expanded upon or invented, wholly or partly, over fifteen species of ponies and over twenty other species, ranging from Scythian-Neanderthal ponies to bicorn zebras to ponies that live in the Earth's core, the mesosphere, and the moon; from sapient coats of skin to dark, telepathic parrots to flying creatures that resemble UFOs. And once I've created them, I back off and watch them live. A friend related to me that I am, in a sense, an anthropologist-god; I create a species and then study it. I detail a clear biology, both general and specific, for each species. I take note of their histories, their cultures, and their societies, and list their interactions with other species and how they fare in the world against the obstacles I create for them to surpass.

As for my own species—bronies—I have plenty of interactions with them, too. I maintain a social group of about twenty bronies with whom I interact daily. These range from lifelong friends I know in real life to people I've only ever known through Twitter or Facebook. We write together, we talk about ideas and have roleplaying sessions, and we watch the episodes together and laugh. I find bronies to be a very rewarding community—almost always optimistic, well-meaning, kind, and thoughtful. It really means a lot to me that I have "found my people," and that they have accepted me. It's not too odd to me that the show we all care about is supposed to be for little kids, or that the show has a primarily female character population.

So in the end, I suppose you could say that what really drew me to writing fanfiction for *My Little Pony* was that it offered such an enticing opportunity for my specific kind of obsessive, unstoppable creative flow to flourish. This fandom lets me bail out my brain—floating in a tumultuous, briny sea of golden ideas—with an extra-large bucket rather than a rusty soup ladle as I did in other fandoms before *My Little Pony*. It gives me an outlet to melt and smelt all my thoughts and whimsies into gleaming architecture or fine-edged weapons. Many of my ideas—I'd say a large percentage of them—will never see the light of day or the eye of any reader. Sometimes that hurts, but usually I can deal with that and instead concentrate on the stories that I definitely want to release into the world.

I wouldn't say my life is too hectic to get all the writing done I need to. I have ample free time on most days, although it varies with my schedule and the general course of events in my life. My afternoons and weekends are usually completely open, but I don't spend all of that time writing. Often, though, I need to strike a balance between my real life and the life I live when my brain is plugged into the computer through my hands. Spending too much time writing and reading fanfiction keeps me from getting my homework done and being with my family and friends...but spending too much time in meatspace keeps me from draining myself of ideas, and then I have to pour those ideas all over my family and friends, even though they'd much rather not hear about that sort of thing. After all, I don't know many bronies in real life, and even fewer who have the same passion I do for this particular constellation of ideas, this universe that I've half borrowed, half birthed. That is why I turn to my friends online.

There, I'm not only a member of the *My Little Pony: Friendship Is Magic* fandom. I'm a member of the SCP Foundation (a collaborative sci-fi/horror fiction-writing website), several internet poetry and art groups, and a cabal of professional jokesters and idiot-savant madmen on Twitter. I dip my tentacles into every social network in the hopes of making new connections. The more I can make, and the more options for new friends and communities I explore, the more outlets I have to express my ideas. This gives me more people off of whom to bounce notions and with whom I can discuss Big Issues—the Biggest Issues that concern me as a person and the internet realms I inhabit. The friends I've made through all of these websites and fandoms act as a support network to keep me afloat and sane amid the infernal busy buzzing of my head full of ideas.

An early note from my editor: "This is such an important issue, and one you haven't touched on much earlier in the book." Sigh. I know. And neither has fanfic—not that much. Not enough, I'd say. There have been some moments, and this exchange between Rukmini Pande and Samira Nadkarni, two fan-studies critics based in India, touches on several of them. Overall, however, media fandom engagement with racial and ethnic difference in fanfiction has been minimal.

As far as I've seen—and please take this as a challenge, a heartfelt invitation to prove me wrong—fanfic hasn't done the kinds of deconstruction and reimagining of race and ethnicity that it's done for gender and sexuality, occasionally social class, and, more recently, disability. In fic fandoms that do feature characters of color, the fanfic surrounding those characters still doesn't typically engage their race or ethnicity, and for all the genderswapping and biological tinkering I've seen, I don't see many Spocks of color, for instance. In this area, commercial entertainment's reimagining of sources has outpaced fan culture: witness CBS' casting of Lucy Liu as Joan Watson on Elementary, and New Paradigm Studios' digital comic Holmes and Watson that recasts the duo as African American detectives in Harlem.

Whereas some series that have inspired vast fic fandoms have made important inroads in diverse casting and representing racial and ethnic differences—the original Star Trek being the most obvious and groundbreaking example—the fic itself has not necessarily followed suit. In science fiction and fantasy franchises, furthermore, racial and ethnic issues are often explored via divides between imaginary species or synthetic and biological humans—approaches that, while fascinating, place the issue of race as we experience it at a certain remove. That's fine; that's how those genres engage culture and politics, and I'm a big fan of that engagement. But dealing with tension between werewolves and vampires or between Cylons and humans doesn't confront race head-on in the way a show like The Wire does.

On the other hand, when Western media culture or fanfic does imagine characters in some nonwhite or non-Western scenario, it's not always sensitively or tastefully done. Of course it isn't. The history of cultural appropriation and exploitation is as obvious as it is extensive and egregious—Charlie Chan and Gunga Din don't know nothin' bout birthin' no babies, and so on. If people are writing fic for fun, it makes sense that they might stay away from these issues—race isn't nearly as much fun to talk about as sex. It feels *heavy, and people who appear to take fanfiction very seriously can open themselves to ridicule. Moreover, fic gets feedback, and inviting feedback on racial issues can be scary. Writers don't want to field accusations of racism or find they have actually been, however unintentionally, racist or insensitive. I have spoken to many writers (of various backgrounds) who are interested in portraying more diverse characters or playing with racial and ethnic difference, but are wary of giving offense, getting flamed, or simply having their work ignored. I've heard from many fans of color who tire of always feeling like the only nonwhite in the virtual room, even as I've also spoken to those who embrace online fandom as a venue where they don't have to interact or write primarily through their ethnic or racial identity. Most often, however, I've heard comments akin to the following, from an email exchange with a fandom blogger and critic:*

> *For me, online fandom has not been a place in which I don't have to deal with race. In my experience, online fandom has simply been a smaller subset of the larger culture (which, of course, is not exactly the healthiest place in which to exist if you're any shade that isn't White). I've been fortunate enough to have a cluster of cool, mellow, socially aware people of all shades with whom I can share my fandom love (although, that doesn't necessarily make the uncomfortable feeling of being a fan of color [FOC] in a sea of White ones go away). I've seen many, many other fans of color be attacked, degraded, and threatened for expressing legitimate criticism of the problematic elements in the shows/books they love (or of the frequently oppressive behavior of other fans).*[135]

Racial and ethnic dynamics play out differently in manga, anime, and other fandoms with non-Western origins that haven't been my focus here. But all of the Western, predominantly white media properties Fic has discussed have vast global fandoms. Every one of these shows, movies, and books has inspired fans from many different cultures and ethnicities to read and write fic. Some evolve their own localized fan cultures, as we saw earlier in this volume with the 1950s Irish fandom. Some don't develop local communities, having strong cultural reasons for not acknowledging in person the kinds of materials they like to read and write online. Some read and write in English; some expand the diversity of fandom's readership by donating labor to translation projects, garnering, say, Chinese or Thai or Indonesian readers for fic writers from London or Utah or Finland. There are many, many different experiences of global fandom outside the cultural centers where the media properties are produced. The following dialogue gives two perspectives from two individuals who do not speak for vast, undifferentiated demographics, but only for themselves.

From a Land Where "Other" People Live

Perspectives from an Indian Fannish Experience

Rukmini Pande and Samira Nadkarni

It is a truism that no person experiences or "does" fandom in any one way. When it comes to race in fandom, this is perhaps even more true. As aca-fen who started our journeys as academics and members of media fandom at almost the same time (in 2002) and in the same place (Mumbai), we wanted to look back at the different experiences we've had while coming to terms with our identities as fans, and in particular as fans of color. While Samira left India in 2008 and has navigated fan communities in the UK, Rukmini went on to Delhi and found fellow fans there, too.

Fanfiction in particular has been examined as a site of subversion by various aca-fen and critics, and it is where we both would have expected racial dynamics to be explored as well. Our conversation here is an attempt to map out our differing experiences, while also touching on how contemporary fan communities try (and, it has to be said, very often fail) to come to grips with issues like equitable representation and cultural appropriation in the popular media texts that are their focus.

Finding Fandom in India

RUKMINI: Samira, you were my introduction to media fandom and for a long time you were my only actual "IRL"[136] fan person. Do you think your distance from the larger, mostly Western fandom

344

communities affected the way you viewed fandom, and your own identity as a participant? And further, race in fandom?

SAMIRA: It's the oddest thing, because my original fandom community, and indeed, the fandom community I still identify strongly with, is the community that I built within my own preexisting social circles—people I knew outside of being a fan and brought into fandom, not people I met because I was a fan. As a result, race and culture didn't really enter into this early stage of my fandom persona as an issue quite as much as age and gender did—I found it far easier to talk to young women about my growing interest in slash simply because they were more likely to be receptive to it. Indian culture is very concerned with machismo, and homosexuality itself was extremely taboo until July 2009.[137] So, in many ways, you were my first experience of what a real-world fandom community entailed as well.

My own introduction to fandom had come about only in 2002, about a year before we met, thanks to my attempts to make sense of the anime *Weiss Kreuz*. I accidentally ended up on a LiveJournal (LJ) community that, at the time, I believed to be discussing the actual events of the series. It wasn't until a few weeks into watching the show itself that I came to understand the basics of fanworks and what that sort of engagement with canon might mean in terms of manipulating and/or producing a narrative. In this early phase, I didn't really know anyone online and didn't have an LJ account myself. It made sense then to discuss it with friends I already knew, in an effort to come to terms with the slash community I'd accidentally stumbled into and grown compelled by.

As a result, when I met you, Rukmini, and realized we had similar interests, I bombarded you with information about *Weiss Kreuz* and the slash pairings, and we sort of began our own independent community, each of us trying to figure out how to reconcile the content and media styling with our own experience of what writing and culture entailed. At this time, I associated my identity with a gender- and race-neutral online persona that I inhabited as a fandom lurker.[138] It wasn't until you and I parted ways in 2006—I stayed in Mumbai and you moved to Delhi—that I realized race, gender, and culture were very much coded into the fandom experience. This was largely because you met other people, both online and in person, who also produced or consumed fanworks, integrating into a larger preexisting Indian fandom community, while I continued to visit online forums. As a result, your experience of fandom in terms of ethnicity is quite different from my own: you met people in person in Delhi who had been, and continue to be, involved in fandom for just as long, if not longer, than us, whereas I mostly ended up trying to locate myself within multiracial and ethnically diverse fandom communities online. And, as you have always said, Delhi really changed your experience of fandom…

RUKMINI: I think we just didn't know there could be a local fandom community, really, outside of the two of us. First, of course, our identity as lurkers was a factor, and I think that element of subterfuge carried into IRL interactions with potential fandom people. Additionally, we were both slashers and that carried (and to an extent still carries) its own taboo.[139] I met other fan people in Delhi very gradually, and while I joke now about the strange verbal maneuvering each encounter involved before we recognized each other as "those kinds of people," that hesitant caution was motivated by a very real fear of discovery. I continued to lurk for a long time, and only got an online journal when badgered into it by a local (Indian) fandom friend in 2010. Gathering confidence from her experiences, I reached out to other fans in online spaces after that, but I continued to view fandom communities as something that was "out there," mostly in America or the UK.

However, as I realized that fan culture was what I was going to work on professionally, I also began to realize that I had collected quite a few "people like me" at home in Delhi, and the idea that an Indian fan community might already exist slowly filtered in. The first time approximately five of us met and talked about fandom was fairly recently, in early 2012. And it was quite an experience! Coincidentally, 2012 was also the first time Delhi had its own Comic-Con! I think the idea that fandom was, and is, here too continues to be pretty slow to sink in, but it has certainly been a turning point in the way I think of my fannish identity.

SAMIRA: You're so right that the subtle taboo of slash fandom, coupled with the cultural taboo of homosexuality in India, made it really hard to locate others who might be willing to discuss their interest in slash fandom without running the risk of being considered "deviant." When in India, I still find it easier to discuss heterosexual pairings when discussing my interest in fandom with anyone who identifies as being outside of a fan community. And this is mostly because people are more willing to discuss the subject openly and in fair terms when dealing with what is seen to be the sexual norm. In contrast, my experience was that slash fanworks necessitated a stealthier approach and so largely occurred online or in places where we felt we wouldn't be overheard as easily. We're not alone in this: I've had conversations with fangirls from Iran, Romania, and Sri Lanka who have indicated similar experiences.

Cultural Diversity (or Not) and How Slash Fandoms Address It (or Don't)

SAMIRA: The issue of slash aside, I never really encountered fanworks with a great deal of racial or cultural diversity. I certainly haven't read any good ones set in India that don't somehow "exoticize" the region or the culture, or devolve into the ridiculous with chases in jungles riding elephants. Personally, I find that fanworks of this nature annoy me, and I tend to steer clear of any that even hint at this sort of appropriation of an Asian culture or subculture.

RUKMINI: Yes, I know. I think it was RaceFail '09[140] that really got me to start thinking about race in fandom and how my identity, which I was always discussing critically in terms of my academic life, was interacting with my fannish behavior.

I think to an extent I had compartmentalized my media-fandom identity (that was based on the consumption of primarily American shows and movies) as separate from my cultural and racial identity, as I had never lacked for a media representation of my culture; Bollywood (and other Indian cinema) and literature being produced in India saw to that. Media fandom was a very different part of my popular-culture consumption habits.[141] Not that I hadn't noticed that there was a severe lack of diversity in the fanworks I consumed, but I hadn't critically engaged with that lack yet. I think that the conversations RaceFail started (or rather brought to the forefront, since it was far from the first time these issues had been talked about) were critical, not only in terms of what was being discussed but the fact that they became a way for fans of color to find each other and build communities as well.

SAMIRA: It's true that a lot of the shows that spark fandom trends—for example, current booming slash fandoms include *Teen Wolf*, *Skyfall*, *Supernatural*, and so forth—don't really tend to have more than a character or two who are racially or culturally othered, and when they do, these characters are largely sidelined, in the show and in fanworks, in favor of a dominant white-only pairing. For example, I have huge issues with *Supernatural*, particularly in its fourth and fifth seasons. The show's two major angels of color, Uriel and Raphael, send a clear but really problematic message: the former's language and interactions—referring to humans as mud-monkeys, and so on—depicts a sort of racism[142] that appropriates and reverses racist terminology used toward POCs, and he eventually reveals himself as a double agent acting on behalf of Lucifer in "On the Head of a Pin" (4-16); the latter acts as a major angelic antagonist (also shown to be clearly in the wrong) of the good guys (the Winchester brothers and Castiel). While it's possible to argue that Uriel's racism indicates that POCs might have their own inherent racial biases, gesturing toward this by placing him beyond his depiction as an African American male to his role as an angel of the Lord, this argument is hard to sustain in the face of *both* angels of color being depicted as antagonists. Given the viewers' carefully nurtured sympathy for the Winchester brothers and Castiel—all white men (or depicted as such)—Uriel and Raphael's casting as "the bad guys" clearly displays a deeper agenda that, at least partially, points toward race.

In addition to this, the episode "Hammer of the Gods" (5-19) appropriates a number of mythologies from across the globe—Indian mythology being clearly represented in the use of Ganesh and Kali—and, despite their depiction as *not* subordinate to Christianity, a white Christian icon, Lucifer, kills them all ... except Kali, who flees in fear with the Winchesters. The suggestion that Kali, arguably one of the strongest Gods in the Hindu pantheon, would flee in fear from a confrontation is both ludicrous and offensive. It devalues not only the strength associated with a female symbol of power (notably the only female God in that episode) but also the cultural power associated with her mythos. This just underlines the absolute devaluation associated with races and cultures that don't fall within the dominant Western, white, Anglo-centric (and distinctly American) hegemony. It's something that is repeated almost every time the show appropriates a mythological figure, vilifies it, and then sends in two Western white men to kill it and save the person/city/world while refusing to link these events to any historical or cultural context that might disrupt an easy interpretation of the plot.[143] Fandom that then takes up this storyline, in which existing racism and cultural prejudice are not-so-subtly promoted, and continues with it fails to really challenge it or engage with it on different terms. And that's just very, very wrong.

RUKMINI: Oh yes, absolutely! *Teen Wolf* is currently pressing all kinds of buttons for me in terms of race and cultural appropriation. There are many, many ways in which the show has sidelined its characters of color.[144] But even more than the failings of its creator, Jeff Davis, it's been fandom's reaction that is of concern to me. As you pointed out, slash fandoms have often been accused of sidelining characters of color to concentrate on white pairings. However, *Teen Wolf* fandom's dismissal of that unicorn, an actual queer character of color (Danny Mahealani), while aggressively campaigning to make the main slash ship of the show (Derek Hale and Stiles Stilinski, both white) canon, ostensibly to further the cause of queer representation on television, has been especially jarring.

I also have to comment on the ongoing use of the character of Kali in various media as something that has really hit close to home! Eric Kripke's *Supernatural* wasn't the first to butcher her representation by any means, and I'm afraid the same thing is happening with *Teen Wolf*—only *Teen Wolf*'s representation might be worse because their Kali will be a recurring character. (As of this conversation, the episodes featuring her haven't aired yet.) I know why Kali is such an attractive figure to Western writers; her link to the forces of chaos in Hindu mythology, the violent iconography that surrounds her, and the sexual elements of the Tantric philosophy that she is associated with are almost irresistible. As I've said before, what hurts me is not really the failure of the writing itself, as my cynicism toward Western writers appropriating my culture is almost an automatic lens. What hurts is the insistence of the *Teen Wolf* fandom that Kali is "just a name"—that the character is a werewolf, and not supposed to be the goddess herself—in the face of Indian fans writing many, many well-argued pieces of meta about why that is just not true.[145] The fact that the actress cast for the part is not Indian (Felisha Terrel is half black) just adds salt to the wound!

SAMIRA: In many ways, we've both come to feel really strongly about this issue of cultural appropriation that verges on a negation of culture itself[146] because it is constantly sidelined even as it's being discussed, and it is annoying that there doesn't seem to be a distinction being made between engaging with a culture and its people and appropriating these. And that's what we're hoping to draw attention to here: both Davis and Kripke *chose* to appropriate rather than engage, and it's upsetting when parts of fandom follow suit. It's far too simple to consider the problem of racial and cultural othering as simply ingrained, or inescapable within the media, because at some point, when we're consuming, reproducing, or repurposing this content for fanworks, we're also buying into it simply by supporting it financially or systematically. And we need to think about that, about our complicity in these systems.

Fanworks can be an amazing space within which to negotiate these boundaries because the limits become permeable. Gender-bending, race-bending, age-bending, alternate universes—all of these provide the opportunity to engage with, challenge, reposition, or remove these ideologies as depicted in the original media.

Cultural Diversity: Fanworks Can Do Better and Sometimes Do

RUKMINI: The debate over the difference between appropriation of and engagement with other cultures is a heated one, both in media fandom and larger society. But it is one that is vital if media fandom is going to uphold its claim to resisting dominant societal narratives. Fans of color often find their fannish communities silent on the topic of race, and that definitely hurts the idea of inclusiveness many of us hold dear. I think the basic idea that keeps coming up in discussions, prompted by events like RaceFail, is the need to explore the idea of white privilege and not shut down discourses around it through defensiveness. Disengagement is certainly not the answer, and there are plenty of resources available to help people out if they truly do want to learn.

One fandom that has been extremely engaged in discussions of race has been the one formed around *Avatar: The Last Airbender* (2005–2008) and its sequel, *The Legend of Korra* (2012–). The original animated series was hailed for its depiction of various different racial and ethnic groups in Asia (the airbenders, for example, have been seen as representative of Tibetan Buddhism, with their decimation at the hands of the Fire Nation paralleling the actual history of Tibet). While not perfect, ATLA was a genuine attempt at working with "foreign" cultures without exoticizing them; for example, each nation's "bending," or special power over the elements, was carefully individuated to correspond to specific martial arts styles, avoiding the one-size-fits-all approach of most Western depictions of martial arts.

The fandom that built up around ATLA was also extremely attuned to the nuances of that representation and, notably and rather gratifyingly, took action when that core principle was forgotten by the show's Powers That Be. When the live-action film of the series was announced in 2007, the fandom reacted with outrage at the news that white actors had been cast to play all the positive leads. They made their displeasure clear through the very tools they had used to celebrate the series: transformative fanworks. Combining wit and social critique, some fans used internet memes to show how ludicrous the whitewashed casting was, while others used the casting failure as a springboard to extend the critique to other fandoms. For example, in 2010, the Dreamwidth community Dark Agenda launched "The Racebending Revenge Ficathon," which challenged fans to write a fanfic in a fandom of their choice, in which they changed the race of a central white character to show how that would affect the show's universe. The film's controversy also lead to the establishment of Racebending.com, a grassroots organization that continues to point out problematic racial elements in popular cultural texts. So it's clear that fandom can contribute significantly to exposing racially flawed texts and building a resistance to them; there just needs to be a continual will to make that a priority.

SAMIRA: It's clear that media and the society that produces it are in a symbiotic relationship, and that given the current rapid growth and awareness of fandom, and fanfiction in particular, as a recognized subset of media, producers of fanworks are in an enviable position to engage with these concerns, and not simply reproduce the systems of thought that function as the canon (either in terms of the media itself or the society that produces it). They can interact with these, if not as equals, then as new contenders, and actually produce a space where race and culture are thoughtfully and respectfully engaged.

The Look of Fic: 2013

Wattpad's fanfiction homepage, August 2013[K]

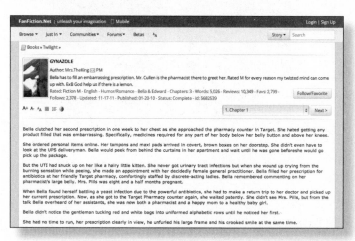

Mrs.TheKing's Twilight fanfiction "Gynazole" on FanFiction.Net. Although "Gynazole" was originally posted in 2010, this screenshot depicts the archive as seen in 2013. Most of the story has been removed by the author.[L]

The most popular fanfiction tags on Archive of Our Own, August 2013. Tags enable searching for specific kinds of fic within or across fandoms.[M]

A fanfic post reblogged to the SuperWhoLock Tumblr. The image-intensive blogging platform Tumblr has transformed the fanfic interface to include more direct interplay between fan art or GIFs and text. It has also made it easier for fandoms to merge and overlap. Most fanfiction posts on Tumblr are short forms (often called "drabbles"), often responses to image prompts, or teasers that link to longer works on other platforms or archives.[N]

part five

FANFICTION AND WRITERS WHO DON'T WRITE FANFICTION

But Who Do Something Related. I Think.

The post-modernist always rings twice.

—@EricIdle

POSTMODERNISM: Parody and pastiche. Disrupting grand narratives. Rejecting Enlightenment and Romantic genius. William S. Burroughs cutting up novels. Kathy Acker plagiarizing Dickens. And Sade. And everyone else.

Appropriation. It's been avant-garde...for a long time now.

E. L. James wrote a kind of pastiche of Stephenie Meyer and popular Twilight fanfictions. She took phrases, character traits, plot points, structures—even scenes. It is not *even a little bit* avant-garde. It's the enemy the avant-garde scares its children with at night.

Fanfiction isn't the first appropriation- and pastiche-based writing culture to go mainstream. Think Don DeLillo: literary, but published by mainstream commercial houses, widely taught and consumed, his work adapted as a movie starring Robert Pattinson. E. L. James started out in a writing subculture and wrote her fic *based* on a movie franchise starring Robert Pattinson. Coincidence? Yeah, totally. But wouldn't you love to be a guest at a dinner party with *those* two authors?

A tête-à-tête between DeLillo and James probably isn't happening any time soon except in the pastiche fanfiction I'm writing in my head, "Blood and Guts in Twi-School." Still, you might think fanfic and postmodernism, as appropriation-based writing cultures with somewhat fraught relationships to the mainstream, would have plenty to talk about—besides young British actors. Something I've learned since turning my attention to contemporary writing cultures: they don't talk to each other, and when they do, they don't speak quite the same language.

A case in point: I live with a pioneer in the field of "conceptual writing"—an avant-garde practice that Darren Wershler describes in his essay here. When I first heard about it, I thought: Oh! *Conceptual*—based on ideas, or maybe something Kantian. I get it.

I *so* did not get it. Conceptual writing has nothing to do with Kant. Conceptual writing has everything to do with appropriating other people's material and reframing it—which sounds like a description of fanfiction that a lot of people would agree with. These communities (by and large) have nothing to do with each other, however. They appropriate different material to different ends, produce very different kinds of texts, share few if any of the same concerns or goals, and would likely be insulted—on either side—by the insinuation of any association whatsoever.

Well, I *say* "would likely be." So I asked someone else to write that essay, and Darren has teased out some much more thought-provoking questions and parallels than I have in the course of picking arguments with my avant-garde partner (as one does).

To continue.

As I say, I live with "conceptual writing" on a daily basis. I embrace it (and one of its pioneers). I also like doing philosophical (possibly conceptual) readings of literary texts. So when, in the course of looking at yet another writing culture, commercial publishing, I saw so much discussion of and desire for something called "high concept" novels, I was surprised, but pleased. I wondered if they meant conceptual writing like well-known psychology test questions presented as poetry, or conceptual writing like maybe Wallace Stevens when he goes all phenomenological about a jar.

Guess again. By "high concept," commercial publishing means, essentially, books that can be pitched in four words or less. The literary equivalent of *Snakes on a Plane*. See, I wouldn't have thought that.

"Can be pitched in four words or less" is not an airtight definition. "Retyped the *Times*" could pitch a well-known work of conceptual writing in three words (Kenneth Goldsmith's *Day*, which consists of a single issue of the Sunday *New York Times* retyped and reformatted as a book), but it's not going to get agents into a bidding war. As it happens, a lot of these short pitches for high-concept novels sound like fanfiction crossovers. *Buffy* meets *Brideshead*. Edward Cullen, Squire of Downton. When I started talking to people in the mainstream publishing world a few years back, however, I found that most of this world had no idea what fanfiction was. Those who had heard of such a thing did not embrace the idea that what *they* did (publishing and promoting stories they hoped would be popular) had anything in common with what fanfiction communities did (posting and promoting stories they hoped would be popular). I'm basing these generalizations on personal conversations and informal exchanges. I've since spoken to several agents who were also well-known fan writers, but I stand by my claim. Until *Fifty Shades of Grey*, fanfiction was on the margins of the New York–based publishing world's hive mind. At best.

I tried to interview a writer of literary fiction about basing a character on a well-known political figure. I didn't ask her questions about fanfiction, but I did explain the context of this book. I wanted to identify different motivations and processes for writing about real people who are alive and might not consent. Writers can make use of apparently analogous processes, but conceive of their projects very differently, to very different ends, and I want this book to make that clear. This writer wasn't familiar with fanfiction, but she still wanted very much to distinguish what she did as a literary writer from it. She wanted to make clear that she didn't write about just famous people, but only about people she felt had a kind of mythic or philosophical resonance and importance. I agree with that assessment of her work, and I understand not wanting to discuss something you don't know about. However, the exchange still hovered at the edge of some perplexing prejudices that adhere to notions of celebrity and to the word *fan,* and which seem to operate even in the absence of any direct knowledge or experience of fanfiction.

What if a fanfiction writer had shared more than an interest in writing about characters based on mythic or particularly resonant real people? I'm thinking of a very talented fic writer who has written characters based on political figures; her work is deeply psychological as well as political. I could imagine the writer describing these characters as working through archetypal American and British myths. Now, she may be a "fan" of some of the inspirations of her work—but does that make it less serious? Is the work automatically less serious because of the way she shares it? Or is it less serious because in addition to being kind of mythic and archetypal and political, her characters are also having all kinds of explicit sex and end up together rather than in tragedy? I think literary critics and writers sometimes make that kind of judgment automatically. I wonder if it can be traced back to an ancient genre distinction from classical drama: comedy ends in marriage and lacks the weight of tragedy. But *Middlemarch* ends in marriage and mixes politics with a romance plot, and I can't think of anyone who has ever thought George Eliot wasn't serious. Ever.

I've been thinking about fanfiction for a long time now, but I've been thinking about literature and writing for longer. I believe distinctions matter. The dramatic conventions that separate tragedy and comedy do lead to important differences, and I don't actually think that *A Midsummer Night's Dream,* say, has all the political and psychological resonance of *Hamlet* or *King Lear*. But then we also get something like *The Tempest*, which incorporates elements of tragedy and comedy but is probably best described as a kind of proto-sci-fi/fantasy. I don't like lines in the sand that divide literary from genre fiction, but I also don't like to erase all lines—genre fiction has some distinctive elements I don't think it should be ashamed of. What I do like is comparing literatures. I have a PhD in that. I like crossing lines without erasing them.

I like, for example, that Jonathan Safran Foer "wrote" a book that cut out pieces of *The Street of Crocodiles*, one of our favorite books (we talked about it when we were students), to make my favorite book of his, *Tree of Codes*. It's a stunning book and a stunning object—and to my mind, more original than the novels he's most known for. I don't think this project makes him a different, more elevated *species* than a girlfriend of mine who makes stunning fanvids or any of the people in this book who write fic. But that's how the culture has been treating them—like different species.

It isn't, of course, all about genre prejudice. Because there's also gender prejudice to contend with. When *Vogue* did a photoshoot in honor of Edith Wharton, they dressed up Foer, his teacher, Jeffrey Eugenides, and the writer Junot Díaz as Wharton's intellectual and writer friends. They dressed up a model to play Wharton.

In this volume, Wharton is played by fanfiction.

The high echelons of the literary are dominated by men. It's less true in genre fiction, and I think it's no accident that the professional writers in this volume who have come out of fanfiction are genre writers and are women.

I like to think of this final section of the book as a (nonfiction) crossover fic between postmodernism and a particular panel at the 2010 San Diego Comic-Con. This panel, "The Power of Myth," featured a range of professional writers whose work revisits and retells mythology—among them Amber Benson and Lev Grossman, whose names are now on the cover of this book. At the time, I was live-tweeting Comic-Con to my pop culture theory class, who were "meeting" that day on Twitter. As I'd been doing throughout the day, I asked a student's question and relayed the answer back to the class. The question: "What, besides copyright, was the difference between what these writers were doing and fanfiction?"

Not all the panelists were entirely pleased. One bluntly answered, "Quality"—which I don't *think* was meant to be self-deprecating. Seanan McGuire, author of the October Daye and InCryptid series, had the most complete answer—unsurprisingly, as she is or at least has been a fan writer and fan singer-songwriter (or filk) artist, herself (for *Buffy*. *Firefly*. *Veronica Mars* and Shakespeare. *Veronica Mars* and *Josie and the Pussycats*. My kind of fangirl). It makes sense that she would have given a great deal of thought to the question of how professionally published work related to fic.

McGuire felt the difference essentially came down to specific character and characterization. If she were to (hypothetically) write a Cinderella story, she explained, she wouldn't use Andrew Lang's exact characterization—or if she did, it would be fanfiction for his *Blue Fairy Book*. But if she wrote one in which Cinderella goes to Comic-Con dressed as, say, Batman, that's a different story entirely. She explained that she'd read books and said to herself, "Hey, this totally started as *Battlestar Galactica* fanfiction," to which her response was essentially—good for you!

In this section, then, I wanted to juxtapose a range of writers who celebrate and actively pursue techniques associated with fanfiction. They represent the avant-garde, the literary, and the popular. They write poetry, criticism, literary novels, genre fiction, drama, musicals, movies, and comic books. There's not that many of them, and they all mix it up a bit—one of them has even written and acted the same character. I don't want to efface all these distinctions of genre, because again, I like comparing things. And it's much more fun and interesting to compare apples to oranges than it is to compare a big vat of applesauce to itself.

But it's perfectly fine—and possibly more productive—to compare a Granny Smith to a Golden Delicious to a particular kind of Macoun that grows only in Upstate New York. Acknowledging basic similarities doesn't mean effacing the fact that we might cultivate and prefer different flavors. Or that we might truly believe that spending years honing a rare varietal in our backyard is better than just stocking up on popular supermarket varieties. Or that we might consider that heirloom apple elitist and a waste of time, and just want something we can buy in bulk that will hold up in a pie...

You get my meaning. There's plenty to argue about, even if we're all apples, eating each other...and we exhaust our metaphor in both tenor and vehicle, which has apparently driven us to a fruit orgy and left us there.

That is not what I meant, at all.

Let's try it this way. Let us go then, you and I... back to the Harry Potter fandom, for a minute. Or visit *The X-Files*. Fandoms carve up their output and their writing cultures—and sometimes their friendships—along their works' portrayal of relationships: whether romantic or sexual, and with whom. Entire archives are often divided that way, and fandoms bicker and worse about why people should or should not represent certain relationships, and in what ways. It seems natural in the context of fandom that Mystrade and Wincest are important generic categories, or that Kirk and Spock is an entirely different fictional animal from Kirk/Spock. And in fact, these are important descriptive terms that people will not only defend but advocate for above all others. But when outsiders see a fan community so polarized by its feelings about, say, writing Hermione with Harry or Ginny with Harry that these groups can't even talk to each other, and don't even want to share the same (digital) shelf space—well, frankly, to the people who aren't caught up in that conflict, it looks a little absurd.

So maybe this is what the rest of us look like:

The people who ship writing/difficulty and writing/revolution don't talk to the people who ship writing/entertainment or writing/romance. The writing/money shippers have an uneasy détente with the writing/literature folks in the prose fandom, but almost none of them talk to the poetry people because how could you even? The writing/YA folks have a strong community or are cliquish, depending on who you ask, and everyone knows not to invite the writing/genre people to the same party as writing/literary folks because it just ends up in a shouting match.

Fandom would explain that this is why we can't have nice things.

There are some important legal distinctions between what (some) of the writers in this section do and what (some) of the writers in other sections do—there are permissions negotiated, works transformed, criticisms made. But by and large it's a lot blurrier than you might think. *Fanfiction* doesn't designate a legal status or a specific kind of work. Lots of it is parody, lots of it is critical and transformative, and most of it (still) isn't for sale. I'd probably be fine to publish parts of a *Buffy* fic I wrote as a work of gender criticism—it's pretty explicit(ly critical). Reusing portions of my own scholarly work without very explicit citation, on the other hand, would constitute fraud. Yet fiction writers rework their own short stories into novels and there's no problem at all. Citation is everything—but in terms of the creative process, how does citation change anything?

And what if a work *is* illegal? I can tell you: nothing in literary history suggests we can reliably discount a work's cultural or literary value on the basis of its legal status. Quite the opposite. Works that break laws or otherwise offend the ethics and morals of their day often end up having tremendous literary, cultural, intellectual, and political significance. On the other hand, being illegal and ethically horrifying hardly guarantees value or significance. There's plenty of cheesy, dodgy rip-offs. There's no easy line we can draw. We seem as a species to operate under some kind of imperative to categorize, but there's no categorical imperative—a judgment that would always be right in all circumstances—about any kind of writing from sources.

And as Amber Benson will explain, even the lines we used to be able to draw are only getting blurrier. Fanfiction and its media have already changed the way people are writing, reading, finding, and thinking about stories. It won't change back. Fanfiction will be coming to the party and probably saying all kinds of awkward things polite company would leave unsaid.

You can imagine the Christmas dinners.

And if you can't, it's probably time to start trying.

Darren Wershler is an experimental poet, essayist, and cultural critic. Best known for The Iron Whim: A Fragmented History of Typewriting, *he is also Research Chair in Media and Contemporary Literature at Concordia University. Darren has been active on the forefront of what's come to be known as conceptual writing—a contemporary movement in avant-garde literature that involves copying, manipulating, reformatting, and otherwise appropriating found text. Aside from using material in ways that often occupy a legal gray area, what can fanfic have in common with the avant-garde? Are there ways in which this avant-garde is fannish? This essay considers how these very different writing and interpretive communities have evolved in relation to digital media, the mainstream literary establishment, and their own marginal status.*

Conceptual Writing as Fanfiction

Darren Wershler

Conceptual writing and fanfiction are the bearded Spocks of their respective universes.

If you're reading this book, you probably already know more about fanfiction than I do.

What I know about is a thing called conceptual writing. And I think that one useful way to think about conceptual writing is as fanfiction about conceptual art.

Another might be to say that, in neighboring universes that overlap slightly, both fanfiction and conceptual writing play the role of bearded Spock. What I want to consider in this brief essay is the value of a kind of forced cultural exchange. In the event of an unexpected ion storm and a transporter accident, or its prose equivalent, is there anything useful that writers of fanfiction and conceptual writing might learn from each other? It'll take me a few hundred words to get to the point where we can find out.

363

Conceptual writing is a term that has come to describe the work that my friends and I have produced over the last dozen years. One major example is Kenneth Goldsmith's *Day*, which consists of the entire text from the September 1, 2000, issue of the *New York Times*—stock quotes, ads, captions, and all—reset in nine-point type, reproduced line by line, and bound as a massive paperback book, with Goldsmith listed as the author.[147] In more general terms, conceptual writing is a catchall description for a mixed bag of writing techniques used by people who are interested in the impact of networked digital media on the creative process, the social function of authorship, and the economy of publishing.

This sort of writing is fannish in the sense that it draws much of its inspiration from things that were happening in the art world from the mid-1960s to the late 1970s. Conceptual art is a big, complex category, but Alexander Alberro usefully describes it in terms of four major "trajectories": a deemphasizing of the importance of the artist's technical skill and the cohesiveness of the final product; an increasing emphasis on the importance of text over images; a shift away from the aesthetically pleasing toward the conveyance of that odd modern invention we call *information*; and a questioning of how art is "supposed" to be framed, and the notion that there is a "correct" context (like a gallery) in which people are supposed to encounter it.[148] Conceptual writing follows these trajectories because, with a few exceptions, they had been largely ignored by literary writers.

Before there was a clear consensus about what it was or what it was going to be called, what conceptual writing did was to draw attention to the rhetorical aspects of writing that canonical literature usually neglects: weather reports, legal transcripts, social media feeds, stock quotes, Usenet posts, and so on. These texts are the "dark matter" of literature; they make up the bulk of everything that's written, but we habitually pretend that they don't matter in any capacity other than the moment.

John Guillory describes such texts as belonging to what he calls "information genres." In order to use them to convey that peculiar modern invention we call "information," we have to pretend that they have no rhetorical value of their own that might taint it.[149] By repackaging great swaths of information in media and formats other than the ones in which it initially appeared—again, think about Goldsmith reformatting the *New York Times* as a book—conceptual writing drew attention to the fact that all writing is poetic. It is poetic in that it always says more than we intend, and we assign value to it in keeping with large sets of external factors that sometimes have little to do with the ostensible content.

What conceptual writing does now is produce more poetry.

Over thirty years ago, legendary avant-garde poet and small-press publisher Bob Cobbing remarked that "there is no point whatsoever in adding to the quantity of poetry in this world. The world has quite enough poetry already. Probably too much. Far too much. The only excuse for being a poet today is to add to the quality of poetry, to add a quality which was not there before."[150] From Cobbing's perspective, the job of the writer is not to produce more of something already recognizable, but to constantly shift approaches and techniques, literally *making difference*. Rather than simply adding to the bulk of unread books on the shelf, conceptual writing, like Cobbing's work—and, I'd argue, like fanfiction—reframes big chunks of culture in a different context than they originally appeared, so that we can think about just how odd they actually are.

As is the fate of all successful cultural interventions, conceptual writing no longer exists on the margins of culture; it has become (semi-) respectable. Conceptual writers have performed in the Whitney Museum of American Art and the White House, and Goldsmith was selected as the Museum of Modern Art's Poet Laureate for 2013. Say what you want about these institutions and whether or not conceptual writing deserves a place in them, but they're very definitely not the margins. Conceptual writing has also produced the inevitable signs of cultural legitimacy: two giant, doorstop-sized anthologies, *Against Expression: An Anthology of Conceptual Writing*[151] and *I'll Drown My Book: Conceptual Writing by Women*.[152] Conceptual writing has become a big tent, and all sorts of people have laid claim to it (which is not particularly surprising, for reasons I'll get to shortly).

From my perspective, this isn't an occasion for either celebration or mourning. I'm trying to provide a relatively dispassionate description of a process of cultural circulation that has happened many times before and will happen many times again. Monet was a radical before he was a calendar. What interests me—and is of relevance to both conceptual writing and fanfiction—is what happens next: how a community based around a formerly marginal writing practice deals with its own relative success.

It's certainly possible to argue that fanfiction follows at least some of the trajectories of conceptual art, too, but that would take more space than I have here. The similarities between fanfiction and conceptual writing that I want to consider right now have nothing to do with tone, style, or subject matter. What interests me are particular similarities in the practices of their respective communities, and how cultural policing keeps them separate. In some respects, I think that conceptual writing has more to learn from fanfiction than the reverse.

Conceptual writing, like fanfiction, grows out of particular kinds of interpretive communities.

In his Introduction to the *UbuWeb Anthology of Conceptual Writing,* Craig Dworkin coined the term *conceptual writing* in its present usage.[153] (It has since been revised and expanded for *Against Expression.*) Dworkin emphasizes that even though the majority of the anthology's writers "were participants in the set of contemporaneous practices that came to be known as 'Conceptual Art'" (see Lippard[154]), "conceptual writing" does not refer exclusively to "writings by conceptual artists." Instead, Dworkin is after something that he calls "distinctly conceptual writing."[155]

This deft rhetorical maneuver allows for a bit of anticipatory plagiarism on Dworkin's part. The invention of the category of "distinctly conceptual writing" means that regardless of era, nationality, form, politics, or aesthetic allegiances, Dworkin can now claim the works of modernists like Alfred Jarry, Gertrude Stein, and Samuel Beckett, as well as texts from various neo–avant-garde individuals and groups, such as Fluxus and the Oulipo. What's going on here is an attempt to imagine a community.

All arts communities try to situate themselves within a larger history of the kind of work that they admire. Dworkin's invention of the notion of "distinctly conceptual writing" means that he can expand his canon into the present, to include work by twenty-first-century writers. Those people, whose names have been listed in different combinations at different times and different places (Dworkin included), are my friends, and here we arrive at the crux of the matter. Regardless of where it is now or what was happening elsewhere (and I know for a fact that in Vancouver and England at least, other communities were developing their own ideas about what could eventually be included under the big tent of conceptual writing), my experience of conceptual writing began with friendships more than with a sense of stylistic affinity. If you don't like the people you're talking to and writing with and for, you find another group. (I suspect this is true of fannish writing communities and fannish friendships, too.) Family resemblances are superficial at first, and develop as you and your friends discuss and debate, then work to find commonalities and ponder differences with the other communities you encounter along the way.

Dworkin's essay, of course, first appears in the context of UbuWeb. The closest thing to the online home of conceptual writing, UbuWeb is a massive repository of avant-garde art, writing, audio, and video: everything from anonymous street flyers and outsider art to digital copies of early films by directors like Gus Van Sant. Much of the material on Ubu-Web infringes on various copyrights. All of it has been collected and posted without permission and has been maintained through thousands of hours of labor without remuneration—except, perhaps, in the form of increased online reputation. I'd argue that this sort of unauthorized and quasi-authorized categorization, sorting, and positioning of one's literary heroes in order to contextualize one's own work is functionally indistinguishable from fannish activity, including fanfiction.

What makes the difference between conceptual writing and fanfiction are the respective cultural fields in which they occur.

Conceptual writing is located within literature and is ambivalent about wanting out. Fanfiction is located without literature and is ambivalent about wanting in.

American architectural and cultural theorist Charles Jencks expands on Umberto Eco's notion of "double coding" to describe hybrid styles that deploy popular *and* elitist connotations simultaneously. Double-coded texts communicate with the public and "a concerned minority" at the same time.[156] Sometimes called "dog whistles," such texts contain references that will usually only be recognized by those "in the know." When Omar quotes a line from Steve Earle's song "New York City" to McNulty in an episode of *The Wire* ("The Cost," 1–10), and Steve Earle is already a recurring cast member in the show, that's a dog whistle. Morrissey's use of the Polari phrase "Bona Drag" for the title of one of his albums is another type of double coding. Like Cockney rhyming slang, Polari was developed to indicate to members of specific communities (gays, carnies, etc.) that you were one of them. Different manifestations of double coding can achieve very different ends.[157] Conceptual writing and fanfiction both partake of double coding in a way that creates a strong but slightly skewed resemblance—think Spock versus bearded Spock. When encountered by chance against the backdrop of everyday life, both fanfiction and conceptual writing can easily be mistaken for something more mundane, unless you know the subtle signs (Spock's beard) that indicate that what you're looking at means something profoundly different from what you think it does.

Conceptual writing formed within the world of small-press poetry, though many of its practitioners are ambivalent about identifying their work as poetry or themselves as poets (witness Kenneth Goldsmith's frequent refrain that he's not a poet, even though he's been published largely by poetry presses). Dworkin mentions instances in which "one of the central figures of language poetry—a writer who had in fact himself incorporated transcribed texts into poetry"—repeatedly excluded conceptual writing from poetry.[158] This same language poet told me, on another occasion, that what I wrote wasn't poetry, but was "some sort of conceptual art." If it was a compliment, it was backhanded at best. I think he meant it as a kind of policing gesture, to exclude my work from the set of things he wanted to consider important. But it's hard to tell, because in North American culture, poetry itself is already a marginal activity. Books of poetry account for only 0.12 percent of total market sales in Canada,[159] (I'm Canadian; given the amount of support Canadian literary presses receive from the government, and the lack of such support in the United States, I assume that the figure is even lower in the states). For all of the newfound cultural capital that some of its members have accrued, in terms of the number of books in circulation, conceptual writing remains a margin of a margin.

Fanfiction also began as the marginal activity around genre fiction (or, as the academy condescendingly calls it, "paraliterature"). There are established pathways between fanfic and genre fiction, especially in science fiction. Not only do some science fiction fanfiction authors become commercial writers, but some commercial science fiction writers do more than support fanfiction—they continue to write it themselves.[160] But fanfiction is making serious incursions into mainstream publishing. Penguin and other prestigious houses are beginning to buy up little publishing operations that publish fanfic and were previously considered "vanity press" services;[161] Amazon is moving into the business of licensing entire fictional universes, presumably in the interest of producing a domesticated version of fanfiction. In a contemporary context, fanfiction has a much more convincing claim to cultural centrality than conceptual writing and even, arguably, poetry in general.

Fanfiction and conceptual writing have both been fueled by the rapid growth of networked digital media.

If fanfic and conceptual writing both have their origins in the small-press circulatory practices of specific interpretive communities, both have taken off as a result of the explosive growth of the internet. Here again we encounter Spock's beard, because there are uncannily similar-yet-different theories to account for this growth in both fanfiction and conceptual writing, each with their respective critical champion.

On one side of the mirror, Henry Jenkins, the preeminent theorist of convergence and transmedia, has made a strong case for the reliance of transmedia on fanfiction.[162] Briefly, transmedia theory argues that storytelling now takes place across multiple media platforms, creating entire fictional universes that require the audience to visit many of them to experience fiction fully, and to actively participate in the telling of its stories. Star Trek, with its multiple series, books, comics, cartoons, websites, and huge, active fan community, is the canonical example; Jenkins' work began with studies of fanfiction in the Star Trek community. On the other, Marjorie Perloff, the preeminent critic of the literary avant-gardes, developed a similar theory of what she calls the "differential text,"[163] which I've expanded elsewhere to a theory of "differential media."[164] Perloff's work on this subject begins with a consideration of Kenneth Goldsmith's *Fidget*, a key early text of conceptual writing. While Perloff emphasizes the differential text is a series of aesthetic possibilities for different kinds of manifestations (*Fidget* has been, among other things, a book, a website, a performance piece, a gallery installation, and two tailored paper suits), Jenkins focuses on transmedia as a business model—but truth be told, both transmedia and differential media rely on the creation and circulation of cultural capital. Moreover, both have demonstrated that reputation and other forms of cultural capital can be translated into *actual* capital.

But there is a substantial difference between fanfiction and conceptual writing that proceeds directly from the relationship of each with transmedia and the differential text. Both fanfiction and conceptual writing can manifest differentially, but they place their emphases on different aspects of their source materials. Where fanfiction uses transmedia as its vehicle, conceptual writing takes as its subject the materiality of the new configurations and forms that transmedia provides.

Where fanfiction shifts characters to other settings, conceptual writing shifts text to other discursive contexts.

The basic move of both fanfic and conceptual writing is the ancient trope of the *clinamen*: repetition with a slight difference. In the form of a diagram, we could represent the respective swerves from tradition of fanfic and conceptual writing as spirals of varying degrees of tightness, expanding out from a point that they nevertheless continue to orbit. However, these spirals operate on different objects. Fanfiction works at the level of what's written or said: for example, by combining characters from two different fictional worlds. Conceptual writing works at the level of the *context* in which something is written or said: for example, by shifting the context of a text's publication from official courtroom transcripts to a hardbound edition published by a literary small press.

If fanfiction always proceeds with reference to some sort of original text produced by a successful commercial writer, conceptual writing begins by referring to gestures and practices produced by generations of successful avant-garde artists who already were calling the notion of originality itself into doubt. And yet, Dworkin notes that conceptual writing acquires a "strong sense of signature" because it makes "irrevocable" interventions into culture.[165] Over time, a canny act of appropriation becomes indistinguishable from Romantic notions of creation out of nothing. W. G. Sebald allegedly gave the following advice to his creative writing students: "I can only encourage you to steal as much as you can. No one will ever notice. You should keep a notebook of tidbits, but don't write down the attributions, and then after a couple of years you can come back to the notebook and treat the stuff as your own without guilt."[166] Creativity and appropriation are two sides of the same coin, and ultimately are inextricable from each other. While both fanfiction and conceptual writing might appear to challenge or threaten originality, they also rely on it and reproduce it at other moments.

Kenneth Goldsmith is the E. L. James of conceptual writing. Or, to put this all another way: This is an essay about E. L. James if I say so.

Both Goldsmith and James are symptoms of whatever it is that has replaced the crumbling narratives that we've used to make sense out of the tatters of modernity—some mutant form of celebrity culture.

Fanfiction is now demonstrably capable of producing bestselling authors. Conceptual writing has had some mainstream successes: the international success of Christian Bök's *Eunoia*, and Kenneth Goldsmith reading for President Obama—and his subsequent lampooning by Jon Stewart—are two of them. If literature retains any of its privilege, it's only so that privilege can be claimed by the Spock-bearded rabble that it traditionally relegated to the hinterlands, now bent on dividing between themselves the diminishing spoils of what we used to call literature.

To avoid reproducing the myopia and narrowness that conceptual writing and fanfiction came into existence to contest, they both need to recognize that they are part of a larger cultural tendency to see all creativity as a process of remixing. Dworkin notes that "in the twenty-first century, conceptual poetry thus operates against the background of related vernacular practices, in a climate of pervasive participation and casual appropriation."[167] The only problem with that sentence, from my perspective, is what counts as foreground and what counts as background.

By recognizing itself as a minoritarian practice (i.e., part of the background), conceptual writing might become capable of doing something that poetry has never been capable of: recognizing the things that look just like it and transpire all around it that are not published as poetry, don't circulate through literary communities, aren't received by people as literary texts, but nevertheless could be formally indistinguishable from conceptual writing... *and not colonizing them for poetry in the process.* There's a price to pay for that, though: actually giving up the last vestiges of the Romantic notion of author-as-lone-genius, the ones that even a century of modernity refused to erase. In its place, we might install some sort of invisible but open conspiracy that's capable of appreciating the tactical efficiencies of the things we want to dismiss as cheesy imitations and knockoffs. If makers of conceptual writing and fanfiction really desire to operate differently from culture at large (and I'm no longer sure that this was ever the case), they'd need to produce writers who are not interested in becoming celebrity authors but are willing to dissolve away into the shadows before the laurels can be handed out. Not Warhol's Factory, but Batman Incorporated.

An Interview with Doug Wright

DOUG WRIGHT IS AN AWARD-WINNING playwright, librettist, and screenwriter who often works with historical material and documentary sources. His play *Quills* (and his screenplay for the film) was based on the life of the Marquis de Sade, and his Pulitzer- and Tony award-winning *I Am My Own Wife* was based on the life of Charlotte von Mahlsdorf, a transgendered antiques dealer who survived the Nazi and East German Communist regimes. Doug has also collaborated on adapting documentary films for the stage, writing the books for the musicals *Grey Gardens* and *Hands on a Hardbody*. I've discussed Doug's work in several courses in the context of adaptation, the ethics of representation, and depictions of non-normative genders and sexualities. Here, I asked him about the differences between working with "real person" sources versus literary sources, between historical persons and those he actually knows, and how he makes the work he builds from these sources his own.

Could you say a little bit about the history of dramatic writing from sources? It seems as if it has a very long tradition.

I don't think that any writing springs fully forged from the mind of the writer; we're all writing from "sources," whether that source is our own memory, an experience we've weathered, a book or poem that influenced us once, a painting we admired, or a nugget of history that lodged in our brain. You can't write without precursors; none of us are immune to influence. In fact, it may be true that no writer can ever claim to be wholly and unequivocally "original."

What kind of work goes into adapting an existing creative work as a play? How, as a playwright, do you make it yours?

I only gravitate to material that moves me in some visceral, absolute way. I have to see myself in it (in a particular character, or in the central human truth the work espouses) before I agree to adapt it. I don't take the assignment and then try to locate myself in it. I have to be there from the start.

In a related question, how transformative would you say it is to rework a short story or novel, say, as a play? (Or a documentary film to a musical?) Does the change in genre always make a big difference, or does the degree of difference greatly depend on the approach of the playwright?

Different forms follow different rules; Broadway musicals, for example, require strong storytelling in a way that cinema verité, psychologically driven documentaries (like *Grey Gardens*) do not. You have to meet the demands of the form you've chosen, even if it means reinventing the source material to a certain degree. A good adaptation is rarely a slavishly fidelitous one.

Creatively speaking, do you find a great difference in working from fictional or creative sources and working from "real person" sources?

A source is a source, and the adaptation process is largely the same. And you have to show the same sensitivity to any living person who is impacted by your work. A novelist may take just as much umbrage with you if you distort his fiction as a historical figure may take if you distort his or her life.

Do you find it changes your process or your attitude to your work when you are writing based on a well-known, iconic (but long-dead) figure like Sade, as opposed to someone like Charlotte von Mahlsdorf, whom you actually knew?

Absolutely. Thanks to other writers like Yukio Mishima and Peter Weiss, Sade is both a historical figure and a literary icon. You can employ him in either way. There are a myriad of biographies about Sade—many of them exquisitely researched and written—which inform the historical record. And if you take liberties with his life, there are plenty of nonfictional works available to the general reader to reposition your inspirational flights of fancy. And an audience is (for the most part) ready to experience Sade as a symbol; they don't really expect straightforward biography. He's already appeared as a semifictionalized character in countless other books, plays, and movies. But Charlotte was largely unknown; I knew audiences would be meeting her for the first time. As such, I felt a heightened obligation not to reinvent the facts of her life, but to represent them as faithfully as I could. She has yet to enter the pantheon of literary devices!

Could you talk about the process of adapting the real people who were the subjects of *Hands on a Hardbody*, but who were (as I understand it) combined and otherwise adapted to suit dramatic purposes? How did you seek their permission? How did they react to the process and the end result?

When we initially approached the original contestants from Robb Bindler's 1997 [documentary] film, we were unequivocally clear with them: we said that our characterizations would endeavor to be true to their essential spirit as people, but that we would take liberties with the raw data of their lives. They understood that we would heighten certain character traits or invent certain biographical details in order to more fully serve our drama. They all gave us permission, and when we flew them first to La Jolla to see the original run of the show, and later to its Broadway opening, they were uniformly pleased. While they acknowledged that we'd taken creative license, no one felt violated or misrepresented in any fundamental ways. Obviously, that was a great relief to me!

Would you have qualms about basing a character (very recognizably) on a living person? Would you feel differently basing such a character on a public figure as opposed to, say, someone you know socially?

It was much easier to write about Sade than Charlotte von Mahlsdorf for that very reason. As a writer, you certainly have moral obligations, but they remain abstract. With a friend, they become intensely personal and you violate them at your peril.

When writing about a historical figure or "real person," how do you balance the demands of the play (dramatically or thematically) with concerns about historical accuracy or being "true to life"?

It depends on the intention that motivates your work. If your primary aim is to provide a biographical but dramatic portrait of a life, then you should do so with close attention to the historical record. If your aim is to create a parable or an allegory that uses the person in question in a metaphorical or symbolic way, then you should feel free to do so, I think, within reason. Obviously, you shouldn't engage in gross distortion or misrepresentation. And the play itself should alert the audience to your authorial intent, so they can experience it accordingly. I'm a great fan of disclaimers in programs ("the play is inspired by but not wholly true to actual events"), but I'm even more heartened when the play's style and tone contextualizes its treatment of real people. For example, given its absurdist style and antic word play, it would be very hard to mistake Tom Stoppard's *Travesties* for a real-life account of the lives of James Joyce, Tristan Tzara, and Lenin. Similarly (I hope), the arch, Grand Guignol style of my play *Quills*—written with all the breathless ghoulishness of a penny dreadful—signals to the audience that they should take its events with a grain of salt.

Would you be concerned about being a recognizable character in someone else's play or novel? What about a character in slash fanfiction?

Since real people have entrusted me to integrate them into my work, I suppose I shouldn't be coy and ask fellow authors to refrain from doing the same to me! That would be more than a tad hypocritical, wouldn't it? :)

Are you aware of *Quills*-based fanfiction? (I found about forty-five stories online.) How do you feel about people writing in and out of characters and settings you created?

I had no idea! As long as the fiction doesn't raise any possibility of plagiarism or copyright infringement, then I think it's the highest form of flattery!

To my knowledge, all of the *Quills*-based fanfiction is offered freely on the internet in the traditional spirit of fanfiction—others "playing in your sandbox" with no intent to profit. BUT, if someone *were*

suddenly to write a fantastically popular *Quills*-based fanfiction but decide to make it all set on, say, Madison Avenue in the early 1960s, and then change all the names and publish or produce it...would that bother you?

Again, as long as they didn't plagiarize me, I don't think I could take issue with it. As I said in my opening answer, no writer writes free of influence. I owe a great deal of *Quills* to the works of the late Charles Ludlam, and *I Am My Own Wife* was born of documentary theater pioneered by Emily Mann, Anna Deveare Smith, and Moises Kaufman.

Given all this discussion of creative use, writing from sources, and writers earning money from work based on other writers' work, is there anything you'd like to clarify about your stance on copyright protection or the relationship between creative use and infringement?

Copyright is a moral imperative for all artists, living or dead, and should be treated with the utmost care. In the age of information sharing, it is imperiled. We must strive to maintain it. It provides the basis for our livelihood and makes our craft an economically tenable one. Writers should be inspired by one another and should be open to artistic influence from our colleagues. But we should never steal one another's work.

An Interview with Jonathan Lethem

JONATHAN LETHEM IS AN AUTHOR, editor, critic, essayist, and Mac-Arthur Fellowship recipient. He's written the National Book Critics Circle Award–winning novel *Motherless Brooklyn,* the *New York Times* bestseller *Fortress of Solitude,* and an entire book on the Talking Heads album *Fear of Music.* He's mixed detective fiction with science fiction; he's edited Philip K. Dick. And for all that, I fangirl in his general direction.

Lethem also hosts the Promiscuous Materials Project, an archive of his own stories that he makes available for adaptation by playwrights and screenwriters. He's not exactly saying "Fic me for fun and profit"—he confers certain rights but not others for his dollar fee, and he does not want to see his fiction republished as fiction by someone else. (He has expressed some interest in being slashed, but that's another story. Or at least a promising prompt.)

Lethem explains his motivation on the Promiscuous Materials website like this:

> I like art that comes from other art, and I like seeing my stories adapted into other forms. My writing has always been strongly sourced in other voices, and I'm a fan of adaptations, ap[p]ropriations, collage, and sampling.
>
> I recently explored some of these ideas in an essay ["The Ecstasy of Influence"] for *Harper's Magazine.*[168] As I researched that essay I came more and more to believe that artists should ideally find ways to make material free and available for reuse. This project is a (first) attempt to make my own art practice reflect that belief.

I absolutely recommend the essay he mentions. It sparked some further questions in my mind about how Lethem might see fanfiction and its relationship to other kinds of creative borrowing and reworking, and how we judged them. I was really curious about how he'd answer them. So I asked him.

In your essay "The Ecstasy of Influence," originally for *Harper's*, you argue that "appropriation, mimicry, quotation, allusion, and sublimated collaboration consist of a kind of sine qua non of the creative act, cutting across all forms and genres in the realm of cultural production." Do you notice a difference in how people react to similar strategies in different areas of cultural production?

Yes, I absolutely notice a difference. It's why I'm so interested in writing across media and discipline, to help people reframe their resistance to quotation. Because it strikes me as so peculiar that things like sampling and quoting seem so natural in one area, but seem inapplicable or unacceptable in another. Much of it has to do with the setting of reception experience—whether it sets up expectations of purity or high culture, and therefore expectations of "originality."

You mention high culture as giving us high expectations of originality, but some of the very artists that most suggest high culture and purity to a lot of people—such as what is known as High Modernism, writers like Ezra Pound and T. S. Eliot—were huge practitioners of quotation and appropriation.

Yes, that's one reason I get irked with those who try to quarantine postmodernism. They really need to subject T. S. Eliot to that test. And the history of visual art in the twentieth century is a procession of collage, appropriation, et cetera, a constant shackling of low vernacular. Virtually every major art movement in the twentieth century has been implicated in appropriation with the possible exception of pure abstract expressionism.

It's everywhere, basic, a native gesture, so for me, I try to universalize these techniques as much as possible. Not that the experience of the new isn't important—the *experience* of the new is very important—but the *truth* of it is probably that the artifact or gesture arousing that sensation is *not* new. We are not the first people to arrive at self-reflexivity or intertextuality. The Greeks had a chorus.

So I get irked at the oppressive self-congratulation of the present in congratulating itself for self-reflexivity and mashup. *Or* decrying the same things. Because in all sorts of folk traditions, self-reflexivity and mashup have *always* been here, especially in those traditions closest to fanfiction. Oral storytellers, for example, were always working with a tapestry of borrowing, references, stories. Like hip-hop, their stories made mosaics, sampled riffs, borrowed extensively.

It's when economies of money or prestige come into it that we see people putting up the fences, balkanizing the territory, and selling what they have done as "defensibly original." Almost always art gestures almost always are borrowing. We live in a common language of culture.

But doesn't plagiarism exist?

Yes, at the extreme margins, there's something pathetic. That's when someone takes something that's nearly everything that makes someone's work interesting, disguises the origin, and presents it. That sucks. But everything short of *that* is much more complicated to talk about. A work derives energy from the way it transforms a source or many sources, the way it combines this material with elements that are native to the teller. This kind of work comprises the enormous preponderance of what we mean by "culture." A tiny wedge of plagiarism, and a vast field of culture. It won't do us any good to suggest the exalted, excused practices are in some way unrelated to what we call plagiarism. Stuff doesn't come out of the vacuum; it comes out of other stuff.

Once you've accepted *that,* you can get into the fascinating region of what is actually before you. Then we can talk about reception feeling. What kind of reference makes you feel good, and what makes you feel like something unfair has occurred?

I often go to music to discuss these reactions. Like, what about Paul Simon's *Graceland*? If you know anything about African music, you know the album *is* African music, with Paul Simon's reedy tenor and lyrics stuck onto it. Some people felt surprise and discomfort when they listened to the album and then went and listened to African music and realized how much the album relied on that music. But on the other hand, Paul Simon never made any secret of it. He named it, made it explicit. If we think of a scale, on the degree of transformation, I'd say *Graceland* gets about 15/100. It's not very transformed. But on transparency? 99/100. Paul Simon showered gratitude and exposure and money on his sources. He performed with them. So in his case, if we have these two scales, Paul Simon did so great on one of them that we excuse the other.

Let's take a different example. Led Zeppelin. They stole songs from Willie Dixon. The biggest monster of a white British band stole music from this more-or-less unknown black guy, put their name to it, and had to be sued to do anything about it, to give any credit or compensation. They scored a 3 on the scale of acknowledgment and transparency. But on the other hand, their music doesn't sound like Willie Dixon. The transformation is extremely vital. Led Zeppelin not only made a new, arresting sound out of these songs, they invented a whole new genre of music. They got heavy metal out of Willie Dixon. So they get a 99 on level of transformation. They made something so utterly new, that you have to give it up to the transformative gesture, and it's hard to want them not to have done it from a musical point of view—even if the way they did it was immoral.

Do you think how much money is involved influences how people react to appropriation—including how they react in the legal arena?

In general, I'm not interested in law; I'm interested in art—but money has everything to do with how people react. If there's no money being made, people don't usually care as much.

Why do you think these practices of appropriation are so much less acceptable to people in terms of the written word? Why is it a much bigger deal to plagiarize writing? Have literary critics (of contemporary literature, I mean—book critics) ceded what should be judgments about aesthetics and effect to the interests of the publishing industry?

I do think that's true [that book critics have ceded those judgments to the publishing industry], but I'd add another diagnosis: literary criticism is too closely intertwined with newspaper journalism. So whereas other fields of art reception are successfully partitioned from ethos of journalists, book reviewers are usually newspapermen who fancy themselves book reviewers. The field of book reviewing so totally overwhelms academic literary criticism in terms of influence, and journalists are of course obsessed with journalistic notions of plagiarism, sources, and inaccuracy. These standards migrate far too much in the realm of literary writing.

Imagine the Ian McEwan scandal in the [visual] arts—it's insane, it would never happen. [McEwan was accused of borrowing too heavily in his novel *Atonement* from Lucilla Andrews' wartime hospital memoir, *No Time for Romance*. McEwan consistently acknowledged he'd used the memoir as source.] But journalists love that stuff. Since *they* write from sources, sometimes very minimally transformed, they need to become police. But their own degree of transformation is pathetically tiny compared to Ian McEwan['s]. It's the narcissism of minor difference; it's overcompensation.

Speaking of differences, how is it different—creatively—when we base a character on someone else's story or character, as opposed to basing that character on someone else's life or personality?

There's no difference. Legally, I know it's totally different ranges, but from the creative standpoint that distinction poses a meaningless quarantine between sources. Because many people—myself included—are largely *themselves* based on literary characters.

My characters were always based on someone real and also resonated with a literary character. That's what it's all about. Fantasies, archetypes. In *Motherless Brooklyn*, it was Raymond Chandler's detective, the Tourette's guy I saw [on] a bus, case studies I read in Oliver Sacks' work—and me, he's based on me, too. And Elliot Gould, in Altman's *Long Goodbye*! How could anyone think it's any less complicated (apart from lawyers)? The dream that this complexity could be neatly sorted out is a very typical American, pragmatist, anti-intellectual fantasy, based on suspicion of the artist or intellectual.

When someone tells a fanfiction writer that they're "not a real writer," I say to that that person, "You don't have the slightest idea of what it means to write a scene and a character in the English language, with images and words chock full of received meaning." I do think there's an innocent bravery to saying, "I'm going to write another Sherlock Holmes story," but of course it's already a new Sherlock Holmes the moment you start writing it. It's not Doyle's. It's *yours*.

One of the ways avant-gardes and their critics have theorized collage, appropriation, and cut-up is as a disruption of narrative, and even of (an ideologically constructed) self. How can these same strategies work *toward* narrative, and *toward* the construction of (fictional) selves?

I respect this avant-garde position enormously, but I want to poke at it. Take, for example, the French appropriation of Hollywood *film noir* when they invented New Wave. Goddard was adapting these romantic American models, these crime texts. Then he destroyed them, fought them, chopped them up. In interviews, he talks about the resistance to this material, how his films avoided the obvious gestures of his sources. And yes, there's enormous energy in these acts of resistance and disruption. But after they have done this two or three times— and it's an enormous font of material for them—what are they not admitting to themselves about what they love and desire? The things you choose to transform are the things you love, even if you unmake them. You're still participating in them.

Do you think the same critique applies to a writer like Kenneth Goldsmith and his work in reformatting the *New York Times* or traffic and weather reports? Or is he just using material, interested in how formats change how we see the material?

No, that's fair enough. I don't think he has a feeling of closeness to the *Times*. He's transforming his sources into pure language, in a way. But Kenny Goldsmith is at the extreme edge, I'd say. In the other edge, let's say, is a very talented fan writer who writes very delicate, in-character *Star Trek* stories, filling in the detail in a very respectful way, but without transforming the world at all. Identifying those two extremes is like the Led Zeppelin–*Graceland* continuum we discussed. Goldsmith and the respectful fanfiction writer are the limit cases—what everyone else does falls in between.

As a writer and copyright holder, how do you reconcile the "open source" ethos with the need to make a living?

I'm not Lawrence Lessig; I don't have proposals. I make my living partly by propagation of copyright. I grew up in it; I'm attached to it. I don't have the vision, but my instinct leads me to believe there are protections afforded my work that are absurd. It's like there's ten miles of frosting on a cake. I like the cake, I might cling to the cake, but it definitely doesn't need all that frosting.

Some people would say that I have a right not to see certain things done to my characters while I'm still around, and maybe I can see that. But I believe that after I'm gone, my work belongs to the culture. A lot of people's reactions have to do with how long it takes for it to be okay, and I think it starts being okay really quickly. It's nice that I get to make a living, but a lot of artists don't. It is easy to exaggerate making a living into some kind of nativist right. I'm lucky, but I'm in a rare category. Most people participate in culture for free, or it costs them money. I went into it knowing that, and I did it anyway. I got lucky, but I still try to ignore the money and just make and respond to art.

Patricia Storms slashed you with Michael Chabon in comic form, and I know you've expressed an interest in being slashed. Who would you want to be slashed with, Mr. Lethem?

Oh, it's not up to me! Please surprise me. The thing about asking to be slashed, you're begging to be distracted. But you can't protest these things. My tiny share of fame—it puts my name up for grabs. I accept that. It's not that I feel I'm so terribly important, that anyone is obligated to have fantasies about me. But if you accept my view that intellectual property is kind of a chimera, then that includes the names and personae of we who drift into the public sphere. I'm a fiction, inventing myself as I go along—but why should I be the only one with the right?

Amber Benson is an actor, writer, and filmmaker. Much beloved for her portrayal of Tara on Buffy the Vampire Slayer, *Amber seems to create in most media these days. She is cocreator of* Ghosts of Albion, *a transmedia property that began life as an animated web series and continued via novels and a roleplaying game. She has made several films; has written the Calliope Reaper-Jones series of novels and a children's book; and has collaborated on several comic books for the* Buffyverse, *revisiting as a writer the character she'd played for years. Fic writers also revisit this character. A lot. Here, Amber writes about how internet accessibility, participatory culture, and transmedia have transformed highly structured divisions into an atmosphere of (sometimes confusing) creative flux.*

Blurring the Lines

Amber Benson

There used to be a hard-and-fast rule. There was "them" and then there was "us." "Them" was made up of artists—the people who created TV shows, books, films, music, and visual art. "Us" was the group of people who consumed what they made. "Them" was set apart from "us" because "them" was creating material that was then disseminated, on a large scale, to "us" out there in the real world. "Us" could enjoy "them" and their work, but "us" could not contribute to the creations we loved in any appreciable fashion.

But then something interesting happened: the internet took over the world, and this hard-and-fast rule slowly began to disintegrate. All of a sudden, "us" was able to horn in on "them" and their creative process in a very public way—most notably in the form of fanfiction.

fanfiction

All lowercase letters.

No spaces.

No CAPS.

I have a weird perspective on the subject.

I am an actor, sometimes.

And I once played a character who's a fanfiction favorite.

I hear she/I does a whole lot of "slash-ing"...wait, that's not the proper use of the word. This might be better: I hear there is a lot of slash fanfiction about her/me on the internet. Which is kind of sad because this means the fanfiction version of her/me is getting a lot more action than the real me.

Before I get started, I should clarify exactly who/what I am. If the name in the byline is unfamiliar to you, you might recognize the title of the show I appeared in, or the name of the character I played in that show: *Buffy the Vampire Slayer* and Tara Maclay, respectively.

Just FYI, I had to go online and look up whether or not the "c" in Maclay is capitalized. You would think from the amount of time I spent pretending to be this fictional character (three years), I would know how to spell her last name properly. But the truth is, there are a lot of fans out there who know way more about her than I do.

And some of these more knowledgeable fans write fanfiction.

I try not to read fanfiction about her/me. I think it would be awkward and I'd forever be left wondering why she/I am so much cooler on paper/ the internet than I am in real life. I am also leery of reading anything about her/me because I really don't want to read about my pretend-self doing naughty things with characters/people whom I may or may not be attracted to in real life.

When I was on *Buffy* (this was many, many moons ago), not looking at *Buffy* fanfiction was another hard-and-fast rule. People are litigious, so anything written by a fan and sent in to the writers/producers was not supposed to be read. I have retrofitted this rule to fit my own needs— mostly because of the not-wanting-to-think-about-me-doing-naughty- things-with-fictional-characters worry—so just know that when I see you at a science fiction convention and you hand me your fanfiction about Tara/me, I will smile and take it...but I am probably not going to read it if Tara/me is being a dirty birdy.

I have been known to read fanfiction about other things, things I have no creative/personal stake in. I might even read the *Buffy* stuff you write, unless you have Tara Maclay giving cunnilingus to Counselor Troi (who is, by far, my father's favorite Star Trek Betty). If you hand me something like that then I am probably going to take a pass.

Pause.

I must preface all of this with a disclaimer: I have cowritten (along with Christopher Golden) a few Willow/Tara comic books. There is a difference between writing these comics and writing fanfiction and it comes down to two things: the storylines for the comics are carefully vetted by Dark Horse Comics/20th Century Fox, and there is no cunnilingus in them. (Well, at least none that ended up on the page. Maybe some dirty bits were excised before the comics went to print...and now you'll forever wonder if I was just pulling your leg or if there really *was* excised cunnilingus in those comic books, right?)

I think we can all agree there's something meta about my situation, something *Adaptation*-like about the layer upon layer of weirdness. Well, let me just tell you that, though you may think *my* creative life is meta, it's nowhere near as meta as the creative life of my friend Javier Grillo-Marxuach.

Be prepared. This might knock your meta-socks off.

My friend Javi is truly one of the kindest, most gifted writer/producers I've ever had the pleasure of knowing. And he possesses two qualities I very much value in other creative individuals: he treats the business of show like a team sport, and he has a genuine interest in helping others...unlike a lot of the people I've met in Hollywood.

Oh, and there's a third thing, too.

He's an honest-to-God *Fan*.

With a capital "F."

So, to just point out the blurring of the lines here, Javi is not just an artist, he is also a fan. Where he is concerned, the words *artist* and *fan* are synonymous.

A few years ago, Javi created a brilliant television show for ABC Family called *The Middleman*. (To up the meta-quotient, *The Middleman* was a comic book before it was adapted for television.)

The Middleman had (and still has) a dedicated fan following—especially for its plucky, intelligent female heroine, Wendy Watson (played by actress Natalie Morales). So, needless to say, there were a lot of frustrated fans when the show was pulled off the air after only one season.

And one of those frustrated fans was Javi himself.

Three years later, he did something about it.

In the ultimate meta-fanfiction crossover, Javi wrote a fanfiction piece about his own show...and *Doctor Who*.

You can go to The Middle Blog over at LiveJournal and read his fanfiction story in its entirety. I really think you should. It's quite brilliant, weaving together the best of *The Middleman* with Javi's passionate love of

Doctor Who—but what was so intriguing to me was not the piece itself (as cool as it is), but what it represented about the blurring of lines.

I realized that as much as we try to put a divide between the two worlds ("them" and "us"), there really isn't one anymore. Not with the advent of transmedia, the rise of creator-owned content on the internet, the domination of Twitter and Facebook. Not when Twilight fanfiction becomes a bestselling series of erotica novels. Not when the guy who made *The Middleman* decides to write a fanfiction piece about the television show he created because he's still interested in telling stories about his characters.

All of these components have created a perfect storm that will forever knock down the wall of separation between artist and audience.

Would it be crazy to postulate, then, that with the blurring of these lines, the words "artist" and "fan" have become interchangeable in some ways? Just because you created a character, it doesn't mean you get to tell the whole of their story—especially if you sell your characters to studios/television networks/comic book companies. Suddenly, these conglomerates own your creative content and they get to decide its fate. Making you, for all intents and purposes, just another fan of the thing that you happened to create.

This has been going on in the comics world forever. Poor comic book superheroes get passed around like hookers at a gangbang—they've always got someone new writing about them, drawing them, adding to their mythology.

So, by the same token, when a fan writes fanfiction, one might equate them to just another writer for hire on a project—they're just not getting paid in money for their work. For them, the payment is the sheer joy of writing for characters they love. They are no longer just a "fan." Now they are an "artist."

I'm going to insert myself in here again because I'm still trying to figure out where I fit into all of this.

As an actor, I gave my voice and face to a character who someone else created and wrote all the dialogue for. When someone sits down to write fanfiction about my character, they are envisioning and often describing that same face and voice, which happen to belong to me, but which I lent to the character when I played the part.

Working on the Willow/Tara comic books as a writer, I wrote about/for the character I played on *Buffy*. At that point, I became an artist who was using my own face and voice to give continuing life to a fictional character whom I played on television, but did not create.

See? It's all very confusing.

Then add in how accessible everything is via the internet—which is a huge tool when one wants to go about "blurring the lines"—and it's even more troubling. On Twitter, am I just me, Amber Benson? Or am I an actor named Amber Benson who played a character called Tara Maclay? Or am I only seen as Tara Maclay, the character from that television show you loved to watch, who for unknown reasons likes to go around calling herself Amber Benson?

Also, am I somehow creating fanfiction when I interact with people on the internet—adding to my real-life, personal continuing storyline *and* to the now-defunct storyline of the character I played on television? This makes my head spin, and does nothing to answer the real question: If we can't tell who the "artists" are, and if the "fans" are just as hard to categorize, then where does that leave us?

I actually think that—barring my own existential identity crisis—it leaves us in a very good place. Fanfiction has pried open a door, allowing fans a chance to participate in the continuing storylines of the characters they love. The internet has given these fans and their fanfiction a high-profile stage so that the world can find and enjoy their artistic endeavors. It has also given "artists" a chance to create outside of the system—like Javi and his *Middleman* fanfiction—and to address questions, comments, and suggestions from their "fans" directly and in a creative way.

For better or worse, it looks as though the lines have been forever blurred. I just wish this essay had given me a little more personal clarity. Maybe I'll just follow Javi's example and go write some fanfiction. Maybe a little Amber/Tara slash fanfiction—so I can *really* confuse myself...

ACKNOWLEDGMENTS

I WOULD LIKE TO THANK, first and foremost, the many writers and readers of fanfiction who have engaged with me over the years. They are too many to be named and some don't want to be named, but they have all challenged and educated me.

I am enormously grateful to everyone who helped write this book: my coauthors, the *Fic* contributors, and those who agreed to be interviewed. My editor Leah Wilson also felt like a coauthor. Even Twitter sometimes felt like a coauthor as it provided countless tips, links, fact-checks, recommendations, and sustained debates (looking at you, @einfach_mich and @LyricalKris). Gretchen, Ivy Blossom, Jane, and Myg, as well as many contributors were especially generous with their time and insights. My agent, Michael Bourret, has helped me intellectually as well as in very practical ways during what were (for me) difficult days. All the editorial and production folks at Smart Pop have been incredible, supportive, and a pleasure to work with.

Thank you also to all who helped make my summer 2010 Theories of Popular Culture class a real intellectual adventure: the writers BellaFlan, Algonquinrt/d0tpark3r, ItzMegan73, The Black Arrow, Snowqueens Icedragon, Sebastien Robichaud, Anais Mark, AngstGoddess003, Mrs. TheKing, Gondolier, and m81170 shared their fics and, in many cases, time and insights with my class. tby789, LolaShoes, Ms Kathy, HMonster, and Sleepy Valentina were also an important part of the conversation. The students of ENGL 5960—Myles Barker, Kacey Bowles, Elizabeth Cornwall, Molly Daines, Chris Dammert, Edward Granda, Joshua Lund, Jesse Maynes, Michelle McKonkie, Pace Measom, Gillian Nelson, Dai Newman, Katie Prottengeier, Cooper Savage, Mary Jane Snyder, and Richard Wentworth—were in a class by themselves (no, but really) and all made important contributions to a field they had no idea even existed before the beginning of class, as well as to this book. Over the years, the Utah Browncoats and some lovely Spuffy communities on LiveJournal have been generous with my students and me as well.

My family has been very patient and supportive as this project turned out to be a lot more extensive than I'd anticipated. I can't imagine anyone better suited to helping me think through alternative methods of writing and reading than my beloved partner, Craig Dworkin, who also made the coffee that fueled this project from its inception.

ABOUT THE CONTRIBUTORS

Cyndy Aleo (algonquinrt/d0tp@rk3r) is a freelance writer, editor, and book reviewer who still reads more fanfiction than anyone probably should. Her involvement with Twilight has been reduced to rewatching the films with RiffTrax accompaniment, though she still rants on occasion. Her debut novel, *Undying*, is out now in ebook. You can find her on Twitter at @cyndyaleo.

V. Arrow (aimmyarrowshigh) graduated from Knox College in 2008 with degrees in history and creative writing, specializing in twentieth-century pop culture and young adult lit. Under another name, she has previously published at Pop Matters, The One Love, Tommy2. net, and *The Hollywood Reporter*. She believes that pop culture affects, reflects, and informs all aspects of daily life in Western culture and that it is perhaps the most crucial form of media expression to analyze and discuss.

Tish Beaty (his_tweet) was part of the team that in 2010 developed The Writer's Coffee Shop Publishing House. During her time with TWCS, she managed both authors and editors, and edited many titles, including the #1 *New York Times* bestseller *Fifty Shades of Grey*. No topic is taboo on her author blog, tishbeaty.com, and healthy living recipes can be found on her site lusciousandhealthyliving.blogspot. com. When not wrangling her kids, cooking, or blogging, Tish can be found presenting self-editing and character development tips. Recent publications include an essay in *Fifty Writers on Fifty Shades of Grey* as well as a short story in the anthology *We Love NY!*

Brad Bell is cocreator, executive producer, and star of the newlywed sitcom *Husbands*, for which he has won writing and acting awards. Last year, he coauthored *Husbands: The Comic* with Jane Espenson and served as consulting producer for VH1's *Pop Up Video*. Since 2008, Bell has produced short-form satire on YouTube and released electronic music on iTunes as his online persona, "Cheeks."

Amber Benson is a writer, actor, director, and maker of things. She lives in LA and doesn't own a television. Her new urban fantasy series, The

391

Witches of Echo Park, will be out in 2014, but if you like her brand of insanity, you can go pick up her five-book Calliope Reaper-Jones series at your local bookstore. She also codirected the film *Drones*, which you can add to your Netflix queue...right...now!

Peter Berg (Homfrog) is a seventeen-year-old geeky dude with big ambitions. Receiving a 2180 on his SATs and an INTP on the Myers–Briggs, he is a rising senior at the Lab School of Washington in the District of Columbia. He's worked at a community newspaper and led an after-school computer club. His favorite books are *Godel Escher Bach*, *The Phantom Tollbooth*, and *The Cyberiad*. He has written about ten fanfictions in the *My Little Pony* fandom and has many more ideas as-of-yet unimplemented. Besides *MLPFIM*, the fandoms to which he belongs include Homestar Runner; *Adventure Time*; *Gravity Falls*; *Eureka*, *Warehouse 13*, *Alphas*, and *Haven*; the SCP Foundation; and *Supernatural*. Peter's favorite color is orange and his favorite adjective is "hella." He's not the guy who directed *Battleship*. He likes to make other people happy.

Lauren Billings (LolaShoes) splits her time between her research career and her writing passion, where she writes both YA and erotica with Christina Hobbs under the pen name Christina Lauren (christinalauren books.com). You can find their Beautiful Bastard series online or on shelves now. Lauren lives in California with her husband and their two children. Her handle on Twitter is @lolashoes.

Kristina Busse found online media fandom when desperately searching the internet after Buffy sent Angel to hell—and she has been lost since. Her fandoms today include *Generation Kill*, *Hannibal*, *My Chemical Romance*, *Teen Wolf*, and *X-Men First Class*. But ask her tomorrow, and that list may have changed. Kristina has been publishing academic essays on fanfiction since 2002, and her work has appeared in numerous anthologies and journals. She is founding coeditor of the online peer-reviewed academic journal *Transformative Works and Culture* and coeditor of *Fanfiction and Fan Communities in the Age of the Internet* (2006), *Sherlock and Transmedia Fandom* (2012), and the forthcoming *Fanfiction Studies Reader*. Her current book project is *Fanfiction and Literary Theory*.

Rachel Caine is the bestselling writer of the Weather Warden, Outcast Season, Revivalist, and Red Letter Days series in urban fantasy, and the Morganville Vampires series in young adult. She's the winner of multiple awards, most recently a Career Achievement Award from

Romantic Times. She still loves film, television, and all forms of storytelling. Oh, and she wrote a *Stargate: SG-1* media tie-in novel, too. You can find her online at rachelcaine.com or follow her on Twitter at @rachelcaine.

P.S. If you'd like to read her *Prey* fanfic, it's been freshly archived at juliefortune.tumblr.com/prey.

Francesca Coppa is professor of English at Muhlenberg College, where she teaches courses in dramatic literature, performance studies, and mass media storytelling. She is a founding member of the Organization for Transformative Works, a nonprofit organization established by fans to provide access to and preserve the history of fanworks and culture. She is currently the Wolf Professor of Television Studies at the University of Pennsylvania. Follow her on Twitter at @fcoppa.

Randi Flanagan is a writer and publishing sales professional; she has completed several Twilight fics and is currently writing an original work of fiction. She lives in Toronto, Ontario, with her husband, son, and two face-eating miniature pinchers.

Jolie Fontenot has her PhD in communication studies from the University of Texas at Austin. The majority of her research examines the social glue that holds people together in the form of organizational identification. She started studying the Twilight fandom in 2006, and along the way, met many fascinating people and learned their stories. Dr. Fontenot teaches for the University of South Carolina Regional Campus system. She can be reached at jfonteno@mailbox.sc.edu.

Wendy C. Fries (Atlin Merrick) makes her living writing nonfiction by day, and makes herself happy writing fiction by night, including original one-hour TV scripts and short stories. The heads-down goal from here? Making fiction both the source of fun *and* finance. And staying mad as a box of frogs.

Christina Hobbs (tby789) makes her home in Salt Lake City, Utah. She is coauthor of the *New York Times* bestselling Beautiful Bastard series, as well as the upcoming young adult novel *Sublime*.

Ron Hogan is the founder of Beatrice.com and TheHandsell.com. His book projects have ranged from a pop history of 1970s Hollywood to anthologies of stories drawn from the archives of pulp romance magazines. He hosts literary events throughout New York City, including Lady Jane's Salon, the first monthly reading series dedicated to romance fiction. He lives in Queens with his wife, Laura, and their cats. Follow him on Twitter at @RonHogan.

Bethan Jones is a PhD candidate in the Department of Theatre, Film, and Television Studies at Aberystwyth University. Her thesis, tentatively titled "The G Woman and The Fowl One: Fandom's Rewriting of Gender in *The X-Files*" focuses on the ways in which fanfiction writers resist and revise meanings around gender in cult television series. Bethan has written extensively on fandom, new media, and gender, and her work has been published in the journals *Transformative Works and Culture*, *Participations*, and *Sexualities*. Bethan is on the board of the Fan Studies Network, blogs at bethanvjones.wordpress.com, and can be found on Twitter as @memories_child.

Jacqueline Lichtenberg is a professional reviewer, an editor, the creator of the Sime~Gen® Universe, the primary author of *Star Trek Lives!*, the founder of the *Star Trek* Welcommittee, the creator of the term "Intimate Adventure," and the winner of the Galaxy Award for Spirituality in Science Fiction and the first *Romantic Times* Award for Best Science Fiction Novel. Her books are available in ebook, print, audiobook, and dramatization on satellite radio. Her most recent book is *The Farris Channel*, Sime~Gen #12 (Wildside Press, 2012). Sime~Gen is in development as the story-driven, cross-platform science fiction RPG *Ambrov X* (ambrovx.com), taking Sime~Gen into the space age.

Samira Nadkarni is completing her doctorate at the University of Aberdeen. She grew up in Mumbai, India, and has been either a participant or a lurker in various fandoms since 2002. Her publications range from the analysis of contemporary poetry to pop culture. In her spare time she writes terrible poetry and tweets about her cat.

Rukmini Pande is completing her doctorate at the University of Western Australia, Perth, focusing on the construction of the erotic body in slash fanfiction. She has also completed an MPhil in fan culture from Jawaharlal Nehru University, India, on fandom as a means of online identity creation for women. She spends far too much of her time arguing with people on the internet.

Chris Rankin was born in Auckland, New Zealand, and lived there until he moved with his parents to the UK at age 6. In August 2000, he auditioned for the Harry Potter films, and is now recognized internationally for playing the role of Percy Weasley in six of the eight movies. In addition to this, he has appeared in *The Rotter's Club* (BBC2), *Victoria*

Cross Heroes (C5), and a selection of "celebrity shows" including *Celebrity Total Wipeout*. He has also toured the UK playing Edgar Linton in *Wuthering Heights*, Eilert Loevborg in *Hedda Gabler*, and Young Syrian in Oscar Wilde's *Salome* (the latter two he also produced).

Since the age of sixteen, Chris has produced, directed, acted, and led masterclasses. In recent years, he graduated from the University of Lincoln (UK) with a BA in Media Production. He is currently working in Television Production for a major new drama for BBC ONE.

Feel free to follow him on twitter @chrisrankin or visit his website www.chrisrankin.co.uk.

Tiffany Reisz is the international bestselling author of the Original Sinners series from Mira Books. Her debut novel, *The Siren*, won the RT Book Lover's Magazine Editor's Choice Award for Best Erotic Romance 2012. She continues to hope someday Jason Isaacs will read *The Siren* and steal her from her boyfriend.

Andy Sawyer is librarian of the Science Fiction Foundation Collection at the University of Liverpool Library (www.sfhub.ac.uk) and a critic/reviewer of science fiction and fantasy wearing academic and fannish hats, often at the same time. His "Foundation Favourites" column appears in the British Science Fiction Association's *Vector*. He recently coedited (with David Ketterer) *Plan for Chaos*, a previously unpublished novel by John Wyndham (Liverpool University Press, 2009; Penguin, 2010) and (with Peter Wright) *Teaching Science Fiction* (Palgrave, 2011).

From 2002 to 2012 he was director of the MA in science fiction studies for the School of English, University of Liverpool. He was the 2008 recipient of the Science Fiction Research Association's Clareson Award for services to science fiction, and Guest Curator of the British Library's "Out of This World: Science Fiction but Not as You Know It" Exhibition in 2011.

Andrew Shaffer is the author of *Fifty Shames of Earl Grey: A Parody* (a Goodreads Choice 2012 Semifinalist) as well as several works of nonfiction. His website is www.literaryrogue.com. His FanFiction.Net username is andrewshaffer.

Heidi Tandy (Heidi8) has been part of the Harry Potter internet fandom since the day of *Goblet of Fire*'s release, and has since been involved in fanfiction (founding and posting on FictionAlley.org), news websites (The Leaky Cauldron, HPANA), discussions and meta (HPForGrownups), and HPEF fancons from Nimbus in 2003 through Ascendio in 2012. Since at least 2000, Heidi Tandy has advocated for fans, built fansites, organized fan-supported charitable fund-raisers like Help_Haiti on LiveJournal, and advocated that fans' creative endeavors are frequently transformative and therefore protectable under US copyright and trademark law. She's spoken at fan-run and law-focused events on topics including copyright and trademark, as well as written fanfiction, created over fifty fanvids, and crafted mediocre fanart because she really can't draw, for Harry Potter, *The Magicians*, *Doctor Who/Torchwood*, *Heroes*, *Supernatural*, *Sherlock*, *Glee*, Marvel Cinematic Universe, XMFC, *Teen Wolf*, and *Schoolhouse Rock*. Heidi was sorted into Ravenclaw on Pottermore, tweets as TravelingHeidi, and blogs with other fandom-focused lawyers at fyeahcopyright.tumblr.com. "Creativity is magic!"

Darren Wershler, aka Darren Wershler-Henry, is the Concordia University Research Chair in Media and Contemporary Literature (Tier 2). At Concordia, he works with the Technoculture, Art, and Games (TAG) group on video games, comic books, contemporary poetry, and other preposterous things. Darren is the author or coauthor of twelve books, most recently *Guy Maddin's My Winnipeg* (University of Toronto Press) and *Update* (Snare), with Bill Kennedy.

Jules Wilkinson (missyjack) is a fangirl, writer, and comic from Australia who watches a lot of TV. She runs the award-winning *Supernatural* Wiki—a site covering both the show and the fandom of *Supernatural*, which started in 2006 and attracts nearly 1 million visits a month. She coedited the first ever essay collection about *Supernatural*, *Some of Us Really Do Watch for the Plot*.

Jules' fanfic and original writing explores the postmodern self, gender identity, and desire. To be honest a lot of it seems to be about sex.

As an occasional comic, Jules has confused, and occasionally amused, audiences at festivals around Australia.

She is currently editing an anthology of stories by and about fangirls called *SQUEE!* You can find out more about her at juleswilkinson.com.

Jen Zern (NautiBitz) is a native New Yorker and former Los Angeleno who recently washed ashore on the enchanted island of Martha's Vineyard. There, she writes books, walks dogs, serves food, and laughs really loud. At night, she searches for mermaids. You can follow her on Twitter at @jenizee or read her fic at nautibitz.com.

ABOUT THE AUTHOR

ANNE JAMISON is Associate Professor of English at the University of Utah. She holds a PhD in Comparative Literature from Princeton and is the author of *Poetics en passant* (Palgrave, 2009), a forthcoming book on Franz Kafka and Czech culture, a number of essays and articles, and a lot of tweets (as @prof_anne). Her work on fanfiction has been quoted in publications from *The New York Review of Books* to *The Wall Street Journal* to *Entertainment Weekly's* PopWatch. She lives happily in Salt Lake City in a house full of children, basset hounds, and an avant-garde poet. And yes, of *course* she's written fic.

ENDNOTES

1. Jeffery, Morgan. "'Sherlock': Edinburgh TV Festival Masterclass—Live Blog." Digital Spy, 24 Aug. 2012. http://www.digitalspy.com/british-tv/s129/sherlock/news/a401513/sherlock-edinburgh-tv-festival-masterclass-live-blog.html.
2. Lauzen, Martha. "Boxed In: Employment of Behind-the-Scenes Women in the 2011-12 Prime-time Television Season." Center for the Study of Women in Television and Film. http://womenintvfilm.sdsu.edu/research.html.
3. Lauzen. "The Celluloid Ceiling: Behind the Scenes Employment of Women on the Top 250 Films of 2012." http://womenintvfilm.sdsu.edu/files/2012_Celluloid_Ceiling_Exec_Summ.pdf.
4. Vida. "The Count 2012." http://www.vidaweb.org/the-count-2012.
5. de Cervantes, Miguel. *Don Quixote Part II,* John Ornmby, trans. http://www2.hn.psu.edu/faculty/jmanis/cervante/quixote2.pdf.
6. Berk, "Dodgy Don Quixote Sequel," Comic Book Resources, 24 Aug. 2007, http://forums.comicbookresources.com/showthread.php?187694-Dodgy-Don-Quixote-sequel.
7. Richardson, Samuel and Anna Laetitia Barbauld, ed., *The Correspondence of Samuel Richardson.* Cambridge, England: Cambridge University Press, 2011.
8. Judge, Elizabeth F. "Kidnapped and Counterfeit Characters: Eighteenth-Century Fan Fiction, Copyright Law, and the Custody of Fictional Characters." In Reginald McGinnis, ed., *Originality and Intellectual Property in the French and English Enlightenment* (Routledge, 2012).
9. William Makepeace Thackeray (as M. A. Titmarsh). *Rebecca and Rowena: A Romance upon Romance.* London: Chapman and Hall, 1850.
10. "The Truth about Sherlock Holmes," in *The Complete Sherlock Holmes,* vol. 2, 683.
11. As quoted by Green. *The Further Adventures of Sherlock Holmes,* Richard Lancelyn Green, ed. London: Penguin Books, 1985.
12. Richard Green's *The Further Adventures* and Martin Key's *The Game is Afoot: Parodies, Pastiches, and Ponderings of Sherlock Holmes* (St Martins, 1994) were invaluable in preparing this section.
13. Originally delivered as an address to the Baker Street Irregulars in January 1941, Stout's piece was subsequently published in the March 1, 1941, issue of *The Saturday Review of Literature.* http://www.unz.org/Pub/SaturdayRev-1941mar01-00015.
14. Shklovsky, Viktor. "Art as Technique" (originally published in 1917). In *Russian Formalist Criticism,* edited by Lee T. Lemon and Marion J. Reiss. Lincoln: University of Nebraska Press, 1965.

15. greywash. "Confessions: Meta Coda to 'The Sensation of Falling Just as You Hit Sleep.'" 13 Feb. 2012. http://greywash.dreamwidth.org/16168.html.

16. "Katie Forsythe." Fanlore. http://fanlore.org/wiki/Katie_Forsythe. Accessed 23 August 2013.

17. damned_colonial. "Doylist or Watsonian?" 22 Apr. 2010. damned-colonial. dreamwidth.org/470356.html.

18. Berry, John, ed., *A Time Regained (Fables of Irish Fandom Volume 1)*, Halesowen, England: Shoestring Press, 1998; Berry, John, ed., *The If Files (Fables of Irish Fandom Volume 2)*, Halesowen, England: Shoestring Press, 1999; Berry, John, ed., *Tales of Oblique House (Fables of Irish Fandom Volume 3)*, Halesowen, England: Shoestring Press, 1999; Berry, John, ed., *Each Charter'd Course (Fables of Irish Fandom Volume 4)*, Halesowen, England: Shoestring Press, 1999; Berry, John, ed., *Fandom Denied (Fables of Irish Fandom Volume 5)*, Halesowen, England: Shoestring Press, 1999.

19. Berry, *A Time Regained*, 1.

20. Around the same time as Cheslin reprinted the "Fables," he reprinted another collection of fan-based fiction, described later in this essay: spoof detective stories that also featured fans as characters, featuring "Goon Bleary."

21. Berry, *Tales of Oblique House*.

22. Ibid; ellipses are Berry's.

23. Willis, Walter and Bob Shaw. *The Enchanted Duplicator*. Belfast, Northern Ireland: printed by Walter Willis, 1954. http://fanac.org/fanzines/Enchanted_Duplicator/Enchanted-00.html.

24. Hansen, Rob. *Then* (1988–93; 4 vols). London: Rob Hansen, 1988–1993. http://www.dcs.gla.ac.uk/SF-Archives/Then/Index.html.

25. Berry, *Tales of Oblique House*.

26. Berry, *The If Files*.

27. Berry, John, ed., *The Bleary Eyes: The Early Years,* Halesowen, England: Shoestring Press, 1993; Berry, John, ed., *The Middle Ages (The Bleary Eyes Volume 2)*, Halesowen, England: Shoestring Press, 1993; Berry, John, ed., *Nor the Years Condemn (The Bleary Eyes Volume 3)*, Halesowen, England: Shoestring Press, 1994; Berry, John, ed., *Kitsch in Sync Legends (The Bleary Eyes Volume 4)*, Halesowen, England: Shoestring Press, 1995; Berry, John, ed., *The Bleary Eyes Volume 5*. Halesowen, England: Shoestring Press, 1996.

28. *The Bleary Eyes*.

29. *Retribution 15, 1960/Bleary Eyes: Volume 2*.

30. *Bleary Eyes: Volume 2*.

31. Ibid.

32. Ibid.

33. *Fandom Denied (Fables of Irish Fandom Volume 5)*.

34. Shatner, William, Sondra Marshak, and Myrna Culbreath. *Shatner: Where No Man... The Authorized Biography of William Shatner.* New York: Ace Books, 1979.

35. Roddenberry, Gene. *Star Trek: The Motion Picture.* New York: Pocket, 1979.

36. Did the Luke Skywalker figure in his X-Wing uniform fit inside the prop plane from Fisher Price's Wilderness Patrol? I'm sure my brother and I must have at least tried. I do remember that Gonk the Power Droid became a valued member of the Adventure People TV Action Team.

37. My wife and I have a running mock debate as to whether I'm a Trekker, an ex-Trekker, or, as I sometimes put it, a guy who knows Harry Mudd's middle name is Fenton because it's a matter of basic twentieth-century American cultural literacy.

38. The short version of the Wold Newton family hypothesis is that a meteorite that really did fall in the outskirts of that Yorkshire village in 1795 exposed sixteen "fictional" characters in a passing carriage to radiation that gave them and their descendants superpowers; Tarzan, for example, is the great-great-grandson of Elizabeth and Darcy from *Pride and Prejudice* on his father's side and the Scarlet Pimpernel on his mother's. Though Farmer generally confined himself to tracing the intertwined lineages of that core group, later scholars—most notably Win Scott Eckert—would expand the "Wold Newton Universe" to bring their favorite characters from literature, television, and film onto the playing field.

39. Dobbs, Michael Ann. "Learn to Be a Better Writer by Reading Fanfiction." io9.com, 1 Jan. 2013. http://io9.com/5972357/things-you-can-learn-about-writing-by-reading-fanfiction.

40. Personal email communication, March 2013.

41. Ibid.

42. Personal email communication, December 2012.

43. Reed, Jessica. "David Duchovny and Gillian Anderson: A Dream Couple?" *The Guardian,* 9 Aug. 2012. http://www.guardian.co.uk/commentisfree/2012/aug/09/david-duchovny-gillian-anderson-dream-couple.

44. Wills, Emily Regan. "The Political Possibilities of Fandom: Transformational Discourses on Gender and Power in *The X-Files* Fandom." Accessed 21 Nov. 2009. http://www.allacademic.com//meta/p_mla_apa_research_citation/3/6/2/9/2/pages362928/p362928-1.php.

45. Knowles, Chris and Michael Hurwitz. *The Complete X-Files: Behind the Series the Myths and the Movies.* New York: Insight Editions, 2008.

46. Den of Geek. "The 10 Most Disappointing Female Characters in Sci-fi TV." 1 Jul. 2010. http://www.denofgeek.com/television/525697/the_10_most_disappointing_female_characters_in_scifi_tv.html.

47. Scodari, C. and J. L. Felder. "Creating a Pocket Universe: 'Shippers,' Fan Fiction, and The X-Files Online." *Communication Studies* 51, no. 3 (2000).

48. Ibid.

49. Ibid.

50. wendelah1. "Fic Recs: Diana Fowley (The X-Files)." 6 Feb. 2012. halfamoon.livejournal.com/270567.html.

51. Maidenjedi. "Something Strange." Accessed 6 Feb. 2012. http://users.pdsys.org/~maidenjedi/fanfic/something_strange.txt.

52. Ibid.

53. Penley, C., "Feminism, Psychoanalysis, and the Study of Popular Culture," in *Cultural Studies,* edited by L. Grossberg, C. Nelson, and P. A. Treichler, New York: Routledge, 1992; Jenkins, H., *Textual Poachers: Television, Fans and Participatory Culture,* New York: Routledge, 1992; Jenkins, H., *Convergence Culture: Where Old and New Media Collide,* New York: New York University Press, 2006.

54. Brooker, W. *Using the Force: Creativity, Community and Star Wars Fans.* New York: Continuum, 2002.

55. Lamb, P. F. and D. L. Veith, "Romantic Myth, Transcendence and Star Trek Zines." In *Erotic Universe: Sexuality and Fantastic Literature,* edited by D. Palumbo. New York: Greenwood, 1986.

56. Bacon-Smith, C. *Enterprising Women: Television Fandom and the Creation of Popular Myth.* Philadelphia: University of Pennsylvania Press, 1992.

57. Green, S., C. Jenkins, and H. Jenkins. "Normal Female Interest in Men Bonking: Selections from the *Terra Nostra Underground* and *Strange Bedfellows.*" In *Theorizing Fandom: Fans, Subculture, and Identity,* edited by C. Harris and A. Alexander. Cresskill, NJ: Hampton Press, 1998.

58. idella. "The Future's So Bright I Gotta Wear Shades." 8 Jan. 2010. xf-santa. livejournal.com/48315.html.

59. Tosenberger, C. "Homosexuality at the Online Hogwarts: Harry Potter Slash Fanfiction." *Children's Literature* 36 (2008): 185–207.

60. idella, "The Future's So Bright."

61. Bronze Archive for 2–3 Jan. 1998. http://www.cise.ufl.edu/cgi-bin/cgiwrap/ hsiao/buffy/get-archive?vip=joss-whedon.

62. Bronze VIP Archive for 18 Nov. 1998. http://www.cise.ufl.edu/cgi-bin/cgiwrap/ hsiao/buffy/get-archive?date=19981118.

63. Joss Whedon, comment dated 29 Jan. 2000, 16:37:03. Bronze VIP Archive for 29 Jan. 2000. http://www.cise.ufl.edu/cgi-bin/cgiwrap/hsiao/buffy/ get-archive?date=20000129.

64. Joss Whedon, comment dated 6 Feb. 2000, 09:50:47. Bronze VIP Archive for 6 Feb. 2000. http://www.cise.ufl.edu/cgi-bin/cgiwrap/hsiao/buffy/ get-archive?date=20000206.

65. Ibid.

66. Jenkins, *Convergence Culture.*

67. Bronze VIP Archive for 18 Nov. 1998.

68. "Joss Whedon Speaks about 'Grave.'" The Bronze Beta, 22 May 2002. http:// www.bronzebeta.com/Archive/Joss/Joss20020522.htm.

69. Bianculli, David. "Joss Whedon: Slayers, Dolls and Singing Villians." NPR interview, 12 Feb. 2009. http://www.wbur.org/npr/100601869/ joss-whedon-slayers-dolls-and-singing-villains.

70. Bronze VIP Archive for 18 Nov. 1998.

71. Jane Espenson, comment dated 12 Dec. 1999, 15:23:00. Bronze VIP Archive for 12 Dec. 1999. http://www.cise.ufl.edu/cgi-bin/cgiwrap/hsiao/buffy/ get-archive?date=19991212.

72. Jane Espenson, comment dated 12 Dec. 1999, 15:58:14. Bronze VIP Archive for 12 Dec. 1999. http://www.cise.ufl.edu/cgi-bin/cgiwrap/hsiao/buffy/get-archive?date=19991212.

73. Barnet, Barbara. "A Conversation with Jane Espenson: Part One." Blogcritics, 29 Sep. 2012. http://blogcritics.org/a-conversation-with-jane-espenson-part/.

74. Lewis, Lisa A., ed. *The Adoring Audience: Fan Culture and Popular Media.* London: Routledge, 1992. http://www.scribd.com/doc/47984716/The-Adoring-Audience-Fan-Culture-and-Popular-Media.

75. HPEF Presents: Ascendio 2012. "About HPEF." Accessed 16 July 2013. http://hp2012.org/?page_id=3064.

76. LeakyCon. "Special Guests: A Quick Who's Who of LeakyCon 2012." Accessed 16 July 2013. http://www.leakycon.com/london/special-events/.

77. Gunelius, Susan. *Harry Potter: The Story of a Global Business Phenomenon.* New York: Macmillan, 2008.

78. Melissa Anelli, personal email communication, April 2011.

79. Ibid.

80. Ibid.

81. Heidi Tandy, personal email communication, April 2011.

82. Russon, Mary-Ann. "HP Webmasters Interview: Heidi Tandy, FictionAlley.org." UrbanWire, June 2004. http://www.theurbanwire.com/jun04/heiditandyprint.html 2004.

83. Heidi Tandy, personal email communication, April 2011.

84. Ibid.

85. The Harry Potter Alliance. "What We Do." Accessed 16 July 2013. http://thehpalliance.org/what-we-do/.

86. The Harry Potter Alliance. Sample chapter page. Accessed 16 July 2013. http://thehpalliance.org/chapters/featured-chapter-sample-page/.

87. Noxon, Christopher. "Oh Harry, You Naughty Boy." Inside.com, October 18, 2001. http://www.christophernoxon.com/index.php/cnsite/clip/oh_harry_you_naughty_boy/.

88. Odlyzko, Andrew. "Content Is Not King." *First Monday* 6, no. 2 (5 Feb. 2001). http://firstmonday.org/ojs/index.php/fm/article/viewArticle/833/742.

89. FictionAlley.com forums. Comment dated 28 June 2004. Accessed 17 July 2013. http://forums.fictionalley.org/park/showthread.php?s=&threadid=64277.

90. Ventre, Michael. "Devoted 'Twihards' Get Their Fix Online." *Today Movies.* 16 Nov. 2009. http://www.today.com/id/33921402/ns/today-entertainment/t/devoted-twihards-get-their-fix-online.

91. Astraea, "BUFFY Fans: Can a Buffy Fan Watch Twilight?" The Trek BBS. 3 Oct. 2011. http://www.trekbbs.com/showpost.php?p=5264523&postcount=6.

92. Jamison, Anne. *Fifty Shades of Pop Culture Theory: Twilight Fan Fiction Unit from Theories of Popular Culture (ENGL 5960)* (blog). http://fiftyshadesofpopculturetheory.blogspot.com/.

93. "Legitimate Concerns about Breaking Dawn." PetitionOnline. Accessed 16 July 2013. http://www.petitiononline.com/petitions/BDFailed/signatures.

94. Kelly Hardy (autumnblossom1972). Comment to "Reviews for 'Sacrifices,'" 14 June 2009. www.fanfiction.net/r/3940174/0/60/.

95. bronzed topaz. Comment to "Reviews for 'Waiting for Dawn.'" 26 June, 2012. http://www.fanfiction.net/r/3766104/33/1/.

96. Lewis, Andy. "25 Most Powerful Authors: EL James Opens Up about Her 'Roller Coaster' Year Since 'Fifty Shades' Hit Big." *The Hollywood Reporter*, 30 Nov. 2012. http://www.hollywoodreporter.com/news/ fifty-shades-writer-el-james-395588.

97. Icedragon. "Re: Master of the Universe by Snowqueens Icedragon." *Twilighted Forum*, 27 Oct. 2009. http://www.twilighted.net/forum/viewtopic.php?f=44&t= 6627&start=200#p759242.

98. Scalzi, John, "My Policy on Fanfic and Other Adaptations of My Work," *Whatever* (blog), 25 May 2007, http://whatever.scalzi.com/2007/05/25/ my-policy-on-fanfic-and-other-adaptations-of-my-work; Scalzi, John, "Quick *Fuzzy Nation* Addendum," *Whatever* (blog), 7 April 2010, http://whatever. scalzi.com/2010/04/07/quick-fuzzy-nation-addendum/; Scalzi, John, "Wil Wheaton/John Scalzi Fan Fiction Contest to Benefit the Lupus Alliance of America" (Scalzi-Wheaton [or non-explicit Scalzi/Wheaton] contest post), *Whatever* (blog), 30 May 2010, http://whatever.scalzi.com/2010/05/30/ fanfic-contest/.

99. Personal email communication, 2013.

100. Neil Gaiman. "Fair Use and Other Things." 19 April 2008. http://journal. neilgaiman.com/2008/04/fair-use-and-other-things.html.

101. einfach mich. "Open Letter to the Fan Fiction Fandom." 11. March 2012. http://einfachmich.tumblr.com/post/19146182920/open-letter-to-the-twilight -fan-fiction-fandom.

102. Personal communication, July 2013.

103. Archive of Our Own. "FAQ." Accessed 21 August 2013. http:// transformativeworks.org/faq#t456n26.

104. Personal communication, December 2012.

105. Braden, Kara. "Filing off the Serial Numbers—from Fanfic to Novel (Part 1)." 23 May, 2013. http://karabraden.tumblr.com/post/51153188418/ filing-off-the-serial-numbers-from-fanfic-to-novel.

106. de Sade, Marquis. *Juliette*. Grove Press: New York, 2000. First published 1797.

107. Braden, "Filing off the Serial Numbers."

108. Scalzi, John. "Amazon's Kindle Worlds: Instant Thoughts." *Whatever* (blog). 22 May 2013. http://whatever.scalzi.com/2013/05/22/amazons-kindle -worlds-instant-thoughts/

109. JaneDavitt. "Reunion." 14 Sep. 2005. http://supernaturalfic.livejournal. com/550.html.

110. Estimates of proportions of genres and pairings in *Supernatural* fanfic are based on analysis of the fic listed on the daily "*Supernatural* Newsletter" (http:// www.spnnewsletter.livejournal.com), which covers only stories posted on LiveJournal.

111. As of June 28, 2013.

112. As of June 28, 2013.

113. Black Samvara @supernatural_fic. Accessed 16 July 2013. http://delicious.com/supernatural_fic.

114. spn_anna commuity homepage. Accessed 16 July 2013. http://spn-anna.livejournal.com/.

115. Winchester Mpreg community homepage. Accessed 16 July 2013. http://mpregwinchester.livejournal.com/.

116. "Knotting." *Supernatural Wiki*. Last modified 29 June 2013. www.supernaturalwiki.com/index.php?title=Knotting.

117. The SPN J2 Big Bang challenge can be found at spn-j2-bigbang.livejournal.com.

118. Analyses of stories, and a list of other *Supernatural*-centric Big Bang challenges, can be found at www.supernaturalwiki.com/index.php?title=Big_Bang.

119. "Drinking with the Stars: 'Supernatural''s Misha Collins." YouTube.com, 21 Oct. 2009. http://www.youtube.com/watch?v=TGl-hkjcZRU.

120. "Cockles" is the mashup pairing name in fanfiction for stories featuring Misha Collins and costar Jensen Ackles. Ryan, Maureen. "'Supernatural' Season 8: Misha Collins Talks Castiel's Big Return and More." HuffPost TV, 31 July 2012. http://www.huffingtonpost.com/2012/07/31/supernatural-season-8-misha-collins_n_1726114.html.

121. Samlicker81. "Burning Desires," posted under "The Completion of My Fic from Sympathy for the Devil." 13 Sep. 2009. http://wincest.livejournal.com/2647212.html.

122. Chuck Shurley writes under the pen name Carver Edlund, which is a portmanteau of two of the show's writers at the time—Jeremy Carver and Ben Edlund.

123. Jenkins, Henry. "Supernatural: First Impressions." *Confessions of an Aca-Fan*. 15 Jan. 2007. http://www.henryjenkins.org/2007/01/supernatural.html.

124. "Robdam." *Supernatural Wiki*. Last modified 30 April 2013. http://www.supernaturalwiki.com/index.php?title=Robdam.

125. Walschots, Natalie Zina. "Teenage Dread." *Toronto Standard,* 12 July 2012. torontostandard.com/culture/teenage-dread.

126. Arrow, V. "Real-Person Fanfiction: Looking at Band Fandom(s), One Direction Edition." *Survey,* 28–31 Oct. 2012.

127. Colazitron. Personal interview, 29 Dec. 2012.

128. Jones, Lucy. Personal interview, 30 Dec. 2012.

129. Elle. Personal interview, 30 Dec. 2012.

130. Thomas, Kayley. "Remediating Reality in Real Person Slash Fiction." (Master's thesis, University of Florida, 2010). http://www.worldcat.org/title/remediating-reality-in-real-person-slash-fan-fiction/oclc/741565148.

131. Mitchell, Ramona. Personal interview, 30 Dec. 2012.

132. Shrew. Personal interview, 26 Dec. 2012.

133. Cat. Personal interview, 31 Dec. 2012.

134. Darcie. Personal interview, 30 Dec. 2012.

135. Personal Communication, 2012.

136. "IRL" is fandom speak for "in real life."

137. On July 2, 2009, homosexuality was decriminalized in India after a long fight by the queer movement on behalf of the Indian LGBT populace. It's worth noting that the 2009 law pertains exclusively to sodomy as per article 377 of the Indian Penal Code; lesbianism was never included within either the law or its repeal, as it was beyond taboo—it was considered practically unthinkable in a culture that emphasizes a traditional nuclear family and the patriarchal structure this entails.

138. A fandom lurker is someone who consumes fanworks but does not produce any themselves, and who does not interact with other producers or consumers of fanworks online. The term is used for someone who exists on the fringes of fandom activity and has refrained from identifying themselves to the community.

139. Slash carries a taboo across the world as current global socio-sexual movements clearly indicate that homosexuality is still a fraught subject. To be a slasher is, loosely speaking, to entangle your own personal sexuality with these different threads. It's not an easy subject to launch into with someone who lies outside of the community, who might not understand that element. The taboo of being a slasher in fandom isn't a taboo merely within the fandom community but extends beyond these bounds to interactions with the world at large; that is, I might choose to disclose my identity as a slasher to people I meet, but their own stances on sexuality (within or outside of fandom) might influence our interaction.

140. "RaceFail '09" refers to a series of blog posts initially written in response to SF/F author Elizabeth Bear's advice about "writing the other" in fiction. These posts pointed out both Bear's apparent hypocrisy, critiquing her record of portraying people of color, and encompassed the failings of the SF/F genre as a whole when dealing with the issue of race. The term also includes the responses the blog posts generated and the resulting (sometimes heated) discussions. More information on RaceFail '09 can be found at http://fanlore.org/wiki/RaceFail_'09 (accessed January 2, 2012). We found that our own experience of fandom resonated quite strongly with Deepa D's "I Didn't Dream of Dragons": http://deepad.dreamwidth.org/29371.html (13 Jan. 2009).

141. Bollywood has its own fanworks; there is a specific subsection on the collected fanfiction archive, FanFiction.Net, and there are numerous online journals that contain fanworks devoted to Indian cinema and literature specifically, although, notably, the majority of these are produced in either English or Hinglish.

142. Arguably, this can be traced back to the idea in Anne Jamison's introduction to this essay wherein race as an issue is subverted in favor of alien races or cyborgs. In *Supernatural*'s case, racism, while still present as a global issue, is also taken beyond those bounds to an issue that deals with the theological divide of angels, demons, and humans.

143. James, Kendra. "What's Not Going Bump in the Night?: The Missing Folklore of *Supernatural*." 14 Apr. 2011. http://www.racialicious.com/2011/04/14/

whats-not-going-bump-in-the-night-the-missing-folklore-of-supernatural-tv-
correspondent-tryout.

144. This information is documented by Kendra James at Racialicious.
com, 1 Aug. 2012. http://www.racialicious.com/2012/08/01/
this-show-was-supposed-to-be-a-gift-teen-wolf-race.

145. Included here is just a small sample of the pieces available online regarding
the casting and appropriation of "Kali" in *Teen Wolf* fandom: "Kali,
Motherfuckers...or You Know Vengeance, Motherfuckers," 22 Oct. 2012,
http://zorana.tumblr.com/post/34110118173/kali-motherfuckers-or-you-
know-vengeance; "For Every One of You Who Thinks...," 29 Nov. 2012,
http://beliel.tumblr.com/post/36801233111/for-every-single-one-of-you-
who-think-kali-is-an; Joseph Lamour and Kendra James, "*Teen Wolf*: I Came
for the Hot Guys, I Stayed for the Consistent Race Fail...and I Wish I
Could Quit," in "The Racialicious Entertainment Roundup: Nov. 23–29,"
Racialicious.com, 30 Nov. 2012, http://www.racialicious.com/2012/11/30/
the-racialicious-entertainment-roundup-nov-23-29/#more-26472.

146. The negation of culture arises when the propagation of cultural references
for that particular society privileges populist notions rather than any truthful
or factual understanding. It prioritizes a false history that is often historical
propaganda and that itself carries a great deal of racial, social, and political
prejudice. For example, people watching *Indiana Jones and the Temple of
Doom* might now cringe at the assumption that South Asia is a land of ritual
sacrifice and the eating of monkey's brains. If that makes viewers cringe, why
should they not also cringe from the fact that Davis is using populist notions
of a South Asian deity to add cultural flavor to the depiction of a villainous
werewolf?

147. Goldsmith, Kenneth. *Day.* Great Barrington, MA: The Figures, 2003.

148. Alberro, Alexander. "Reconsidering Conceptual Art, 1966–1977." In
Conceptual Art: A Critical Anthology, edited by Alexander Alberro and Blake
Stimson. Cambridge, MA: MIT Press, 1999, pp. xvi, xvii.

149. John Guillory, "The Memo and Modernity," *Critical Inquiry* 31 (2004).

150. Cobbing, Bob and Steven Ross Smith. *Ballet of the Speech Organs: Bob Cobbing
on Bob Cobbing.* Saskatoon/Toronto: Underwhich Editions, 1998.

151. Dworkin, Craig and Kenneth Goldsmith. *Against Expression: An Anthology
of Conceptual Writing. Avant-Garde & Modernism Collection.* Evanston, IL:
Northwestern University Press, 2011.

152. Bergvall, Caroline, et al., eds. *I'll Drown My Book: Conceptual Writing by Women.*
Los Angeles: Les Figues Press, 2012.

153. Dworkin, Craig Douglas. "The UbuWeb Anthology of Conceptual Writing."
*UbuWeb.*Accessed 9 June 2013. http://www.ubu.com/concept/.

154. Lippard, Lucy R. *Six Years: The Dematerialization of the Art Object from 1966 to
1972; A Cross-Reference Book of Information on Some Esthetic Boundaries.* New
York: Praeger, 1973.

155. Dworkin, "UbuWeb Anthology."

156. Jencks, Charles. "From 'The Death of Modern Architecture' from *What Is Post-Modernism?*" In *From Modernism to Postmodernism: An Anthology,* edited by Lawrence Cahoone, expanded 2nd ed. Malden, MA: Blackwell.

157. Ibid.

158. Dworkin and Goldsmith, *Against Expression.*

159. CBC Books. "To Read or Not to Read: Fresh Air Considers the State of Poetry in Canada." *CBC Books,* 11 Apr. 2011. http://www.cbc.ca/books/2011/04/to-read-or-not-to-read-fresh-air-considers-the-state-of-poetry-in-canada.html.

160. Romano, Aja. "10 Famous Authors Who Write Fanfiction." *The Daily Dot,* 30 Aug. 2012. http://www.dailydot.com/culture/10-famous-authors-fanfiction/.

161. Sonne, Paul and Jeffrey A. Trachtenberg. "Penguin Group Dives into Self-Publishing." *Wall Street Journal,* 19 July 2012. http://online.wsj.com/article/SB10000872396390444464304577537092288601370.html.

162. Jenkins, Henry. *Convergence Culture: Where Old and New Media Collide.* New York: New York University Press, 2006. See especially chapter 3.

163. Perloff, Marjorie. "'Vocable Scriptsigns': Differential Poetics in Kenneth Goldsmith's *Fidget.*" In *Poetry, Value, and Contemporary Culture,* edited by Andrew Roberts and John Allison. Edinburgh: Edinburgh University Press, 2002.

164. Wershler, Darren S. *Guy Maddin's My Winnipeg (Canadian Cinema vol. 6).* Toronto: University of Toronto Press, 2010.

165. Dworkin and Goldsmith, *Against Expression.*

166. Skinner, Richard. "Max Sebald's Writing Tips." *Richard Skinner* (blog). 14 Jan. 2013. http://richardskinner.weebly.com/2/post/2013/01/max-sebalds-writing-tips.html.

167. Ibid.

168. *Harper's,* Feb. 2007. http://harpers.org/archive/2007/02/the-ecstasy-of-influence.

Image Endnotes

A. falling_voices. "fic: the theory of narrative causality; i." 31 July 2011. http://falling-voices.livejournal.com/18360.html. Accessed 21 August 2013.

B. falling_voices. "fic: the theory of narrative causality; iv." 31 July 2011. http://falling-voices.livejournal.com/19055.html. Accessed 21 August 2013.

C. Lichtenberg, Jacqueline. Kraith Collected, volume one. 1976 reprint of 1972 first edition.

D. Lichtenberg, Jacqueline. "Spock's Argument." Kraith Collected, volume one. 1976 reprint of 1972 first edition.

E. Han, Steven. "The Calamari." Posted to alt.tv.creative.x-files.creative. ftp://ftp.gossamer.org/stories/c/Calamari. Accessed 21 August 2013.

F. Homepage. The Slayer's Fanfic Archive. 25 January 1999. http://web.archive.org/web/19990125092016/http://slayerfanfic.com/.

G. Mediancat. "There Are No Willows Here." The Slayer's Fanfic Archive. 13 October 1999. http://web.archive.org/web/19991013153553/http://slayerfanfic. com/Mediancat/willows1.html.

H. Homepage. FictionAlley.org. 01 August 2001. http://web.archive.org/ web/20010801160819/http://www.fictionalley.org/

I. AliciaSue. "An Unlikely Coven." Schnoogle.com (part of FictionAlley.org). http://web.archive.org/web/20071209151302/http://www.fictionalley.org/ authors/aliciasue/AUC01.html.

J. d0tparker. "Dear D0t: What's With the Love for Abusive Edwards?" 26 April 2010. http://web.archive.org/web/20110209051702/http://www.twificnews. com/dear-d0t/dear-d0t-whats-with-the-love-for-abusive-edwards/. Accessed 21 August 2013.

K. Mrs.TheKing. "GYNAZOLE." http://www.fanfiction.net/s/5682539/1/ GYNAZOLE. Accessed 21 August 2013.

L. Wattpad. "Fanfiction Stories and Books Free." http://www.wattpad.com/stories/ fan-fiction. Accessed August 2013.

M. Archive of Our Own. "Tags." http://archiveofourown.org/tags. Accessed August 2013.

N. cumberchameleon. "AU - The Bet (Part One)." http://cumberchameleon. tumblr.com/post/52644335369/au-the-bet-part-one-after-an-argument-about. Accessed 21 Aug 2013.

Index

Some key concepts, especially those relating to gender and sexuality or their representation, are not included in the index. Due to the high frequency with which such issues are discussed, their entries would be so long as to be unhelpful.